The crisis of British Protestantism

Manchester University Press

Politics, culture and society in early modern Britain

General editors

DR ALEXANDRA GAJDA
PROFESSOR ANTHONY MILTON
PROFESSOR PETER LAKE
DR JASON PEACEY

This important series publishes monographs that take a fresh and challenging look at the interactions between politics, culture and society in Britain between 1500 and the mid-eighteenth century. It counteracts the fragmentation of current historiography through encouraging a variety of approaches which attempt to redefine the political, social and cultural worlds, and to explore their interconnection in a flexible and creative fashion. All the volumes in the series question and transcend traditional interdisciplinary boundaries, such as those between political history and literary studies, social history and divinity, urban history and anthropology. They thus contribute to a broader understanding of crucial developments in early modern Britain.

Recently published in the series

Chaplains in early modern England: Patronage, literature and religion
HUGH ADLINGTON, TOM LOCKWOOD AND GILLIAN WRIGHT *(eds)*

The Cooke sisters: Education, piety and patronage in early modern England
GEMMA ALLEN

Black Bartholomew's Day   DAVID J. APPLEBY

Insular Christianity   ROBERT ARMSTRONG AND TADHG Ó HANNRACHAIN *(eds)*

Reading and politics in early modern England   GEOFF BAKER

'No historie so meete'   JAN BROADWAY

Republican learning   JUSTIN CHAMPION

News and rumour in Jacobean England: Information, court politics and diplomacy, 1618–25   DAVID COAST

This England   PATRICK COLLINSON

Sir Robert Filmer (1588–1653) and the patriotic monarch   CESARE CUTTICA

Doubtful and dangerous: The question of succession in late Elizabethan England   SUSAN DORAN *and* PAULINA KEWES *(eds)*

Brave community   JOHN GURNEY

'Black Tom'   ANDREW HOPPER

Impostures in early modern England: Represensations and perceptions of frauduent identities   TOBIAS B. HUG

Royalists and Royalism during the Interregnum
JASON MCELLIGOTT AND DAVID L. SMITH

Laudian and Royalist polemic in Stuart England   ANTHONY MILTON

Full details of the series are available at www.manchesteruniversitypress.com.

The crisis of British Protestantism

Church power in the Puritan Revolution, 1638–44

HUNTER POWELL

Manchester
University Press

Published by Manchester University Press
Altrincham Street, Manchester M1 7JA, UK
www.manchesteruniversitypress.co.uk

British Library Cataloguing-in-Publication Data
A catalogue record for this book is available from the British Library

Library of Congress Cataloging-in-Publication Data applied for

ISBN 978 1 5261 0673 5 *paperback*

This edition first published 2017

The publisher has no responsibility for the persistence or accuracy of URLs for external or any third-party internet websites referred to in this book, and does not guarantee that any content on such websites is, or will remain, accurate or appropriate.

Typeset in Scala with Pastonchi display by
by Koinonia, Manchester

Printed in Great Britain by
Lightning Source

Contents

Acknowledgements

This book is the product of nearly six years of work and is immeasurably better because of the people and organisations that have generously helped along the way. I have benefited from the knowledge and assistance of staff at the Bodleian Library, the British Library, National Library of Scotland and New College Library. However, I must single out the staff of the Rare Books Room at the University of Cambridge and particularly Stella Clarke, Clair Welford and Helen Hills. I spent the majority of my research in the Rare Books Room surrounded faithfully assisted by all three librarians.

Some scholars read parts, or all, of this book and provided invaluable input. Others have happily engaged in useful conversations, either in person or through email. I am extremely grateful to John Adamson, Josef Ansorge, Francis J. Bremer, John Coffey, John Collins, Tim Cooper, Mark Dever, Simon Gathercole, Lee Gatiss, Crawford Gribben, Polly Ha, Joel Halcomb, Simon Healy, Ann Hughes, Clare Jackson, Mark Jones, Vivienne Larminie, Michael Lawrence, Paul C. H. Lim, Anthony Milton, William O'Reilly, Jason Peacey, Jacqueline Rose, Richard Serjeanston, David Smith, Laura Stewart, Carl Trueman, Elliot Vernon, Tom Webster, Peter Williams, Michael P. Winship, Blair Worden and Avihu Zakai. I wish to express my thanks to both the Early Modern British and Irish History Seminar at the University of Cambridge and the Institute of Historical Research for allowing me to present early versions of chapters from this dissertation. Cambridge's Early Modern Seminar and its conveners was a welcome support network of scholars and colleagues who modelled congenial scholarship and academic camaraderie. I am extremely grateful to Gerald Bray who helped with all of my Latin translations and Dirk Jongkind who translated my Dutch sources. Bringing in an international component to the book would have been impossible without their assistance. Jonathan Warren helped with the index. Megan Wenger did a careful editorial read of the manuscript, and all mistakes and typos in the final product are purely mine.

There are three historians and friends who deserve special mention here. Joel Halcomb has been a regular source of wisdom for all things congregational and a general support in all things academic. Elliot Vernon's unparalleled knowledge of English presbyterianism has helped me to clarify my own thoughts on this topic. Chad Van Dixhoorn made sure I was a precisionist whenever I engaged the minutes of the Westminster assembly.

As John Morrill's one hundred and seventeenth graduate student, it is hard to know what accolades I can offer John that he has not already received. As his student I learned how to study History, as a friend he has made me a better person. It was a true privilege to learn from John and this book is very much the result of his careful guidance.

Most of all, I want to thank my family. My parents were supportive throughout and encouraging throughout. I have written this book for the majority of my children's (Whitefield, Hudson and Kate) lives and their presence, love and kindness made the

Acknowledgements

process so much more enjoyable. Laura has been a more loving and supportive wife than I could have dreamed of. This book was completed in large part because of Laura's hard work behind the scenes. She helped me carry this burden every step of the way, and this book is as much hers as it is mine.

Introduction

On 14 October 1644, the Earl of Pembroke, one of Charles I's more moderate if persistent opponents in the 1640s, told the Westminster assembly of divines that '[T]he kingdome was on fire. The burning of our consiences & soules. If we doe not setle a government, how many religions shall we have?'[1] He believed that settling the issue of church government was necessary to prevent the breakdown of religious orthodoxy. England had been engaged in a war for over two years, a war that had engulfed three nations and pitted Parliament against its own king. The Westminster assembly – charged by Parliament with reforming the Church of England – had been meeting for almost a year. Whatever the reasons England had for entering into the Civil War, Pembroke believed religion could be a solution to the conflict.

Pembroke's comment captures the essence of the crisis that had been brewing in England for some forty years and would remain unresolved until the end of the Interregnum. For many puritan divines, since the reign of Elizabeth the evolution of the Church of England into a truly reformed church had been stunted: its theology had reformed, but its structures were tainted by a prelatical, and thus Catholic, system of church government. Charles I's enforcement of this system threatened to undermine the evangelical orthodoxy enshrined in England's thirty-nine articles of religion, which had been established in 1563. It was at the nexus of church government and religion where governance and theological purity collided. Heterodoxy flourished where orthodoxy was not enforced; chaos waxed where ecclesiology waned. For puritan divines, church government was the only way to protect the church, and thus the state, from heresy. This was always the case, but it was even more so during England's revolution.

The fundamental ecclesiological issue in the years 1638 through 1644 was the question of church power. Once Parliament concluded that ecclesiastical power did not reside in the diocesan bishop, the state, along with its leading divines, needed to identify where church power existed and how that power was to be executed. It was a question fraught with difficulty. Indeed, even two hundred years later, the great Scottish presbyterian historian James Bannerman, referring to the early 1640s, conceded, '[P]erhaps, in the whole range of ecclesiastical theology, there is no question in regard to which a greater diversity of judgment among competent divines has prevailed; and none, probably, in regard to which it is more necessary to speak of caution and

1

diffidence ... [than the question of church power].' These 'competent divines' are amongst the subjects of this present study. The complexity that Bannerman noted is largely the reason why the topic has not been treated thoroughly.[2] Approaching the question of church power through England's most influential divines, we find an entirely new way of understanding six pivotal years in British history. When we focus on the years 1638–44 and on the question of church power, and examine how the leading congregational divines, emerging English presbyterians and Scottish presbyterians represented themselves in the early part of the Revolution, how they perceived each other, and *how they worked together*, a picture emerges that militates against what Anthony Milton has called the 'over application of polarizing labels'.[3] In other words, this book comes to terms with the fact that our typical ecclesiological categories are far less clearly delineated than many have been comfortable with.

The years 1638 through 1644 straddle a crucial divide in British history, as calls for religious reform and renewal mutated into political revolution. This book seeks to bring coherence to a pre-revolutionary historiography that focuses on questions of conformity to and semi-separatism from 'the church by law established' and a post-1642 historiography built around a coarse polarity between 'presbyterianism' and 'independency'. It recognises that the 1640s brought new men to the fore and an intense interaction between religious divines and lay Members of Parliament (MPs) who struggled for control of a nation and the future of its church.

The 'high orthodoxy' of revolutionary puritans with their heightened theological precision constitutes a story far more interesting and challenging than the one accommodated in the reductionist ecclesiological categorisations we are normally offered. The freedom of the press and general collapse of authority during the revolution allowed debates over church government to receive a public hearing; therefore, divines finally had a true opportunity for religious reform.

While the historiographical rediscovery since the 1980s of Protestant scholasticism has helped to rescue post-Reformation English puritanism from the realms of pietistic platitudes, it has not been equally applied to the field of ecclesiology. Indeed, church government is regarded as *non*-theological. Political and intellectual historians approach church government with little interest in, as John Coffey and Alistair Chapman have noted, understanding that 'religious ideas (like political, philosophical, or scientific ideas) need to be understood first and foremost on their own terms'.[4] As we attempt to study these divines 'on their own terms', we will call into question several prevailing beliefs about the congregationalists, the Scottish presbyterians and the English presbyterians, and about the context of religious reform in the early 1640s.

THE APOLOGISTS

We will primarily focus on a group commonly referred to as the 'Dissenting Brethren', who became known as such for their official dissent to the only proposition the Westminster assembly ever passed regarding presbyterian church government. The Dissenting Brethren, or Apologists – Thomas Goodwin, Jeremiah Burroughs, Philip Nye, Sidrach Simpson and William Bridge – were a small group of congregational ministers who went into exile in Holland together in the late 1630s, and published a famous tract during the Westminster assembly entitled the *Apologeticall Narration.*[5] No group in the history of the Puritan Revolution had a more disproportionate impact on the course of events than this vocal minority. Whether it was their exploits during the period of William Laud's ascendancy and subsequent experience of exile in Holland in the 1630s, their helping to craft the *Solemn League and Covenant*, their impact on the Westminster assembly and its outcome, their participation in the Whitehall debates, or their rise to power under Oliver Cromwell where they helped design and lead his national church settlement, this small band of congregational divines had an uncanny ability to appear at every revolutionary flashpoint. Indeed, their famous (or infamous) *Apologeticall Narration* receives an obligatory mention in most major histories of the British Revolution, and it is a touchstone in virtually all histories of seventeenth-century puritanism. Remarkably, they remained a cohesive group, writing numerous pamphlets, manuscripts and confessions of faith together between 1635 and 1658.[6]

As a group they have fascinated historians for years. Yet the very fact that they crossed so many paths, and partook in so many pivotal events during the Puritan Revolution, has meant that our understanding of them has been largely tangential to, and derivative of, other narratives. Their importance in the 1630s can be seen in their celebrated non-conformity, membership in the Hartlib circle and involvement in emerging colonial ventures. Nevertheless, their flight to Holland during the Laudian ascendancy has led to the conclusion that they were less important in, and less central to, Revolutionary religious debates than those divines who chose to stay behind. The Apologists' later intimate involvement in church reform during the era of 'Root and Branch' debates over whether to completely abolish or reform episcopacy and during the Westminster assembly is vitiated in the historiographical efforts to link them to the shadowy world of London 'radicalism'. Their belief in ecclesiastical accommodation during the 1640s is swept into scholarship attempting to find the birth of broad religious toleration.

Historians of the Westminster assembly, often guided by the belief that 'presbyterianism' was England's only hope for religious stability, have dismissed the Apologists' involvement as an unwanted nuisance. It is said that the Apologists' behaviour in the assembly showed an 'intractableness and rigid adherence to formal principle with iron resolve and utter carelessness for the consequences marked'.[7] Uncritically accepted as the leaders of independency in the 1640s, their polity is regarded as the logical fulfilment of Jacobean separatist and semi-separatist polities.[8] Their importance in the Revolution is seen in their ability to stop a rigid presbyterian settlement and to give hope to radically new notions of the separation of church and state that carried with it the birth of religious toleration. Conversely, when they rise to power under Oliver Cromwell, they are then regarded as the opportunistic architects of religious intolerance who systematically tighten the Calvinistic screws on the 'extremists' they used to support. In terms of the broader historiography of the Puritan Revolution, the Apologists are the tail that seems always to wag the dog.[9]

Richard Muller has recently argued that the historians of the sixteenth and seventeenth centuries must 'avoid the enormous pitfalls of a decontextualised or badly contextualised history'.[10] The Apologists have suffered from both extremes. Historians have decontextualised the Apologists by a selective reading of their writings and anecdotal analysis of their behaviour based on modern assumptions of relevance.[11] For example, William Haller and W. K. Jordan have seen them as harbingers of religious liberty and toleration, and one scholar has suggested that their ecclesiological 'middle way' was a major flashpoint in a larger early modern trend towards 'moderation'.[12] Historians of radicalism, exemplified by Murray Tolmie, have the Whiggish tendency to isolate – indeed create – what we will find to have been an overly dramatised, relevant narrative of how schismatic ecclesiology brought forth the modern concepts of separation of church and state. The denominationalism of 'radical' religion fails to assess the linguistic, theological and conceptual distinctions used by these divines during this period of 'high orthodoxy'.[13]

It has been argued that the Apologists did not develop their version of the congregational way until 1643 and that they refused to bring forth a promised platform of church government. The Apologists have been portrayed as opportunistic and peripheral, indeed duplicitous, participants of Edmund Calamy's Aldermanbury house group, which was working to reform the Church of England. Their *Apologeticall Narration* has been described as a declaration of ecclesiastical warfare that sought to break the Aldermanbury alliance in order to secure a broad toleration for independent churches.

PRESBYTERIANS VERSUS INDEPENDENTS

The axiomatic binary conflict model of 'presbyterian versus independent' is a dominant historiographical leitmotif of the early 1640s. This is most notable in the historiography of the Apologists' publication the *Apologetical Narration*, which W. M. Hetherington's foundational work on the Westminster assembly – followed more recently by the work of Robert S. Paul – viewed as the first shot in an ecclesiastical war with the presbyterians: a document that ripped asunder any alliance that existed with the presbyterians and made any future accommodation between the two parties impossible.

Studies on church government have tended to find those narratives that they set out to look for. Presbyterianism and independency have been portrayed as essentially monolithic and static categories into which historians must plug their theses. For example, historians have seen intense scholastic debate as conflict between these two parties. Studies of the Westminster assembly debates over church government have oddly overlooked the fact that the methodological rules of scholastic debate were a fundamental part of the way these divines thought and argued. Being sensitive or gentle to one's opponent was utterly foreign to those trained in scholastic disputation. The scholastic debater 'was rather a proselytiser for his own opinions, eager to divide truth from error, to best his adversary here and now, to secure acceptance of his ideas by his disciples and contemporaries'.[14] This methodology also meant that divines could, and often did, change their minds when presented with persuasive argumentation: this happened regularly within the assembly.[15] What may seem like ecclesiastical warfare to the modern reader was exactly what these divines were trained to do.

DENOMINATIONALISM AND THE PRESBYTERIANS

The study of presbyterianism in the 1640s has particularly suffered on this point. The dogged belief that England's only hope was a presbyterian settlement has unduly turned our focus to the 'independents' of England who must necessarily be blamed for the delay of that settlement.[16] However, the myth of a unified presbyterian majority needs to be challenged. There were marked, and important, ecclesiological differences between the Scottish and English presbyterians, and also within those two groups. The Scots were no more the vanguard of presbyterian polity, as is commonly believed, than the English were acquiescent ecclesiological infants in need of a helping hand.

The tendency towards denominationalism in the historiography of Scottish presbyterianism in England, along with a failure to understand it in its Scottish context, has done a particular disservice to our understanding of men like George Gillespie and Samuel Rutherford. If we take a step back from the prevailing historiography of 'presbyterian versus independent', a very different and far more complex scenario arises. A recent historiographical question has focused on whether or not there was presbyterianism in England prior to 1640.[17] We shall see that the question we should ask is not merely whether or not presbyterianism existed in England before 1640, but also what types of presbyterianism emerged at the Westminster assembly. We will try to isolate a few of those presbyterian strains of ecclesiological thought, in context, and consider how they related to one another.

The Scottish presbyterians have been regarded as the inflexible juggernaut, who wanted uniformity at all costs.[18] This image has partly been reinforced by denominational historians of the Westminster assembly.[19] By and large, the Westminster confession was only implemented in Scotland, whereas it was dead on arrival in England.[20] However, there continues to be a historical position that believes, as one historian has recently stated, that by the time England and Scotland had covenanted together against Charles in 1644, Scotland was in the 'driving seat in British revolutionary politics'.[21] Hence, it is thought, there was a political dimension in which Parliament saw a Scottish-type kirk established in England as fair trade for Scottish troops. The Scottish divines are portrayed as the mortal enemies of the Apologists, with whom they had irreconcilable differences. This was true of certain Scottish divines, but not all, and certainly not of the most influential Scottish ministers at Westminster. Furthermore, the Scottish divines are viewed as the catalyst through which English presbyterianism, and indeed the Westminster assembly, would stand or fall. The English presbyterians, Erastians aside, are simply judged by when they decided to fall in line with the Scots. All of these conclusions need to be challenged.

SOURCES

This book will call into question the use of various pamphlet sources and also engage in a careful analysis of several well-known, but relatively unused, texts. A close inspection of the pamphlet literature coming from these groups of divines will show a more nuanced interplay of source material and ideas than has been typically noticed. Pamphlets have always played an important role in our understanding of religious debate in the 1640s, but the overuse of a highly selective group of sensational pamphlets has distorted our views of debates within Westminster.

The only pamphlets that directly addressed the *Apologetical Narration* and early debates at the Westminster assembly were written by five arguably peripheral figures, none of whom were assembly members or had any major impact on assembly debates. Yet the historiography of the *Narration*, and indeed of the assembly as a whole, has been dominated by the use of the external pamphlet debates as sources for what occurred in the assembly. In this way, they have created an image of all out ecclesiological war within the assembly.

One hallmark of the pamphlet debates outside of the assembly is the blame shifting over who actually started the debates. A typical example is Rosemary Bradley's conclusion that the presbyterians were unanimous in their distaste of the *Narration* and in blaming the pamphlet war on its publication. But she bases this on a reading of Adam Steuart and Thomas Edwards – who were not members of the assembly.[22] Assembly presbyterians remained silent in print, as did the Scots.[23] The pamphlet warfare in early 1644 was essentially a debate between five men who kept egging each other on. On the independent side there was John Goodwin and Nathaniel Holmes. John Goodwin, by his own admission, was not in dialogue with the Apologists in 1643 and 1644. His independent polity and politics was markedly different from that of the assembly congregationalists, and his relationship with them would grow to the level of hostility over the course of the 1640s. Nathaniel Holmes, as we will see, became an incessant cause of frustration and embarrassment for the Apologists in particular and the assembly in general.

On the 'presbyterian' side, we have Adam Steuart, Alexander Forbes and Thomas Edwards. The Scottish divine Adam Steuart was primarily focused on attacking John Goodwin. Alexander Forbes was living in Holland and would later admit that he did not fully understand England's debates over church government. The English minister Thomas Edwards was a peripheral figure, and that fact in and of itself was the source of much of Edwards's vituperation. Edwards repeatedly condemned the Apologists for breaking the alliance that they were said to have formed with the presbyterians, while continually praising the 'virtuosity' of the presbyterians.[24] We could include the English divine William Rathband in this list, but his pamphlet, written before he became a member of the assembly, was primarily aimed at the New England divine Thomas Welde. When he became a member he disengaged.

We will make extensive use of private correspondence, including a collection of letters by the Scottish divine Robert Baillie. Baillie's private letters and journals provide an invaluable resource for scholars of this period. But his accessibility has coloured the way we understand his fellow commissioners, Gillespie and Rutherford. We will call into question Baillie's reliability as a source for either the congregational divines *or* the Scottish commissioners.

The influence of Thomas Edwards's well-known responses to the *Apologeticall Narration* cannot be overstated. In this book we will carefully avoid letting Edwards lead the discussion, primarily, again, because he was not at Westminster and not part of the circle of divines we will focus upon. Murray Tolmie's work relied heavily on Thomas Edwards for his source material and painted a very misleading yet influential picture of the Apologists. The Apologists, for Tolmie, were a group of clandestine, 'separatist' operatives representing 'organised radicalism' in London. Thus the Apologists were willing to go to great lengths to undermine a national church.[25] Like Edwards's use of guilt by association, Tolmie sees friendships, advice or even brief encounters between the Apologists and separatists as tantamount to the Apologists endorsing and encouraging 'radical' ecclesiastical and political policies.[26]

Historians utilise Steuart, Forbes, Edwards, John Goodwin and Holmes to explain what Scottish presbyterians, English presbyterians and the Apologists

at Westminster believed, instead of actually studying what men like Rutherford, Gillespie, Thomas Goodwin, Burroughs, Herle and Calamy actually said
and wrote.[27] The point here is not to avoid those pamphlets, but to generate
a narrative using the characters *in* the story. In doing so, we will see an intellectual dialogue and debate that moves us away from scurrilous anecdotes and
purely polemical rhetoric.

THE WESTMINSTER ASSEMBLY OF DIVINES

The recently transcribed minutes of the Westminster assembly will also play
an important role. The minutes provide a rich, un-mined source for how
these divines engaged with each other. One failure in the historiography of
the Westminster assembly is that no effort has been made to merge what
was said in private with what these divines actually had printed in books
and pamphlets. In this way, this book will provide a methodology for how to
approach the published volumes on the Westminster assembly edited by Chad
Van Dixhoorn.

In historians' efforts to codify the presbyterian and independent distinction, they have eliminated a variety of other distinctions. While it makes for
more exciting – and less messy – history to place the black hats and white
hats on our subjects, it can be severely misleading. Though there were most
certainly categories we can broadly label 'presbyterian' and 'congregational',
there were a number of distinctions within these categories that these divines
considered to be important. By the 1640s there was not one presbyterian and
one congregational mould. The point at which a congregationalist crossed
over to presbyterianism (or vice versa) was by no means a static line of demar-
cation. A careful analysis of the extensive ecclesiological texts of the period
reveals a far more complex understanding of church government than we are
accustomed to. The texts may seem messy at times, but we should try to trace
out the logical coherence that existed in the minds of those who wrote them.

Studying the minutes has been a notoriously difficult problem for historians. A debate over a seemingly innocuous proposition or its prooftext can
go on for days or weeks, and it is not always easy to distinguish between
individual divines' competing positions. For example, a divine will occasionally utilise the scholastic strategy of arguing his opponent's position in order to
expose an inconsistency. I will show that the best way to approach the assembly's discussions on church government is to take a particular topic – in this
case, church power – and trace it through the minutes. Furthermore, the most
elucidating moments in the assembly are when the divines debate how to
proceed and what topic they should address next. These are turning points in
the assembly, and in these instances we gain the clearest insights into various
parties' positions and their strategies. It becomes much more difficult to study

the minutes once the assembly is committed to debate a particular proposition. At that point, the scholastic procedures have begun and the reader can get stuck in a mire of points and counterpoints. We will focus on three pivotal moments in the assembly, October 1643, February 1644 and September 1644, which taken together will help the historian better understand the first, and arguably most important, year at Westminster.

PARLIAMENT'S ASSEMBLY

Historians of revolutionary England have tended to focus on the extremes of the ecclesiological spectrum in an effort to define elusive terms such as 'radicalism' and 'religious toleration'. However, when the Long Parliament called the Westminster assembly, it knew that one of the most destabilising elements of the body politic was an inchoate national church, where heterodoxy presented as much of a threat as prelacy. This was Parliament's assembly of divines, and the state needed a church that would stymie a clerical usurpation of state control, but could equally fend off the burgeoning call for separation of church and state. Very few MPs sought an assembly that would replace one (prelatical) clerisy with another (high presbyterian) one, but most sought an assembly that would protect Reformed orthodoxy and see off independent assaults on the very existence of a uniform national, reformed confession of faith.[28] As Chad van Dixhoorn puts it, after the abuses MPs had experienced from the Laudian church, the two Houses designed the summoning ordinance for the assembly as a pre-nuptial agreement where they would be the dominant partner.[29] In other words, the Houses made a nearly impossible request for an assembly that they could both trust and manage, and that could create and maintain an 'ecclesiological centre' knowing it was simultaneously bound in its Solemn League and Covenant with Scotland to model the 'best reformed churches' (i.e. foreign) in a national English context.

Most MPs believed that they needed Scottish troops by the time it signed the Solemn League and Covenant in 1644. That they were willing to bend the religious will of England to Scotland's brand of presbyterianism as part of that bargain was entirely different. Presbyterianism, much less Scottish presbyterianism, was not a forgone conclusion when the Westminster assembly first met.[30] The Westminster assembly was no side-show to the political drama playing out in Parliament and on the battlefield. Nor were its members simply mouthpieces for powerful individuals or groups in the Palace of Westminster. Many members of the assembly had received protection in noble households or had been placed by lay patrons in out-of-the-way country parishes in the 1630s and heavily promoted by lay patrons since 1640, but they were never puppets. This book will seek to show that the dynamics in the assembly owes far more to esprit de corps within a body confident in the calling of its members by God without any need to seek puppet-masters across the road from the Abbey Church of St Peter.

TERMS

Throughout the book I will refer to the Apologists as congregationalists, rather than 'independents'. The latter was a title repeatedly eschewed by the Apologists as sounding politically insubordinate and rejecting any sort of communion with a wider network of churches, or even a national church. Assembly members were careful to avoid addressing the Apologists as 'independents' during their debates, and indeed, in the minutes the word was also used in reference to the Scottish presbyterian system of church government being 'independent' – or alongside – of the magistrate.[31] Independent was a word used regularly in print and private diaries in reference to the Apologists, often – but not exclusively – as a pejorative. However, I will show that there was an acknowledgement, particularly amongst the groups studied in this book, of theological distinctions between the congregationalism of the Apologists and many other independents. The assembly repeatedly recognised that the congregationalists favoured a *type* of presbyterian church government. Indeed, after months of the most intense debates over church government, the presbyterian Charles Herle said of the assembly, 'That which is right Indepen[dency], all of us are opposite to'.[32]

In general, I will label the presbyterians as Scottish, English and clerical English. The clerical English presbyterians have not been studied in detail, and there is virtually no discussion of them in the pre-revolutionary puritan historiographies. As I use it, 'clerical' is merely a descriptive, and not a pejorative term. I mean only that the perceived right to partake in a synod resides not in a principle of representative eldership, but in the teaching office of the minister. These clerical English presbyterians believed that all church power could reside in a synod of elders over multiple churches and not in the local church. They wielded a considerable amount of influence at Westminster and seemed to be followed by a silent group of backbench voters in the Jerusalem Chamber. Another influential voting block within the assembly was the Erastian English presbyterians. Though we will discuss their influence on certain ecclesiastical debates, the major impact of Erastianism on the assembly took place after the period covered in this book. Within each group there were a variety of views on any number of important ecclesiological issues, and therefore we should hold lightly to each category. I have attempted, where possible, to isolate and describe those views when they arise.

When the words synod, presbytery or national assembly are used, they will refer to a group of elders from various churches convening to govern or discuss matters pertaining to the churches in their regions – or country. In the primary source material, the word presbytery has several meanings, and of course, the powers given to such assemblies was a heavily debated topic. Many parties at Westminster agreed that it could refer to a local group of elders from one particular church that had a unique responsibility to care for that body. The meaning of the word often has to do with the context, and for the reader – particularly using the minutes of the assembly – it can be difficult to know how the word is being used. Therefore, I have made an attempt to clarify when we are discussing local church presbyteries as opposed to any group of elders meeting outside the context of the particular church.

There are innumerable ways to re-theologise ecclesiological studies, particularly in this complex period of 'high orthodoxy'. We currently lack a detailed history of biblical exegesis and interpretation across the early modern period, and this is particularly noticeable in texts relating to church government. As Willem van Asselt has noted, if we are going 'to recover the intentions of the Reformed scholastics', then we must understand that they 'cited a text when they considered it to be intrinsically important because of its truth'. A biblical text 'did not function "historically" (a notion absent in premodern times), but it was interpreted according to one's own frame of thought ... and as an authority of truth'.[33] One way to untangle the complexities of this period is through the concept of the ecclesiastical 'keyes', as they are understood through the foundational verses of Matthew 16:19 and Matthew 18:17, 18.[34]

These two passages, and particularly the former, outline what Thomas Goodwin called the '*substratum*' of all church government. They instruct on the notion of church power and how that power should be allocated in any church system. The tendency to focus on the more well-known passage in Matthew 18 – where Christ ordains how the church should handle matters of discipline – without first developing categories of church power stemming from Matthew 16 has introduced a host of reductionistic categories into the historiography. Together they are arguably the most fundamental verses to understand if we are to begin to untangle the complexity of ecclesiological studies and to begin to provide scholastic terminology for the relatively understudied debates of the early 1640s; and as a conceptual tool the keys will unlock several of the most important pamphlets on church government written between 1638 and 1644 and clarify vital, but altogether overlooked, debates at the Westminster assembly. They will also provide a way to begin to tease out the real and important differences within what we popularly call independency and presbyterianism.

OUTLINE

The main arguments here are threaded throughout the book. Each chapter presumes points made before and anticipates subsequent narratives. Thus, while it is hoped that each chapter contributes a unique and significant historical perspective, they are not intended to be read in isolation. The first two chapters are background studies of the Westminster assembly. We will explore the relationships and theological connections between the Apologists, the Smectymnuan divines ('Smectymnuus' was a publishing acronym for the important group of English presbyterians that included Stephen Marshall, Edmund Calamy, Thomas Young, Matthew Newcomen and William Spurstow), and the Scottish commissioners who were sent to negotiate with Parliament in 1640 and 1641. These relationships will force us to rethink the dynamic interplay between these various groups in the assembly. The third chapter moves into the beginning of the Westminster assembly and examines a brief, but crucial, debate at Westminster in late October 1643. That debate sets the ecclesiological stage for the rest of the book, for in it we find the basis of the Apologists' polity and the emergence of a variety of English presbyterian positions. Chapters 4, 5 and 6 will look at the pivotal first half of 1644 from three different perspectives. Chapter 4 is an important reassessment of the *Apologeticall Narration*'s place in the immediate political and theological climate of 1644. Having set the political stage, we will then furnish the story with theology, without losing sight of the larger narrative contours of 1644. Chapter 5 will begin to analyse the uniqueness of the Apologists' understanding of the keys through New England divine John Cotton's enormously important *Keyes of the Kingdom of Heaven*. We will situate Cotton's *Keyes* in the wider pamphlet disputes and assess its relationship with the wider independent movement. Chapter 6 will be a more nuanced and in depth study of the Apologists' (and Cotton's) unique congregational polity and how it was received by reformed orthodox theologians *outside* England. Chapter 7 will go back into the assembly and see how the previous three chapters converge in the Westminster disputes, and thus challenge some important misconceptions about the Apologists and their place in England's push for religious reform. The final chapter will address the question of religious accommodation in the Westminster assembly and how its failure was as much a result of presbyterian factionalism and political exigencies as it was a refusal of the Apologists to submit to a presbyterian church settlement.

SUMMARY

The narrative that unfolds is a crucial reassessment of some of the most important puritan divines at a pivotal moment in British history. The years 1638 to 1644 uncomfortably straddle a seismic shift, where religious reform morphed into political revolution. When we focus on these years and how the Apologists, emerging English presbyterians and Scottish presbyterians represented themselves, how they perceived each other, and *how they worked together*, a very different picture emerges than the one commonly portrayed. This is not a comprehensive study of any particular group or church government.

A contextualisation of their ecclesiological writings will demonstrate that they actually reflected a framework of intellectual discourse that has been lost in the crude binary categories of 'presbyterianism' and 'independency'.

NOTES

1 C. Van Dixhoorn, *The Minutes and Papers of the Westminster Assembly, 1643–1652 (MPWA)*, 5 vols (Oxford: Oxford University Press, 2012), vol. 3, p. 392.

2 J. Bannerman, *The Church of Christ*, 2 vols (Edinburgh: T & T Clark, 1868), vol. 1, p. 263.

3 A. Milton, *Catholic and Reformed: Roman and Protestant Churches in English Protestant Thought, 1600–40*, Cambridge Studies in Early Modern British History (Cambridge: Cambridge University Press, 1995), p. 4.

4 J. Coffey & A. Chapman, 'Introduction: Intellectual History and the Return of Religion', *Seeing Things Their Way: Intellectual History and the Return of Religion* (Notre Dame, IN: Notre Dame University Press, 2009), p. 15.

5 Although they are commonly referred to as the Dissenting Brethren, I will refer to these five divines as the Apologists, since technically they did not officially dissent from a presbyterian system until late 1644.

6 See T. M. Lawrence, 'Transmission and Transformation: Thomas Goodwin and the Puritan Project 1600–1704', University of Cambridge, PhD thesis (2002), Bibliography, pp. 245–252. Also see *Principles of Christian Religion* (Oxford: Bodleian Library: Nalson MSS, 22).

7 J. R. De Witt, *Jus divinum: The Westminster Assembly and the Divine Right Of Church Government* (Kampen: J. H. Kok, 1969), p. 106.

8 See M. R. Watts, *The Dissenters* (Oxford: Clarendon Press, 1978), p. 98; Y. Chung, 'Parliament and the Committee for Accommodation', *Parliamentary History*, 30 (2011), 289–308, p. 290.

9 For the Apologists' views on toleration, see H. Powell, 'The Last Confession: A Background Study of the Savoy Declaration of Faith and Order', University of Cambridge, MPhil thesis, deposited in Seeley Library (2008).

10 R. A. Muller, 'Reflections on Persistent Whiggism and its Antidotes in the Study of Sixteenth- and Seventeenth-century Intellectual History', in A. Chapman *et al.* (eds), *Seeing Things Their Way: Intellectual History and the Return of Religion* (Notre Dame, IN: University of Notre Dame Press, 2009), p. 150.

11 Ibid., p. 139.

12 W. Haller, *Liberty and Reformation in the Puritan Revolution* (New York: Columbia University Press, 1955), p. 119; W. K. Jordan, *The Development of Religious Toleration in England: Attainment of the Theory and Accommodations in Thought and Institutions (1640–1660)* (London: George Allen & Unwin Ltd., 1938), p. 371; E. Shagan, 'Beyond Good and Evil: Thinking with Moderates in Early Modern England', *Journal of British Studies*, 49 (2010), 488–513, pp. 504–505; E. Shagan, 'Rethinking Moderation in the English Revolution: The Case of An Apologeticall Narration' in G. Tapsell and S. Taylor (eds), *The Nature of the English Revolution Revisited* (Martlesham: Boydell & Brower, 2013); J. S. Morrill, *The Nature of the English Revolution* (London: Longman, 2013).

13 For more on these distinctions, see W. J. van Asselt & P. Rouwendal, 'Introduction: What Is Reformed Scholasticism', in J. v. A. Willem (ed.), *Introduction to Reformed*

Scholasticism, trans. A. Gootjes (Grand Rapids, MI: Reformation Heritage Books, 2010), chapters 8 and 9.

14 W. T. Costello, *The Scholastic Curriculum at Early Seventeenth-century Cambridge* (Cambridge, MA: Harvard University Press, 1958), pp. 8–9.

15 Van Dixhoorn, *MPWA* (vol. 1), p. 21.

16 This is the tenor of De Witt's study of the Westminster assembly, *Jus divinum*.

17 See P. Ha, *English Presbyterianism, 1590–1640* (Stanford, CA: Stanford University Press, 2011); and T. Webster, *Godly Clergy* (Cambridge: Cambridge University Press, 1997), pp. 303, 311.

18 D. G. Mullan, '"Uniformity in Religion": The Solemn League and Covenant (1643) and the Presbyterian Vision', in W. F. Graham (ed.), *Later Calvinism: International Perspectives* (Kirksville, MO: Northeast Missouri State University, 1994), p. 260.

19 This is discussed in Van Dixhoorn, *MPWA* (vol. 1), p. 26.

20 Ibid., p. 86.

21 A. I. Macinnes, 'The "Scottish Moment", 1638–45', in J. Adamson (ed.), *The English Civil War: Conflicts and Contexts, 1640–49* (Basingstoke: Palgrave Macmillan, 2009), p. 125.

22 R. D. Bradley, '"Jacob and Esau Struggling in the Wombe": A Study of Presbyterian and Independent Religious Conflicts 1640–48', University of Kent, PhD thesis (1975), pp. 201–202.

23 J. L. Kim, 'The Debate on the Relations between the Churches of Scotland and England during the British Revolution (1633–1647)', University of Cambridge, PhD thesis (1997), p. 219.

24 Bradley, '"Jacob and Esau"', chapter 1.

25 M. Tolmie, *Triumph of the Saints* (Cambridge: Cambridge University Press, 1977), p. 96.

26 For a more lengthy discussion on the flaws – both conceptually and factually – in Tolmie's work, see H. Powell, 'The Dissenting Brethren and the Power of the Keys, 1640–44', PhD thesis, Faculty of History, University of Cambridge, Cambridge (2011), pp. 255ff.

27 For a recent example, see Shagan, 'Rethinking Moderation in the English Revolution: The Case of An Apologeticall Narration'.

28 See R. A. Muller, *Calvin and the Reformed Tradition: On the Work of Christ and the Order of Salvation* (Grand Rapids, MI: Baker Academic, 2012), p. 51; A. J. B. a. W. d. Boer (ed.), *The Reception of John Calvin and His Theology in Reformed Orthodoxy, Church History and Religious Culture* (special double issue), 91.1–2 (2011), esp. pp. 255–274.

29 Van Dixhoorn, *MPWA* (vol. 1), pp. 11, 12.

30 Bradley, '"Jacob and Esau"', p. 66.

31 Van Dixhoorn, *MPWA* (vol. 1), p. 30.

32 Van Dixhoorn, *MPWA* (vol. 3), p. 265.

33 W. J. van Asselt, 'Scholasticism Revisited: Methodological Reflections on the Study of Seventeenth-century Reformed Thought', in A. Chapman *et al.* (eds), *Seeing Things Their Way* (Notre Dame, IN: University of Notre Dame Press, 2010), p. 167.

34 Matthew 16:15–19, 'He saith unto them, But whom say ye that I am? And Simon Peter

answered and said, Thou art the Christ, the Son of the living God. And Jesus answered and said unto him, Blessed art thou, Simon Barjona: for flesh and blood hath not revealed it unto thee, but my Father which is in heaven. And I say also unto thee, That thou art Peter, and upon this rock I will build my church; and the gates of hell shall not prevail against it. And I will give unto thee the keys of the kingdom of heaven: and whatsoever thou shalt bind on earth shall be bound in heaven: and whatsoever thou shalt loose on earth shall be loosed in heaven.' Matthew 18:17–18. 'Moreover if thy brother shall trespass against thee, go and tell him his fault between thee and him alone: if he shall hear thee, thou hast gained thy brother. But if he will not hear thee, then take with thee one or two more, that in the mouth of two or three witnesses every word may be established. And if he shall neglect to hear them, tell it unto the church: but if he neglect to hear the church, let him be unto thee as an heathen man and a publican. Verily I say unto you, Whatsoever ye shall bind on earth shall be bound in heaven: and whatsoever ye shall loose on earth shall be loosed in heaven.'

Chapter 1

Prelude to a debate

By the time of the first meeting of the Long Parliament in November 1640, England was at a crucial juncture in its ecclesiastical and political history. Charles's enforcement of new ceremonial policies of the Church of England in the 1630s resulted in widescale harassment of puritan pastors. Through Laud's stewardship, the king was perceived to be turning back the clock on the Reformed orthodoxy endorsed by his father, James I. Since the Elizabethan Religious Settlement in 1559, there had been a recurrent – if at times latent – fear that a Roman Catholic church structure (governed by archbishops and bishops) was a naive placeholder for a future return of Catholicism. Charles's marriage to a Catholic queen did nothing to assuage these fears. For an increasing number of puritans and politicians, England's king was failing in his most important duty, protecting the nation from a papal (i.e. *foreign*) invasion.

Perhaps Charles's greatest misstep had been attempting to enforce Laudian 'innovations' in the Scottish kirk. His failure – or unwillingness – to recognise Scotland's potent mixture of national pride and religious zeal resulted in rebellion, as Scottish presbyterians covenanted together to reject both ceremonialism and England's prelatical church. For the Scots, England's church was itself foreign – both to their kirk and reformed orthodoxy. Charles's lack of regard for Scotland's grievances was highlighted by the fact that the Scots had to invade England twice between 1638 and 1640 to get his attention. The second time, however, Scotland was not to be placated by the king's ultimately empty promises. Charles was forced to either agree to the demands of the Scottish Covenanters or engage the rebels on the field of battle. He fatefully, if not foolishly, chose the latter. When the Scots occupied north-east England Charles lacked the manpower and the finances to dislodge them. In order to pass bills to acquire the necessary resources, he had to call what would be known as the Long Parliament. By this point, however, Parliament had its own extensive list of grievances against the king. Scotland capitalised on this political rupture and sent commissioners to treat directly with sympathetic parliamentarians in London. England's revolution began to take shape.

In the winter of 1640 and 1641, debates over removing episcopacy 'Root and Branch' from England were well underway. As of yet, civil war was not on the horizon, and Parliament was months away from appointing an assembly of divines to restructure the Church of England. There was no widespread agreement on how to reform, or rescue, England's church from the perceived dangers of arminian theology and Catholic ecclesiology. Parliament was loosely divided into those who wished merely to purge the current structure from its Laudian innovations, and those who wished to replace it completely. They were unified in their rejection of arminianism, but far from united in what – if anything – should be done about the prelatical structure of England's church.

The question for Parliament was whether they could go backwards and forwards at the same time – could England go back to a pre-arminian episcopacy without changing the structure that may have allowed for heterodoxy in the first place? In the minds of puritans, faith and order were bound together, and while the latter was certainly of secondary importance, it was nonetheless agreed that a rightly ordered church was the only thing that could fence the boundaries of orthodoxy.

THE GODLY ALLIANCE

While Parliament tackled matters of state and religious grievances, certain parliamentarians and religious divines began a polemical attack on the core tenets of Laudianism. The lack of unity in Parliament, however, meant that those who had a semblance of ecclesiological clarity had to be more aggressive in their efforts to influence church reform. This was particularly true of the 'junto' of ministers and peers meeting at Edmund Calamy's Aldermanbury house during those pivotal months. When we look specifically at this small group of influential divines and peers in 1641, we see a polity that was far more clearly delineated than scholars have previously assumed. There was a distinct movement away from prelatical bishops towards locating church power in the particular church. What was uncertain was the nature and type of power that should be located above those churches, and on that point there was widespread disagreement. There was, however, agreement that church power could not be located in the person of the bishop, and that as long as the prelate retained binding jurisdiction in matters of the church, reformed orthodoxy, and thus the body politic, could not be safe from Catholic innovations and foreign invasions. This was not a burying of differences that emerged in non-conformity, but an alliance based on genuine exegetical conviction and agreement.

In late 1640, the Apologists took advantage of Parliament's conflict with Charles and began to return from their self-imposed exile in Holland with the high hopes of religious reform. They quickly assimilated into the Calamy house group. They had personal relationships with English puritans and parliamentarians at Aldermanbury and quickly developed a close working relationship with the newly arrived Scottish commissioners. Surprisingly, given the current historiography, the Scots and the Apologists, at this stage, had the most in common ecclesiologically. The Apologists were not moving in separatist circles, nor were they peripheral to the 'Root and Branch' debates. This chapter will highlight how the Apologists' congregational platform of church government, clearly articulated in the winter of 1641, was known to the Calamy circle and was supported as a church model that could unite the godly. In the next chapter we will see how this platform engendered a close working relationship with the Scottish presbyterians based upon similar biblical exegesis. While the congregational divines exhibited a clear, and widely accepted, form of church government, the rapidly changing religious and political context in England gave birth to variegated presbyterianisms both north and south of the border.

John Adamson has provided a political account of the pivotal months between December 1640 and February 1641 – and beyond. He recovers the central role of a 'junto' of peers in bringing about the civil wars. We can also note here how intimately involved these peers were with the Aldermanbury divines in general and the Apologists specifically. Referring to those crucial months in late 1640, the English divine Cornelius Burgess much later stated that the nobles, including the Earl of Warwick, Lord Saye and Sele, Lord Brooke and others, were meeting twice weekly with divines such as Stephen Marshall and Calamy to discuss church reform.

> a number of Lords and Commons, with whom (by their appointment) Mr. <John> White of Dorchester, Mr. <Stephen> Marshall, Mr. <Edmund> Calamy, my self & one or two ministers more, mett twice ever week, at some of their lodgings. Among them, was the late Earle of Warwick, the Lord Say, Lord Brook, with some other nobes, Mr. <John> Hampden , Mr. Pim, &c.[1]

Nobles did not have idle time on their hands, yet in spite of their busy parliamentary schedule, they made time for these divines. Carol Schneider has shown that the Calamy coterie helped draft the *Ministers' Petition and Remonstrance*, and Adamson argues that there is 'little doubt that he [Calamy] was acting with at very least his patron's [Warwick's] consent'.[2] The *Ministers' Petition*, however, was only one piece of a larger, more systematic and collective effort at parish reform. This effort drew together an old network of ministers and patrons, friendships and allegiances forged in the fires of Laudian persecution. As we analyse their collective effort at parish reform we shall see that these moderate divines acted in concert with these nobles, not simply with their tacit consent.

Burgess does not mention any congregationalists by name in his letter to Baxter, but evidence demonstrates that 'the one or two ministers' included Burroughs and perhaps Thomas Goodwin.[3] We know from a letter dated 28 December 1640 from the Scottish divine Robert Baillie that

> There was some fear for those of the new way, who are for the Independent congregations; bot after much conference, thanks be to God, we hope they will joyne to overthrow the Episcopacie, erect Presbyterian government and Assemblies, and, in any difference they have, to be silent, upon hope either of satisfaction when we can gett more leasure, or of toleration, on their good and peaceable behaviour.[4]

Calamy himself said a few years later that 'My house was the receptacle for godly ministers in the worst of times: here was the *Remonstrance* framed against the Prelates ... [where we demonstrated to Parliament that] a Bishop and Presbyter were all one.'[5] The idea of bishops and presbyters being one was a common thread that connected the major documents coming out of the meetings in Calamy's house. It was at Calamy's Aldermanbury home a year later that the Holland Brethren and the Smectymnuus group would allegedly codify what Baillie had only hinted at, an agreement not to publish or preach ecclesiological polemics until the issue of the episcopacy had been resolved.

Frank Bremer has done a thorough analysis of the relationships between Smectymnuans and congregational divines going back as far as their years at Cambridge.[6] These relationships were still vital in 1641, and can be traced throughout the Hartlib manuscripts.[7] Calamy and Burroughs represent one of these longstanding relationships. In the 1630s Calamy and Burroughs had preached together in Bury St Edmunds. Both men were under the patronage of the Earl of Warwick. Kenneth Shipps, who has written extensively on the puritan patronage network in East Anglia, believed there was a competitive conflict between the two ministers.[8] Yet evidence outside of Shipps's period of study exhibits an extremely close and abiding friendship between Calamy and Burroughs. Calamy would bring a series of Burroughs's sermons – which he preached in early 1641 – to publication, stating, 'These Sermons are to be prized for their own worth and intrinsecall excellency, whoever was Author. And this Author is to be honoured for his reall worth, whatsoever he is the authour of.'[9] In his funeral sermon for Simeon Ashe, Calamy cited Burroughs in a small list of divines whose death was a great loss to the ministerial community in England.[10] Indeed, Burroughs and Calamy preached together in 1643 supporting an Anglo-Scottish alliance against the Royalists.[11] There were two parish churches in Bury St Edmunds in the 1650s, and we know from a letter written to Oliver Cromwell from the congregational parish church that its members asked him to allow both churches (presbyterian and congregational) to continue to worship within Bury, using the peaceable relationship of Burroughs and Calamy as their example.[12]

Burroughs, along with Calamy, was one of Warwick's protégés, and Warwick sheltered Burroughs prior to his exile in Holland. Burroughs was brought into the Warwick circle through Lord Brooke and via a chaplaincy with Lord Mandeville, who he met in Bury St Edmunds.[13] When Burroughs came under the investigative gaze of Matthew Wren, Bishop of Ely and Norwich, the bishop was forced to handle the case with care due to the divine's powerful connections.[14] Burroughs himself was the divine who was at Warwick's bedside when the nobleman was near death in 1638, as Burroughs says in the dedicatory to his book *Moses his Choice*.[15] This work was published, probably not coincidentally, the same month as the *Petition Examined* (the document we will focus on in this chapter) and was dedicated to Warwick.[16] But this preface was more than just sycophantic prefatorial praises. Burroughs called Warwick to remember his deathbed covenant with God to reform the church of God should he live: 'It is now mere three yeares since that your Lordship lying sick not without apprehension that God's time to call you from the Land of the living was come.' Burroughs reminisced, 'I was then for some time dayly with your Lordship, and all the desires of you expressed for life were, that you might live to doe God service here.'[17] And connecting that deathbed covenant to the present circumstances in England, Burroughs reminded Warwick, 'those Covenants you made with God if ever he restored you ... [,] surely those Vowes of God are upon you'. God has 'now put an opportunity in your hand to fulfill them', and 'now he expects the performance of them'.[18] Burroughs had left Warwick with a covenant of church reform on what he believed to be his dying lips, and now, three years later in 1641, Burroughs felt emboldened by events to remind Warwick to honour that covenant.

It has been argued that the Apologists were uncommitted to a particular polity and that Burroughs was effectively a presbyterian, arguments that do not hold when considering the protection offered to him by Warwick.[19] There were numerous intersecting storylines during this brief period that would indicate Warwick was familiar with the polities of the ministers he watched over, particularly Burroughs's. It was while he was staying in Warwick's home that Burroughs received his pastoral call from Bridge's congregational church in Rotterdam.[20] Given that Burroughs had already travelled back and forth to Holland, it seems probable that he was congregational prior to his departure to Rotterdam. He would have known the government structure of Bridge's church before he accepted the offer to be its minister. Warwick would have known the type of church to which Burroughs had gone. And Warwick himself, under the guise of the Providence Island Company, had already provided safe passage to New England for the puritan ministers Thomas Hooker and Nathaniel Ward.[21] We must remember that it was in Warwick's garden that Burroughs fell foul of the Court of High Commission when he voiced his support for the Scottish Covenanters and indicated the people had a right to take up armed resistance against the king. These are topics Burroughs would probably have discussed with his patron as he sat by him in what he believed to be his deathbed.

The Apologists' connection to the dissident peers extended well beyond Warwick. Burroughs had already published his *Excellency of a Gracious Spirit* in 1638 and dedicated it to Lord Mandeville, crediting Mandeville and his wife for giving him the idea for the treatise.[22] Thomas Goodwin was connected to Mandeville through his relationships with Marshall, Burroughs and Bridge. Goodwin was publishing pamphlets in the late 1630s dedicated to Lord Brooke, and he dedicated republished tracts to Mandeville in the early 1640s.[23] These were probably the works on practical divinity that Baillie praised in March 1641.[24] Goodwin's network was expanded through the extraordinarily well-connected Philip Nye. Nye's network of influence was almost without peer, and perhaps matched only by that of his close friend and relative, the Smectym-nuan Stephen Marshall. As early as 1632 Nye was involved in the Massachu-setts Bay Company, and he became assistant scribe, with William Jessop, of the Providence Island Company, which brought him into contact with Saye and Sele, Lord Brooke, Warwick, Mandeville, along with Sir Nathaniel Rich, John Pym, Oliver St John, Sir Arthur Hesilrig and Sir Thomas Barrington.[25] Simpson was also involved in the Bay Colony venture.[26]

When Nye and Goodwin moved to their Arnhem church in Holland, powerful Yorkshire gentlemen and future MPs – soon-to-be central figures in the struggle against Charles – went with them. Among them were Sir William Constable, Sir Matthew Boynton, Sir Richard Saltonstall, Sir Thomas Bourchier and Henry Lawrence, Oliver Cromwell's landlord and an elder in Goodwin's congregation.[27] 'The roster of Arnhem', as one historian put it, 'composed the most prestigious colony-in-exile to be found in the Netherlands.'[28] These were simultaneously members of Nye and Goodwin's congregations, and they were the very same men who David Scott has argued acted in collusion to draw Scotland into England during the Bishops' Wars.[29] Sir William Constable of Yorkshire was brother-in-law to Fernando Fairfax, the influential Parliamen-tarian and future Civil War commander.[30] Boynton, whose daughter married Saye and Sele's son, was certainly back in Yorkshire in August 1640.[31] Along with Thomas Alured, Boynton attempted to disrupt Charles's war efforts against the Scots.[32] Alured and Boynton probably remained members of Goodwin's church in London and Nye's church in Hull after they returned from Holland.[33] Thomas Alured was connected to Nye through the Providence Island Company and was probably Nye's patron when he returned to Hull, and Alured was a distant relation of Lord Brooke.[34] According to Adamson, many of the conspiratorial activities of these nobles were happening under the guise of the Providence Island Company.[35] Arthur Newton has gone so far as to say Nye was Mandeville's protégé, and notably it was Mandeville who presented Nye with his parish living in 1643.[36] We can safely assume, therefore, that Nye and Goodwin had some idea of the 'treason' going on in Yorkshire and their parishioners' involvement. Parliament would lean heavily on Bridge to give their theological defence for taking up arms against Charles.[37] In 1638 Saye and Sele wrote to John Cotton in New England informing him that Thomas Goodwin had already fled to Holland and that he knew Nye was about to join him. Saye and Sele offered to pass along any writings by Cotton to the Holland exiles.[38]

It was this group, then, the Smectymnuans and the Holland Brethren, with at the very least the knowledge of, but probably the support of this group of nobles, that united around a common cause for church reform. Carol Schneider has helpfully noted that there was a spectrum of ecclesiological persuasions in this house group, ranging, as she says, from 'congregational independency' on the one end, all the way to supporters of reformed episcopacy, like Cornelius Burgess, on the other. She believed, quite accurately, that many in the Calamy house group were looking for a 'middle way', but she failed to apprehend that they had found one.[39]

'WE ALL SEE A PLATFORM BEFORE US'[40]

In January 1641, the Scottish commissioner Alexander Henderson stated, 'It will seem nothing strange, that amidst so many petitions against the Prelacy, from all parts of the Kingdom, some should set forth and appear for [the Prelacy].'[41] This was in reference to what he called the 'Prelatic Petition', also known as the *London and Westminster Petition*, a seven-point defence of diocesan episcopacy.[42] Henderson made this statement at a critical time in England's brewing crisis over religion. As the conflict between Charles I and his parliaments escalated throughout 1639 and 1640, religious grievances had begun to reach the political foreground.[43] Whether his shock was genuine or feigned, Henderson sought to project an image that petitions in favour of episcopacy were scarce. His statement was appended to a response to this 'Prelatic Petition', written by Jeremiah Burroughs and possibly Thomas Goodwin, entitled *The Petition for the Prelates Briefly Examined*. This document was written on behalf of an alliance between congregationalists recently returned from Holland, dissident noble peers, soon-to-be-Smectymnuan presbyterians and Scottish commissioners, who held meetings at Edmund Calamy's house in Aldermanbury. Due to some surprising – and overlooked – historical evidence the *Petition Examined* will form the centrepiece of how this chapter will analyse efforts for religious reform in England during the 'Root and Branch' debates. Each group connected to the *Petition Examined* had their particular grievances against Charles. They were united in their revulsion towards Charles's religious policies. What has not been recognised is the extent to which certain members of this small band of divines and politicians actually agreed on a platform of church government in England.

The *Petition Examined* provides the earliest known platform of government by the Holland Brethren. Part of the reason this tract has been overlooked is that it has been too closely identified with its less ecclesiologically specific sister document, the Smectymnuan *An answer to a book entituled, An humble remonstrance*, which was written in response to Bishop Joseph Hall's *An Humble Remonstrance to the High Court of Parliament*. Carol Schneider devoted most of her time to the Smectymnuan pamphlet and assumed its vague presbyterianism must also have been reflected in the *Petition Examined*. She stated that the vagueness in both pamphlets was intentional in order to cohere with the concurrent parliamentary debates in 1640/1641.[44] Tom Webster, who views the *Petition Examined* as merely a response to pro-Episcopal pamphlets and not as containing its own platform of church government, spends more time analysing the Smectymnuan work (which he mistakenly believes to have preceded the *Petition Examined*). He sees the *Petition Examined* as portraying a false unity on the part of the Holland Brethren and Smectymnuans, calling it 'a superbly constructed presentation of unity, masking the issues that were to prove irreconcilable at the Westminster assembly'.[45] He argues that the *Petition Examined* cannot be called a 'proto-congregationalist' document.[46]

Scholars should not expect a congregational document to appear in a form that would not have existed in 1640/41. Congregational polemic at this stage was not written in response to presbyterianism, and we should not expect to find a point-for-point rebuttal of presbyterianism in a time when Episcopal reform was in view. The differences between the English presbyterians – if indeed we can call the Smectymnuans that – and the Holland Brethren were not hidden behind some intentionally vague effort to unite the godly in parish reform. In the *Petition Examined* the congregationalists made no effort to hide the fact that there were differences between the two groups.

And what of the dating of the *Petition Examined*? The George Thomason catalogue states June 1641. However, in a letter from Baillie dated 28 February 1641, we learn that a petition to Parliament for the upholding of the bishops received a 'solid and pertinent answer to it be Mr. Barroues [Burroughs] and his colleagues, with Mr Hendersone's preface, is walking up and doun the earth, which I here send yow'. He mentioned Burroughs's piece along with several other works written by the Scottish commissioners in favour of presby-terianism. We also learn that the piece was quite popular, being read 'up and doun the earth'.[47] Baillie never mentioned the Smectymnuan *Answer* to Hall, which would be odd if it had already been written and emanated from the same group of ministers and nobles, as Tom Webster alleges.[48] But, within the *Petition Examined* Burroughs stated, '[these points] ere long you shall have them discussed more largely upon another occasion', which seems to anticipate the *Answer*.[49] The *Petition Examined* and the *Answer* drew on many of the same sources, including St Jerome, St Cyprian, Polydore Virgil and John Rainolds's Letter to Sir Francis Knolles, to make many of the same points.[50] This, along with other source material connections, indicates Burroughs had pre-publication access to the Smectymnuan tract and that the documents were written in collusion.[51] So, where did the Thomason dating come from? A copy of the *Petition Examined* in Union Theological Seminary, which is not the same as Thomason's copy, indicates on the title page, 'the fourth Edition, Corrected according to the Authors own coppy'. This was also dated 1641.[52] So we know that the *Petition Examined* went through at least four editions in 1641 alone. It seems Thomason picked an edition between the first and fourth editions.

Yet there is another overlooked and more significant piece of evidence written three years later that corroborates and expands upon what we learn from Baillie's letters. *Automachia*, published under the pseudonym Irenaeus Philalethes and mistakenly attributed to Lewis du Moulin, is believed by some scholars to have been written to reconcile presbyterian and Episcopalian forms of church government.[53] Actually, the pamphlet was written in response to the *Petition Examined*.[54] External and internal evidence shows that *Automachia* was written not by du Moulin but in fact by Christopher Harvey, a Church of England vicar. In 1641 du Moulin was using the pseudonym Irenaeus Philadelphus, not Irenaeus Philalethes. More important, however, is that in 1662 Christopher Harvey, vicar of Clifton upon Dunsmore, claimed he was using the name Irenaeus Philalethes as his pseudonym in 1642 – the year *Automachia* was published. Both the author of *Automachia* and du Moulin seemed to be in favour of a reformed episcopacy, but du Moulin seemed to have more interest in presbyterianism with an occasional deference to diocesan bishops who were chosen by the elders.[55]

Automachia was written as a scholastic discussion between Reason, Religion, Prejudice and Partialitie. On page 8, Prejudice (who represents the author of the *Petition Examined*) makes a clear reference to the *Petition Examined*, saying, 'What say you then to those eight reasons urged from Scripture against Episcopacy in the examination of the Petition for the Prelates'. Earlier in the book, Religion has asked, 'Where shall we then begin [this debate]?' Prejudice responds with a striking sentence, 'If you will at the last report we received (Febr. 27 1640 [sic]) which was that the London Petition, and the Ministers generall Petition, and their Remonstrance are Committeed, and that onely the point of Episcopacy is reserved to the Houses.'[56] The date 27 February was the day before Baillie wrote his letter to Scotland commending the *Petition Examined*.[57] It was also the day that the *London and Westminster Petition* – the basis for the *Petition Examined* – was republished along with Cheshire's first pro-Episcopal petition.[58] This indicates that the petitioners anticipated the Calamy house group response.

Furthermore, Harvey lumped the *Petition Examined* in with the *Ministers' Petition and Remonstrance*, authored by Marshall and Calamy, which is further evidence that the Holland Brethren were working with Smectymnuan divines in late 1640 and early 1641. Although not published until 1642, we can show that *Automachia* was written in 1641, between the *Petition Examined* and the Smectymnuans' *Answer* to Bishop Hall. In *Automachia*, Harvey recognised that the *Petition Examined* anticipated a larger refutation of diocesan episcopacy. More startling, not only does Alexander Henderson preface the *Petition Examined*, but Harvey also believed it to be published in collusion with Henderson's *The Unlawfulnesse and Danger of Limited Prelacy*, also written in January 1641, and that Burroughs was 'of [Henderson's] minde'.[59] Thus Harvey, writing during early 1641, clearly sees the connections within the Calamy house members – especially between the Scots and the Apologists – that we have been arguing for in this chapter.

Harvey never once mentioned congregationalism or independency; rather, he referred to the ecclesiology in *Petition Examined* as 'Presbytery Parish discipline'.[60] Indeed, both Carol Schneider and Rosemary Bradley assumed that, if anything, the *Petition Examined* seemed to support, if not promote, a type of presbyterianism.[61] However, that the *Petition Examined* presented a congregational platform of church government is indisputable. Burroughs says as much, and, although he did not use the term 'congregational', Harvey recognised the platform of church government in the *Petition Examined*.[62] Harvey cited numerous examples within the pamphlet where Prejudice [Burroughs] insists that power for all matters of discipline and polity resides in the particular congregation.[63] Harvey also recognised that this particular strand of congregational polity emphasised the role of the particular presbytery in that church. Below is the platform transcribed in full:

[1] Church discipline is to be learned from the plaine and perfect Word of God, and in such particulars as are common to the Church with other Societies, is to be directed by the light of nature, the Church observing alwayes the generall rules of the Word.

[2] A particular Church consisteth of such as in the use of the ordinances of Christ, doe joyne together in one body and society to walke in all the wayes of Christ; neither are there any other members of a particular Church but such as in profession are beleevers and Saints.

[3] The Church may have no office nor officer-bearers, but such as are by divine appointment, which are Elders or Deacons, or more particularly, Teachers, Elders, and Deacons, by which Christ hath provided for all the necessities of the Church.

[4] Although the civill and Ecclesiasticall government be different kinds of governments, yet it is a principall part of the civill Magistrate, who is the keeper of both Tables, to have a care of the Church, and to exercise his authoritie for the preserving of Religion, and for the peace and safety of the church: and where the Magistrate doth his duty, it is a speciall blessing of God, and he is to be obeyed in all things lawfull.

[5] Each particular Church hath her owne power and authoritie, and the use and benefit of all the Ordinances of Christ; neither is there any thing to be done without the expresse or tacite consent of the Congregation, in matters which are proper and peculiar to a particular Church, whether in election or ordination of Ministers or admitting or excommunicating of members.

[6] It is in many respects expedient both for the members of each Church, whether Ministers or people, and for the right governing and well-being of the particular Churches in a Nation professing Christian Religion; that besides their particular assemblyes and Elderships, they conveene by their Commissioners, Ministers, and Elders in greater Assemblies, that matters that concerne all the Churches within their bounds respective may with common advice and consent be agreed upon for their good and edification.[64]

The emphasis in the pamphlet centres around two connected themes. Firstly, that the individual congregation is the primary church in the New Testament. Citing Cyprian, Burroughs says, 'The bounds of a Church were not greater than a Bishop might call together the whole multitude about the affayrs of it.'[65] The other theme, common to all the Calamy house pamphlets, was, as Burroughs quoted 'Doctor Whitaker' to have said, 'that jure divino, a Presbyter and Bishop are both one'.[66] He also cited the continental divine Johan Gerhard, who was very influential in the Apologists' thinking on polity. From Gerhard's use of Acts 20:17, 18, Burroughs claimed, 'Wee doe not acknowledge any inequality of jurisdiction that Bishops have over Presbyters.'[67] Each church must have multiple elders, who are called to rule the church. And indeed, the *Petition Examined* claimed that according to Acts 20, 'the whole charge of all the affaires of the church of Ephesus was left to the Elders'.[68] Hence, although Harvey saw congregationalism in the *Petition Examined*, he referred to its ecclesiology as 'Presbytery Parish discipline'.[69]

The emphasis on the role of the particular church's presbytery was a predominant issue surrounding the anti-prelatic pamphlets, and has thus contributed greatly to the confusion over what the congregationalists were after. The emphasis in all the pamphlets was on a congregational presbytery, with very little – if any – emphasis on synods. In terms of the power of the church, Burroughs repeatedly cited Ambrose as having said that people have the power to elect their elders, and Augustine and Jerome, who said that people have a role in church discipline.[70] We should also note that Burroughs quoted the Utrecht theologian Gisbertus Voetius's very influential book *Desparata Causa Papatus*. Burroughs probably knew Voetius, and the Dutch divine will play an important role later in this book.[71]

The prelacy was built around the notion that the bishop could exercise church discipline alone on behalf of the churches under him. Burroughs, along with most others in the Calamy circle, rejected this argument. He stated that Matthew 18 could not mean the power of discipline belongs to the bishop alone because 'our Saviour Christ saith, *Goe tell the Church*, which Church to interpret of one man, is against that place'.[72] Furthermore, 'whosoever yee binde' means necessarily that one person alone may not perform discipline.[73] The church cannot be understood as one man; therefore, one man cannot exercise discipline over the church.[74] In Scripture, 'one man is never called a Church, and against common sense, because the word Church, there signifies an assembly'. Harvey understood Burroughs's reference to 'an assembly' to mean 'the whole community and multitude of the faithfull in a particular Congregation'.[75] Thus in a perceptive effort to divide the alliance behind Burroughs's platform, Harvey stated that the power of the keys is given not to the whole assembly, but to 'the Guides and Officers onely'.[76] And this is an argument that 'is well maintained against the Separatists'.[77] Harvey was well aware that the standard line that divided the separatists and the presbyterians was whether the 'church' in Matthew 18 meant an assembly of believers or just the elders of that church.

There are two points that we should emphasise here, because they will be central themes throughout this book. First, Harvey's understanding of 'separatism' in relation to other reformed polities. Harvey concentrated on what he considered the ambiguity in Burroughs's rejection of the unique power of bishops in discipline and ordination. He noted that Burroughs 'pretends' that 'each particular Church hath her own power and authoritie and the use and benefit' of all matters pertaining to that particular church, 'whether in election or ordination of Ministers or in admitting or excommunicating of members'.[78] Harvey claimed that Burroughs contradicted his own beliefs, for Burroughs also claimed that 'Jurisdiction and Ordination belong onely to the Elders', and they only need the 'expresse or tacit consent of the whole congregation'.[79] From Harvey's perspective, Burroughs was trying to have it both ways, elders with power and people with power. But what Harvey perceived as an inconsistency is actually an important ecclesiological stance that separated the Apologists from separatists and many independents, and made them more similar to many presbyterians, particularly, as we shall see, the Scots. The Apologists believed that the people had power in church government, but they believed church authority (jurisdiction) belonged only to the elders. Second, Harvey claimed that the power of the keys was given 'immediately unto the Apostles, and mediately through them to the ordinary Ministers of the Church'.[80] Harvey's clerical emphasis here would be taken up by some English presbyterians in the Westminster assembly, over and against other presbyterians and congregationalists to emphasise that the particular church had no role in the disciplinary process.[81]

The *Petition Examined* contained a defined platform of *national* church government, one of the earliest of the Puritan Revolution; it was understood by all parties involved in the pamphlet's writing and not a source of tension. The

Petition Examined anticipated the publication of the Smectymnuan pamphlet, although it did not 'defer' to the Smectymnuans.[82] In *An Answer*, the Smectymnuans' polity was far more in line with the congregational platform espoused by the *Petition Examined* than many of these emerging presbyterian divines would be two years later. The Smectymnuans argued that the individual church was the fundamental structure argued for in the New Testament, that the seven Asian churches in Revelation were considered particular congregations, and like the *Petition Examined*, that the church in Ephesus was but one flock.[83]

For the Smectymnuans, 'the knowledge and approbation of the body of the Church' was required before any act of 'excommunication [or] absolution' could be performed.[84] Thus the people had more power in church discipline than simple concurrence with the elders' decisions. The Smectymnuans also argued on the basis of a consociation of churches, which, following celebrated non-conformist divines Paul Baynes, Robert Parker and John Davenport, meant that any power in synod was derived upward from the basic unit of church power, namely a particular congregation.[85] The particular church, they argued, had a role in the government of the church, but how that power was actuated and allocated, although clearly different from 'separatism', was not addressed. This was not undefined church government; it was undelineated notions of church power – which are related, but distinct, topics.

Burroughs admitted that this was a unique platform of church government, but saw within it aspects that all parties in opposition to episcopacy could unite behind. These are the broad contours of the Apologists' platform of church government, and continued to be the basis for their vision of church government for the next twenty years. Burroughs stated,

> we all see a platform before us amongst our brethren in the reformed Churches, which we conceive would give satisfaction in the maine, being according to the former six Propositions, and what alteration is to be made in such things wherein one reformed Church differs from another ... may be effected with more peace than the Episcopacy can be continued.[86]

In other words, as Burroughs stated elsewhere, 'They who seeme most to differ, yet they differ not one from another so much as they all differ from the Episcopacy', and furthermore, 'there is not so vast a difference amongst us as you think, in these things wee are all agreed'.[87] Smectymnuans echoed this, when they wrote that Joseph Hall and the prelatic party 'odiously' exaggerate our divisions, with their Machiavellian attempt to divide and conquer.[88] The Smectymnuans published in collusion with the Apologists, fully aware that the Apologists were promoting a discernible church polity. It does not mean the Smectymnuans were congregationalists, but, as Elliot Vernon will show in his forthcoming work, they still saw the type of congregationalism espoused by the Apologists, with its clerical emphasis, as biblically viable and practicable. And we should note that this attempt at a broad platform that the godly could unite behind is almost exactly what this same coalition of English presbyterians and congregationalists embraced when they led Cromwell's state church twelve years later.

THE 'ALDERMANBURY ACCORD'

Before proceeding to the Scottish side of this story, we should take a brief look at how this Calamy group related to each other between 1641 and the beginning of the Westminster assembly two years later. It has been argued that the Apologists flouted their commitment (the 'Aldermanbury Accord') to refrain from promoting their polity publicly.[89] This disregard for the alliance, so it has been argued, reached its apex with the publication of the *Apologetical Narration* – something we will address in chapter 4. It has also been argued – perhaps in contradiction to the first point – that the Apologists had promised a platform of church government and opportunistically refused to deliver. As we saw in the previous chapter, a platform indeed had been presented, and as we shall see in chapter 3, they made at least one more attempt in October 1643.

The 'Aldermanbury Accord' itself presents historiographical problems, largely because our best evidence for its existence and parameters come from the biased accounts of the English biographer John Vicars and the presbyterian Thomas Edwards. I doubt the claim that the parties agreed never to discuss polity. It is more probable, given the writings across the period of the Accord, that their agreement was to tone down the specific ecclesiological issues that were most contentious. Rosemary Bradley's detailed study of the citations that Edwards used to 'prove' that the Apologists were flouting the Accord shows that nothing they said rose to the level of ecclesiological proselytising.[90] It is also noteworthy that Edwards used the standard polemical methodology of lumping all types of 'independents' together, many of whom were not even part of the Accord, to prove that it was broken.

I have read all the citations used by Edwards, and there is nothing said by the Apologists that the Calamy presbyterians would have found particularly offensive or radically different from their own positions. And of course Edwards failed to cite the presbyterian sermons, which were equally cryptic, or only occasionally overtly presbyterian, in their ecclesiological comments, or to note that Charles Herle, a presbyterian member of the Calamy house group, was the first of the moderate group of ministers to come out against independency in May 1643. Strangely, Edwards only gave a passing mention to Thomas Goodwin's sermon before Parliament in April 1642, which is perhaps the most congregational document to come out from the Apologists. The sermon was published by an order of the House.

The most significant oversight in the previous analyses of this sermon, *Zerubbabels Encouragement*, is the verse cited on the front page, Revelation 11:4, which differs from the sermon text, Zechariah 4:6–8. It was not unusual for the verse on the front page to differ from the sermon text in printed sermons of the period, though they were always related. In this case, the connection is not only striking, but vitally important to unlocking the rest of the text. *Zerubbabels Encouragement* was preached using Zechariah as an Old Testament recapitulation of Goodwin's commentary on Revelation 11 – which was written in the 1630s and well known to the Aldermanbury group. Michael Lawrence has shown that the exegesis in this commentary had been the basis for Goodwin's migration towards congregationalism.[91] When one reads *Zerrubbabels Encouragement* one sees that all the elements Lawrence cited for Goodwin's views of purifying the Church of England along boundaries of the local, visible church are present. Certainly, the explicit references to a particular congregational polity are sufficiently buried in the sermon. However, if Goodwin's commentary on Revelation was as widely known as Lawrence suggests, then many would have readily recognised the connections in the sermon. If the traditional understanding of the Aldermanbury Accord is true, this sermon would represent the most egregious violation of the Calamy house agreement.

However, in the effort to find a break in the ecclesiastical alliance, the fact that the Calamy house members continued to work together and with Parliament in capacities outside of Root and Branch reform has been overlooked. Indeed, it was Calamy house members that Parliament relied upon to give a theological justification for their war with the king. Much attention has been given to the debates between Henry Ferne and Charles Herle over the right of Parliament to take up arms against the king. However, it was Bridge's and Burroughs's books that were printed for Parliament, not Herle's.[92] It is clear that these writings of Bridge, Burroughs and Herle were all part of a larger group of pamphlets, again from the Calamy house group, that also included pamphlets written by Stephen Marshall and the English presbyterian Herbert Palmer. They cite each other's writings against Ferne, and some of this was apparently done in connection with Warwick, and certainly with the approbation of Parliament.[93]

There is no evidence – apart from a select number of vitriolic pamphlets – that there was a cataclysmic breakdown with this Calamy group. The working relationship between these divines continued up until, and indeed well into, the Westminster assembly. The relationship between the Smectymnuan divines and the Apologists as seen through the *Petition Examined* helps us readjust our view of the forthcoming debates at Westminster. However, as we shall see in the next chapter, it is the Apologists relationship with the Scots that forces us to reconsider one of the dominant ecclesiological motifs of revolutionary England.

NOTES

1 Burgess also claimed, 'not one was for total abolishing of all, or any, but usurped Episcopacy'; 'Cor<neilus> Burges to Richard Baxter From, 10 Sept. 1659', R. Baxter, G. F. Nuttall & N. H. Keeble, *Calendar of the Correspondence of Richard Baxter* (Oxford: Clarendon, 1991), vol. 2, p. 409.

2 J. S. A. Adamson, *The Noble Revolt: the Overthrow of Charles I* (London: Weidenfeld & Nicolson, 2007), p. 174.

3 Goodwin was preaching his sermons on Ephesians in London throughout 1641. See F. Cheynell, *The rise, growth, and danger of Socinianisme* (London, 1643), p. 66.

4 R. Baillie, *The letters and journals of Robert Baillie: M.DC. XXXVII.-M.DC.LXII*, 3 vols (Edinburgh: R. Ogle, 1841), vol. 1, p. 287.

5 E. Calamy, *A just and necessary apology against an unjust invective* (London, 1646), p. 9.

6 F. J. Bremer, *Congregational Communion: Clerical Friendship in the Anglo-American Puritan Community, 1610–1692* (Boston: Northeastern University Press, 1994), chapter 1.

7 Lawrence, 'Goodwin', pp. 127ff; V. T. Wells, 'The Origins of Covenanting Thought and Resistance: c. 1580–1683', University of Stirling, PhD thesis (1997), pp. 151, 172.

8 K. W. Shipps, 'Lay Patronage of East Anglian Clerics in Pre-revolutionary England', Yale University, PhD thesis (1971), pp. 316, 42.

9 J. Burroughs, *The Saints Treasury ... Being sundry sermons, etc.* (London, 1654), dedicatory, not paginated.

10 E. Calamy, *The righteous man's death lamented. A sermon preached at St. Austins, London ... At the funeral of ... Mr. Simeon Ash, etc* (London, 1662), 22–24. I am indebted to Elliot Vernon for this citation.

11 T. Gardiner, *Foure speeches delivered in Guild-Hall on Friday the sixth of October, 1643* (London, 1646).

12 J. Browne, *History of congregationalism and memorials of the churches in Norfolk and Suffolk: By John Browne* (London, 1877), pp. 416–417.

13 Lawrence, 'Goodwin', p. 177.

14 Shipps, 'Lay patronage', p. 177.

15 J. Burroughs, *Moses his Choice, with his eye fixed upon heaven: discovering the happy condition of a self-denying heart. Delivered in a treatise upon Heb. II. 25, 26* (1641), dedicatory, not paginated. See also, J. Burroughs, *A Vindication of Mr Burroughes* (1646), p. 20.

16 It was registered on 20 Feb, 1641, S. W. Carruthers, Presbyterian Historical Society (United States) & Presbyterian Historical Society (England), *The Everyday Work of the Westminster Assembly* (Philadelphia: Pub. jointly by the Presbyterian Historical Society (of America) and the Presbyterian Historical Society of England, 1943), vol. 1, p. 14.

17 Burroughs, *Moses his Choice*, The epistle dedicatory, not paginated.

18 Ibid., The epistle dedicatory, not paginated.

19 T. Webster, 'Burroughes, Jeremiah (bap. 1601?, d. 1646)', *Oxford Dictionary of National Biography* (Oxford: Oxford University Press, 2004). See also Webster, *Godly Clergy*, pp. 303, 327.

20 Burroughs, *Vindication*, pp. 21, 22.

21 Shipps, 'Lay patronage', p. 184.

22 J. Burroughs, *The Excellency of a Gracious Spirit* (London, 1638), preface not paginated.

23 H. Powell, 'The Dissenting Brethren and the Power of the Keys, 1640–44', Faculty of History, University of Cambridge, PhD thesis (2011), pp. 22–23.

24 Baillie, *Letters and Journals*, vol. 1, p. 311.

25 A. P. Newton, *Colonising activities of English Puritans* (New Haven: Yale University Press, 1914), pp. 176–179. See also H. R. Engstrom, 'Sir Arthur Hesilrige and the Saybrook Colony', *Albion: A Quarterly Journal Concerned with British Studies*, 6 (1973), 157–68.

26 J. Peacey, 'Seasonable Treatises: A Godly Project of the 1630s', *English Historical Review*, 113 (1998), p. 675.

27 K. L. Sprunger, *Dutch Puritanism: A History of English and Scottish Churches of the Netherlands in the Sixteenth and Seventeenth Centuries* (Leiden: Brill, 1982), pp. 226, 227. See also D. Neal, *The history of the Puritans or Protestant non-conformists ... In Two Volumes*, 2nd edn (London, 1754), vol. 2, p. 623.

28 Sprunger, *Dutch Puritanism*, p. 226.

29 D. A. Scott, '"Hannibal at Our Gates": Loyalists and Fifth-columnists during the Bishops' Wars – the Case of Yorkshire', *Historical Research*, 70 (1997), 269–293.

30 D. Scott, 'Constable, Sir William, baronet (bap. 1590, d. 1655)', *Oxford Dictionary of National Biography* (Oxford: Oxford University Press, 2004).

31 Scott, '"Hannibal at Our Gates", p. 279.

32 Adamson, *Revolt*, p. 60; D. Scott, 'Alured, John (bap. 1607, d. 1651)', *Oxford Dictionary of National Biography* (Oxford: Oxford University Press, 2004).

33 M. Tolmie, *The Triumph of the Saints: the Separate Churches of London, 1616–1649* (Cambridge: Cambridge University Press, 1977), p. 105.

34 Scott, '"Hannibal at Our Gates"', p. 278.

35 Adamson, *Revolt*, p. 54.

36 Newton, *Colonizing activities*, p. 178.

37 See Powell, 'Dissenting Brethren', pp. 60–61.

38 S. Bush (ed.), *The Correspondence of John Cotton* (Chapel Hill, NC; London: Published for the Omohundro Institute of Early American History and Culture, Williamsburg, Virginia, by the University of North Carolina Press, 2001), p. 283.

39 C. G. Schneider, 'Godly Order in a Church Half-reformed: The Disciplinarian Legacy, 1570–1641', Harvard University, PhD thesis (1986), p. 436.

40 Cited from J. Burroughs, *The petition for the prelates briefly examined* (London, 1641), p. 33.

41 J. Burroughs, *The petition for the prelates briefly examined. Wherein you have these pleas for prælacy, discussed, and answered, etc* (London, 1641), preface.

42 J. D. Maltby, *Prayer Book and People in Elizabethan and Early Stuart England* (London: Cambridge University Press, 1998), p. 239. The published version of the petition is probably a reprint for reasons that will be discussed later in this book. T. Aston, *A petition delivered in to the Lords Spirituall and Temporall, by Sir Thomas Aston, Baronet, from the county palatine of Chester concerning episcopacie* (London, 1641).

43 J. S. Morrill, *Nature of the English Revolution: Essays by John Morrill* (London: Longman, 1993), p. 69.

44 Schneider, 'Godly Order', pp. 444–475.

45 Webster, *Godly Clergy*, p. 330. Webster wrongly concluded that the Scottish commissioners were not part of the Calamy house meetings, ibid., p. 330.

46 Ibid., pp. 326–328, 330.

47 Baillie, *Letters and Journals*, vol. 1, p. 303.

48 Webster, *Godly Clergy*, p. 330.

49 Burroughs, *Petition Examined*, p. 24.

50 See ibid., pp.10, 14–15, 25–27.

51 Bremer, *Congregational Communion*, p. 133.

52 Burroughs, *Petition Examined*, frontispiece, Wing P1749A.

53 Vivienne Larminie, 'Du Moulin, Lewis (1605?–1680)', *Oxford Dictionary of National Biography* (Oxford: Oxford University Press, 2004); online edn, September 2010, www.oxforddnb.com/view/article/19428, accessed 5 April 2011.

54 Philalethes, *Automachia* (London, 1642), p. 8.

55 For Harvey claiming the use of Ireneaus Philalethes, see C. Harvey, *Self-contradiction censured* (London, 1662), p. A3.

56 Philalethes, *Automachia*, pp. 8, 5.

57 Baillie, *Letters and Journals*, vol. 1, pp. 303, 304.

58 Maltby, *Prayer book and people*, p. 239; Aston, *A petition delivered* .

59 Harvey stated, 'but it may be they think there is enough said to that purpose by others, and are of his minde, who taking it upon him to discover the unlawfulnesse and danger of a limited prelacie'. Harvey then went on to cite pages from Henderson, Philalethes, *Automachia*, pp. 25–27.

60 Philalethes, *Automachia*, p. 6.

61 Bradley, 'Jacob and Esau', p. 42; Schneider, 'Godly Order', pp. 475, 436.

62 Burroughs, *Petition Examined*, p. 33; Philalethes, *Automachia*, p. 12.

63 For examples see Philalethes, *Automachia*, pp. 12, 15, 22.

64 Burroughs, *Petition Examined*, pp. 31–32.

65 Ibid., p. 24.

66 Ibid., p. 15.

67 Burroughs, *Petition Examined*, p. 27. Acts 20:17, 18, 'And from Miletus he sent to Ephesus, and called the elders of the church. And when they were come to him, he said unto them, Ye know, from the first day that I came into Asia, after what manner I have been with you at al seasons.'

68 Burroughs, *Petition Examined*, p. 34. Carol Schneider read this quote to mean that the Apologists actually affirmed a 'presbyterial principle.' Schneider, 'Godly Order', p. 475.

69 Philalethes, *Automachia*, p. 6.

70 Burroughs, *Petition Examined*, pp. 24, 26.

71 Ibid., p. 28; G. Voet, *Desperata causa papatus* (Amstelodami, 1635).

72 Burroughs, *Petition Examined*, p. 34. Matthew 18:17, 18. 'And if he shall neglect to hear them, tell it unto the church: but if he neglect to hear the church, let him be unto thee as an heathen man and a publican. Verily I say unto you, Whatsoever ye shall bind on earth shall be bound in heaven: and whatsoever ye shall loose on earth shall be loosed in heaven.'

73 Burroughs, *Petition Examined*, p. 34.

74 Ibid., p. 34.

75 Ibid., p. 34; Philalethes, *Automachia*, pp. 14–15.

76 Philalethes, *Automachia*, p. 15.

77 Ibid., pp. 15–16.

78 Ibid., p. 21.

79 Ibid., p. 21.

80 Ibid., p. 16.

81 See below, chapter 3.

82 Contra Schneider, 'Godly Order', p. 462.

83 Smectymnuus, *An answer to a book entituled, An humble remonstrance* (London, 1641), pp. 48ff.

84 Ibid., p. 40.

85 Ibid., p. 80.

86 Burroughs, *Petition Examined*, p. 33.

87 Ibid., p. 31.

88 Smectymnuus, *An answer*, p. 82.

89 See Bremer, *Congregational Communion*, pp. 132–135; Schneider, 'Godly Order', pp. 466–467; E. Vernon, 'The Sion College Conclave and London Presbyterianism during the English Revolution', University of Cambridge, PhD thesis (1999), pp. 67–68. For primary sources that mention the Accord, see T. Edwards, *Reasons against the independant government of particular congregations* (London, 1641), p. 25; T. Edwards, *Antapologia; or, a full answer to the Apologeticall Narration* (London, 1644), p. 238; J. Vicars, *The schismatick sifted* (London, 1646), pp. 15–16.

90 Bradley, 'Jacob and Esau', pp. 175ff.

91 T. Goodwin, *Zerubbabels encouragement to finish the temple. A sermon preached before the honourable House of Commons, at their late solemne fast, Apr. 27. 1642* (London, 1642); Lawrence, 'Goodwin', chapter 3.

92 Powell, 'Dissenting Brethren', p. 60.

93 S. Marshall, *A plea for defensive armes* (1643), not paginated.

Chapter 2

George Gillespie and
the congregational alliance

A t some point during their exile in Holland Jeremiah Burroughs and his fellow congregational divines read a book written by a young and relatively unknown divine by the name of George Gillespie. That fact that they approved of that document forces us reassess some of the most widely accepted story-lines of the early Revolutionary period. If it is true, as most historians assume, that the Scots, led by George Gillespie, were the enemies of the congrega-tional divines at the Westminster assembly, then the previous chapter presents us with some significant problems. We have established that on the eve of the Civil War the *Petition Examined* presented a widely recognised congre-gational platform of church government that many Aldermanbury house divines and peers could unite around. But, given the congregational founda-tion of Burroughs's *Petition Examined*, why did Robert Baillie commend the document, and why did Alexander Henderson write the preface?

David Mullan and John Coffey have commented that in the 1630s in Scotland, the 'impulse in the direction of something like independency was certainly strong and militated against the pretensions of a [Scottish] national church' and, in Samuel Rutherford's case, there was 'a fundamental tension between [his] idea of the church as a pure gathering of the godly and the idea of the church as a comprehensive national institution'.[1] Yet Mullan sees this common thread of church purity as merely ironic, given that 'presbyterians recoiled in horror from the congregational covenant', and 'none of these Scottish presbyterians divines were conscious friends of independency'.[2] Thus Mullan, whose work ends in 1638, dovetails nicely into the prevailing Civil War ecclesiastical warfare motif, where Scots lead presbyterians in an ecclesiological war against the Apologists. The *Petition Examined* did state, 'there are ... [no] members of a particular Church but such as in profession are beleevers and Saints'.[3] Similar views on churches of professing believers, however, was not the basis for this orchestrated pamphlet campaign and the alliance between the Scots and the Apologists in the winter of 1640/41.

Christopher Harvey, as we have seen, believed Henderson's *Unlawfulnesse and Danger of Limited Prelacy* was published in conjunction with Burroughs's *Petition Examined* and that Henderson endorsed the polity espoused in the *Petition Examined*. We know from Baillie that the commissioners were already meeting with the Holland Brethren in the winter of 1640/41.[4] Baillie claimed that those of the Holland Brethren who were in favour of the 'Independent congregations' had agreed to be silent in any differences they had with the Scots.[5] Indeed, we have established that within a month of Baillie's writing those comments, the Apologists had written up a congregational platform which was prefaced by Henderson, and Baillie himself was praising Burroughs's *Petition Examined*. Although, as we shall discuss, it is impossible to take Baillie at face value, it seems that the congregational polity in the *Petition Examined* did not break the Apologists' promise (if there ever was such a promise) to refrain from highlighting any real differences with the Scots.[6] We cannot explain away the alliance between the Scots and the Apologists via a collective effort at united ambiguity until the prelacy was pulled down, nor can we say they were papering over their mutually perceived differences. There was something more fundamental that connected them.

We should first note that the *Petition Examined* explicitly rejected a 'moderated' episcopacy.[7] There is no doubt that the *Petition Examined* was published as part of the Calamy coalition, but this does not mean every single member of that group would have agreed with the polity it espoused. The Calamy house group certainly contained some who were still 'supporters of a reformed episcopacy'.[8] Harvey himself was in favour of a modified episcopacy, and thus his frustration with the *Petition Examined*. It would make sense then that the Scots and the Apologists united against retaining any sort of reduced or modified Episcopal structure. Alexander Henderson was particularly mortified by the potential retention of any semblance of Episcopal government in England. The Scots, with the exception of Baillie, would never have been fully comfortable with a working relationship with those divines like Cornelius Burgess who would continue to retain a strong clerical impulse in their polity. The Smectymnuans were also clearly against any type of reduced episcopacy, which further explains the close relationship between the Smectymnuan pamphlet and the *Petition Examined*.[9] However, it was not, as one historian has suggested, 'merely political expediency which led [the Scots] to co-operate with the Independents'.[10]

When Burroughs returned from Holland in November 1640, he had already read *Against English Popish Ceremonies*, published in Leiden in 1637, and written by the Scottish theologian George Gillespie, who came to England as a chaplain to the Scottish commissioners. Burroughs asked Henderson and the other Scottish commissioners – who had just arrived in London – 'Whether we might not take that Book as the judgement of the most godly and able Ministers of Scotland, for matters of Church-discipline'? The Scottish divines responded that 'we might'.[11]

There are numerous ways, textually and ecclesiologically, to explain the affinities between the Apologists' polity and Gillespie's *Popish Ceremonies*. Here I will focus on how Scottish views of church government were far more congregational at the time than they would be three years later at the Westminster assembly – there was so much commonality, in fact, that the alliance between the two parties was based as much on a genuine ecclesiological common ground as it was on political opportunism. Amazingly, there is no evidence that these two groups were in dialogue prior to 1640. And yet they independently arrived at similar views of the power of the local church, based on their readings of the Bible and of the writings of the same English and continental reformers, including Johan Gerhard, David Pareus, Wilhelm Zepperus, William Fulke and most conspicuously Girolamo Zanchius.

Gillespie's *Popish Ceremonies* argued for congregational positions, and several contemporary divines noticed this fact. As Gillespie built his case for the power of the keys existing in a particular church, he began not with the bedrock Christological commands in Matthew 16, but instead with Matthew 18:17 and 1 Corinthians 5. Gillespie stated, 'The power and authority of Binding and Loosing, Christ hath delivered to the whole church, that is, to every particular church, collectively taken.'[12] For Gillespie, the 'particular church, collectively taken' meant the entirety of the people within the particular congregation, for when Christ says, 'tell the church' he means tell 'the particular church' where one 'shall happen ... to be a Member'.[13] And citing 1 Corinthians 5:4, 5 Gillespie reiterated, 'Every particular Church or Congregation hath power to Excommunicate.'[14] Therefore, 'It pertaineth to the whole Church, collectively taken, to deny her Christian Communion ... [and] [t]herefore, it pertaineth to the whole Church to Excommunicate them ... the whole Church hath the power of judging [the person who] ought to be so punished. The whole church hath the power of remitting this punishment againe.'[15]

In commenting that the power of excommunication belongs to the whole church, Gillespie was particularly influenced by Thomas Cartwright, Fulke, Gerhard and Zanchius.[16] Zanchius's understanding of the power of a local church in the disciplinary process had a powerful influence on Gillespie. All four commentators interpreted 1 Corinthians 5 as Paul writing to the whole church as a body who possessed the power to excommunicate. Fulke provided an important exegetical connection between the power of the keys in Matthew 16:19 and excommunication in 1 Corinthians 5. Peter received the power of the keys on behalf of all the Apostles, 'And the church hath the same power after them.'[17] Fulke then stated, 'The authoritie of excommunication pertaineth to the whole church, although the judgment and execution thereof is to be referred to the governors of the church' who are appointed 'to avoid confusion'.[8] These authors' understanding of the power that existed in the local church, which was influential on a wide swath of non-conformist divines, would continue to be cited authoritatively by the leading congregational divines in the 1640s.[19] Significantly, where Gillespie articulated a more 'independent' theological distinction of the 'first subject of the power of the keys', he embraced the practical distinctions articulated by Fulke, Zanchius and Pareus between the power of the keys in the whole church and the use of the keys in the elders.[20] Gillespie believed that Christ delivered the power of the keys to the whole church, collectively taken, but an authority to exercise those keys was given to the elders of the church.

This is a crucial distinction for Gillespie, and vital for us to grasp as we approach the rest of this book. In his schema, there is a difference 'betwixt the power it selfe, and the execution of it'.[21] The former belongs to the whole church, whereas the latter belongs to the elders. These distinctions place Gillespie closer to Robert Parker than to the Apologists. Parker himself argued that church power was in the body of the church, but exercised in the elders as representatives. Gillespie stated, 'we have proven, that the power of binding and loosing, pertaineth to every particular Church collectively taken. But the execution and judiciall excercing of this power, pertaineth to that company and assembly of Elders in every Church'.[22] Yet the congregation was not divorced from the elders' ability to exercise their power. Gillespie cited Gerhard's famous *Summe of Christian Doctrine*, where Gerhard stated, 'The Power of excommunicating belongeth unto the whole Church and is pronounced by the Minister', and the consent of the entire congregation was required, when the church is 'gathered together'.[23]

Gillespie also cited a story told by Bullinger, as related by Zanchius, in which the particular churches of 'Helvetia' (Switzerland) would choose for 'themselves a certaine Senate of Elders, or company of the best men in the Church, which might ... exerce the Discipline of Excommunication'.[24] Gillespie referred to Fulke's comments on 1 Corinthians 5 as an authority on these issues of the power of the keys and the execution thereof by the elders. Fulke stated, 'The authority of excommunication pertaineth to the whole church, although the judgement and execution thereof is to be referred to the governors of that church.'[25]

This quote was also used by the Elizabethan divine Andrew Willet, who was a favourite source for Bridge and Burroughs. Willet, in the same passage where he cited Fulke, added that according to Christ, 'If he wil not heare thee tell the Church: this place proveth, that although the exercising of the keys be referred to the governours of the Church; yet the authoritie and right is in the whole Church: for the keys were given to the whole Church.' Thus Willet was cited in order to reject what would become a presbyterian position in the 1640s: 'The pastors and governors, although they be excellent and principall members of the Church, yet are they improperly called the Church.'[26]

Gillespie believed this power of execution must reside in the context of the particular church, since the people were necessary in the final acts of church government. Again citing Gerhard, Gillespie concluded that 'the Church consisteth of two integrant parts, *viz.* Pastors and Sheepe, Teachers and Hearers', therefore 'the representative church [is] ... the Ecclesiastical Consistory wherof we have spoken'.[27] Arguing here against diocesan bishops, Gillespie denied that Christ would allow excommunication to proceed through the bishop inasmuch as Christ denied a bishop's power absent from his congregation. Gillespie argued that the proper and primary subject of church power was the church, constituted with both people and elders, not elders alone. The elders were connected to the people as their representatives.

According to this position, procedurally, the disciplinary process would initially involve the elders, who would investigate, admonish and attempt to bring about reconciliation and repentance. But, the power and authority of binding and loosing would reside in the particular gathered church if there was to be an excommunication, because for 'the right execution of this Discipline the manifest consent of the whole Church is also necessary', and 'that [for] excommunication ... [to] fruitfully succeed the consent of the people is necessary'.[28] Gillespie hinted that it is not only the issue of excommunication that should be brought to the church, but citing Zanchius and Gerhard, he stated that 'waightie matters in the Church ... ought not to be undertaken without the consent of the whole Ecclesiastical body'.[29]

Similarly, in terms of ordination, Gillespie believed, 'The wholle Church hath the power of Ordination communicated', for 'It is most certaine (and among our Writers agreed upon,) that to the whole Church collectively taken, Christ hath delivered the keyes of the Kingdome of Heaven, with power to use the same.' Therefore, Christ 'hath also delivered unto the whole Church, power to call & ordaine Ministers for using the keyes: otherwise the promise might be made void, because the Ministers which shee now hath, may faile'.[30] When the 'Ministery of the Church faileth or is wanting, Christian people have power to exerce that act of ordination, which is necessary to the making of a Minister'. Citing Pareus, Gillespie added, 'The Church hath by Divine institution delivered the Power of ordaining ordinary Ministers, to the Presbitery, whereof the Church consisteth representative.'[31] In other words, like Robert Parker, Gillespie believed that ordination was an act that was properly performed by the elders, but only as they were acting in the capacity of representatives of the church's power. We will remember that for Burroughs, the power and exercise of ordination resided in the elders alone. It was not a power shared with the people as Gillespie believed.

It was not only Burroughs who perceived these congregational impulses in Gillespie's writing. Baillie claimed that he did 'myslike much of [it]', although given that Baillie was still in favour of a modified episcopacy in 1638 there was much in *Popish Ceremonies* for him to 'myslike'.[32] Baillie originally believed, as he had heard, that Alexander Henderson had written *Popish Ceremonies*, until he was told Gillespie was the author – an indication Baillie was not ecclesiologically allied with Henderson and Gillespie in the late 1630s.[33] Nor were Henderson and Gillespie entirely unique within the Covenanting movement in Scotland. Archibald Johnston of Wariston, who was also a lay commissioner sent to negotiate with Parliament in 1640 and 1643, had helped Henderson draft the Scottish National Covenant, which was signed in 1638. When writing a public defence of the Scottish Covenanters relating to their grievances against Charles, Wariston included the complaint that bishops had taken away the people's rights in ordaining their own ministers.[34] By 1644 the Westminster assembly's presbyterians would vote that ordination was something wholly reserved to the elders.

Baillie was not the only Scot to have concerns about Gillespie. The Aberdeen divine and anti-Covenanter John Forbes decried *Popish Ceremonies* for its emphasis on the particular church and how it promoted the role of the people in excommunication. In his pamphlet dispute with the Covenanters Forbes saw a congregational emphasis in Gillespie's work and he associated it with the Scottish divines Alexander Henderson and David Dickson. In a response to Henderson and Dickson, during a series of questions and answers regarding his refusal to sign the Covenant, he cited this very section of Gillespie. Forbes wrote, 'Excommunication requyre the presence of the whole Congregation, because the power of binding and loosing, is delyeered by CHRIST to everie particular Church, or Congregation, collectiuelie taken as it is affirmed in the Dispute agaynst *Popish Ceremonies*, Part. 3. Cap. 8. Pag. 182.'[35] He associated the Gillespie pamphlet not only with Henderson and Dickson, but with all the Covenanters, and called *Popish Ceremonies* one of 'your Wrytinges'.[36] Henderson and Dickson did not deny their association with the teachings of *Popish Ceremonies*. This gives further credibility to Burroughs's statement that all the commissioners from Scotland acknowledged *Popish Ceremonies* as representative of their position. Forbes was later exiled to Holland for opposing the Solemn League and Covenant and was also banned from taking communion in Scotland. Importantly, this stridently anti-Covenanter attitude would not stop Baillie from employing Forbes in his behind-the-scenes pamphlet against the 'independents' during the Westminster assembly.[37]

We should be careful, however, not to isolate Gillespie's thoughts on the particular church from Scottish polity in its wider historical context. Although, as we shall see, there would be a diversity of opinions between eminent Scottish divines such as David Calderwood and Baillie on the one hand, and Gillespie and Rutherford on the other, Gillespie did not consider himself to be articulating anything different than what the Church of Scotland had historically prescribed. Gillespie would later claim that there were 'sessions' (i.e. particular elderships over particular churches) who were 'elected with the consent of their oune congregations ... in Scotland 20 years before there were Presbyteries, so the Sessions, were continued with their pouer after the erecting of Presbyteries'.[38] Gillespie cited instances in the Acts of the General Assembly, from 'both before the Second Book of Discipline was agreed upon and after'.[39]

Regarding particular Scottish churches, in 1586, 'If they be laufullie ruled by sufficient Minister and Session, they have power and jurisidiction of their oune congregation in matters ecclesiasticall, to take order therewith; and things that they cannot decide, to bring them to the Presbytery.'[40] And in 1597, the Assembly at Dundie stated that sessions cannot be elected without the 'consent of their oune congregations'.[41] This is very similar to the Scottish *First Book of Discipline*, ca. 1560, which stated that the particular church is 'of fundamental importance'.[42] *The First Book of Discipline* gave considerable emphasis and 'unqualified freedom to elect annually its own elders and deacons by whatever method it chooses to adopt'.[43] And notably, regarding 'the final decision in a matter of excommunication ... the congregation is required to assume responsibility and the ministry is compelled to act as the executive of the congregation's wishes'.[44] Synods, functioning as ecclesiastical courts, only existing in their embryonic form, received no mention in the *First Book of Discipline*.[45] Indeed, there was no mention of bishops in the covenant, and as Austin Woolrych has noted, this tactical decision was 'aimed at accommodating the many who hated Caroline innovations ... but had no quarrel with the Jacobean synthesis of episcopacy and presbyterianism'.[46]

JOHN BALL AGAINST GILLESPIE

Scottish scholars were not the only divines sceptical about Gillespie's views on the church. Perhaps the most important statement about *Popish Ceremonies* came from an unexpected source. John Ball, one of England's most astute observers and critics of separatism, had read Gillespie and found what he believed to be serious fundamental problems in the Scottish divine's view of church power. The third section of John Ball's *Friendly Triall of the Grounds tending to separation* is a critique of John Robinson's understanding of the 'first receptacle of the power of the keys'.[47] Robinson, a celebrated non-conformist in many Jacobean and Caroline semi-separatist circles, believed that Peter received the keys of church power on behalf of believers and therefore the whole gathered church had the power of the keys. This was a common separatist interpretation of the power of the keys.

John Ball was aware of this understanding of the distribution of power and would have none of it. But, more importantly – and something that has been completely overlooked by historians – he saw the same distribution in George Gillespie's *Popish Ceremonies*, which Ball silently cited. There has been a great deal of confusion as to Ball's theological position. The historiography focuses on whether or not he was a full-fledged presbyterian.[48] Those questions tend to revolve around his understanding of synods. We will later see that his views on synods were not too dissimilar from the Apologists'. Nonetheless, very little attention has been given to how he understood the power of the keys allocated at the local level.

Ball began his section by refuting Robinson's argument on the first immediate receptacle of church power. As he stated, 'the ordinary power of the keyes or government, with the execution thereof is not given to the community of the church'.[49] Nor was this power of the keys, as Robinson and Henry Ainsworth alleged, given to the church and derivatively to the elders. The church cannot convey to the elders what she never had in the first place.[50]

Ball disagreed with Gillespie's assertion that the power of excommunication had been delivered to the particular church. He offered his dissent by silently citing Gillespie, stating, 'for those Divines which hold power and authority of binding and loosing to be delivered by Christ to the whole church, that is, to every particular church collectively', those divines 'generally with one consent maintain, that the execution and judicial exercising of this power perteineth to that company and assembly of officers or governours in every church the Apostle calleth a Presbytery (1 Tim. 4.14)'.[51] This quote was taken from page 185 of Gillespie's *Popish Ceremonies*. Ball struggled to understand how the whole community could be considered recipient of church power, because it would implicitly mean a church without officers could have the power of the keys if the elders were absent.[52] A comparison of two passages further illustrates how Ball was citing Gillespie. In *Popish Ceremonies* Gillespie stated:

> For this authority of binding and loosing, though it pertained to the whole Church, in actu primo sive in esse, yet it pertained to the Presbitery alone, in actu secundo sive in operari: and even as the act of speaking, pertaineth to a man, as Principium quod, but to the tongue alone, as Principium quo.[53]

Ball was clearly referencing this statement in the following passage:

> For that power agreeth not to the whole body in actu primo or in esse (as they speak) ... [I]f the authority of binding or loosing pertain to the whole church in actu primo sive in esse, and to the Presbytery alone in actu secundo in operari, as the act of speaking perteineth to a man as the principium quod, but to the tongue alone as the principium quo, yet the church cannot be taken for the whole community.[54]

According to this viewpoint, 'our Savior,' said Ball, '[in Matthew] speaketh of the actuall execution of this power (not of the power it self), which belongeth to the governours'.[55] For Ball, the idea that power and the actual exercise of that power could be separated was not provable from Scripture.

The focus in John Ball's polemic was Robinson's rebuttal to Richard Bernard's *The Separatists Schism*.[56] Robinson embraced what would later be considered the more separatist interpretation of Matthew 16. According to Robinson, Christ gave Peter the keys of the kingdom right after Peter confessed Jesus was the Christ. Therefore when Christ committed the power of binding and loosing to Peter as the rock upon which the church will be built, the disciple stood as the federal representative of all confessing believers throughout history. As Robinson stated, 'Two or three or more people making Peters confession, Matt 16, are the Church. But two or three may make this confession without officers. Therefore such a company is a Church.'[57]

Herein lay Ball's fear of what Gillespie was teaching. Robinson argued that a church exists prior to the elders being 'ordeyened' into the church.[58] Gillespie agreed with that principle, as we have seen. Ball was unclear as to his own beliefs on how Christ allocated the power of the keys, although he rejected outright that the congregation has any power regarding binding and loosing. For a better understanding of Ball's position, we must turn to his response to New England congregationalists written a year later, but not published until after his death.

In 1637 fears of sectarian tendencies in colonial churches prompted thirteen ministers in England to send nine questions to clergy in New England.[59] According to Tom Webster, 'The questions stimulated a major defence of New England's practices to which John Ball replied on behalf of his friends', the English ministers.[60] Ball enumerated the various protestant positions on the power of the keys. This list was interesting because it demonstrated an awareness of the various positions and indicated that the English presbyterian position was not fully settled. The first position Ball articulated distinguished 'betwixt the power it self which they give to the Church and the execution and exercise of it, which they confine to the Presbytery'.[61] Ball attributed this position to Robert Parker and to Dudley Fenner, and it was closest to the one held by Gillespie in 1637. The second position was held by those who 'give the power of the keys with the exercise therefore to the whole body of the Church, or if in the dispensation they attribute to the Officers' who are servants of the church and derive their authority from the church.[62] In other words, the gathered church was the first subject of the ecclesiastical power of the keys. This was a position Ball attributed to separatists such as John Robinson. Ball then vaguely, and tantalisingly, referred to those who hold the church to be 'the communitie of the faithful, together with their officers and their guides'.[63] Ball did not elaborate on this point, nor did he offer any citations. Possibly, he was aware of a position in which the church without elders could not properly be considered a church. In other words, all the power of the keys could not exist in a church without officers, contrary to what the separatists believed.

Ball moved on to reiterate that the power of the keys 'and the execution thereof, Christ hath not given immediately to the whole multitude, but to some persons and Officers designed and appointed thereunto'.[64] Citing Matthew 28 and John 20, Ball articulated what would become the standard line against congregational and independent churches, namely that binding and loosing is on a par with the administering of the sacraments and preaching, which Christ never committed to the whole community.[65] Anticipating the objection that a church may elect their pastors, which would connote a power in the whole church, he stated that the church, however, may only apply that 'authority and power' to him whom they choose. This ability to elect was not to be understood as a power and authority that existed in the community of the faithful. If, as Robinson believed, 'the church doth not onely call, but make Officers out of power and vertue received into her selfe, ... then should the Church have truly lordlike power in regard of her ministers'.[66]

Against Robinson and Gillespie, Ball believed the people could not have the power because power must always carry with it the ability to exercise that power.[67] This formulation would be the argument of many English presbyterians by the time of the Westminster assembly. The distinction between the people's role in election and the elders' unique power was going to be the source of unending confusion in the debates to come over the next three years.

Tom Webster argues that Ball sided with Parker against the New Englanders. Yet there is nothing to indicate that Ball did so; indeed, his tortured phraseology makes it nearly impossible to determine the extent to which he embraced Parker's position. Ball's arguments against Gillespie can equally be used against Parker. Although there is no doubt that Ball was trying to protect the Parker tradition from accusations of separatism, yet John Allin and Thomas Shepherd, who responded to Ball on behalf of the New Englanders three years later, conceded that they could not apprehend the point that Ball was trying to make in reference to Parker.[68] Nor, as they say, could Ball decide what to do with Robert Parker, stating, 'it appeares that how ever the author [Ball] began professedly against us as Separatists in this point, yet he followes the cause against Mr. Parker, with whom hee seemes to be friends'.[69] Ball was accusing the separatists of giving the power of the keys to the people; Allin and Shepherd (who themselves share Parker's understanding of the keys) claimed that Ball's arguments against the separatists equally accrued to Robert Parker.

Carol Schneider, who has provided the best overview of John Ball's pamphlet debates, noticed a subtle shift in Ball's understanding of the particular church in his last pamphlet, written against the English separatist John Canne. 'Ball's new task', observed Schneider, 'was to restate that the orthodox non-conformist position in such a way as to exclude any possible conclusion that church power was derived *from* the congregation *to* its elders.'[70] On this point, Ball had decidedly shifted away from Robert Parker. It is clear Ball had already stated this position in his work against Robinson. He wrote, 'The ministers and guides of the church are immediately of Jesus Christ, from whom immediately they derive their power and authority.'[71] Polly Ha, against

Carol Schneider, has argued that 'there is no basis for assuming that congregational views lurked' in Ball's '"Cartwrightian tradition"'.[72] Ha is certainly correct about Ball's *later* position. It was Ball's movement away from Parker that made him more 'presbyterian', but only from a certain perspective. Depending on who was reading Parker, he could be understood as either an 'independent' or a 'presbyterian'. Furthermore, Ball would also 'insist upon the direct derivation of church authority from Christ to his ministers'.[73] This sounds like the ecclesiology of the Apologists.

GILLESPIE, 1641: STRAINING TOWARDS 'PRESBYTERIANISM'?

By 1641 we see a shift in the focus of Gillespie's writing. While he does not disown his previously articulated positions, Gillespie only indirectly argues for the rights and privileges of the particular church. Gillespie's *An Assertion of the Church of Scotland* (1641) was also a product of the pamphlet campaign generated by the Calamy house group, and therefore was connected to Burroughs's *Petition Examined* and the Smectymnuans' *Answer* to Joseph Hall.[74] We must not miss this fact: the *Assertion* was a direct attack on the independency of men like John Canne, and yet it was written by a member of the same group of divines that included the Apologists. It represents a shift in Gillespie's thought away from the Scottish polity described around the particular church and towards the authority of 'presbyteries and synods'. However, he was far from articulating the *jure divino* presbyterianism he would be known for at the Westminster assembly. Indeed, even after exposure to the congregationalists of England he exhibited a great deal of empathy with their understanding of a particular church. In *Assertion*, we can see him embracing the use of the local presbyters and gathered synods while trying to retain aspects of the polity he would articulate three years later. Whereas the Scottish National Covenant had masked the differences between those who wanted an end to ceremonial innovation and yet still supported a Jacobean ecclesiastical equanimity, and those who wanted to be rid of bishops altogether, that unity was evaporating by 1640.[75] It became clear that if Scotland were to influence English religious politics, it would have to articulate principles that were prescriptive, not simply proscriptive. One can sense this transition in the writings of Scottish commissioners and particularly in the writings of Gillespie. Yet with higher precision there was inevitable division.

Gillespie's *Assertion* would be too congregational for Rutherford, who in the following year would have to refute aspects of Gillespie's polity and reject Gillespie's influences, such as Robert Parker, Girolamo Zanchius and Wilhelmus Zepperus. Rutherford delineated the differences between Scottish presbyterianism and what he saw as English independency. Gillespie's *Assertion*, once again, helps us to understand the genuine common ground between the Dissenting Brethren and the Scottish presbyterians prior to the Westminster assembly.

It is not our goal to trace out the entire scope of Gillespie's polity, much less to suggest he was not really a 'presbyterian'. Our intention is to continue the analysis of his evolving understanding of the keys of the kingdom. This is because, as Gillespie himself would come to state, debates about synods were unintelligible if the allocation of the keys within a particular congregation were not understood.[76] It should be stressed that even during Gillespie's discussions on the role of synods, he avoided any mention that ecclesiastical synods or assemblies were *jure divino*. He exhibited indebtedness to Robert Parker in his defence of the use of synods. And Gillespie readily recognised, without dissent, that Parker was a 'tender friend of congregations', and although 'the exercise of ecclesiastical power [was] proper to the Rulers of the Church', Parker placed 'the power it selfe originally in the whole Church', precisely the distinction Gillespie had made three years earlier.[77] Furthermore, Gillespie conceded that the primitive churches were indeed single congregations in villages and they could indeed manage their own affairs.

Gillespie was very careful with his wording. He did not abandon the polity he had espoused in *Popish Ceremonies*; he simply changed his emphasis. He saw that the ecclesiastical jurisdiction was in the elders, but he made no mention of the power of the keys. He exegeted Matthew 18:17, 'goe tell the church', to mean tell the elders, where that church exists representatively. Indeed, he left aside the issue of Peter and his commission from Christ in Matthew 16. In 1637 Gillespie had distinguished between the power that resides in the church and the ecclesiastical jurisdiction that exists in the elders, who act as the church's representatives. In 1641 he confirmed the latter without denying the former.

Gillespie was desperate to maintain the distinction between church and elders, and he cited various verses from the epistle to the Hebrews and Paul's letters to Timothy and the church in Thessalonica to show that 'in every Christian Congregation there are some Rulers, some ruled, some Governors, some governed, some that command, some that obey'.[78] This is consonant with what we know about Gillespie's later positions; he operated from the premise that the particular congregation, consisting of elders and people, was the *ecclesia prima*, and developed his polity from that starting point.

Gillespie used Parker's view of the keys against the separatist John Canne, the same view that was eventually condemned by Rutherford. For Gillespie, Canne went farther than merely placing the power in the church. Gillespie wrote, 'Now this seemeth not enough to those with whom wee have now to doe. They will have the people freely to vote in all judgments of the church.' This would mean the 'exercise of jurisdiction by the people, which is the democracy of Morellius, condemned by Parker himself'.[79] Parker would go on to say that the power of the keys 'is primarily in the church but secondarily in the rectors'.[80] With this distinction in place, Gillespie defended those who 'put a difference betwixt the power it selfe, and the exercise of it, ascribing the former to the collective body of the Church, the latter to the representative'.[81]

In this context Gillespie silently cited himself from four years before. He stated that 'some [*viz.* himself in 1637!] who make the whole Congregation the first subject of the power of spirituall Jurisdiction' do nonetheless hold 'that the whole Church doth exercise the said jurisdiction as *Principium quod*, the Eldership alone, as *Principium quo*, even as the whole man seeth, as *Principium quod*, the eye alone, as *Prinicipium quo*, and so of all the rest'.[82] Gillespie had not entirely abandoned his position from three years earlier, but he also was only willing to refer to his previous position as an observant and acquiescent third party. In fact, Gillespie wished to bypass the question of the original subject of the power altogether, stating there are 'many learned men [who] deny the power of Church government to be originally in the people, though others (and those very learned too) doe affirme it'.[83]

Gillespie was still giving signals that the congregation had all the powers necessary for self-governance. In terms of church discipline and excommunication, Gillespie supported Henry Jacob's 1616 confession of faith (which he called the separatists' confession). Article 14 of the confession stated that the pastors 'ought to bee trusted by the Congregation, with the managing of all points of their Ecclesiasticall affaires and Government' provided 'that in matters of waight, the whole Congregation doe first understand thereof ... [and] before any thing be finished, and the finall act bee done in the presence of the whole Congregation' to make sure that congregation 'doe not manifestly dissent' from it.[84] Gillespie argued that '[w]e are heartily content, that Congregations doe fully enjoy all the Christian liberty, which here is pleaded for in their behalfe, yea and much more also'.[85]

In fact, citing Robert Parker's use of Zepperus, Gillespie stated that the elders must not proceed to excommunication if the congregation does not agree that the excommunication is valid. And returning to one of his favourite authorities, Zanchius, Gillespie stated 'that without the consent of the church no man ought to be excommunicated'.[86] As we shall see, Rutherford would condemn such views expressed by Parker, effectively stealing him from the English presbyterians and calling him a separatist. Nonetheless, Rutherford himself exhibited an understanding of the keys that brought him closer to the Apologists than to many of his English presbyterian counterparts.

In conclusion, we should see some ambivalence in Gillespie's thought as he attempted to articulate his presbyterian polity after having been exposed to an English context. Gillespie would long be remembered as being most sensitive to the rights and prerogatives of the particular church, and we will see this again and again throughout this book. Our intention is not to deny his belief in the vital nature of synods. Rather, we see that, for some Scots, synods were impacted by their understanding of the particular church. Gillespie did not deny that power exists in the church, and if anything he seemed closer to the Robert Parker mould than to what would become a standard – if we can still use the term 'standard' – presbyterian understanding of the elders alone being the first proper subject, and sole possessor, of the keys. When Burroughs asked Alexander Henderson if Gillespie's *Popish Ceremonies* could be taken as representative of Scottish polity, it was because he recognised a commonality between the beliefs of the Apologists and the viewpoints articulated by Gillespie, built on real exegetical consensus. Within a year of the publication of *An Assertion* the Scottish presbyterians would articulate their polity in opposition to Robert Parker, the great hero of English non-conformity. Adding to the confusion, John Cotton and the Apologists could also claim Robert Parker as an influence; nonetheless, they believed him to be too 'independent' when compared to their understanding of the power of the keys. As the Scottish presbyterians moved back from the Parker position, they would find themselves in alignment with the Apologists.

RUTHERFORD INTERVENES

Rutherford's *A Peaceable and Temperate Plea for Paul's Presbyterie in Scotland*, published in London in 1642, represented an episodic shift in the church government debates in England. In it we find a marked move towards Scottish presbyterianism as it would come to be known in 1645. In England the Aldermanbury Accord was holding. The Calamy house presbyterians and the Holland Brethren studiously avoided any public debates on the power of the keys or on the jurisdiction of synods. Into this silence came Rutherford's pamphlet. While it seems Rutherford was cleaning up a congregational mess left behind by Gillespie, Rutherford nonetheless exhibited a great deal of respect, affection and indeed sympathy with what would become known as 'the middle way' position. Indeed, from a personal perspective, Rutherford had only praise for the congregational men both in print and in his private letters. He was more circumspect when talking about, or even citing, English presbyterian divines – which he rarely did.[87]

We will briefly study Rutherford's *Peaceable Plea* in order to understand his view of the keys before he encountered Cotton, or indeed, the Holland Brethren. Later in this book, we will expand our understanding of Rutherford's polity when he began to engage Cotton in print, and use that engagement to expand into a full description of the Apologists' understanding of the keys. We can tentatively claim that Rutherford's *Peaceable Plea* precipitated the breakdown of certain alliances within the English non-conformist community, in that he effectively called one of the English presbyterians' greatest non-conformist heroes an 'independent'.

The thrust of Rutherford's *Peaceable Plea* was a rebuttal of Robert Parker's assertion that believers received church power directly from Christ. Rutherford interpreted Parker as arguing that the 'power of the keys is in the believers immediately, and in the Rulers at the second hand, and borrowed from them'.[88] The basis for Parker's error, according to Rutherford, was his understanding of Peter's relationship to the church in Matthew 16. Parker taught that believers received the keys through Peter's confession that Jesus was the Christ. Peter stands as the federal representative of all believers throughout all time and the keys were therefore given to all believers in the church.[89]

The precise dating of the writing of Rutherford's *Peaceable Plea* complicates the way we understand the timing of Gillespie's *Assertion*. In a letter written in 1640, two years prior to the publication of the pamphlet, Rutherford indicated that he had a book in the London press against the Brownists' beliefs.[90] The editor of Rutherford's letters says that this is undoubtedly referring to *Peaceable Plea*.[91] There are two problems with this conclusion. First, in 1640/41 Baillie made a catalogue of the pamphlets written by the Scottish commissioners who were in London and made no mention of Rutherford's *Peaceable Plea*.[92] Rutherford was in Scotland, and given the political tumult in England during the winter months of 1640/41, we would have to assume that any pamphlet written by Rutherford in the London press would have been brought to the capital by the commissioners, and therefore would have been included in Baillie's catalogue. Secondly, this could mean Rutherford pulled his pamphlet from the press and waited until 1642 to publish it, which would indicate an implicit deferral to Gillespie's *Assertion* (which appeared in 1641), a document which was not unassailably presbyterian.

Pointedly unlike Parker and Gillespie, Rutherford argued that 'the adequate and proper subject of full power of the keyes is the presbytery of Pastors and Elders'. The church does not receive the power of the keys and then 'give over the use of them ... to the officers'.[93] Rutherford stated that it is against reason and Scripture 'that the power of the keyes essentially, fundamentally and originally is in the Church of beleevers, and the exercise only, and some borrowed acts of the keyes should be in the officers'.[94] Echoing John Ball's critique of Gillespie, Rutherford argued, 'It is absurd that one should essentially, and actu primo, have the power of the keyes, and yet he may not preach, nor baptize'. For Rutherford, the problem remained that if the whole church received the power of the keys, then the church must, by definition, have the power to exercise those acts of church government that are essential parts of the keys. 'If the power of the keyes be originally in the Church of Beleevers, and the exercise only in the officers, then Pastors in rigor of speech are the Churches [sic] servants, and so not over them Lord.'[95]

In terms of excommunication, Rutherford disagreed with many of the divines who had influenced Gillespie. Rutherford wrote, 'In a matter of

Excommunication Zepperus, Zanchius, Beza, Bucanus, Pareus, thinke the Eldership should not excommunicate ... [but] I see not how believers have a negative consent.' He believed the people may only affirm and cannot overrule the elders.[96] Gillespie in both 1638 and 1642 argued that elders cannot excommunicate without the people's consent.

In terms of installing officers, Rutherford believed that the power to ordain resided solely in the elders. The members of the church may elect, but for Rutherford this was not a power of the keys. Interestingly, Rutherford was willing to call the power to elect a 'popular power about the keys' but denied it any formal power.[97] Those who, like Parker, believed that the power of the keys was given to the church of believers, had conflated ordination and election. '[T]hey make the election of Elders (which by Gods Word is due to all the faithful) an act of jurisdiction.'[98] Rutherford argued that because the power of the keys was not given to the church of believers as the formal subject, they did not have the authoritative power to make and ordain officers. On this distinction Rutherford cited Martin Bucer, who 'judiciously distinguisheth power from authoritie' and claimed that this was Augustine's conclusion when he stated, 'the keyes were given in Peter to the whole church'.[99]

What Rutherford did do with the keys is important. He did not deny that keys are given to the church, but he did delineate what those keys are and how they function. He fundamentally rejected what he considered two extremes. Firstly, he rejected that the universal church was the first subject of the power of the keys, something believed by some English presbyterian divines. 'This mistake hath beene, that some Doctors believe that the power of the keyes ... must have some common subject, viz. the universall Church', and that power must reside there 'before it be given to certaine guides.'[100] He also rejected the position of Robert Parker, William Best and Henry Jacob, who saw believers as the first subject of the keys and the elders in a particular church as representatives of that power. Rutherford demurred, 'neither Scripture, nature, nor reason requireth such a shifting of the keyes from hand to hand, seeing Christ can keep them, and immediately put them in their trust, whom he liketh best'.[101] Like Gillespie, he believed the elders were representatives of people in the church, but Rutherford clarified the positions by stating that the elders' powers were wholly distinct and of a different kind than the believers' in a church.

Therefore, Rutherford described a variety of powers of the keys. There is a 'physical power of the keys' that Christ gives to men as they are believers and members of the visible church. '[B]ut this is not formally a power of the keyes, but a popular power about the keys, whereby popular consent may be given to key-bearers, for their election.'[102] This popular power was not to be confused, as Robert Parker and the 'independents' had done, with 'authoritative power' of the keys which resides only in the elders. Popular power was limited to the people of the church, but ordination, which was an 'act of jurisdiction' and therefore a matter of authority, belonged only to the elders. This is the same distinction Burroughs made in the *Petition Examined*. According to Parker's model, jurisdiction would first reside in the believers, who would give it to the church. For Burroughs the keys of jurisdiction and order – along with the use of those keys – were limited to the elders as the first subject of that power. These keys of church power were given subjectively to the elders, but objectively to the church of believers for their benefit.

Rutherford moved beyond Gillespie's interpretation of church power. Gillespie believed the 'whole church collectively taken' was the first subject of all church power, but he limited the exercise of that power in most cases to the elders. On first blush, it may seem that Rutherford was closer to John Ball, who argued that power could not be separated from the ability to exercise that power; therefore, the whole church could not receive the keys. However, unlike Ball, Rutherford was still willing to talk about the people possessing a type of power of the keys. Associating the power of the keys with the people was something that many English presbyterians would reject entirely. The London ministers, who chaffed at any mention of keys associated with the people, spoke unequivocally against Gillespie's language when they stated, 'the power [of discipline] cannot be placed in the whole Church collectively taken'.[103]

It may seem on the surface – indeed, it has been presumed – that Rutherford had written only against 'Independents'. However, the type of independency Robinson and Ainsworth advocated was not a serious political option for the Church of England in 1641. Rutherford had a different group in mind. The Scottish divine was serving notice to a strong contingency of English presbyterians who were attached to the tradition of Robert Parker. Tom Webster has said that the debates between congregationalists and presbyterians were squabbles among those who followed William Ames, who he dubbed 'Amesians'.[104] Although I would caution against this reductive view of ecclesiological indebtedness, if any non-conformist divine had a singularly influential role in the formation of revolutionary English presbyterianism, it was Robert Parker. By calling Parker's polity 'independent' Rutherford was, by implication, saying that at least one tradition of English presbyterianism was standing on shaky theological ground. However, for a man like Stephen Marshall, as long as the elders, and thus the presbytery over multiple churches, represented the power of the people and exercised that power for them, Parker's position was not problematic.

For Rutherford, it was not as simple as rejecting the exegesis of Peter standing in for believers throughout all time. Rutherford did believe that the individual church was the *ecclesia prima* and that a particularised church contained all the keys necessary for a fully functioning, rightly ordered church.

In this way, he was anticipating a brand of English presbyterianism that went in the other direction and over-emphasised the clerical aspect of presbyterian polity. By calling the role of the people a 'power' from Christ, even although it did not rise to a power of 'jurisdiction', Rutherford was protecting the people's rights in a way that would be rejected by men like Lazarus Seaman, Cornelius Burgess and even the 'London presbyterian' ministers, whom Rutherford would argue against at the Westminster assembly. Rutherford argued for the rights of the particular church, stating 'the Church hath the keys to bind and loose from Christ equally independent upon any mortall man in discipline'.

While Rutherford's *Peaceable Plea* undoubtedly had an impact on the ecclesiological debates in England, it did not alter the course of English presbyterianism. As Polly Ha has shown, there was a strong, erudite strand of presbyterianism that preceded Scottish involvement in England. Contrary to the prevailing historiography of the 1640s, the Scots were not the 'vanguard' of presbyterianism in England, nor, as we shall see, would the English divines simply fall in line with their northern counterparts.[105] Ha has noted that presbyterians 'recognised power to have originated in the congregation'.[106] She was right, but by 1640 at least, this was only true of *certain* English presbyterians.

We should note that Rutherford was writing against Independency, but not directly against the Apologists. This is evidenced by the association of the Apologists with the Scottish commissioners. Baillie, upon meeting the Apologists in 1641, claimed that 'our only differences are in the matter of the jurisdiction of synods', and even that difference was 'very small in speculation'.[107] We should take this comment seriously. Baillie did not draw this conclusion because he misunderstood the Apologists, nor were Burroughs and his colleagues purposefully ambiguous. While the Apologists' platform was written as broadly as possible, it nevertheless contained all the hallmarks of the Apologists' congregational polity. Henderson, although admitting that he did not embrace the Apologists' polity *in toto*, was nonetheless happy to preface it. If indeed the Apologists believed in the same type of independency that Ainsworth, Robinson or even Henry Jacob espoused, then Baillie's comments, and Henderson's Preface, contradicted the arguments of Rutherford's *Peaceable Plea*.

There was no doubt in Rutherford's mind that Parker's, Ainsworth's and Robinson's exegesis of Matthew 16:19 was the hallmark foundation of independent thought. Of course, it is possible that Rutherford felt that the Scots had conceded too much to the congregationalists and Rutherford was attempting to correct their polity by writing *Peaceable Plea*. But this is highly improbable given that Baillie had only recently moved away from reduced episcopacy and that he would have a continued revulsion of independency. Baillie by his own admission in 1641 saw a clear difference between the 'Holland Brethren' on the one side and Brownism and separatism on the other.[108] In terms of the power of the keys in the particular church, the Apologists had an exegesis that brought them very close to the Scots. The Scots, not having experienced a separatist controversy like England had experienced, came to England articulating their polity in such a way that probably gave too much credibility to the more 'extreme independents' that all parties in this Calamy house group eschewed. It fell to Rutherford to clarify their thoughts and adjust their language – not necessarily their polity – for an English context.

CONCLUSION

In all the pamphlets generated by the Calamy house group, only one had a platform of church government. Both the author and the pamphlet's detractor Christopher Harvey recognised that it was a platform. It was a congregational platform, but distinguishable from the more extreme versions of independency that English divines had come to fear. It was a set of positions that all those who opposed diocesan episcopacy, at least in 1640/41, could unite around. Contrary to Murray Tolmie's thesis, the Apologists had not abandoned the concept of a national church. The Calamy house group, and especially the Scots, would not support a platform of government that rejected national church reform. Tom Webster has stated that we cannot even see proto-presbyterianism or proto-congregationalism in the early 1640s, but that argument itself is based on a myth of uniformity. Each polity had a variety of permutations.[109] Years of ecclesiological debate had not resulted in binary clarity between two opposing polities; it had resulted in an increasingly complicated spectrum of polities, all to be understood as presbyterian or congregational depending on how one understood those categories. We are not arguing that the Scots were congregationalists, nor are we arguing the congregationalists were crypto-presbyterians. We are beginning to see that polities varied in fundamental ways that generated varied ecclesiologies within the monolithic categories we are accustomed to dealing with.

In terms of uniting the godly, there were extremes on the either end of the ecclesiastical spectrum that were certainly ruled out of bounds, but there was a variety of polities between those extremes that could indeed unite around a broad platform. In fact, a broad platform of church government was the only way to hold the centre, for with every added layer of specification there was an alienation of a particular aspect of church polity. The assembly of divines, to which we will now turn, tried to codify the centre with extreme precision. But, taken from a twenty-year perspective, the Westminster assembly was a disruptive moment that broke into the effort to unite the godly. It was only when England returned to a broad platform of church government in 1652, involving many of the same people from the Calamy house group, that the divines could hope to settle the ecclesiastical differences within this wide array of polities. All of this gives sharper relief to a comment Nye would make on the assembly floor only a year later that the Apologists came closer to Scottish church government than many English presbyterians.[10] Nye knew, with good reason, that the Apologists had a better chance of accommodation with the Scots than they did with many English presbyterians.

NOTES

1   D. G. Mullan, *Scottish Puritanism, 1590–1638* (Oxford: Oxford University Press, 2000), p. 131; J. Coffey, *Politics, Religion and the British Revolutions: The Mind of Samuel Rutherford* (Cambridge: Cambridge University Press, 1997), p. 189.

2   Mullan, *Scottish Puritanism*, p. 133.

3   Burroughs, *Petition Examined*, p. 31.

4   Baillie, *Letters and Journals*, vol. 1, p. 287.

5   Ibid., vol. 1, p. 287.

6   Perhaps we should take Baillie literally when he stated, 'Our *only* considerable difference will be about the *jurisdiction* of Synods and Presbyteries ... As for Brownists and Separatists of many kinds, they mislyke them weell near as much as we'. Ibid., p. 311 [italics mine].

7   Burroughs, *Petition Examined*, p. 33.

8   Schneider, 'Godly Order', p. 448.

9   See Smectymnuus, *An answer*, p. 58.

10 W. S. Hudson, 'The Scottish Effort to Presbyterianize the Church of England during the Early Months of the Long Parliament', *Church History*, 8 (1939), 255–282, p. 269.

11 J. Burroughs, *Irenicum, to the Lovers of Truth and Peace. Heart-divisions opened in the causes and evils of them: with cautions that we may not be hurt by them, and endeavours to heal them* (1646), pp. 155–156.

12 G. Gillespie, *A dispute against the English-Popish ceremonies* ([Leiden], 1637), p. 181.

13 Ibid., p. 182.

14 Ibid., p. 183.

15 Ibid., p. 181.

16 D. Parei, *Theologi Archi-Palatini in S. Matthaei Evangelivm Commentarivs* (Genevae, 1641), 1 Corinthians 5:4; W. Fulke, *The text of the New Testament of Iesus Christ* ([London?], 1582), I Corinthians 5:4; G. Zanchius, *Opera Theologica Hieronymi Zanchi* (Heidelberg, 1613), vol. 4, p. 756.

17 W. Fulke, *The text of the New Testament of Iesus Christ* (London, 1601), p. 60.

18 Ibid., p. 497.

19 J. Norton, *The Answer to the Whole Set of Questions of the Celebrated Mr. William Apollonius*, D. Horton (Cambridge, MA: Belknap Press of Harvard University Press, 1958), pp. 84–85.

20 Gillespie, *English-Popish ceremonies*, pp. 181ff. See also Norton, *Answer*, pp. 85, 84; cf.

Zanchius, *Opera Theologica*, vol. 4, book 1, section 4, question 3; Fulke, *New Testament*, 'Annotation on I Corinthians 5:4', Norton, *Answer*, p. 4.

21   Gillespie, *English-Popish ceremonies*, p. 181.

22   Ibid., p. 185.

23   J. Gerhard, *The Summe of Christian doctrine* (Cambridge, 1640), p. 264.

24   Gillespie, *English-Popish ceremonies*, pp. 185–186.

25   Norton, *Answer*, p. 84; Gillespie, *English-Popish ceremonies*, p. 181.

26   A. Willet, *Synopsis papismi* (1592), pp. 209–210.

27   Gillespie, *English-Popish ceremonies*, p. 186.

28   Ibid., p. 190.

29   Ibid., p. 190.

30   Ibid., pp. 169–170.

31   Ibid., pp. 170.

32   Baillie, *Letters and Journals*, vol. 1, p. 90.

33   Ibid., p. 90.

34   A. Johnston, *A Short Relation of the State of the Kirk of Scotland* (1638), not paginated.

35   J. Forbes, *Duplyes of the ministers & professors of Aberdene* (Aberdeen, 1638), pp. 133; see also 59, 61–62, 83, 88, 93, 95, 97.

36   Ibid., p. 88.

37   Baillie, *Letters and Journals*, vol. 2, pp. 65, 92, 166, 313.

38   Ibid., vol. 2, p. 505.

39   Ibid., p. 505.

40   Ibid., p. 505.

41   Ibid., p. 505.

42   J. K. Cameron, *The First Book of Discipline: With Introduction and Commentary* (Edinburgh: Saint Andrew Press, 1972), p. 68.

43   Ibid. p. 68; *The first and second booke of discipline. Together with some acts of the Generall Assemblies, clearing and confirming the same: and an Act of Parliament* (1621), p. 55.

44   Cameron, *The First Book of Discipline*, p. 68; *The first and second booke of discipline*, pp. 50–53.

45   Cameron, *The First Book of Discipline*, p. 69.

46   A. Woolrych, *Britain in Revolution, 1625–1660* (Oxford: Oxford University Press, 2002), p. 100, see also Morrill, *Nature of the English Revolution*, p. 105.

47   J. Ball, *A Friendly Triall of the Grounds tending to Separation* (London, 1640), pp. 231ff.

48   See Ha, *English Presbyterianism*, p. 60.

49   Ball, *A Friendly Triall*, pp. 232–233.

50   Ibid., pp. 234, 239.

51   Ibid., p. 265.

52 Ibid., p. 265.

53 Gillespie, *English-Popish ceremonies*, p. 188.

54 Ball, *A Friendly Triall*, pp. 266–267.

55 Ibid., p. 267.

56 J. Robinson, *A justification of separation from the Church of England* (Amsterdam, 1610).

57 Ibid., p. 126.

58 Ibid., p. 127.

59 Webster, *Godly Clergy*, p. 301.

60 Ibid., p. 302.

61 S. Ashe & W. Rathband, *A Letter of Many Ministers in Old England, requesting the judgement of their reverend brethren in New England concerning nine positions* (London, 1643), p. 71.

62 Ibid., p. 71.

63 Ibid., p. 71.

64 Ibid., pp. 71–72.

65 Ibid., p. 72.

66 Ibid., p. 74.

67 Ibid., p. 75.

68 Shephard and Allin themselves had a different understanding of the keys than the Apologists. J. Allin & T. Shepard, *A Defence of the Answer made unto the Nine Questions or Positions sent from New-England* (London, 1648), p. 169; see also, T. Shepard & J. Allin, *A Treatise of Liturgies, Power of the Keyes, and of matter of the visible church* (London, 1653), p. 176.

69 Shepard & Allin, *A Treatise of Liturgies*, p. 176.

70 Schneider, 'Godly Order', p. 365.

71 Ball, *A Friendly Triall*, p. 235.

72 Ha, *English Presbyterianism*, p. 60.

73 Schneider, 'Godly Order', p. 366.

74 Gillespie may have also written, Anon, *Certain Reasons tending to prove the unlawfulness and inexpediency of all Diocesan Episcopacy (even the most moderate)* (1641).

75 Morrill, *Nature of the English Revolution*, p. 108.

76 G. Gillespie, *An Assertion of the Government of the Church of Scotland* (Edinburgh, 1641), p. 109.

77 Ibid., part 2, pp. 36, 25.

78 Ibid., 110.

79 Ibid., 110.

80 R. Parker, *English Translation of Robert Parker's De Politeia Ecclesiastica.* (Oxford: Bodleian Library: Parker MS, The.158), 95r.

81 Gillespie, *An Assertion*, p. 111.

82 Ibid., p. 111.

83 Ibid., part 2, p. 15.

84 Ibid., p. 119.

85 Ibid., p. 119.

86 Ibid., p. 121.

87 S. Rutherford, *A peaceable and temperate plea for Pauls Presbyterie in Scotland* (London, 1642), To the reader, not paginated.

88 Ibid., p. 24.

89 Ibid., p. 22.

90 A. A. Bonar (ed.), *Letters of Samuel Rutherford: with a sketch of his life and biographical notices of his correspondents* (London: Oliphant Anderson & Ferrier, 1891), p. 610.

91 Ibid., p. 612.

92 Baillie, *Letters and Journals*, vol. 3, p. 303.

93 Rutherford, *Peaceable plea*, p. 56.

94 Ibid., p. 59.

95 Ibid., pp. 61–62.

96 Ibid., pp. 50, 218, 223.

97 Ibid., p. 3.

98 Ibid., p. 4.

99 Ibid., p. 5.

100 Ibid., p. 3.

101 Ibid., p. 3.

102 Ibid., p. 3.

103 *A Vindication of the Presbyteriall Government, and Ministry* (London, 1650), p. 71.

104 Webster, *Godly Clergy*, p. 328.

105 See J. R. Collins, *The Allegiance of Thomas Hobbes* (Oxford: Oxford University Press, 2005), p. 101.

106 Ha, *English Presbyterianism*, p. 58.

107 This may also reflect Baillie's evolving attitude towards presbyterian polity.

108 Baillie, *Letters and Journals*, vol. 1, p. 311.

109 Webster, *Godly Clergy*, p 327.

110 Van Dixhoorn, *MPWA* (vol. 3), p. 285; Gillespie recorded, 'Mr Ney said ... that were the goverrment of Scotland laid before us, he and his party would come nearer to it in many things than divers of this assembly will do in other things', G. Gillespie, *Notes of debates and proceedings of the Assembly of Divines and other commissioners at Westminster. Febuary 1644 to January 1645*, p. 68.

Chapter 3

The 'builders' of the new Church of England

By 1642 war had broken out between Charles and Parliament, and there was little hope that either would acquiesce to the other's demands. The king would not remove his protection from those whom Parliament wished to prosecute, and Parliament could not – or would not – trust their monarch as long he was protecting people they perceived to be traitors. By the beginning of 1643 it had become clear that neither side could win the war alone: both Charles and Parliament had to seek allies outside England. Charles looked across the Irish Sea for assistance, which only validated fears that there was truly a Catholic plot. Parliament looked north, for assistance from the Scots. Both were fateful choices. The conflict was now a war in three kingdoms with an inescapable religious dimension. By the time the Solemn League and Covenant was signed, Parliament had become a divided body: divided on how to prosecute a war, divided on the level to which the Scots could intervene in English affairs, and divided on how aggressively to reform religion. All these issues impinged upon the calling of the Westminster assembly and its subsequent debates.

The debates in the autumn of 1643, and the ecclesiological disputes that followed, reveal the varieties of presbyterianism that were represented at Westminster and force us to reassess some popular misconceptions about the ecclesiological alliances in the assembly. The main focus of this chapter will be a crucial debate that took place at the end of October 1643. This debate gives the most accurate depiction of the uniquely English controversies of the Westminster assembly and demonstrates Parliament's attempt to stay ahead of the Scottish influence in England's new church without alienating their northern neighbours. In this debate we witness the assembly's brief foray into the 'substratum', as Thomas Goodwin called it, of all ecclesiological discourse. These days also provide a helpful model for entering into the complicated world of the assembly's debates. We will see time and again, that it was at the beginning of discussions, before the assembly unalterably committed itself to debate a particular proposition, that we get the most unguarded glimpses into what various divines believed and how they viewed one another. At the end of October, the Scottish commissioners were not yet contributing to debates in the assembly and therefore a foreign party was not present to convolute the discussion – it would be the last time English divines debated with English divines on the issue of church government.

By the time the Westminster assembly of divines first met in the summer of 1643, Parliament had decided unequivocally that though the prelacy had not been officially abolished, its ultimate demise was a given. The summoning of the divines was further validation of this fact: Parliament, within a span of three short years, 'had heeded the almost constant calls from its most ardent supporters for a more radical reform' of the Church of England.[1] This was not, initially at least, a call to reform the religion of the church. Insofar as theology was concerned, the assembly of divines was called to 'vindicate' and 'clear' the doctrine of the church. Therefore, their first order of business was to work through the existing *Thirty-Nine Articles*. Many divines had long argued that the theological articles of the Church of England were already 'Reformed', and that it was Laud's interpretation of them that smacked of arminianism. Others believed there were too many theological loopholes in the *Articles* that could easily allow for a wider interpretation of its theology. The Westminster divines eventually realised that in order to fend off heterodoxy they would have to construct an entirely new confession. It was the exigencies of war that forced the assembly to turn its attention to church government, as we shall see in this chapter.

THE SOLEMN LEAGUE AND COVENANT

Throughout 1642 and 1643 those nobles and Members of Parliament who had been part of the initial revolt against Charles found themselves divided over how to settle the conflict.[2] The fiery spirit of religious reform was not shared equally across the peerage. Charles's more moderate opponents – led by Northumberland, Pembroke and the Earl of Holland in the Lords and by Holles in the Commons – were naturally less interested in a protracted conflict. For them tempering the king's belligerency was one thing; permanently overhauling England's entire religious and political complexion was quite another. This group had thrown its lot in with the Parliamentary cause in 1642, believing that the Royalists would be quickly crushed by Lord General Essex's army. They were opposed by the junto who initiated the revolt – Manchester, Saye, Wharton, Pym, Vane junior and St John.[3] Not surprisingly, the group led by Northumberland and Holles pursued peace through proposals to Charles, whereas the junto knew that a negotiated peace from a position of weakness meant beheading.[4] Both groups wanted peace, but they weighed the risks – and their ultimate objectives – differently.

Hence, from very early in the Revolution, historians have divided these two groups into the 'peace party' and 'war party'. The war party was led by the interests of Saye and Pym (who would be replaced by Oliver St John upon his death), and the peace party was led by Northumberland and Holles. A tug of war began between these two bicameral groups in early 1643 when the group led by Northumberland and Holles sought a quick settlement with the king. They offered to leave his powers largely intact and keep some semblance of episcopacy in England.[5] The king rejected these proposals, known as the Oxford treaty, thus empowering Saye and the war party to push forward with a military alliance with the Scots.

Parliament's military leader, Essex, was one of the greatest sources of tension between these groups. The war party was initially supportive of Essex and his army and hoped he would deal a quick and decisive blow to the Royalists. His orders were 'to rescue His Majesty's person, and the persons of the Prince and the Duke of York out of the hands of those desperate persons who were then about them'.[6] In early 1643 Jeremiah Burroughs, in one of his responses on behalf of Parliament to Henry Ferne, dedicated his *Glorious Name of God, the Lord of Hosts* to Essex, stating the Lord General was 'Raised by Parliament in defence of the true Protestant Religion, His Majesties Person, the Laws and Liberties of the Kingdom, and the Privileges of Parliament'.[7] However, Essex's military defeats in the summer of 1643 made it clear to many in Parliament that in order to stave off a protracted war (or, worse, an outright defeat), an alliance with the Scottish Covenanters was inevitable.[8]

The religious foundation for such an alliance had already been laid. The idea of a national assembly of religious divines had been in gestation since 1641.[9] The Commons had been in favour of a meeting of divines, and Parliament's Grand Remonstrance in 1641 specifically requested that Charles consent to 'a general synod of most grave, pious, learned and judicious divines of this island; assisted with some from foreign parts, professing the same religion with us'.[10] The Commons could not move forward without the Lords' approbation, and the Lords dragged their feet on the matter of an assembly until 1642. As John Morrill has noted, this was not only because of the procedural hurdles and recurrent mutual distrust between the two houses, but also because true religious reform could only receive an official parliamentary sanction once the bishops were expelled from the House of Lords.[11]

Parliament was by no means committed to a particular form of church government, but there was widespread agreement that Scottish presbyterianism was a foreign polity that threatened to compete with Parliament's carefully guarded rights to oversee the Church of England. However, the need for troops after the string of military defeats in 1643 forced Parliament's hand.[12] Ultimately, the calling of the assembly was bound to the war: Parliament needed Scottish troops, Scotland wanted uniformity of religion – the calling of the Westminster assembly solved both problems.

The Saye-Pym war party knew that religion had to be a basis for bringing the Scots into the fray. As early as 1642 the war party in England had been planning for a more cohesive alliance with the Covenanters in Scotland.[13] The passing of the Ordinance summoning the assembly of divines in June demonstrated that Parliament was already planning for an alliance. Parliament had communicated to the General Assembly in Scotland in July 1642 'that Parliament's main concern in the war was "the glory of God by the advancement of the true religion, and such a reformation of the church as shall be most agreeable to God's word"'.[14] This language portended the wording of the Solemn League and Covenant, and already hinted that while Parliament wanted to change England's church, it was by no means committed to the Scottish model.

For the peace party, the threat of an alliance with the Scots was tolerable, insofar as it would increase pressure on Charles to expedite peace. Beyond that, the peace party saw an actual Scottish military intervention as a dangerous escalation of the conflict.[15] By the summer of 1643, however, both sides recognised the need of the other. As long as prelatical government remained in place, Scotland felt its very self-preservation was at stake.[16] Like England, Scotland's nobility was divided into two groups that differed in how to achieve a lasting settlement with Charles, but it became increasingly apparent an alliance with England was the only way to protect the Scottish kirk and kingdom. Around the same time as the Oxford treaty, Charles rejected a peace proposal from Scotland and effectively told them to stay out of English affairs. Royalist troops (which included Catholic soliders) occupied the northern English counties of Yorkshire, Cumberland, Westmorland, Northumberland and Durham, and a plot had been uncovered indicating the king planned to attack Scotland with Irish troops.[17] Taken with the plots uncovered in London, both sides truly believed Charles intended to 'extirpate true Protestant religion in England, Scotland, and Ireland'.[18]

No doubt the calling of a religious assembly sweetened the deal Parliament offered to Scotland. However, it is also true that calling the Assembly of Divines *prior* to the actually signing of the Solemn League and Covenant put Parliament in a position to invite commissioners to England's religious assembly. Parliament was not forced to call an assembly of divines as a result of the Solemn League and Covenant. Indeed, it became a parliamentary parlour game to allow the Scots to believe they had more influence than they really did.

When Parliament decided they needed Scottish assistance in their war effort against Charles, they chose Stephen Marshall and Philip Nye as the two divines to travel with the English commissioners who were sent north to negotiate the Solemn League and Covenant. David Stevenson can be taken as represen-

tative of the wider scholarship when he states that Nye, 'a leading independent', along with one of the commissioners, Henry Vane, in order to keep the
door open for 'independency in England', cleverly inserted the clause that the
church of England should be reformed 'according to the Word of God'.[19] This
ploy was seemingly so obvious one scholar has wondered 'why the Covenantors so easily agreed to the amendments'. Indeed, he goes on to say that even
at this stage, 'the independents were ready to declare war against the presbyterians'.[20] C. V. Wedgwood notes that Nye preached an 'offen[sive] sermon in
Edinburgh ... of strong independent flavor'.[21] The only evidence for either of
these claims is from the writings of Baillie who, by 1643, strongly believed that
uniformity must be in the form of Scottish presbyterianism. Yet Henderson
himself would acknowledge, 'We are neither so ignorant nor so arrogant, as to
ascribe to the Church of Scotland such absolute purity and perfection; as hath
not need or cannot admit of further Reformation.'[22] The English presbyterian
Thomas Case recoiled at the thought that the English were bound to follow
the Scottish model of presbyterianism. Burgess 'protested vigorously' for the
removel of the phrase 'according to the Word of God' because it presumed that
the Church of Scotland was of divine origin.[23] Parliamentarians were equally
cautious. Sir Simond D'Ewes wrote in his diary, 'I conceived this to be a very
strange clause, that we should declare in our law that the Church of Scotland
was reformed according to the word of God.'[24]

Certainly, political dynamics played a part in the debates within the
Westminster assembly. This was, after all, Parliament's assembly, and over
and over again, the divines would be reminded that they served the state –
something that would infuriate different assembly members. Nonetheless,
the divines were required to define England's church according to biblical
principles. Indeed, the assembly members frowned on the use of citations
from commentaries (even from their most revered reformed predecessors)
during their debates. Certainly, divines would, when they could, cite sources
that validated their point, but assembly members were often quick to rebuke
each other when getting too far afield from the scriptural proofs needed for
each proposition. Whatever subterfuge was suspected in the insertion of the
phrase 'according to the word of God' would have paled in comparison to the
ensuing fiasco had it been left out. No doubt divines entered the assembly with
their own beliefs in theology and polity, but it is also remarkable when reading
through the minutes of the assembly just how much divines were willing to
change their minds when confronted with a biblical proof-text.

When we take into consideration the discussion in the previous chapters
on the debates of 1640/41, we can see reasons why Nye and Marshall were
selected to be sent to Scotland. Most obviously, they were leaders in the
Calamy house group. In addition, it is probably not coincidental that Marshall
and Nye were related through marriage. There is also the overlooked fact that

along with Nye – who was ministering in Kimbolton – all four of the Parliamentarians who were dispatched northward – Sir Henry Vane Junior, Sir William Armyne, Henry Darley and Thomas Hatcher – were either Yorkshire or Lincolnshire men.[25] Moreover, their views of church government were far more similar to the Scottish presbyterians than were the views of many other English presbyterians, whose clerical impulses would unnerve many of the Scots, especially Gillespie and Rutherford. The Scots already knew Nye and Marshall personally, had worked with them, and knew their ecclesiological leanings. Henderson himself had already prefaced a congregational platform written by Burroughs and Goodwin. In October 1643, Burroughs would be sent with Edmund Calamy to plead with the City of London to provide money to support the Scottish troops in the war. Burroughs was effusive in support of the Scottish church and the Scottish cause. He compared the church of Scotland to the church of Philadelphia in the book of Revelation, saying, 'When was there ever a Nation, such a Church, that joined together in such firm Covenants as they have done? had wee the like union amongst us, O what great things had wee done long before this time.'[26] Given this attitude, the picture is not one of Nye and his companions going to Scotland in order to slow their enemies' inevitable advance; rather, they were emissaries without a tincture of clerical presbyterian impulses.

OCTOBER 1643: 'YOU ARE NOW UPON THE FOUNDATION OF ALL'[27]

In October 1643 the assembly quickly fell into a debate on the topic of 'the power of the keyes'. This was arguably one of the most important ecclesiological debates the assembly would ever have, yet remains largely ignored in the historiography. As complex as the debates were, they are essential for understanding the forthcoming church government discussions at Westminster. The verse at the heart of the debate was Matthew 16:19, where Christ tells Peter, 'And I will give unto thee the keys of the kingdom of heaven: and whatsoever thou shalt bind on earth shall be bound in heaven: and whatsoever thou shalt loose on earth shall be loosed in heaven.' Few divines doubted that this verse got to the very heart of what a church was, and virtually all interpreters agreed that Jesus was founding his church through Peter. From there, exegesis diverged greatly. As the English divine Thomas Gataker noted early in the debates, '[as to] what the keyes are. This is a metaphoricall word & debate amongst the learned what they are. A poynt of much use for the stating many controversyes'.[28]

Although we will primarily tease out the Apologists' position in these crucial discussions, we should also note that the minutes convey a great deal of confusion, and indeed, uncertainty in the assembly concerning how to address Matthew 16:19. Since the divines were trained to ferret out inconsistencies as well as to promote their own positions, gathering a linear narrative out of any Westminster debate is difficult: a difficulty compounded by the fact that the style of disputation is already foreign to the modern observer. We will therefore draw heavily on Thomas Goodwin's *Government of the Churches of Christ*, for it is evident that he was organising and citing his own personal assembly notes when writing it, something that has gone unnoticed in the scholarship of the assembly.

Two things were necessary for understanding what Matthew wrote: what the keys were and in what regard Peter received them. To put it another way, what was church power (the keys), and who had the right to use that power. Up until the revolution, the Church of England was built upon the ideat that the Bishop could exercise church power alone. With the bishops removed, the assembly was free to redefine the fundamental question of church power. This chapter is concerned what (or who) was the *primum subjectum* (first subject) of church power. Secondly, this chapter will demonstrate that the Apologists' position was distinctly different from that of most 'independents'. These were not new concepts the Apologists were introducing to the assembly. Indeed, over a year before, Goodwin had stood before Parliament and preached an uncontroversial sermon in which his view of Matthew 16:19 and his understanding of national church reform along congregational lines were fully present. The October 1643 debate materialised out of a seemingly innocuous proposition by the English presbyterian Lazarus Seaman, namely that the apostles had the power of the keys and also exercised those powers. Because Seaman attempted to use Matthew 16:19 as his proof-text, he exposed decades of ecclesiological positioning against opposing spectres of prelatic tyranny and separatist anarchy. For the Apologists Matthew 16:19 represented the '*substratum*' of all church power, and therefore could not so easily be passed over without putting one of their bedrock theological tenets at risk.

On 12 October 1643 Parliament sent an order 'enjoining our [the assembly of Divines'] speedy taking in hand the discipline and liturgy of the Church'.[29] The House of Lords ordered that the divines find the 'Discipline and Government' that is 'most agreeable to God's Holy word' and that is nearer in 'Agreement with the Church of Scotland and other Reformed Churches abroad, to be settled in this Church in Stead and Place of the present [prelatic] Government' which Parliament 'is Resolved to be taken away'.[30] With the arrival of the Scottish commissioners in London, Parliament had to accelerate the reforming of England's church. A debate on church government, and more specifically a church government to replace the prelatic Church of England, had been forced upon the assembly.

On 17 October an agitation arose amongst the divines over how to proceed upon the topic of church government.[31] The primary concern for the assembly was whether or not to establish a general rule and model for church government in Scripture and then proceed to specifics, or to proceed to specifics (e.g. church officers) and build a model derivatively from each specific as it arose. Charles Herle aptly summarised the mood of those who wished to go straight to the discussions of officers: 'The question is not whether Christ hath instituted a government, but whether constituted such a government as that the officers and exercises of them be set downe in the word. It is not to spend time about the subject of the church.'[32] Therefore the assembly should first find out what offices, and how many of those offices are set down in the Scripture, and subsequently explore their powers and how that power is exercised.[33] Dr Thomas Temple agreed with Herle, stating that the general rule of church government can only be found by examining the particulars of the church first.[34] Seaman claimed that to proceed with officers first was in keeping with the model of all other churches.

Those opposed to this methodology were the Erastians and the congregational divines. That the Erastians, fearful of *jure divino* presbyterianism, wanted to discover first whether there was a clear rule of government in the Scriptures is not surprising.[35] However, at first glance we are more surprised to see the congregational divines asking to begin with an exploration of the general rule for church government. It was certainly not for the same reason as the Erastians. Goodwin, Bridge and Simpson believed there was a rule in Scripture, and asked that the assembly examine and find the rule of church government first.[36] The congregational divines considered it fruitless to debate 'perticulars' without having ascertained the broader parameters and boundaries of church government. As Goodwin stated, 'We must first agree on the rule & how this rule binds.'[37] Or, to use Simpson's construction metaphor, 'For the rule of builders, they must have a platforme & that is first drawne before the materialls are prepared.'[38]

One of the accusations levied against the Apologists by the anti-independent pamphleteers was that they refused to bring forward any platform of church government between 1640 and 1644.[39] The evidence indicates that during this period the Apologists did try to bring forth a platform in the context of the assembly debates, as an effort to protect the godly alliance. This happened twice, first in late October 1643 and again four months later, as we shall see, in February 1644.[40]

It may seem foolhardy that the congregational divines wished to dive headlong into the debate on church government in general, particularly when there was broad agreement in matters of church officers. From the perspective of Edmund Calamy, this was precisely the point. 'All assert their government & discipline to be jure divino,' and therefore to go to this 'greatest thing' would only, as the majority said against John Lighfoot – who also requested that the rule be explored first – expose the assembly to 'too sudden of a trial of the differences in opinion that are like to shew among us'.[41] Seaman summarised the majority's response to the Erastians and congregational divines when he stated, 'I take it for granted that ther is a sufficiency in the scriptures concerning matter of government, & therfore not dispute that that it [sic] is in a great measure agreed on.' However, 'We shall not fall into this question in the generall, but in the perticulars.'[42] The problems with this decision were again encountered the following month. In debating whether the Church of England was a true church – which the Apologists believed – the assembly struggled to understand in what sense it was a true church. Simpson chided the assembly for adding to this confusion by having failed to establish a platform first. 'When we are inquiring about a perticular rule in the word of God, that was waved by many in the assembly', and now the assembly was left trying to decide what ministers may have a living in the church of England 'for that which you have not [yet] declared to be Jure divino.'[43]

Ironically, by focusing on officers, rather than a platform of church government, some presbyterians actually prejudiced the debate over Matthew 16:19 that would take place the following week; it limited the discussion to whether Matthew 16:19 was a proof-text for the Apostles receiving the keys immediately from Christ, rather than whether Matthew 16:19 had anything at all to do with the church. The congregational divines, anticipating this, were quick to state that while they conceded the methodology proposed on 17 October, they nonetheless asserted their right to, as Nye said, 'if ther be a necessity to returne to the rule, let it not be a grievance to the Assembly'.[44] A more portentous – albeit completely ignored – comment came from the French minister Samuel De la Place. He considered this tack taken by English presbyterians to be a 'blemish upon Christ' and requested that the assembly instead '[b]egin to examine the power of the keyes'.[45] De la Place gave voice to the latent concerns undoubtedly permeating the assembly members. They were diving headlong into debates that would, on the surface, draw out the similarities on particulars such as church officers, but at the expense of sorting out the most complex and contentious issues of the previous twenty years, namely the power of the keys.

A few days later, on 27 October, Seaman brought this proposition to the assembly: 'That the apostells did Immediately receive the keyes from the hand of Jesus Christ and did use & exercise them in all the churches of the world upon all occasions.'[46] Strictly speaking, was the power of the keys (i.e. all ecclesiastical power) given to all the apostles? The proposition itself was not particularly contentious, as Burroughs would say, 'This proposition may be granted by all without any further debating.'[47] The question, of course, was how this verse related to the church, for all knew that the power of the keys was a power of church government. Was this an extraordinary power, limited to the Apostles, or did it include the ordinary ecclesiastical power subsequently conveyed to elders? Did this power include the congregation? The central, unavoidable question was whether or not, as Seaman asserted, Matthew 16:19 could be used as a proof-text. For clarification, we should note that the assembly was only meant to debate the validity of Seaman's proposition, and whether or not Matthew 16:19 could be used as the proof-text. This is far from what actually happened.

Bridge stated what was obvious to any divines who had lived in England for the previous twenty years: 'ther ... [are] great disputes concerning the keyes'.[48] Dr Joshua Hoyle echoed De la Place's request from ten days before, 'If [the keys] must be determined, why not now?' Thomas Case broadened the question to consider both 'what those keyes ware' and whether 'the apostles did use [them] qua apostells'.[49] Seaman knew exactly where this would lead and quickly tried to stop any further debate. Referring to Burroughs's comment, Seaman stated, '[He] moved that we take that propounded for granted. Let it be soe resolved.' Gataker similarly tried to shoehorn the proposition through, stating, 'I conceive we need not to inquire any further.'[50] Given the protocol set forth by the assembly the previous week, a general discussion about Matthew 16:19 was bound to be tense. They were meant to debate officers, and therefore Seaman attempted to prove the apostles did indeed receive the power of the keys from Christ, without any reference to the church. Interestingly, it was some of the presbyterians who struggled with the proposition, whereas the Apologists were fine with it, provided Matthew 16:19 was not attached to it. In John's Gospel, Christ did indeed give the Apostles the power to bind and loose, and this meant the Apostles had an extraordinary power that did not accrue to ordinary elders.[51] But by citing Matthew 16:19, Seaman was removing the very verse that was widely considered to be the foundation of all church government. As Nye stated, 'the proposition is granted. Whether this scripture prove it is doubted'.[52]

Everyone in the assembly knew they were dealing with a fundamental, and highly problematic, ecclesiological text, but they were less clear on where the debates would lead. Of course, the more clerically minded English presbyterians were not as alarmed by the prospect of using Matthew 16:19 as a proof, for whenever the assembly did revisit the general issue of church government it would have been established that Peter as Apostle received the power of the keys apart from the church. However, the proof for the proposition was not nearly as benign as Seaman and Gataker intimated. No one doubted the Apostles had an extraordinary power of the keys: they had a special commission from Christ to spread the gospel, and they had this as a universal commission not rooted to a particular church or location. These extraordinary powers died with the Apostles and therefore were not conveyed to the elders or the church. But to limit Matthew 16:19 to the extraordinary power of the keys effectively removed the question of the ordinary power of the keys and the ordinary subject (viz. the church). Limiting the exegesis in this way was a first step in fending off separatism, for by protecting the unique power of the apostles, it would be only a small exegetical step to protect the unique power of the elders, quite apart from reference to the whole particular church. For the Apologists the problem was not that claiming Matthew 16:19 proved Seaman's proposition, but the risk that the verse would be *limited* to Seaman's proposition.

Ultimately, the Apologists, and even Gataker and Seaman, were content to pass the proposition and move on to debate the proof-text. But, Charles Herle intervened: 'I thinke that to know what those keyes are is not here pertinent or seasonable', although he nevertheless went on to enumerate the various prevalent opinions as to who received the keys. Herle's speech ultimately forced Seaman to concede that a discussion of Matthew 16:19 prior to the passing of the proposition was inevitable. He stated, 'now we are hard put seeing our Brethren have brought it in'.[53]

This made the resultant debates disorganised and chaotic. The assembly swerved back and forth between discussions about the recipient of church power and the definition of the keys. Often members were unclear as to whether they were debating the proposition or the proof for that proposition. Bridge, helpfully, organised the chaos into three distinct categories. 'One: whether the words of proposition be true. [2]. Whether that place 16 Math. prove it. [3]. What is the *primum subjectum*.'[54] The assembly found it nearly impossible to isolate one of those three points from the other two. We will briefly look at the salient points made about the first point, before taking a closer look at the Apologists' understanding of the last two.

John Lightfoot recorded that Herle thought it 'very questionable whether the keys were given to the apostles or the church'. Herle cited the Catholic Sorbonnists of Paris who 'thinke that the keyes ware not Immediately given to the apostles, but to the church, as they quote most of the fathers, &c'.[55] They stated that 'in a naturall body all facultyes not given to the severall instruments', the subject by which (*subjectum quo*) is the eye, but the subject which (*subjectum quod*) is the whole man.[56] Herle was essentially saying what many presbyterians had long believed, the keys were given 'to the church formally and subjectively, and not only finally for the benefit of it'.[57]

By saying this, Herle was not so subtly introducing the great English divine Robert Parker into the debates. Parker had noted, 'So that primarily all is in the church, secondarily in her rectors for her sake, as the end which is before the meanes intention, and as the whole which is before the part', and therefore 'God and nature intend the whole first and more immediately then any part how noble soever, say the Paris divines illustrating it by the eye induced with sight for the whole, etc.'[58] Parker was himself indebted to the Sorbonnists, following them in acknowledging that the keys, as Herle also noted, 'ware not Immediately given to the apostles, but to the church, as they quote most of the fathers'.[59] It is a fascinating moment, given, as we noted in chapter 2, that

Robert Parker had been effectively labelled an 'independent' by Rutherford. Rutherford rejected the interpretation of the Sorbonnists for the same reason that he rejected Parker. But, of course, Rutherford was not yet there at the assembly to object to Herle's statements. The assembly debates demonstrated how much English presbyterian thought was influenced by Parker.

The Sorbonnists, represented in the writings of Jacques Almain, John Major and Jean Gerson, believed that Christ had given the power of the keys immediately to all the believers, and through them to the pastors.[60] Almain stated that the power promised to Peter in both Matthew 16:19 and Matthew 18:18 'are to be understood as referring to the faithful' and that 'Christ conferred ... power immediately on the Church, understanding the Church as being a gathering of all the faithful'.[61] Bridge claimed the keys could '[e]ither [be] given to him [Peter] as representing the church or else in *commodum ecclesiae ad ecclesiam* or *pro ecclesia*'. That is, 'for the benefit of the church, towards the church or on behalf of the church'. He cited Almain's use of Augustine to prove his point: 'Alman proving that cannot be the sence of Austin that the keyes ware given to the church *finaliter*'.[62] In Almain's own words:

> I prove that Augustine did not say that the keys were given to the church in that sense, because, on that basis, [to say that] the keys were given to the church would mean that they were given for the eventual benefit of the Church, not that they were given to the Church as such – which is manifestly contrary to what Augustine says.[63]

Although Parker believed that all believers gathered into a particular fellowship were the proper first subject of the keys, the guides were not excluded because the believers could give power to certain guides (i.e. elders). This was a relatively standard independent argument, and one not held by the Apologists. But Herle was nonetheless opening the door to the Apologists' position, for he conceded the strength of the Parisian argument, namely that the 'the whole church' seemed to be the formal subject of the keys. His concern was that when Jesus states, upon Peter's confession, that the 'gates of hell not prevail against' the church, he cannot mean simply the officers. For it was a matter of fact that officers, as men, certainly fell into sin and would fall into sin. This was not the case for the universal church, which by definition, could not be defeated by Satan.

Herle's arguments only confused the debate further and brought a variety of presbyterian opinions out of the woodwork. The only clear fact was that Matthew 16:19 was about to be used to defend a proposition that made no reference to the church. Burgess attempted to steer the assembly back to Seaman's proposition 'that is before us'.[64] And Jeremiah Whitaker, in response to Herle's argument regarding the 'gates of hell', stated that therefore it must only be the Apostles receiving extraordinary power, rather than the officers.[65] The Apostles had an extraordinary gifting from Christ, and this could be proved by Matthew

16:19. Extraordinary Apostles, who had the power of the church, would indeed withstand the 'gates of hell', because their great commission from Christ would be invariably fulfilled. However, William Gouge saw the strength of Herle's statement and sought to defer the entire question regarding the 'universall militant church', which 'will come better to be discussed at another time'.[66] Gouge concluded, 'Though it be granted that the church had the power of [the keys], yet if the apostells had them Immediately from Christ, it is the question in hand.'[67] The assembly went ahead and voted in approval of the proposition. But it was not the end of the debate. The proposition needed a proof-text, and the Apologists were on the verge of losing the basis for their whole ecclesiological position. They needed to convince the assembly that the proposition could stand, but that Matthew 16:19 could not stand with it.

THE GRAND CHARTER OF THE CHURCH

Thomas Goodwin aptly summarised the relatively uncontroversial exegetical starting point for Matthew 16:19: 'The first Charter granted by the Founder, and the Patterns of those Master Builders the Apostles'. Therefore, he believed the true import of the verse was vital to any further establishing of church government. When Peter had made his confession he effectively inaugurated the Church of the New Testament. The church was moulded anew by the Son, and as the builder of the church, Christ says two things to Peter, 'I will build my church' and 'I will give Keys.' By 'the Keys he means, the Keys of the Kingdom of Heaven (as the State of the Church under the Gospel is called;) which, to shew he is the Son, and hath all power committed to him, he professeth to dispose anew (as the Keys themselves were new)'.[68] In doing so, Christ was doing away with the Old Testament church, as it were, under the Mosaic Law and building a new church. 'For Christ the Son, being come, shews his Prerogative by declaring the Old to be done away, saying I will build, I wil give the keys, &c whilst he speaks of a New, the Old is done away', and further, 'the Persons to whom, and the Extant and Limits of the power are to be set out by him'.[69] Christ singles Peter out 'electively, [and] it argues his special Designation of the Subject or Persons (whoever they be) to whom he will bequeath them'. That 'Peter here in this promise of the keyes for the future to be given, should stand in a Representative Respect and not meerly Personal', Goodwin continued, 'all Writers in all Ages, and all sides, though in Peter's name, laying several claims unto these keys, do universally acknowledge and observe'.[70] Charles Herle conceded this topic would 'aford a great deale of discussion.' He noted that there were '4 wayes' to interpret Peter in Matthew 16:19: Bridge and Thomas Goodwin claimed there were five. The minutes are incomplete in Herle's speech, but we can fill them in using Goodwin's description of the variant interpretations. Through understanding

70

these interpretations, we can begin to understand the schools of thought that were emerging in the assembly debates.

The first three positions were immediately passed over. Firstly, there were those who argued that Peter stood as Peter only.[71] This position, proffered only by Lightfoot, argued that Peter was merely being commissioned to take the gospel to the gentiles. Herle dismissed this position outright, although Bridge acknowledged it was a position held by the Scottish theologian John Cameron.[72] The second interpretation of the keys was held some 'papists' who assert that Peter was the prince of apostles, thus vindicating the power of the bishop of Rome.[73] This 'Romish' position would imply the keys were given to Peter for the church, but 'they do not make the Church the first subject to which the keys are given'.[74]

The third position passed over illustrates an important point for this book concerning how the Apologists distinguished themselves from the 'independents'. In this category the keys were given to Peter, 'considered as a Believer, having made Confession of his faith, that Christ was the Son of God, and therefore Representing the Church of Believers, as unto whom all Church power should first be given'.[75] This was the standard position held by most 'independents', such as Jacob, Ainsworth, Robinson, Canne, Henry Burton and New England divines like John Davenport and Thomas Hooker. For example, John Canne stated, 'Jesus Christ, Lord & King of his Church, hath given said [church] power of his to all his saints, and placed it in the body of every particular congregation.'[76] Thomas Hooker argued, 'The power of the Keyes take it in the compleat nature thereof, its in the Church of beleevers, as in the first subject.'[77] This was also Robert Parker's belief, and, to some extent, it was held by many English presbyterians that followed him, although they drew different practical conclusions. None of these three options were seriously debated on the floor. Although the Apologists were intent on distancing themselves from this third option, there were nonetheless some assembly presbyterians who were reluctant to totally dismiss it.

The fourth position was that 'this grant [was] made to Peter as an Apostle, and so Representing the Apostles and Ministers only'.[78] It was a central tenet of some English presbyterians that 'the Proper Subject wherein Christ hath seated and intrusted all Church-power, and the exercise thereof, in Only his own Church-Officers'.[79] This position was latent within Seaman's proposition and was, at least in part, held by all English presbyterians. Of course, Seaman's proposition made no mention of elders or church power. On the surface of it, his proposition meant to address the uncontroversial question of the extraordinary power vested in the Apostles. There was little doubt in the assembly, however, as to what lay behind the proposition. Cornelius Burgess, ignoring the obvious desire to keep unity, cut to the chase and claimed, 'Peter, as is generall[y] held, represents the pastors.'[80] Dr Temple echoed the sentiment of many English presbyterians when he stated, 'They who ware called Immediately & had commission Immediately from & by Christ without mention of the church.'[81] The design behind Seaman's proposition was made manifest: if the verse meant that the keys were given to the Apostles without the church, then it meant they would be subsequently given to the elders without the church.

THE MIDDLE WAY

The fifth position reflected the Apologists views and found many sympathisers in the assembly. Recent scholarship continues to argue that the Apologists, along with other independents and anabaptists, 'saw the power of the keys lying in originally in the whole congregation, who merely delegated that power to the elders'.[82] As we shall see, this was not the belief of the Apologists, and was actually closer to the belief of many English presbyterians. Thomas Goodwin introduced the Apologists' central tenet, which was the fifth position on Matthew 16:19. Goodwin stated, 'If the question be whether the apos[tle] be *subjectum totale* or the church *subjectum totale*', this is a 'distinction I doe not soe well understand. They received apostells and the church had his power afterwards'.[83] From Goodwin's perspective, there were three questions: 'Whether Peter Represented the Apostles and Ministers only; or whether he Represented the Church also, or whether Peter is here personally taken, as the sole and single Subject of a personal privilege.'[84] And his solution to this debate takes us to the heart of the Apologists' understanding of the keys: 'We say all these here are intended ... in this his [Christ's] first promise, uttering it himself in this indefinite way, which was afterwards to be further and more distinctively divided.'[85]

For the Apologists this promise made to Peter was done in an indistinct, general and comprehensive way. As William Carter stated, 'it will hardly be proved that what is said to Peter is to be aplyed as a beleiver or rather as an apostell, pastor & beleiver; what is given to Peter as the *proton decticon* must comprehend all these'.[86] Nye would repeat this very comment on the floor a few months later.[87] For the congregationalists the word 'Church' in Matthew 16:19 was taken indefinitely 'and for the Church Universal; but yet not as an Institution Political, and therefore he [Jesus] doth not say, he will give the keys to it [the church political] but to Peter', and Peter is taken, as we have seen, 'as Representing both Saints and Minister, to be divided into several Bodies, as afterwards Christ should appoint it'.[88] 'This was', as Goodwin told the assembly, 'the first promise that ever Christ uttered, that he would build a church; & the first expression that he would give the power of keyes out of himselfe, & because Peter made the first confession.' Peter therefore represented 'all power whatsoever. The first grand charter of the gospell which is afterwards to be branched out as Christ hath placed it'.[89] This branching out and delimitating of church power would occur in Matthew 18, which will be the subject of chapter 7.

For Goodwin, when Christ gave Simon Bar-Jonas his new name, Peter, it was not so much a 'Personal, as a Mystical consideration'.[90] It was a grand charter, taken federally and yet indefinitely, for all the aspects of the church that was to be built. And the strength of this argument came from redemptive history, where God had on other occasions singled out one man 'in whose Name the Grand Charter should eminently run'. Goodwin offered Adam and Abraham as examples. 'Adam was fixed upon, when God, in his Name, gave the Earth unto the rest of the Sons of men; So Abraham was singled out to represent ... the Jews who were his children' and who would inherit the land of Canaan.[91] In this way Peter bore 'the persons of all sorts, that were to have any portion of power, whether his Apostles, Extraordinary officers; or ordinary Officers, as also of the Church of Believers, and even to all to whom ever any portion of the keys was for the future to be given'.[92] Goodwin followed Paul Baynes in stating that Peter was a typical representation of both the church and its officers, who would receive the power afterward.[93] The Greek term for 'give' was in the future tense, and therefore when Christ said, 'I will give', it meant that there was to be a further clarifying and constituting of a specific church. This indefinite promise included the 'mystical church', for Christ tells Peter that the gates of hell would not stand against her, which must refer to the mystical church. But the promise must also include particular churches, for, as Goodwin noted, 'the Mystical general Church, hath not the power of the exercise of all the keys; but only as divided into particular Churches'.[94]

The more clerically minded English presbyterians, consumed with the fears of separatism, tried to assert that the decision over Matthew 16:19 was black and white. Either Peter as an Apostle stood in for all elders, or Peter was a representative believer and therefore the power of the keys was given to believers. No one disagreed with the former position, but there was great confusion as to whether it included the latter position. There was concern that including believers as recipients of the power of the keys would ultimately lead to anarchy in the church.[95] Edmund Calamy, in expressing his concerns over denying Matthew 16:19 as a proof-text for Seaman's proposition, demonstrated an acute awareness of the complexity of the positions of the Apologists, and the potential dangers inherent in them. If believers were included as recipients, it would seem they must also have the power to exercise the keys. Calamy stated, 'ther is a promise of the use of the keyes, not only the power; if the power, then exercise, & then all that professe the faith of Christ' would be able to exercise that power.[96] This was the same argument John Ball had used against Gillespie, and it would lead to a Brownist position where the pastor has no unique authority over the church.

Goodwin countered, 'We doe say that every officer hath power Immediately from Christ, but not church power ... Officers doe not exercise the power of the church but the power of Christ.'[97] This was clearly a position distinct from that of the 'independents', who argued that Peter received all the powers of the keys standing in the place of believers, and therefore any elders who were put in place over the church only had the power the church of believers was willing to give to them. In contrast, the presbyterians were postulating that 'because all beleivers have not all church power, therfore they have none'.[98]

Goodwin would go on to explain the numerous types of power to prove his point. There is a power in the people, but it is not the same power that is in the elders, and that power in the elders is given to them directly by Christ alone, not derivatively through – or from – a gathered church.[99] And in the same language the Apologists would use in the *Apologeticall Narration* two months later, Goodwin affirmed that this was a 'midle way' between purely clerical rule and the anarchy of Brownism. The elders have power over the church, not from the church.[100] These are the types of distinctions that would draw the Scottish presbyterians closer to the Apologists. The Apologists respected the distinction between the elders and the people, and they attempted to prevent the people from ruling over their leaders, while nonetheless protecting the prerogatives of the people. Indeed, the evidence suggests that one reason the Apologists were included in the assembly was that they did not believe the faithful in a church were the first subjects of all church power.[101]

Whereas some of the English presbyterians were horrified by the idea of any power belonging to the people, the Apologists found sympathisers in men like Charles Herle who warned the assembly against the danger of pushing the denial of Peter's representing the faithful too far. Herle said, 'many of the fathers & scoolemen have understood ... [Peter as representing the faithful] & yet are farre from anarchy'.[102] He noted that the 'consent of the people in election of officers [is] absolutely necessary'. And if this was true, Herle conceded, there must be some sort of power in the church, although not necessarily an exercise of power. This debate shows that fears of anarchy, coupled with clerical impulses, caused many of the English presbyterians to feel caught between two extremes. On the one hand, it was clear that many 'fathers and scoolemen' believed that Peter represented the faithful. For Herle, if the 'power' was not first in the people, 'then the officers cannot represent the church'.[103] On the other hand, Herle could not accept a government by the people beyond their right to elect church officers, for 'such a popular way ... [would be] anabaptisme'.[104]

The only way for Herle to cut this Gordian knot was to embrace the position where 'power' was in the church as the '*primum susceptivum* not of that exercise but of that power'.[105] Therefore, the only way to salvage Matthew 16:19 in favour of the presbyterian position, without sacrificing Parker-type representation, was to join it to John 20:23, where Jesus gives the extraordinary power to bind and loose specifically to the Apostles. That way Matthew 16:19 could be further restricted to the Apostles, without having to address the power of the church at all. So, Herle concluded, either 'Wave it [Math. 16:19] or joyne it with Joh[n].'[106]

The assembly was clearly burdened with trying to make sense of various questions regarding power. Time and again they had to ask each other for clarification. And indeed, because Seaman's proposition seemed so simple in its request, many divines simply ignored the request to clarify – for as we have noted, clarification only opened pre-existing debates. Even towards the end of the discussions, divines would exasperatedly come back to the same questions. John Ley stated, 'It was well moved before to find out what is the keyes which will prevent a great deale of this debate', and later that day Lightfoot claimed, 'We cannot extricate ourselves unlesse we unlocke this text & inquire: 1. What is meant by the "kingdome of heaven"?'.[107]

ECCLESIAE PRIMAE AND *ECCLESIAE ORTAE*: 'AN UNTRODDEN PATH'

The issue of the visible universal church is an important concept for us to address. It has been usual to make it a distinguishing mark between congregational and presbyterian polity.[108] What we learn in the 1640s, however, is that the notion of a universal church also served to highlight the fundamental differences between various presbyterian positions, distinctions that have been missed in the historiography of the presbyterian polity. The presbyterians believed the general universal church, in some regard, to be a political body (although pragmatically delimited in national or provincial churches). Seaman's proposition effectively left the door open for an assertion made by some presbyterians that Matthew 16:19 also meant the keys to a visible universal church. The Apologists wanted to keep the universality of the keys without the institutional church. This may seem tangential to the discussion of the keys, but it actually accentuates how the nature or power within the church was a uniquely English source of division. If the English divines could prove that there was one general visible church, then necessarily, the keys of jurisdiction would be given to the whole universal church.[109]

The Apologists were adamant that they believed in a visible catholic church, and it is helpful to note Nye's understanding of it. When Nye wrote his manuscript on church government, possibly in the summer of 1644, he claimed that the congregations are members of the 'Catholick' visible church specifically through 'preaching, praying, and Breaking of bread'.[110] But, for the 'orderly & more edifying administration, wee ought also to be members of some particular church'.[111] Indeed, taking of the ordinances of the church, 'wee [do so] within the compass of the whole Catholick. So much and so neare is our affinitie with a member of the membership of the Catholick church in such a performance'.[112] Citing the Scottish presbyterian David Calderwood, Goodwin even went as far as to say that communion with the universal church was through membership in a particular church.[113] This communion, however, does not extend to matters of jurisdiction, including 'elections, censures, &c ... which are properly kept to that one Individual church whereof wee are members of'.[114] The Apologists flatly denied that the 'keys of jurisdiction' could be committed to the universal church.[115]

Some English presbyterians began to fear that Seaman's proposition would mean the particular church's power was derivative of the power given to the visible universal church as the *primum subjectum*. And this fear was fully realised only five months later when Seaman pressed the assembly to agree that the 'keys' were given to the universal visible church. Bridge pointed Seaman back to these October debates and retorted, 'You have voted the power of the keyes to the apostells Immediatly, & how can it be now to the church visible?'[116]

Because presbyterians argued for a universal church that was pragmatically organised into a series of national, regional and local churches Goodwin prioritised his rejoinder to presbyterian views of the universal church *before* his discussion on the keys in his *Government of the Churches of Christ*.[117] For the congregationalists the church universal was not instituted as a political body, and therefore the particular church did not derive its power from it. According to Goodwin, those 'who assert the General Church to be a Political Body, seem to be divided into ... two several ways of explaining it'.[118] There were those who made the particular church to be the *ecclesia prima*, and they believed that synods, classes and national assemblies are 'but *Ecclesiae ortae*, removes from, and representations of those that are Ecclesiae Primae, the first Churches which are Congregations'.[119] Therefore church power, as Goodwin says, is '*ascendendo*'. Conversely, there were also presbyterians who believed church government 'to be *descendendo*, as asserting the first principal Charter, to be given to the Church Universal, so as that by institution first a Church, and particular Congregations have it but by derived right, as lesser Leases have their's out of a greater Charter'.[120] Gataker, for example, rejected the ascending position, denying that the shepherd 'received his power from the sheepe'.[121] Seaman similarly denied the Apostles could 'represent' the church because that would mean 'the keyes belong to every perticular individuall christian'.[122] Gataker and Seaman, rather, believed in a descending position. William Gouge similarly stated, 'the promise [of the keys] is made to the universall militant church'.[123]

Rutherford also saw these distinctions when he observed English presbyterianism in late 1643: 'some derive all Church-power from a single congregation to presbyteries and classes, *ascendendo, by ascending*, others derive it from presbyteries to a Congregation *descendendo'*, and the latter believe power begins from 'the *Catholick visible Church* to nationall assemblies, and from nationall assemblies to *provinciall Synods*, and from *Synods* to *Presbyteries*, from *Presbyteries* to Congregations'.[124] For those who hold this position, according to Goodwin, the church was at one point able to meet 'by vertue of being the Church Universal; but that it afterwards was multiplied to so many, as they must meet in several places, which is the occasion of forming particular Churches'; yet this separation was 'accidental and occasional, and so they are to be regarded as one Church still, and so that first fundamental Institution still goes on'.[125] To Goodwin's mind, it seemed a contradiction for those who held the universal church to be a political church with jurisdiction, to also believe that synods acted their particular churches' power by representation.[126] We will discuss the ascending position later in this book. The latter position, however, is more difficult to pin down. It seems to be the position held by those clerical presbyterian ministers, and Seaman, Gataker and Burgess, whose positions, distinct although they were, may have reflected residual traces of their Episcopalian tradition.

Nevertheless, this particular English presbyterian position on the church universal was unique in the Reformed orthodox tradition. The London ministers' *Jus Divinum Ministerii Ecclesiastici* is largely representative of at least one major strand of English presbyterianism.[127] In their views of the universal visible church they refer the reader to Samuel Hudson, whom they cite as their authority on the matter.[128] Yet it does expose us to a uniquely English debate that does not seem to have been a source of tension prior to 1643. According to Thomason, Hudson's *The Essence and Unitie of the Church Catholike Visible, and the Prioritie thereof in regard of Particular Churches Discussed* was brought to publication in March 1645. However, in the preface Hudson himself states, 'This Thesis was compiled about a yeare agoe, for the accommodation of private friends.'[129] In other words, this document that defined the English presbyterian position was written around the same time that the assembly was debating the universal church. More interestingly, given the assembly's effort to conform to the best Reformed churches, Hudson also declared that 'many Divines of great worth both English, French and Germane ... affirme that there is no Church Catholike visible, but that the Church Catholike is the invisible church only'.[130] In other words, there was not a debate about the creedal belief in catholicity of the invisible church, but only in catholicity of a visible church with the power of jurisdiction. In regards to Matthew 16:19, Hudson is unequivocal: the keys were given to the 'Church Catholick', not to any 'particular church'.[131]

Hudson's main goal was to refute those who believed 'particular Churches to be the prime Churches' – or, to put it another way, he argued against congregational churches retaining power prior to synods over them.[132] He claimed the distinctions between *ecclesiae primae* and *ecclesiae ortae* were not ancient conceptions, but were first deduced by Robert Parker. The question, similarly posited by Goodwin on the assembly floor, was 'Whether in our apprehension of Churches we are to begin at the Church Catholike and descend to particular Churches, or begin at the particular Churches, and ascend to the Church Catholike.'[33] Hudson readily recognised that there were those such as Zanchius, Gerhard, Chamier, Whitaker and Ames who, against the 'Pontificans', denied a Church Catholique to be visible.[34] In Hudson's opinion, they rightly denied the visible catholic church as 'conspicuous, glorious and manifest, specious and flourishing'.[35] In denying the church catholic, these divines denied one institutional church, viz. the Church of Rome, 'comprimizing the universality of the Church in it selfe, all that will be members of the Church Catholike must submit to them, and be members of that Church', and that that one church must be 'under one visible universall head' (viz. the Pope).[36] Nonetheless, the English presbyterians did assert that there was a universal visible church, made up of all the 'visible beleevers throughout the whole world'.[37]

So, as he began to distinguish between *ecclesiae primae* and *ortae*, Hudson offered the caveat that he did not see distinctions between church visible and invisible, but he saw differences 'between Churches of the same kinde, viz., The Catholick visible, and the particular visible Churches'. Therefore Hudson concluded, 'I conceive, the Church Catholick is Prima, and the particular Churches are Orta.'[38] Hudson offered his position cautiously, knowing the 'ascendendo' position was also tenable. This reticence to disavow the opposing position was most probably due to the influence of Robert Parker within the English presbyterian community. Parker had believed in synods of elders gathered from several churches, but only insofar as the particular church of believers – the *ecclesia prima*, and the first subject of church power for Parker – was willing to give over its own power to synods. For Parker, the universal church was unable to exercise the power of the keys, and therefore cannot be the first subject of the keys.[39] Hudson, conversely, believed that all promises, including the keys, were given to the catholic visible church as the first subject. As Hudson stated, 'that promise that the gates of hell shall never prevail against the Church; is primarily given to the Church-Catholike visible here on earth'.[40] All particular churches derive their power and rights from that catholic church.

Edmund Calamy described Hudson's argument in logical terms: 'if there be a Church-Catholick visible, and this Church be not onely a Church-Entitive but a Church-Organical, and a *Totum Integrale*, having all Church power habitually seated in the Officers of it'. These officers are part of particular congregations, and these 'congregations are integrall parts and members of the Church-Catholike, as the Jewish Synagogues were of the Jewish Church. And if the Ministry, Ordinances, and censures were given by Christ to the

Church-generall-visible', then Calamy concluded, 'the particular Congregation is not the first receptacle of Church power'.[41] In this regard, Hudson could see common ground with John Norton, who in his response to the Dutch divine Wilhelm Apollonius published by the Apologists and Cotton, argued that the 'Church Catholik is an integral ... and that the particular churches are similar parts of that integral.' Indeed, Norton conceded, 'Political visibility is an adjunct in respect of the Church Catholick.'[42] This may indicate another difference that existed within congregational groups. Samuel Stone, for example, argued that the 'catholike' church was not integral and was actually a *species* of the particular church, and the particular church was the genus.[43] What is important to emphasise on this point, is that while Calamy agreed that the particular church was not entirely independent in terms of church government, he refused to say whether he believed, like Hudson, the particular church was *ecclesia orta*, or like Parker, it was *ecclesia prima*. Calamy readily acknowledged this topic was 'an untrodden path' and full of 'difficulty and intricacy'.[44]

And, indeed, for Hudson, Matthew 16:19 speaks of the universal church, but not indistinctly, as the Apologists would have it. Because, as Hudson asserted, the gates of hell would not prevail against the church established in Matthew 16:19, it not only means the invisible church, but the 'to-be' established 'Church Catholik', which comprised visible members of the invisible church.[45] The Apologists also saw Matthew 16:19 as related to the 'mystical' church, but they believed it was nonetheless indefinite and not the establishment of an 'institutional political' church.[46] For the Apologists Matthew 16:19 imported various types of keys (knowledge, faith, jurisdiction, power). There was indeed a key of faith that is given to the church universal, but the key of jurisdiction was limited to the particular church, as constituted with elders and believers into one body.

Goodwin specifically raised the question of the universal visible church in March 1644 when the assembly debated the proposition 'There is one general church visible held forth in the New Testament.'[47] According to Lightfoot, 'Mr. Goodwin suspected there might be some snare in this proposition.' Goodwin pointed out that some 'rise to church-government, "ascendendo," from particular congregations to the church universal, some "e contra descendendo;" ergo, there may be some scruple or entanglement' in the debate over this proposition.[48]

Interestingly, it was Rutherford who responded to Goodwin with two views of the church universal. Whereas the English presbyterians debated amongst themselves as to the first subject of all church power, the universal or the particular church, Rutherford offered a third option. The 'ecclesia presbyterialis' (meaning the elders in a particular church) is 'ecclesia prima' and 'the church catholic is "totem integrale," and what power is given to it is neither 'ascendendo,' nor 'descendendo', but immediately from Christ on every part.[49] As early as 1642, Rutherford was already arguing against this *descendendo* position, 'The mistake hath beene, that some Doctors believe that the power of the keyes ... must have some common substance, viz. the universall Church, in which it must for orders cause first reside, before it be given to certaine guides.'[50] Rutherford believed the particular church was the *'ecclesia prima'*, something we will discuss more at length in the following chapters. But, unlike many of his English counterparts, he believed that a power could reside in a synod over multiple congregations, and the power in that assembly was directly given to it by Christ. Goodwin similarly argued that Christ had specifically ordered that a particular gathered church was given a specific charter from Christ. This charter was the complete seat of church government; it was not derived from the church universal, nor was it a power that could be passed onto greater assemblies. Rutherford argued that each level of church government, from the particular church to the national assembly also had their specific charters from Christ. The Apologists, as we shall see, also believed power was not shared; a power was given to believers and a power was given to elders, each directly from Christ.

The differences between Rutherford and the Apologists were clear, but the similarities should be noted. Both Rutherford and the Apologists believed that the particular gathered church and the elders of that church had specific charters from Christ. The elders had their charter, the church members had their charter, and neither were derivative from the other. This belief, however, was different from that of the majority of English presbyterians. A strain of English presbyterianism was emerging that saw all power as derivative from the universal visible church, and therefore whether power trickled down to the particular congregation was not vital, in their mind, to a functioning presbyterian government.

The assembly effectively left these fundamental questions about Matthew 16:19 unanswered. They eventually voted that the verse was indeed a proof-text for Seaman's position. The power of the keys was given to the Apostles, but they had failed to address the question that actually dominated the debate: how any of this related to the church. After only a few days of debate, on 1 November, the whole issue was shuffled to the side, never to be revisited again as a topic unto itself. For, if the way power was allocated to the particular church was left unresolved, it was nearly hopeless to find a resolution to the kind of power allocated to synods of elders gathered from various congregations. They did not deny it was related to the church. Despite, and perhaps because of, the intense debate, they just ignored the question altogether. As it stood, the assembly was perilously close to claiming that Matthew 16:19 simply meant that the apostles were the extraordinary first subject of the power of the keys.[51]

A BREAK FROM 'THE FATHERS & THE SCOOLMEN'

On 1 November, Bridge, who had been sick the day before when the proposition had been voted in, requested that 'church' be added to it, thereby adjusting the proposition to mean the keys were 'given to Peter & apostels with the church'.[52] Stephen Marshall retorted, rather naively given what had just transpired over the preceding three days, 'Whether the church did receive it is yet a question undebated.'[53] Charles Herle had warned the assembly against application of the terms Brownism and separatism towards those who believed Peter received the keys on behalf of believers. Herle had noted that 'many of the fathers & scoolemen have understood it thus & yet are soe farre from anarchy.'[54] Bridge desisted from pushing a debate. Therefore, what these keys were, what their functions were, in what sense the Apostles received them, whom the Apostles represented, and how the keys concerned the church, were questions left entirely unanswered.

In the Apologists' minds, and indeed to many in the assembly, discussing Matthew 16:19 without any reference to the church seemed extraordinary in the history of exegesis. Time and again in the debates, although the proposition dealt only with the Apostles, the members kept bringing up the church. Many in the assembly failed to see any precedent for limiting Mathew 16:19 to Seaman's proposition. Simpson tried to warn the assembly that it would be outside the reformed tradition to use Matthew 16:19 to prove Peter as an apostle, excluding the church. He cited Gerhard, who said, 'from the time of Christ that 16 Math. Understood [as] concerning the church in all ages'.[55] Gerhard himself had argued 'that unto the Church ... [Christ] hath given the keyes of the kingdom of heaven'.[56] Cornelius Burgess, knowing Gerhard's wide influence regarding the power of the local church, quickly dismissed this statement, saying, 'we are not to looke what Gerrard hath affirmed but never proved'.[57] We have already noted that Fulke interpreted Matthew 16:19 to mean that Christ gave the keys to Peter, and after him both to the Apostles and to the church. Whitaker summarised Augustine, who said 'that in Peter they [the church] did receive them [the keyes] properly, truely, and more principally then Peter himself'.[58] We have already noted the Sorbonnists of Paris who believed that the church, upon Peter's confession, was the first subject of all church power, as did the German Catholic John Wild (Ferus).[59] If we look at the Dutch annotations on the whole Bible, written as a result of the Synod of Dort, we see the writers believed that 'upon Peter's confession ... power is also given to the Church ... and to all the Apostles'.[60] Theodore Beza's annotations stated that Peter's confession 'is the churches as well as his' and the keys were given to 'ministers of the word', but there is no mention of the Apostles.[61]

It was clear that the congregationalists had lost a debate that centred on the most fundamental tenet of their polity. The Apologists' fears were not unfounded. Within two years the London presbyterians were claiming that the 'keyes' only belonged to elders, and thus 'the Keyes of the Kingdom of Heaven, with all their Acts, were immediately committed to the Church-guides, viz. to the Apostles aud [*sic*] to their Successours to the end of the world; compare these testimonies, Math. 16.19 and 18.18'.[162] The problem was never whether the elders received authorial power of the keys, but it was how that power was connected to, and in the context of, the particular church. And hence, as we shall see, the ability to argue for congregational power on the basis of Matthew 18:18 was severely curtailed due to the constraints placed on Matthew 16:19. It was not that the Apologists disagreed with ministers receiving unique ministerial keys, it was that the proposition and proof-text may result in neutering power in the church.

This account also indicates how important it is to make careful ecclesiological distinctions when engaging these debates. Both Robert S. Paul and J. R. De Witt claimed that Seaman accused the 'independents' of being 'Brownists'.[163] Yet Seaman clearly stated that 'here hath been none of the opinions [of] the Brownists'.[164] Paul and De Witt had collapsed Seaman's following comment, that 'not one argument used about this text but used by Robinson', into their own belief that 'independency' and Brownism were essentially the same.[165] Seaman was not calling the Apologists 'independents' or Brownists. He was using a rhetorical trick to show that those who read Matthew 16:19 as referring to the church of believers, which included Charles Herle and those who followed Robert Parker, were exegeting the verse in the same way as the independent John Robinson.

After that, 'The Grand Debate' to come was effectively moot. Nye and Goodwin, in their Preface to Cotton's *Keyes of the Kingdom*, asserted, 'many of our friends, and some that are of a differing opinion, [have] knowne our private judgments long, as likewise our owne Notes and transcripts written long agoe, can testifie; besides many publike professions'; but that did not stop them from fearing the implications of believers having any share of the keys.[166] In the middle of their debates on church government in March 1644, William Price articulated what was undoubtedly the position of many in the assembly: 'That which hinders us in this debate is the want of acurate distinction betwixt authority & jurisdiction.' And Charles Herle lamented, '[we lost] much time by mistaking one another'.[167] As it stood, the power of the keys would only reappear as it related to various aspects of church government, but never again as a topic unto itself.

CONCLUSION

The variety of interpretations espoused on the floor of the assembly cut across the ecclesiastical spectrum. The divines had different opinions; they all knew they had different opinions; they were all evidently squeamish about debating the keys in the first place; and, at times, they equivocated in order to placate. What is most striking is that none of these discussions were new; each divine was keenly aware there was a variety of opinions being postulated, and they all to varying degrees tried to steer the discussion back from the brink of discord. It was the English presbyterians who triumphed, not because the congregational divines deftly hid their polity, but because the presbyterian majority knew that any further specificity in the proposition or the proof-text would force many presbyterians to take sides against each other. The Apologists' positions were fully united, whereas the presbyterian majority was by no means united. Where one believed the first subject of the keys was placed did not dictate whether or not one was a presbyterian; it did dictate, however, what type of presbyterian one was.[168] For example, the debates highlighted how unique in the Reformed tradition was the position on the universal church that was held by some of the more clerical presbyterians. On the other hand, there were those presbyterians who believed the particular church received the keys, but the elders acted as their representatives. These two positions understood church power as being generated from two opposing theological starting points that would have practical implications for how the national church would be designed. Even here, the congregationalists were the middle-way men.

This was a pyrrhic victory for the various polities of English presbyterians who were coalescing to form a majority for practical purposes. What is clear is that by this stage a variety of interpretations of arguably the most important verse for biblical polity was exposing numerous versions of presbyterian polity. Presbyterianism in England was clearly variegated. Some presbyterians argued with the congregationalists that power began at the local level and moved up through an ascending ladder of sessions, presbyteries and national synods (though even the definitions of those assemblies was still up for grabs). Other presbyterians argued the inverse. That power first resided in the universal church and descended downward. How far down would prove to be a huge source of tension between certain English presbyterians and the Scottish presbyterians. What was emerging in the assembly was a strong contingent of English divines who did not believe the local church should necessarily receive its share in church power. The Aldermanbury divines, both congregational and presbyterian, continued to exhibit the exegetical common ground that brought them together in 1641. The presbyterians could not disavow the congregational exegesis of Matthew 16 without simultaneously disowning some of their most influential ancient, medieval and reformed scholastic forebears. Given the freedom to debate foundations of church power, the Westminster assembly fractured in such a way that makes the current historiographical divide between 'presbyterian and independent' virtually unintelligible.

As much as presbyterians wanted to sideline the dicey question of church power, the topic would continue to appear throughout the rest of the year. And indeed, reading the debates over excommunication that took place almost exactly a year later, in October 1644 when a presbyterian settlement was a foregone conclusion, we can see how this unresolved issue continued to complicate debates about power in the particular church. Edmund Calamy asked, 'The 16 of Math. gives the power of the keyes to the apostels; true but is it alone?'[69] In that debate, Calamy had become concerned that the assembly had given power to the Apostles at the expense of the church. Citing the case of discipline by the church of Corinth, Calamy stated, 'In this text ... [excommunication] was the act of the church of Corinth. If Jesus Christ did give the power to the church, I see not by what authority they could doe it alone; any one apostell is not a church.'[70]

For the congregational divines the debate on the power of the keys represented one of the two most consequential debates in the assembly. The congregationalists were outmanoeuvred because the assembly had not sorted out what the keys were and who could use them and initially avoiding the question of a platform of church government. The presbyterians knew that codifying a platform of church government would have only crystallised their own differences. Thus, the typical pamphlet critique outside the assembly, that the Apologists feared a platform would divide the independents in England, was actually true of the presbyterians in the assembly. There was still hope for the Apologists, although hope was found in strange quarters. The Apologists would need the Scots, who would find more in common with their polity than the high clerical English presbyterians would. It is to that relationship we now turn, in order to have a clearer picture of what the power of the keys looked like for the Apologists and why it was so palatable to the Scots. The month of October 1643 has enabled us to see the uniquely English complexities of the ecclesiological debates. The English presbyterians, if anything, demonstrate ambivalence towards the Apologists' positions on the keys. We must keep this in mind as we turn to the *Apologeticall Narration*. As we reassess its importance, or lack thereof, in light of these October debates, we will see there was nothing in the *Narration* that, from the assembly's perspective, was particularly surprising or offensive.

NOTES

1 Van Dixhoorn, *MPWA* (vol. 1), p. 13.

2 See J. Peacey, 'Politics, Accounts, and Propaganda in the Long Parliament', in C. R. Kyle and K. Peacey (eds), *Parliament at Work: Parliamentary Committees, Political Power, and Public Access in Early Modern England* (Woodbridge: Boydell, 2002), pp. 59–78.

3 D. Scott, *Politics and War in the Three Stuart Kingdoms, 1637–49*, British History in Perspective (Basingstoke: Palgrave Macmillan, 2004), pp. 40–41.

4 Ibid., pp. 28–40.

5 Ibid., p. 41.

6 C. Hibbert, *Cavaliers and Roundheads* (London: HarperCollins, 1993), p. 65.

7 J. Burroughs, *The glorious Name of God, the Lord of Hosts* (London, 1643), A2.

8 Woolrych, *Britain in Revolution*, p. 268.

9 Van Dixhoorn, *MPWA* (vol. 1), pp. 2–7.

10 Ibid., p. 4.

11 Ibid., pp. 1–10.

12 Woolrych, *Britain in Revolution*, p. 272.

13 Scott, *Politics and War*, p. 42.

14 L. Kaplan, 'Steps to War: The Scots and Parliament, 1642–1643', *Journal of British Studies*, 9 (1970), 50–70, p. 51.

15 Scott, *Politics and War*, p. 42.

16 Kaplan, 'Steps to War: The Scots and Parliament, 1642–1643', p. 51.

17 D. Scott, 'The 'Northern Gentlemen', the Parliamentary Independents, and Anglo-Scottish Relations in the Long Parliament', *Historical Journal*, 42 (1999), 347–75, p. 350; Kaplan, 'Steps to War: The Scots and Parliament, 1642–1643', pp. 54–55; ibid., p. 57.

18 Scott, *Politics and War*, p. 62.

19 D. Stevenson, *The Scottish Revolution, 1637–44: The Triumph of the Covenanters* (Newton Abbot: David & Charles, 1973), p. 285; R. S. Paul, *An Apologeticall Narration* (Philadelphia: United Church Press, 1963), p. 92.

20 Kim, 'The debate on the relations between the Churches of Scotland and England during the British Revolution (1633–1647)' , p. 185.

21 C. V. Wedgwood, *The King's War: 1641–1647: The Great Rebellion* (London: Collins, 1970), p. 258.

22 A. Henderson, *Reformation of church-government in Scotland* (London, 1644), p. 61.

23 Kaplan, 'Steps to War: The Scots and Parliament, 1642–1643', p. 64.

24 Ibid., p. 64.

25 Scott, 'The 'Northern Gentlemen', the Parliamentary Independents, and Anglo-Scottish Relations in the Long Parliament', p. 351.

26 Gardiner, *Foure speeches*, pp. 29–30.

27 Van Dixhoorn, *MPWA* (vol. 2), p. 243 (Sir Arthur Haselrig, 30 October 1643).

28 Ibid., p. 233.

29 J. Lightfoot, *The journal of the proceedings of the Assembly of Divines, from January 1, 1643, to December 31, 1644: and letters to and from Dr. Lightfoot*, The whole works of the Rev. John Lightfoot, D.D v. 13 (London, 1824), p. 17; Van Dixhoorn, *MPWA* (vol. 2), pp. 195–196.

30 House of Lords Journal, *Journal of the House of Lords: volume 6: 1643* (1767–1830), pp. 254–255. Online version. Date accessed: 1 September 2010; Lightfoot, *Journal*, p. 17.

31 Van Dixhoorn, *MPWA* (vol. 2), p. 198.

32 Ibid., p. 199.

33 Ibid., p. 199.

34 Ibid., p. 200.

35 R. S. Paul, *The Assembly of the Lord: Politics and Religion in the Westminster Assembly and the 'Grand Debate'* (Edinburgh: T. & T. Clark, 1985), p. 137.

36 Van Dixhoorn, *MPWA* (vol. 2), pp. 198–206.

37 Ibid., p. 200; Paul, *The Assembly of the Lord*, p. 137.

38 Van Dixhoorn, *MPWA* (vol. 2), p. 203.

39 For a discussion on these claims and who made them, see Powell, 'Dissenting Brethren', p. 68.

40 See below, chapter 7.

41 Lightfoot, *Journal*, p. 20; Van Dixhoorn, *MPWA* (vol. 2), pp. 200–201.

42 Van Dixhoorn, *MPWA* (vol. 2), pp. 200–201.

43 Ibid., p. 308.

44 Ibid., p. 201.

45 Ibid., p. 199.

46 Ibid., p. 231.

47 Ibid., p. 233.

48 Ibid., p. 233.

49 Ibid., p. 233.

50 Ibid., p. 233.

51 John 20:22–23, 'And when he had said this, he breathed on them, and saith unto them, Receive ye the Holy Ghost: Whose soever sins ye remit, they are remitted unto them; and whose soever sins ye retain, they are retained.'

52 Van Dixhoorn, *MPWA* (vol. 2), p. 242.

53 Ibid., pp. 233, 237.

54 Ibid., p. 235.

55 Lightfoot, *Journal*, p. 31; Van Dixhoorn, *MPWA* (vol. 2), p. 234.

56 Van Dixhoorn, *MPWA* (vol. 2), p. 234.

57 Lightfoot, *Journal*, p. 31.

58 Parker, *De Politeia Ecclesiastica [trans.]*, p. 96r.

59 Van Dixhoorn, *MPWA* (vol. 2), p. 234.

60 Rutherford, *Peaceable plea*, p. 3.

61 J. Almain, 'A book concerning the authority of the church', in J. H. Burns & T. M. Izbicki (eds), *Conciliarism and Papalism* (Cambridge: Cambridge University Press, 1997), pp. 134–200, pp. 144, 153.

62 Van Dixhoorn, *MPWA* (vol. 2), p. 237.

63 Almain, 'A book concerning the authority of the church', pp. 158–159.

64 Van Dixhoorn, *MPWA* (vol. 2), p. 234.

65 Ibid., p. 234.

66 Ibid., p. 234.

67 Ibid., p. 234.

68 T. Goodwin, *The Consitution right, order, and government of the churches of Christ* (London, 1696), pp. 44–45.

69 Ibid., p. 45.

70 Ibid., p. 45.

71 Van Dixhoorn, *MPWA* (vol. 2), pp. 210ff; Goodwin, *Government*, p. 45.

72 Van Dixhoorn, *MPWA* (vol. 2), p. 210.

73 Ibid., p. 210.

74 Goodwin, *Government*, p. 66.

75 Ibid., p. 45.

76 J. Canne, *Syons prerogatyve royal* (Amsterdam, 1641), p. 4.

77 T. Hooker, *A survey of the summe of church-discipline* (London, 1648), p. 195. What unites these following examples is that the power of excommunication – the highest act of church power – was given to the church of believers as the first subject. This 'binding and loosing', typically cited from Matthew 18:17–19, was exegetically tied to Matthew 16:19. While some of these divines (particularly Davenport and Hooker) would delineate distinct *functions* of elders and the people in the process of excommunication, yet they either implicitly or explicitly embraced the exegesis that Peter represented the believers and therefore believers were the first subjects of all church power. For examples, see H. Ainsworth, *An animadversion to Mr Richard Clyftons advertisement* (Amsterdam, 1610), p. 10; H. Ainsworth, *An apologie or defence of such true Christians as are commonly (but vniustly) called Brovvnists* (1604), p. 43; H. Ainsworth, *A True Confession of the Faith, which wee falsely called Brownists, doo hould* ([Amsterdam?], 1596), pp. 22–24; W. Best, *The churches plea for her right. Or A reply to an answer, made of Mr. Iohn Paget, against William Best and others* (Amsterdam, 1635), p. 72; H. Burton, *A vindication of churches commonly called Independent* (London, 1644), p. 26; Canne, *Syons prerogatyve royal*, p. 4; K. Chidley, *The Justification of the Independant Churches of Christ* (London, 1641), pp. 10–11; J. Davenport, *The Power of Congregational Churches asserted and vindicated* (London, 1672), pp. 90–106; H. Jacob, *A confession and protestation of the faith of certaine Christians, etc.* (1616), Articles 3, 4, and 10; *The Presbyteriall government examined* (1641), p. 12; J. Smyth, *Paralleles, censures, observations. Aperteyning: to three several writinges* (Middleberg, 1609), p. 36.

78 Goodwin, *Government*, p. 45.

79 *Jus divinum regiminis ecclesiastici, or, The divine right of church-government, asserted and evidenced by the Holy Scriptures* (London, 1646), p. 68; see also pp. 36, 55.

80 Van Dixhoorn, *MPWA* (vol. 2), p. 235.

81 Ibid., p. 238.

82 Shagan, 'Rethinking Moderation in the English Revolution: The Case of An Apologeticall Narration', p. 46; Shagan, 'Beyond Good and Evil: Thinking with Moderates in Early Modern England', pp. 504–505; M. P. Winship, *Godly Republicanism: Puritans,*

Pilgrims, and a City on a Hill (Cambridge, MA: Harvard University Press, 2012), pp. 80–82, see also Winship's dispute with Brachlow on this issue on p. 274, fn. 37.

83 Van Dixhoorn, *MPWA* (vol. 2), p. 236.

84 Goodwin, *Government*, p. 47.

85 Ibid., p. 47.

86 Van Dixhoorn, *MPWA* (vol. 2), p. 236.

87 Ibid., p. 654.

88 Goodwin, *Government*, p. 44.

89 Ibid., Van Dixhoorn, *MPWA* (vol. 2), p. 234.

90 Goodwin, *Government*, p. 45.

91 Ibid., p. 45.

92 Ibid., p. 46.

93 Ibid., p. 46; P. Baynes, *The diocesans tryall* (Amsterdam, 1621), pp. 84–85.

94 Goodwin, *Government*, p. 46.

95 Van Dixhoorn, *MPWA* (vol. 2), p. 240.

96 Ibid., p. 241.

97 Ibid., p. 242.

98 Ibid., p. 248.

99 Ibid., pp. 248–249.

100 Ibid., p. 253.

101 Compare Herle's comment on 'anabaptism' below, and his comments about the *Narration*, p. 107.

102 Van Dixhoorn, *MPWA* (vol. 2), p. 251.

103 Ibid., p. 251.

104 Ibid., p. 251.

105 Ibid., p. 251.

106 Ibid., p. 251; John 20:23, 'Whose soever sins ye remit, they are remitted unto them; and whose soever sins ye retain, they are retained.'

107 Ibid., pp. 225, 229.

108 Ha, *English Presbyterianism*, pp. 66–67.

109 This is what Gouge, for example, was aiming for. Van Dixhoorn, *MPWA* (vol. 2), pp. 234–235.

110 Nye, *A discourse*, p. 184.

111 P. Nye, *A discourse in which the practise now asserted was opposed* (New College Library: MS Comm 1), p. 185.

112 Ibid., p. 185.

113 Goodwin, *Government*, pp. 152, 227.

114 Nye, *Discourse,*. p. 185.

115 Goodwin, *Government*, p. 152.

116 Van Dixhoorn, *MPWA* (vol. 2), p. 650.

117 Goodwin, *Government*, p. 42.

118 Ibid., p. 41.

119 Ibid., p. 41.

120 Ibid., p. 42.

121 Van Dixhoorn, *MPWA* (vol. 2), p. 239.

122 Ibid., p. 238.

123 Ibid., p. 234.

124 S. Rutherford, *The Due right of Presbyteries* (London, 1644), p. 383.

125 Goodwin, *Government*, p. 42.

126 Ibid., p. 155.

127 I am grateful to Elliot Vernon for his discussing the importance – and limitations – of *Jus Divinum* as an English presbyterian document.

128 *Jus Divinum Ministerii Evangelici, or the divine right of the Gospel-Ministry.* (London, 1654), p. 143. See also H. Powell & E. Vernon (eds), *Church Polity in the British Atlantic World, c. 1636–1689* (Manchester: Manchester University Press, forthcoming).

129 S. Hudson, *The Essence and Unitie of the Church Catholike Visible, And the prioritie thereof in regard particular churches discussed* (London, 1644) preface, not paginated.

130 Ibid., preface, not paginated.

131 Ibid., preface, not paginated.

132 Ibid., preface, not paginated.

133 Ibid., p. 10.

134 S. Hudson, *A vindication of The essence and unity of the Church Catholike visible* (London, 1650), p. 26.

135 Hudson, *Essence and Unitie*, p. 11.

136 Ibid., p. 12.

137 Ibid., p. 4.

138 Ibid., p. 25.

139 Hudson, *Vindication*, p. 25.

140 Ibid., p. 220.

141 Ibid., to the reader.

142 Ibid., preface, not paginated. Cotton had a similar view that Hudson cited, ibid., pp. 51–52; J. Cotton, *A brief exposition of the whole book of Canticles, or Song of Solomon* (London, 1642), p. 191.

143 S. Stone, *A congregational church is a catholike visible church* (London, 1652), chapter 5, reason 6.

144 Hudson, *Vindication*. To the reader.

145 Hudson, *Essence and Unitie*, p. 17.

146 Ibid., p. 19.

147 Lightfoot, *Journal*, p. 215.

148 Ibid., pp. 215–216.

149 Ibid., p. 216.

150 Rutherford, *Peaceable plea*, p. 3.

151 Norton, *Answer*, p. 79.

152 Van Dixhoorn, *MPWA* (vol. 2), p. 256.

153 Ibid., p. 256.

154 Ibid., p. 251.

155 Ibid., p. 240. Probably J. Gerhard, *Confessionis Catholicae*, 4 vols (Jenae, 1634), vol. 1, pp. 326–329; book 2, article 3, chapter 9 in vol. 2, pp. 922–923. I am grateful to Dr Chad van Dixhoorn for allowing me to use this citation.

156 Gerhard, *The Summe of Christian doctrine*, p. 255.

157 Van Dixhoorn, *MPWA* (vol. 2), p. 240.

158 Cited in J. Cotton, *The Way of Congregational Churches Cleared* (London, 1648), vol. 2, p. 31.

159 Cotton cites Ferus' commentary on Matthew 16. Likely from J. Wild, *In sacrosanctum Iesu Christi domini nostri Euangelium secundum Matthæum, piæ ac eruditæ iuxta catholicam & ecclesiasticam doctrinam enarrationes* (Antverpiae, 1577), pp. 48–56. Cited in Cotton, *The Way of Congregational Churches Cleared*, vol. 2, p. 31.

160 T. Haak, *The Dutch Annotations Upon the Whole Bible* (London, 1657), Matthew 16:18, 19.

161 *The New Testament of our Lord Iesus Christ, translated out of Greeke by Theod. Beza* (1582), p. 25.

162 *Jus divinum regiminis ecclesiastici*, p. 181.

163 De Witt, *Jus divinum*, p. 70; Paul, *The Assembly of the Lord*, p. 152.

164 Van Dixhoorn, *MPWA* (vol. 2), p. 252.

165 De Witt, *Jus divinum*, p. 70; Paul, *The Assembly of the Lord*, p. 152.

166 J. Cotton, T. Goodwin & P. Nye, *The keyes of the kingdom of heaven* (London, 1644), preface, not paginated; Van Dixhoorn, *MPWA* (vol. 2), p. 230.

167 Van Dixhoorn, *MPWA* (vol. 2), p. 601.

168 We will look more closely at this in chapter 5.

169 Van Dixhoorn, *MPWA* (vol. 3), p. 419.

170 Ibid., p. 418.

Chapter 4

The *Apologeticall Narration*: international politics and the real 'Grand Debate'[1]

The Westminster assembly's leading congregational divines published their *Apologeticall Narration* between 3 and 11 January 1644. For all the historiographical interest surrounding this famous document, it requires an understanding of the events of the previous three chapters if we are to decipher its contents and context. It did not, as often asserted, start an ecclesiastical war or a 'fatal feud' in the assembly, nor was it a call for religious toleration. Far from being a fundamental break with the accord formed by the Calamy house group, or creating an 'irreconcilable rivalry', it was a last attempt to keep the godly united and protect the unity that had been established in 1641.[2]

When it was first published, the *Narration* received no recorded mention on the assembly floor and did not illicit a debate in either House of Parliament. In fact, the only speech we have recorded by Parliament on the *Narration*, some two months later, was in favour of it, and Parliament would ultimately vote to affirm that the Apologists had acted appropriately.[3] It was printed through a publisher officially licensed by Parliament, and did not break assembly protocol. It was never intended to be a comprehensive platform of church polity, and, in that regard, was far less important than John Cotton's *Keyes of the Kingdom*.[4] Indeed, when we encounter comments on the *Narration* inside the assembly, it was cited positively as a potential source of ecclesiological accommodation. The *Narration* did hit a nerve, but not in the place we have come to expect. It revealed a split that would haunt the assembly for months and years to come, but it was not a split between the 'presbyterians and independents'.

To ascertain the impact of the *Narration* on ecclesiological politics we need to relocate the pamphlet in a wider continental context in the month of March 1644 rather than in the domestic disputes of January 1644. The immediate political context of the early months of 1644 is addressed elsewhere.[5] In order to sustain our interpretation, we will need to look closely at who wrote against the *Narration* and when; we will need to question closely the unity not only of the English assembly members, but also of the Scottish commissioners (and look at the duplicitous behaviour of the one seen by historians as their spokesman); and we will need to examine why the *Narration* only became a source of difficulty for the Westminster assembly in the wake of a counter-productive intervention by the Dutch classis of Walcheren (in Zealand). It was only then that the debates on the *Narration* revealed anxieties that divided many in the assembly from the Erastian majority in Parliament. So the story takes us from a story of 'presbyterian versus independent' to one of *jure divino* presbyterianism versus Erastianism, which served to reinvigorate an ecclesiological accommodation between the Scottish divines and the Apologists. We will see that the *Apologeticall Narration* served to divide and unite parties at unexpected intervals and in surprising ways.

JANUARY 1644: A CALL TO ARMS?

In July 1643 the presbyterian Charles Herle was named one of the official licensers for Parliament 'for the printing of divinity books'.[6] He was by no means the licenser most sympathetic to the congregational cause. Nonetheless, Herle commended the *Apologeticall Narration* proclaiming, 'That however for mine own part I have appeared on, and doe still encline to the Presbyteriall way of Church Government, yet doe I think it in every way fit for the Presse.'[7] Although I disagree with recent descriptions of what the accord at Aldermanbury entailed, if there was a break in an 'independent/ presbyterian' alliance to maintain silence, then it was Herle's *The independency on Scriptures of the independency of Churches*, which was a pointed rebuttal of independent church polity.[8] It was published almost eight months before the *Narration*.[9] However, Herle – in a tone that would resonate with many English presbyterians – would claim that the 'difference betweene us and our brethren that are for Independency, 'tis nothing so great as you seemed to conceive', and 'we are as ... brethren still, and ... ready to rescue each other on all occasions against the common enemy', and he concluded, 'our difference 'tis such as doth at most but ruffle a little the fringe, not any way rending the Garment of Christ ... 'tis so farre from being a fundamentall, that 'tis scarce a materiall one'.[10] We should not read this quote as indicating a merely squeamish belief in presbyterian polity, for Herle was notoriously dogged in his defence of presbyterianism. Indeed, the Apologists had few stronger – and more critical – ecclesiological sparring partners in the assembly than Herle. Baillie, who either approved or disapproved of English presbyterians (including Herle) based on their procedural, political, or ecclesiological support of the Apologists, nonetheless 'placed [Herle] first in a list sent to the earl of Loudoun of the ablest English clergy suitable to serve as royal chaplains' and ranked Herle up with Baillie's close friend and collaborator Cornelius Burgess.[11]

The *Apologeticall Narration* became available to the public at some point between 3 and 11 January. We know this from two newsbooks, *Mercurius Aulicus* and *Mercurius Britanicus*, and from when Thomason obtained his copy.[12] The following entry in *Britanicus* is worth quoting at length, for it gives us the only indication of how the *Narration* was immediately – not retrospectively – interpreted by contemporaries. In this case it was a contemporary who indicated he was a persuaded presbyterian. 'There is a late book ... by our Reverend brethren, but by no independents, viz. Master Goodwin, Master Nye, Master Bridges, Master Simpson, Master Burroughs, in this you may see how long they hold us by the hand, and where they let go, and take us by the finger'. In terms of church government, 'they have the same worship, preaching and praying, and forme of Sacrament, the same Church Officers, Doctors, Pastors, Deacons, and same Church censures in the abridgement, but not as large'. The author supposed that the only difference between the congregationalists and the presbyterians was that the congregationalists 'allow a Church to be authoritative over its own Members, but not over another Church'; they did, however, allow 'an equivalency to our Presbytery and Councells and excommunications of Churches, which is consociation of Churches, and non-communion with Churches', and therefore, the author proclaimed, 'is it not pitty we should breake for such a little knot in a golden thread?'.[13]

Robert S. Paul was so convinced that the *Narration* must have been offensive to the assembly that he refused to believe it could have been published in early January because Lightfoot (himself no fan of independency) did not record any frustration in the assembly at that time. Paul had not done research on the background of the assembly (e.g. 1640–43), and therefore failed to see how the *Narration* fitted into the ongoing efforts for church reform. All of this is consonant with what we have come to expect from the Calamy house ministers we have been studying in this book. The most cited quote of the *Narration*, namely, that the Brethren maintained 'a middle way betwixt that which is falsly charged on us, Brownisme; and ... the authoritative Presbyteriall Government' was precisely the language that Thomas Goodwin had used almost three months earlier on the assembly floor.[14] The polity in the book was intentionally vague, because, as we noted in the previous chapter, the assembly had made it clear that there could be no platform until the particulars of church government were settled. Even so, the polity espoused in the *Narration* regarding synods, church power and the magistrate were well known to the assembly divines and not yet a source of real tension. There are several ways we can better understand the *Apologeticall Narration* other than as a controversial statement of congregational polity. Or to put it another way, there were three distinct messages being sent by the Apologists.

First, the *Narration* addressed commonality between the Apologists and the Scots. We need to recontextualise the *Narration* as a part of an ongoing engagement with, if not an appeal to, the Scots. What has been overlooked in the historiography of the *Narration* is that the Scots submitted two separate papers to the Grand Committee between November 1643 and the end January 1644. The papers claimed that the particular church was a true integral church, with 'intrinsical government', and that the particular church had the power of excommunication by divine right. The Scots called the particular church the *ecclesia prima* and believed that any work on church government should begin with the particular church and move up from there. The first paper they submitted on 10 November. A partial transcription is found in Lighfoot's journal.[15] The emphasis of this first paper 'concern[ed] the severall sorts of Church-officers Assemblies'.[16] The second paper was handed in after the publication of the *Narration*, on 24 January, and that document dealt with 'Congregationall Elderships and Classical Presbyteries.'[17] In this chapter we are concerned with how these papers fit within the context of the *Narration*; in chapter 7 we will see how they affected the debates within the Westminster assembly.

In the *Narration* we can see the Apologists clearly addressing their commonality with the Scots, and subtly reminding them of Gillespie's position. '[H]owever the practice of the Reformed Churches is in greater matters to govern each particular congregation by a combined *Presbyterie* of the *Elders* of several congregations united in one for government', nevertheless, those reformed churches outside of England 'allow, especially in some cases, a particular congregation, an entire and compleat power of jurisdiction to be exercised by the Elders thereof within it selfe'.[18] The power of excommunication, which for the Apologists was the highest power of the keys, resided fully in the body of the particular church until that church 'miscarry', and then 'Presbyterial and Provincial Assemblies as the proper refuge for appeales and for compounding of differences amongst Churches'.[19] This 'combination of Churches others of them therefore call *Ecclesiae ortae*, but particular congregations *Ecclesiae primae*, as wherein *firstly* the power and priviledg of a Church is to be exercised'.[20] This, we will prove later in this book, was certainly a reformed position outside of England.[21]

The Scots received a stinging rebuke from the Scottish Covenanter David Calderwood for sounding too much like 'Independencie' in at least one of the papers they handed in to the Grand Committee, and the Scots had to quickly adjust their tactics. What those tactics were in the early January 1644 has caused some confusion in the historiography. There has been some question as to whether the Scottish commissioners responded to the *Narration* with their *Reformation of Church-Government in Scotland Cleared.*[22] Joong Lak Kim has argued that the *Narration* 'threw cold water on the [Scots'] project of covenanted uniformity'.[23] Therefore many have assumed that the Scots could not be responding to the *Narration* with the polemically innocuous *Reformation*

Cleared and its accommodating style. Indeed, Robert S. Paul was so committed to the narrative that the Scots and the independents were enemies that in his opinion the genteel 'tone of the Scottish pamphlet is in complete contrast to the known sentiments of the Scottish Commissioners'. For Paul the mere fact that the Scots supported a 'limited toleration at the end' of the *Reformation Cleared* 'is in complete variance with the fixed determination of the Scots against toleration after the *Apologeticall Narration* appeared.'[24]

Actually, the *Reformation Cleared* was an effort by the Scottish commissioners both to calm the nerves of the Covenanters in Scotland, and to affirm their goals in following the presbyterian majority in the assembly. We should read the *Reformation Cleared*, like the *Narration*, as a minority party's appeal. Only a week after its publication the Scots told the assembly that they need not follow the model set forth in their paper handed into the Grand Committee, and the Scots were quite happy to allow the assembly English presbyterians to take the lead – for reasons we will discuss later.[25]

Second, the *Narration* was a call to keep the godly alliance together, not a definitive break from the alliance as some scholars would have it.[26] This was made clear by one of the most important clauses of the *Narration*: 'the present work of this age, the reformation of worship and discipline, [we] do differ as little from the Reformed Churches, and our Brethren, yea far lesse, then they do from what themselves were *three yeers past*'.[27] This was a direct reference to the Aldermanbury alliance, not, as Robert S. Paul has suggested, a veiled reference to those in the assembly that had previously been willing to conform under Laud.[28] The Apologists' position was one, in 1641 at least, the godly could unite around, and this included the Scottish divines. But we also know that men such as Stephen Marshall were presbyterians of the Parker (and the Dutch) mould, and it was Parker who specifically stated that the particular church was *ecclesia prima* and the synods were *ecclesiae ortae*. This was the tradition held to by many English presbyterians, but not by all, and the pressure to codify, and to clarify, exactly where the first subject of church power rested would only increase as the assembly approached its discussions over the power of synods. The Solemn League and Covenant had not clearly committed the assembly to any particular form of presbyterianism, as Thomas Case himself had stated.[29] Yet presbyterian parties outside the assembly, particularly in London, were putting immense pressure on the divines to follow a model that would rule the Apologists' polity immediately out of bounds. The Apologists, we must remember, considered themselves to hold a type of presbyterian polity.[30] The pamphlet pressure growing outside the assembly was trying to break the godly alliance in favour of a more clerical presbyterianism.

Initially, it seems, the *Narration* was received with wide acclaim and, furthermore, it did not receive a response from any assembly member either in the minutes or in print.[31] Though, as we noted earlier, there were a number of peripheral critiques outside the assembly that attempted to influence Westminster divines and manage public opinion).[32] The only other external commentary on the *Narration* is from the Scottish presbyterian Robert Baillie, who only decried the document in private, agenda-oriented letters. Baillie's public pronouncements would remain circumspect. His first public denunciation of the independents came in 1645, nearly two years after the *Narration* was published.[33] Yet years later he admitted that the 'fair appearance' of the *Narration* brought him to the 'very gates of a fools paradise'.[34] In any event, the assembly would not permit the Apologists to respond to the criticisms they were receiving in print.[35]

None of this is meant to suggest that pamphlets written outside the assembly were unimportant or uninfluential. But, the overemphasis on pamphlet debates has displaced a contextual reading of the *Narration*. These pamphlets have received considerable attention elsewhere, apart from being used as sources to access the internal debates of the assembly. The assembly was by no means hermetically sealed off from the political and religious conflicts surrounding them. The pamphlets certainly forced the assembly members to remind one another to keep their discussions private. Henderson was one such member who, in the midst of the external pamphlet publications, reminded the assembly that any such publication of their private sessions would be a prejudice to the entire assembly.

Third, the *Narration* served to reinforce the Apologists' parliamentary allegiance. Perhaps the only mystery surrounding the *Narration* is why the Apologists published it when they did. Robert Paul has rightly pointed out that the first weeks of January show, if anything, more unity between the Scots and the Apologists.[36] It is probably best to see the publication as the result of several things happening simultaneously in the winter of 1643–44. For one thing, the Apologists had just supported a document to discourage the further gathering of distinct churches in December 1643, and Rosemary Bradley is correct when she states that the *Narration* was, in some regard, a continuation of that effort.[37] For another, for two months Charles I had tried to lure Nye and John Goodwin into an intrigue against Parliament in what would become known as the Ogle plot. According to the diarist Thomas Juxon, the king promised the two men preferments and 'liberty of conscience', and warned them that the 'Presbytery would be bitter against them' and promised that if they joined him, Charles would 'hinder the Scots coming'.[38]

What Charles did not know was that Nye was partaking in a parliamentary subterfuge to lead the king into a trap.[39] In January 1644, the king was engaging in at least two simultaneous plots to split the various ecclesiological parties in London, and to dislodge the Scots from the capital.[40] Baillie reported that the '[independents] have offers from the Court of all they require'.[41] Though, other assembly members did not believe that the Apologists were negotiating with the king. Only days after the *Narration* was published, Light-foot, while recording a speech made by Lord Wharton in the assembly, distinguished between Nye, 'the moderate Protestant', and John Goodwin, the 'fiery independent' who had been used by Parliament to disrupt the king's plot.[42] Only two weeks after the *Narration* was published, Stephen Marshall delivered a stirring sermon to Parliament, the assembly and the Scottish commissioners, reasserting the Apologists' steadfast commitment to unity in the face of the king's efforts at subterfuge.[43]

The pressure outside the assembly was heating up. There were groups who wanted to stop the whole business of a national church. Edward Barbour and Thomas Nutt, two general Baptists, had mounted a campaign in September seeking to deny that the assembly had any legitimacy, and the assembly received a petition in December from separatists demanding a wide berth for religious toleration.[44] Others threatened to undermine the Apologists' credibility and hamper a settlement that could accommodate congregationalism in the reformed Church of England by linking the Apologists to ecclesiological parties they never intended to endorse.[45] The fact that the term 'independents' was often used for both the Apologists and some extremists outside the assembly only strengthened that claim. The *Narration* referred to four pamphlets written by 'learned' divines with much 'ingenuity'.[46] These publications were, for all intents and purposes, causing cracks to form in the godly alliance. One of these was probably Charles Herle's pamphlet against independency, and another may have been Rutherford's *Peaceable Plea*. The Apologists, despite battles outside the assembly, desperately wished to keep the assembly divines together. And it was not only the Apologists who wanted this.

During the first recorded discussion about the *Narration* in the assembly, Herle stated, 'I desire that it may be presented. I think [the *Narration*] doth them very much right that I had eye to in licensing of … it frees thee [*sic*] from anabaptisme.'[47] For Herle anabaptism meant a purely popular government. The assembly perpetually felt the tension between protecting its own divines from being disparaged and preventing their private debates from spilling into the public.[48] The Apologists were often the casualties of the assembly's deference to the latter. In 1644 we never find assembly members publicly attacking the Apologists, and this respect for the Apologists and the tenor of the debates in the assembly reflected this respect.[49] However, the historiography of the Apologists has completely overlooked the fact that at least twice the assembly forbade them to respond to pamphleteers' accusations. In September 1644, after the summer of attacks from Edwards and Forbes, Goodwin stated, 'We are much chalenged & provoked by severall bookes to give an account [of our churches] … Is it your purpose that we must answer none?'[50] By the end of 1644 Goodwin again complained to the assembly, 'the usual way of redressing themselves by public replies to the world, is not agreeable to the ordinance of Parliament'.[51] The Apologists could not defend themselves without revealing internal assembly debates, the assembly could not allow a public response without defying Parliament.

Since we have no evidence that the *Narration* either caused a stir in the assembly, or drew a reprimand from Parliament, we will need to look elsewhere if we are to find a controversy directly connected to the Apologists, the assembly and Parliament. To set the stage for this discussion, we should briefly describe the *Narration's* position on the magistrate. In his preface to the *Narration*, Herle stated that one of the accusations he wished to clear the Apologists from was 'Incompatiblenesse with Magistracy'.[52] The Apologists considered it the most 'abhorred maxime that any Religion ... should further arrogate unto themselves an exemption from giving account' to the 'Christian Magistrate above them, or neighbour Churches about them. So far were our judgements from that independent liberty that is imputed to us'.[53] The role of the magistrate was a fundamental part of their polity, but we should stress that their position was distinctly different from Erastianism and it shared a great deal of commonality with the Scots.[54] The *Narration* claimed the presbytery was not the only recourse to disciplining unrepentant churches, and indeed, was not the most effective.[55] 'The Magistrates power (to which we give as much, and (as we think) more, then the ... Presbyteriall government will suffer them to yeeld)' is meant 'to assist and back the sentence of other Churches denouncing this non-communion against Churches myscarrying', and this method is 'every way as effectuall' as presbyterianism 'can be supposed to be'.[56] Indeed, the magistrate's intervention, as ordained by Christ, was more effectual than the presbytery because the magistrate 'can inflict a more dreadful punishment, which carnal spirits are seldome sensible of.'[57]

While church power, in terms of church debates on the assembly floor, was the central tenet that separated the Apologists from the Brownists and 'independents', this belief in the role of the magistrate was another distinguishing factor. The Apologists believed the word 'independent' was a 'proud' and 'insolent' title that had been affixed to them. For the title 'independent' insinuated an exemption from 'all subjection and dependance, or rather a trumpet of defiance against what ever Power, Spiritual, or Civil; which we doe abhor and detest'.[58] In the assembly the Apologists uniformly rejected the title 'independent', and even used it pejoratively to describe aspects of presbyterian polity. The assembly never deployed the word independent when referring to the Apologists, and the few times the phrase 'independent Way' was used, the assembly 'appears to [have been] speaking about separatist congregationalists and not the positions of the Apologists in the assembly'.[59]

TEN DAYS IN MARCH

It was not until March, three months after it was published, that we have the first recorded mention of the *Apologeticall Narration* on the floor of the assembly. On 4 March 1643 Dr Cornelius Burgess reported to the assembly, 'You have received a lardge & very affectionate letter' from 'Walacria', and he said that the assembly should give the House of Commons both this letter and their [the assembly's] letter to Zeeland, '[t]hat both the Lattin & English may be sent' together to the House.[60] This letter from the Dutch classis of Walcheren is no longer extant, but we can recreate much of its contents by combing various manuscript sources. After Burgess introduced the letter to the assembly, Seaman stated that in the letter, 'something hinted the businesse of the *Apology* [*Apologeticall Narration*]. Because we cannot in a publique way, desire that those may desire that we may have liberty to speake our sence of this *Apology*'.[61] The letter 'hinted' at the Apologists' '*Apology*', but the assembly had avoided discussing the *Narration* in private, and had furthermore agreed not to discuss it in a 'publique way'. Historians have taken for granted that this letter from the classis of Walcheren was strongly critical of the congregational polity espoused in the *Apologeticall Narration*.[62] They have taken this view, by and large, from two comments made by Lightfoot and Baillie. Lightfoot stated that 'classes of Zealand [Walcheren] … exceedingly distate the apology of the Independents'.[63] But, by his own admission, Lightfoot was not at the assembly the day the Walcheren letter was presented. Lightfoot stated, 'This day I was at Munden, but the work of the day was this.'[64]

Lightfoot only reported what he had heard, and when he returned, the letter had already been sent away to be translated. However, Lightfoot was in attendance two days later when the letter, and its translation, was brought back to the assembly.[65] At this point, Lightfoot's description of the letter's relationship to the *Apologeticall Narration* was far more innocuous than his earlier comment. He stated, 'the letter in a special manner, in some part of it, doth nearly concern them [the independents]'.[66]

Baillie's responses to the Walcheren letter were even more divergent. Initially, he bragged to his cousin William Spang that the Walcheren letter was a 'long and sharpe censure of the Apologetick Narration', that it 'wound[ed]' the independents, and that it showed 'how farr their way was contrare to the Word of God, to the Reformed churches, and to all sound reason.'[67] Neither the assembly minutes, nor Lightfoot or Gillespie record anything close to this type of reprimand. However, only a month later Baillie told Spang of the 'great harm' the Walcheren letter had done to the Scots, and how it actually empowered the 'Independents' and moved certain English presbyterians closer to the Apologists.[68] Indeed, the vast majority of Baillie's comments regarding the Walcheren letter, and a subsequent letter from the synod of Zeeland (which oversaw the Walcheren church), demonstrated increasing frustration that the Dutch classes were not harsh enough on the Apologists, and actually served to bolster the congregationalists' cause.

Since Baillie has been uncritically utilised as a primary source for understanding the *Narration*, it is worth taking a closer look at his Revolutionary machinations before proceeding any further. Throughout 1644 Baillie had taken it upon himself to orchestrate an international campaign against independency in general and the Apologists in particular. While many historians have uncritically accepted Baillie's assessment of the Apologists, they have also allowed his personal correspondence to represent the opinions of the other Scottish commissioners. However, John Coffey has rightly called into question Baillie's claim that there were no substantial differences between Baillie and his colleagues Rutherford and Gillespie.[69] Indeed, Rutherford and Gillespie had more personal respect for the Apologists, and were more sympathetic with their polity than was Baillie. There is almost no evidence that Gillespie or Rutherford cast aspersions on the Apologists. Indeed, regarding personal affection, Rutherford privately claimed 'they came closer to God' than most in England, and Gillespie professed to have a great deal of respect, love and affection for them.[70] Baillie, while he also occasionally claimed to appreciate the personal qualities of the Apologists (and at other times disapproved of them), nonetheless felt his calling was to discredit the congregational divines.

Taken from a larger, twenty-year perspective, Baillie's relationship with Gillespie and Rutherford was tenuous at its best, and antagonistic at its worst. Tom Webster has noted that until the late 1630s Baillie's sympathies were with reduced episcopacy.[71] Forthcoming work may demonstrate that Baillie favoured reduced episcopacy in highly couched terminology, allowing for extraordinary and temporary episcopates. A presbytery, for example, could appoint bishops (or moderators), though retain ultimate power over them.[72] At the very least, as I will argue, Baillie sympathised with a version of presbyterianism that emphasised clerical power.

David Stevenson has shown that Rutherford and Gillespie were opposed by Baillie when they tried to offer support to and showed sympathy for the radical party emerging in the kirk.[73] And we will remember that Gillespie's ecclesiological sympathies were far more congregationally inclined in 1638. Baillie, upon reading Gillespie's 1637 book, said, 'I mislyke much of [it].'[74] Even as late as September 1643, it does not seem that Baillie knew Gillespie well.[75] By the 1650s Rutherford would join the Protestors, 'who virtually seceded from the kirk and set up their own church' and effectively sought to create churches of visible saints.[76] Baillie would remain with the Resolutioners, fearing the 'exclusive communion of the protestors'.[77] Therefore Baillie's views should not be uncritically conflated with the views of other Scottish presbyterians. Baillie is a useful – indeed, vital – source, provided we understand his agenda, motivations and context. It seems that while Baillie held a minority viewpoint amongst the Scottish commissioners in the assembly, it was Rutherford's and Gillespie's polities that represented a minority amongst the covenanters.[78]

Since 1641 Baillie had 'been patiently building a party in the City' that he was now beginning to mobilise in his private war against the independents.[79] As Valerie Pearl has noted, 'One of Baillie's self-appointed tasks in London had been to build a party of High presbyterians among the city clergy', including relatively peripheral figures like Thomas Edwards.[80] But the party was not limited to men like Edwards, and it seems Baillie was particularly attracted to more clerically minded presbyterians like Burgess and Seaman.[81] He had little respect for assembly protocol, and in his effort to secure favour on the continent and keep the Covenanters well informed he broke all the 'rules about confidentiality' at Westminster.[82] By his own admission he became the only Scottish commissioner who refused to tolerate the congregationalists, and on that point, decided to align himself with Cornelius Burgess rather than with Gillespie or Rutherford.[83] It may not be an overstatement to say that Baillie was the Covenanters' mole in London.

Baillie was critical of English presbyterians in the assembly who intimated any sympathy with the congregationalists, and he voiced grievances against the Calamy house English presbyterians in particular. He disparaged Herle for being Nye's 'good friend' (despite Herle's polity).[84] He denounced Stephen Marshall as the independents' 'diligent agent' who was for a 'middle way of his own', and Baillie held him responsible for all the concessions the presbyterians had made towards the congregationalists. Years later Baillie would call Edmund Calamy 'feeble-minded' for refusing to write a preface to his attack on the New England divine John Cotton.[85] Baillie used James Cranford to spread rumours and try to discredit parliamentarians whom he believed to support the Apologists.[86] And he quite happily let Cranford get sent to the Tower as his reward. Indeed, as Pearl noted, as soon as Cranford was released from prison, an unapologetic Baillie dispatched another 'five-point memorandum' insisting that Cranford, amongst other things, continue his propaganda campaign and encourage Thomas Edwards and John Bastwick to print their sermons against the 'Independents'.[87]

For Baillie it seems that ecclesiological positions mattered far less than political pragmatism during the assembly. By his own admission he was not well studied in matters of polity and almost never contributed to assembly discussions.[88] This gives some credibility to John Cotton's insinuation that Baillie lacked Rutherford's scholastic abilities.[89] For our immediate purposes, Baillie's gave specific orders to his cousin Spang in Middleburg, Zealand: 'French and Dutch orthodox Calvinists, particularly Voetius, Rivet and Apollonius, must turn their polemical pens against the Anabaptists, independents and Erastians of England.'[90] Although Baillie would by his silence deny it publicly, he was, through Spang, the instigator of this Walcheren letter. As we shall see, Baillie got far more than he had bargained, and far less than he had hoped.[91]

On 6 March 1644, Lightfoot recorded that the assembly received 'a dangerous book called the "Coole conference" which is partially written; and which cost some warm debatings'.[92] In it, the reliably embarrassing Nathaniel Holmes wove the *Apologeticall Narration* and the Scottish commissioners' *Reformation Cleared* together into a scholastic dialogue, where the Scots were portrayed as the antagonistic responders to the *Narration*.[93] At that time the *Coole Conference* was set aside to deal with the more pressing letter received from the classis of Walcheren.[94]

Both the *Coole Conference* and the letter from the classis of Walcheren presented a headache for the assembly, for different reasons. The author tried to conjure up a conflict where none existed, and it was not relevant to Holmes that the Scots' most important reaction to the *Narration* was not *Reformation Cleared*, but their paper on church government that protected the rights of the particular church as *ecclesia prima*. Not only this, but John Goodwin's pamphlet *M. S. to A. S.*, given the assembly debates of March 1644, presented a far more dangerous problem to the Apologists. As John Coffey has noted, the major burden of *M.S. to A.S.* was to attack the 'presbyterian defence of the magistrate's coercive power in matters of religion' and, correspondingly, represented John Goodwin's first defence of religious toleration.[95] This was a particularly public embarrassment for the Apologists, who firmly believed in the role for the magistrate in church matters and were avowedly anti-tolerationists.[96] Gillespie associated John Goodwin with two other notorious tolerationists, Roger Williams and William Walwyn, who publicly disavowed the positions taken by the Apologists.[97] Gillespie associated Thomas Goodwin with the tolerationists' most virulent detractors.[98] Perhaps realising just how impolitic his position was in 1644, and having not yet fully migrated to the point of hostility towards the Apologists, John Goodwin tempered his position when he re-published *M.S. to A.S.*

Baillie, ever anxious to humiliate the Apologists, claimed that *M.S.*, who he said represented the Apologists, denied all power to the magistrate in order to safeguard the liberty of the 'vilest hereticks'.[99] Baillie conceded that the Apologists would never admit that they believed this, but claimed, '"M. S." is of as great authoritie here as any them [the Apologists]'.[100] In a letter written to the Apologists in early May, the Dutch divine Wilhelm Apollonius expressed the belief that the *Coole Conference* was connected to the *Apologeticall Narration* and its authors.[101] This was probably Baillie's doing, who had sent Spang the *Coole Conference* in either March or April 1644. This was a methodological approach that Baillie shared with his friend Thomas Edwards: with some success, he tried to convince continental divines that all independent manifestos represented the beliefs of the Apologists.[102]

The Walcheren letter coupled with an embarrassing pamphlet debate in public caused anxiety in the assembly. On 6 March 1644 the assembly decided it must write a letter to Parliament and make three points clear: firstly, that the assembly had nothing to do with the *Apologeticall Narration*, nor had any knowledge of it until it was published; secondly, the assembly never made any complaints about this apology; thirdly, they did not complain to this [i.e. the Walcheren] church, or any other church abroad.[103]

At this point Herle, the licenser of the *Narration*, stated, 'I desire it may be presented. I think it [the *Narration*] doth them very much right that I had eye to in licensing of ... It frees thee [*sic*] from anabaptisme.'[104] This comment in favour of the *Narration* helps us understand why the Walcheren letter was so unnerving to the assembly. Herle continued, 'But for any commentary, I question whether any such power is given to us. The same things in this letter are the things in our debates.'[105] The assembly had no power to respond to the classis in Walcheren, and therefore any effort to clear their names of having communicated with the Walcheren classis about the *Narration* had to go through Parliament.[106]

In fact, some suspected that the Walcheren letter was the fault of the Scots. Baillie told Spang that some in the assembly who believed the letter 'spake so near to the mind and words of the Scotts, that some said it savoured of them'.[107] If, as the historiography has generally asserted, the letter from Walcheren was against the congregationalists and their polity, then the letter would have spoken nearer to the 'mind' of all presbyterian sympathisers, not just the Scots. In private all the divines denied having any 'correspondence ... [with] any forraigne Churches', and 'none of them had sent ... the *Apologeticall Narratione*, nor ... [the Scots'] Ansuer to it' abroad.[108] Importantly, the divines also denied having requested any 'censure' of the *Narration* from any foreign churches.[109] Indeed, as Robert Paul – assuming the Walcheren letter was about congregationalism – noted, the Walcheren letter was 'a little bit too true to be good'. The letter 'had been written almost as if the Dutch churches had been briefed about what had been happening and how to best word their reply to further the Scots' interest!'.[110]

Baillie claimed providence brought the letter from Walcheren, but Baillie had, as Paul has noted, 'obviously intended to give the Providence of God a helping hand'.[111] Baillie knew full well that the assembly was expressly forbidden from revealing any of the assembly's work to outsiders or from entering into correspondence with foreign churches.[112] Baillie repeatedly broke both rules. This would not be the only time assembly members complained that assembly matters were finding their way into print back in Scotland.[113] Though, it could be that Baillie did not perceive himself to be bound to such rules, since as a Scottish commissioner he was not technically a member of the assembly. Parliament jealously guarded its role in overseeing the assembly, and this letter from the Walcheren classis opened the divines to the accusation that they were engaging with foreign churches without Parliament's consent. In this case, the letter from the Walcheren classis was opening the door to a conflict between the assembly and Parliament that no one was in the mood to have.

The polemical backfire from the Walcheren letter haunted Baillie for months. The letter had the effect of empowering the Apologists' position before Parliament, drawing Gillespie's ecclesiological position closer to that of the congregationalists, and alienating Baillie from the other Scottish commissioners. There are two reasons the letter did this. Firstly, from Baillie's letter to Spang complaining about the Walcheren letter and a second similarly unhelpful April letter from Zeeland, we learn that the Dutch churches had actually affirmed and 'enlarg[ed]' the power of the particular congregation, by giving the power of excommunication and, indeed, all church power into the hands of congregational presbyteries, except in cases of difficulty.[14] On this point, the Walcherens were actually supporting an important statement within the *Narration*:

> Yea and our own Master *Cartwright*, holy *Baynes*, and other old Non-conformists, place the power of Excommunication in the Eldership of each particular Church with the consent of the Church, untill they do miscarry, and then indeed they subject them to such Presbyterial and Provincial Assemblies as the proper refuge for appeales and for compounding of differences amongst Churches.[15]

Seaman was against many presbyterians and congregationalists on this point: he rejected that a particular church had the power to exercise its own excommunication. He dismissed the Walcheren as just being 'one classis'.[16] Baillie either did not understand, or chose to ignore, how the Dutch churches' view of the power of the keys fitted with the view of the Apologists. Baillie took it upon himself to teach continental churches how to attack independency. Quite often his frustration with the foreign churches was due to the fact that they did not view the Apologists' polity as particularly problematic. His method, like that of his friend Thomas Edwards, was to convince continental divines that all varieties of independency in England were representative of the Apologists' polity. This support from the continental churches further shows that the area in which we would normally expect the *Narration* to be controversial turned out to be the point of agreement (Baillie aside). And this point of agreement would be further exemplified in Baillie's failure to get Voetius and Rivetus to write against the congregational divines.[17] Indeed, Baillie lamented that the Holland divines had not learned from Thomas Edwards![18]

The second part of Baillie's lamentations – relevant to the immediate debate surrounding the *Narration* – concerned the magistrate. He had to ask Spang repeatedly to tell the Dutch classes to avoid the 'point of the Magistrate' because it only served to empower the Apologists.[19] The problem Baillie faced was that the Holland churches had indeed obeyed his orders, namely to decry the *Narration*. However, they decried the *Narration* in ways that Baillie had not anticipated, and indeed, with the results that Baillie desperately wanted to avoid. The Walcheren letter, while it supported the Apologists in terms of its local church polity, *disagreed* with their view of the magistrate. And more dangerously, for the assembly at least, was the prospect that someone had written to the continental churches condemning the *Narration* and therefore, by implication, condemning the magistrate's role in religion.

Back in the assembly no one was in the mood to broach the Erastian issue. Two weeks earlier the assembly had flirted with a debate on the role of the state in matters of church practice. In front of a higher-than-usual amount of 'prime nobles and chiefe members of both houses', Nye (continuing a theme begun by the Erastian John Selden) firmly asserted his belief that a presbytery was not equal to, or independent of, the magistrate.[120] The tension in the assembly was perhaps at its highest to date, for, as we shall see in chapter 7, Nye's comments came at the very end of a two-week debate over the first proposition on presbyterianism. The thrust of Nye's argument was that a presbyterian government risked equalling the power of the state and thereby was not subordinate to civil authorities. Baillie capitalised on the debate, and claimed that Nye called the Scots' version of National Assemblies 'as formidable, yea, pernicious and thrice over pernicious to civill states and kingdoms'.[121]

According to Lightfoot the hottest moment of the debate came when Nye began to quote 'Mr Rutherford's preface upon his assertion of the Scotch government'.[122] Lightfoot was wrong about the citation. It was actually Gillespie's *Assertion* that Nye was quoting, and there is no sense of umbrage recorded in Gillespie's journal. Gillespie's *Assertion* as we have seen was produced during – and in conjunction with – the Calamy house meetings that included the Apologists. Nye cited the following Gillespie quotation on the assembly floor,

> It is not to be expected, but this forme of Church government, shall still be disliked by some ... [such as] Machavellians ... who do foresee that Presbyteriall Synodicall government, being conformed not to the Lesbian [flexible] rule of humane authority, but to the inflexible rule of Divine Institution, will not admit of any Innovations in Religion, be they never so conducible to politicall intentions.[123]

The rest of the Scots probably found these sentiments extremely embarrassing, especially with a Parliament already wary of the assembly's power.

Presciently, Nye's comments prefigured the debate soon to take place in response to the Walcheren letter. Stating that the commonwealth could not bear so great a body such as an independent presbytery to grow within it, Nye then stated, 'Look abroad, and nothing troubles men more than to think whether the presbytery shall be set up "jure divino", ... [and] that if it be, it will grow as big as the civil.'[124] Although the word independent was never used against the Apologists in the assembly, the Apologists, however, would occasionally use 'independent' to describe presbyterianism.[125] With far more exegetical skill than this little description conveys, Nye was opening, ever so briefly, the 'grand debate' that would take place between parliamentary Erastians and the assembly in 1646.[126] The assembly knew this debate would cause serious tensions, and with Saye and Sele's intervention, quickly shuffled the debate to the side unresolved, with the topic left to fester.

According to Lightfoot, Henderson was horrified and stated that Nye spoke like 'Sanballat, Tobiah, or Symmachus', who opposed the rebuilding of the temple in Jerusalem.[127] The minutes do not record the chaos, nor does Gillespie, but Lightfoot's Erastian disdain for the Scots' view of church and state no doubt contributed to his unique perspective on the discussion.[128] The Royalist newsbook, *Mercurius Aulicus*, gleefully recorded that the debate between Henderson and Nye was fierce, and Henderson, in his 'usual way', tried to get Nye thrown out of the assembly. *Mercurius Britanicus* countered that Henderson and Nye went to great lengths to defuse any public perception of discord resulting from their heated exchange.[129] The relationship between Gillespie and Nye was not damaged by it. Chad Van Dixhoorn has noted that no two people in the assembly showed each other more respect than Nye and Gillespie.[130] According to Baillie, the whole episode was used by God to do Nye 'some good; for, ever since, we find him, in all things, the most accommodating man in the company'.[131] And indeed, as we shall see in chapter 6 this entente opened a period of greater accommodation efforts.[132] Baillie's assessment of Lord Saye and Sele after the whole affair was less forgiving: 'My Lord Say's credit and reputation is none at all, which wont to be all in all.'[133] Whether by design or not, the danger of the Scots' long-term view of Parliament and its relationship to presbyterianism had briefly been exposed.

Although we will not address questions surrounding the Erastian controversy in 1646, we should carefully delineate the important differences between the Erastian view of the state and the congregationalist's view of the magistrate's role in religion. The congregationalists believed the state was a civil supervisor that protected the peace, promoted the gospel, and prosecuted heresy. However, the Erastians believed the state was a part of the church system based upon Christological fiat, and the state itself had a share in the power of the keys. Some in the assembly would go so far as to argue the church had no role in excommunication – something rejected by the congregationalists.[134] Both groups believed in the state's involvement in religion, but for different theological reasons.[135] Accordingly, Gillespie acknowledged that the 'independents' were among the 'anti-Erastians'.[136] Writing against Ferne, Bridge cited the divines of Scotland, and Rutherford in particular, as representing his views on the magistrate's role in religion.[137] Burroughs, in his *Irenicum*, described the Magistrate's role as '[judging] things as are against the rules of common justices and equity, and the common light of Christianity', and yet 'the things he doe are civill; and he cannot doe the works of a Church-officer'.[38] Although the spiritual sphere was not the jurisdiction of the civill authorities, the state nonetheless 'may exercise of his power upon the outward man, restraine it from the externall act of the evill, or bring it an externall good'.[39] Burroughs's position was not controversial. Indeed, the London presbyterians, who themselves were strong critics of the assembly congregationalists, cited Burroughs's view of the magistrate positively in their stridently anti-Erastian *Jus Divinum Regiminis Ecclesiasticae*.[40] This position actually made the Apologists more similar to the Scots than we typically think. When the assembly revisited these debates over excommunication in September 1644, Gillespie cited Cotton's *Keyes*, published by Nye and Goodwin, as a source in favour of his argument: 'Mr Cotton doth hold the church is independent upon the magistrate in the use of the keyes.'[41]

The Erastians, by arguing the magistrate was part of the church, saw the magistrate as having a share in the power of the keys. The congregationalists, however, separated church power from civil power, although civil power was nonetheless in place to protect and promote the religion of the state. As Cotton stated, church-subjection to the magistrate was a matter of 'civill peace', and this peace 'is [in] the establishment of pure Religion, in doctrine, worship, and government'.[42] Both the Scots and the congregational divines were 'anti-Erastians', yet both believed that the state played a role in protecting and promoting orthodoxy. However, their views on the subject came from different perspectives. The Church of England was established by law, so any Melvillian concept of separation of church and state would have sat uncomfortably in the minds of English divines (whether Erastian or not). Nevertheless, Gillespie himself would claim that Cotton, Goodwin, and Nye argued, if anything, for less ecclesiastical power in the magistrate than the Scots did!'[43]

In this heated context, the assembly acted swiftly and cautiously to explain the Walcheren letter to Parliament. On 8 March 1644 a letter to Parliament had been drafted by the assembly explaining that they had never spoken against or written against the *Apologeticall Narration*, and the letter had been presented to the divines.[44] According to Lightfoot, Nye asked whether the letters from Walcheren really warranted this letter to Parliament, and further, and perhaps more importantly to the Apologists, Nye asked 'whether some passages in it [the letter to Parliament] do not charge the Apologists with some breach of a parliament-order'.[45] Significantly, the assembly voted that the Apologists had not broken any parliamentary order and removed any language that intimated as much.[46] The Apologists were further displeased that the letter to Parliament indicated that the Walcheren classis had 'complained' about the *Narration*, feeling that the word was too strong for the actual tenor of the letter. But, on this point the assembly overruled their requests and 'voted that the word "complain" should stand'.[147] The letter was ready and Burgess, along with other divines, had to explain the assembly's beliefs to Parliament.

On 11 March the House of Lords' Journal recorded that 'Doctor Burgess and divers others of the Assembly' were commanded by the assembly to present the letters they had written to the continental churches, and 'especially to the Churches of Zealand with the Answer to the same'.[148] A letter from the assembly explaining the missives was read in the Lords.[149] The first half indicated that the Zealand churches rejoiced in England's effort in 'Reforming of this Church according to the Word of God, and for Uniformity of Religion, Public Worship and Discipline in all the three Kingdoms'. However, Burgess continued, they did 'complain of a Book, as offensive to the Reformed Churches abroad, lately written and published by the Five Members of this [the Westminster] Assembly ... intituled *An Apologeticall Narration'*. Burgess further explained that the assembly had had nothing to do with the *Narration*.[150] The ill success of any letter from the assembly to the continent was bound to be a problem for Parliament. As Chad Van Dixhoorn has noted, 'the cash-strapped Parliament was fundraising overseas', and in fact, the States General issued 'pre-printed receipts [to] Dutch congregations with blank spaces provided for the names of donors and the amount of donations'.[151] The assembly did not want to get in the way of a parliamentary monetary relief scheme.

The House of Lords seemed to show little interest in Burgess's report and deferred to the House of Commons, since, as they viewed it, 'what the Assembly hath done in this Business hath been by an Order of the House of Commons' and therefore the Commons should be acquainted with the business, and 'when the House of Commons desires their Concurrence in any Thing touching this Business, they will be ready to do what is fit in it'.[152] The next day, 12 March, Burgess dutifully went to the House of Commons, but this time he came with two letters from the continent, for that morning the assembly had received another embarrassing letter from the churches in France. John de la March, who had studied at Saumur, had reported to the assembly that he 'received Information from those to whom our letters ware sent in France, &c'.[153] From what we can reconstruct from Lightfoot, Gillespie and the Commons Journal, de la March had received a letter stating that a church in Paris had refused to open the letter from the assembly until they had received permission from the State. When they had done this they were accused by the authorities of having had prior secret correspondence with the 'State of England' and the Westminster assembly.[154] The assembly added de la March to Burgess's entourage, and for this visit to Parliament the assembly added a request, saying '[we] desire their order for the printing of the said letter sent to the Reformed Churches if to their wisdome it shall seeme meete'.[155] After having explained the situation to the Parliament, Burgess claimed 'there begins to grow some Danger to our Brethren beyond Sea', and so the 'Assembly desires this House, that those Letters may be published, that all the World may see, that nothing is contained in them that may endanger the Reformed Churches'.[156]

Someone, it seems, had been corresponding with the continental churches, professing to be doing so on behalf of the assembly. The evidence suggests it was Baillie, since we know by his own admission he was indeed writing secret letters to Spang.[157] The assembly had felt the need to make clear that no one, to their knowledge, had written to the foreign churches, and more specifically, against the *Apologeticall Narration*. Baillie had done just that. He had been writing to Spang complaining about the 'independents' for months, and more, specifically on 18 February, he had disparaged the *Apologeticall Narration*.[158] He would even engage his friend David Buchanan, who had once lived in France, to 'write to some of the ministers of Paris, Geneva, and Berne' to get them to write against the 'independents'.[159]

These correspondences were yet more examples of Baillie's efforts to promote his own agenda despite the collateral damage. Writing to the Dutch was one thing, for the Scots and the Dutch divines held similar views on the state's role in religion. Encouraging Parisian churches to write against the 'independents' was a different matter – especially since the court of Charles I, including the Queen, was in exile in Paris, which had already plunged the assembly into trouble.[160] Indeed, Baillie could only show disgust for a German church that had written to the assembly lamenting their own perilous plight rather than obeying Baillie and complaining about the 'independents', saying, 'it was but a poor short epistle, all spent upon lamenting their own miseries, and in the little they spoke to our point'.[161]

On 12 March, Whitaker reported in his diary, 'some of the assembly of divines came and acquainted [the house] how they had been informed that the letters sent from them to the ministers in France had brought them and the churches in France into a worse condition then they were in before – this was to be taken up tomorrow'.[162] It was already clear from Parliament's perspective that there was a problem. The letter they had commissioned to the foreign churches had put those churches in a more precarious position than they were in before the letters had been written.

On 13 March, the House of Commons debated what do to next. And it is through this debate that we finally get clarity as to the precise point of concern the Dutch had with the *Apologeticall Narration*. We find this in the two diary entries of Sir Simond D'Ewes and Laurence Whitaker, which made reference to a speech given by John Selden. Although historians have overlooked it, the entries of these men in Parliament give us a window into the first and only debate Parliament had about the *Narration*.[163]

Parliament debated whether or not, as the assembly had requested, both the divines' letter to the continent and the response from the church in Walcheren should be printed.[164] Simond D'Ewes recorded that 'mr selden spoke against' the publishing of both letters 'showing that in that letter they challenged an ecclesiasticall or church government to bee jure divino with which this civil magistrate had nothing to doo'. And therefore, Selden 'advised that wee should forbeare to print that [Walcheren] letter, which after some debate was thought to be the best way'.[165] Whitaker's entry corresponds to, and expands upon, what D'Ewes recorded:

> this day the letter was read in the house; it was sent from the assembly of our divines to the Protestant churches of France and of Zeeland and also the answer of the divines of Zeeland unto it, which did much toch the discourse written by the independent men in the assembly, called *Apologeticall Narration*, which[?] Answer of the Zealand men, bec: it tended to the excepting of spirituall persons from the civil power, was disliked by us, yet it was ordered that the letter sent [from the assembly] should be published.[166]

This diary entry confirms what we have been arguing all along: that the Walcheren letter was controversial. D'Ewes noted that the letter argued for a spiritual government separate from the 'civil magistrate', or, as Whitaker described it, 'tended to the excepting of spirituall persons from the civil power'. This then was the critique of the *Apologeticall Narration*. The Dutch did not like that the civil magistrate retained a power in spiritual matters. It is certainly significant that Selden made the speech, since he would have been particularly offended by any intimation that Parliament should cede all power in religion to the church. Baillie had already associated Selden's view with those of Erastus.[167]

W. K. Jordan and Sears McGee have shown that the parliamentarian Francis Rous had a hand in writing a pamphlet calling for a limited toleration entitled *The Ancient Bounds*.[168] In *Ancient Bounds*, Rous cited 'a cloud of witnesses in favor of limiting the magistrate's roles in religion', and he included the Walcheren divines in this group.[169] Ironically, given prevailing historiography of the *Apologeticall Narration*, the letter critical of the *Narration*'s view of the magistrate's role in religion, had it been published, would have emboldened those seeking religious toleration. The evidence seems to corroborate John Goodwin's claim that, after the speech by Selden, Parliament took the side of the *Narration* against the letters from Zeeland and 'resolved a general acclamation, that the Apologie was to be left as it was found, unblamed'.[170] John Goodwin also corroborated what we see in the assembly's diaries. 'In [that letter] there are many high passages, seeming prejudiciall to our worthy Magistracy', and although the *Narration* claimed to give more power to the magistrate than many presbyterians did the letter from Zeeland gave 'too little to the Magistracy'. Although we need to be careful when using John Goodwin as a source for events in the assembly, he does seem reliably informed of parliamentary machinations, for he concluded that because the letter from

Zealand gave so little power to the magistrate, 'the State of England, I thinke, cannot approve it here among us.'[171]

Parliament decided to only allow the original letter to the continent to be printed. This letter, after all, was relatively benign in content.[172] Publishing the Walcheren letter would only have embarrassed Parliament. After all, the *Apologeticall Narration*'s deferral to the magistrate was a position that Parliament supported. It reemphasised that this assembly of divines was *Parliament's* assembly. Parliament could not allow a letter from a foreign church criticising Parliament's role in overseeing the Church of England to be published. Furthermore, the content of the Walcheren letter seemed to indicate that someone within the assembly, without the assembly's knowledge, had requested this response to the *Narration*. Parliament had no interest in publicly indicating that members of its own religious synod were acting as foreign agents without their permission.

Baillie was not deterred. Nor was he bothered by the prospect of embarrassing Parliament. It simply forced him to be a little more circumspect. Whereas he initially praised Spang for the letter from the classis of Walcheren, he later complained about it in light of the polemical backfire. He eventually forgave Spang for it following a second letter that came from the classes of Zeeland.[173] But the thrill was short-lived. Baillie lamented to Spang that the 'point of the Magistrate' in both the Walcheren letter and the subsequent Zeeland letter meant neither letter would ever be published in England.[174] But Baillie had alternate plans. He requested that Spang have his own letter printed in Holland 'and sent over [to England], with the former of Walcheren: [because] no man here can get a copie of either'.[175] Baillie justified this little bit of subterfuge as being the only fair thing to do; after all, 'We have printed our letter to yow, both in Latine and English, why should not yow doe the lyke with yours to us?'[176]

Baillie was willing to risk exposing the congregational-like polity of the Dutch, along with the assembly's relationship with Parliament, in order to gain support against Parliament's Erastianism. Baillie would continue to ask his agents, with little success, to play down their emphasis on the power of the local church. He nonetheless preferred to have the Walcheren letter in print with their support of the local church's prerogatives along with their rebuttal of the *Apologeticall Narration*'s view of the state than to have no letter printed at all. Such was the anxiety aroused by the question of whether Parliament had power over religion.

We should juxtapose Gillespie's reaction in the assembly to the Dutch letters to Baillie's criticism of the Zeelanders for their overemphasis on the particular church. When the assembly began debating the power of the particular church on 1 May Gillespie recorded, 'My desire was concerning this debate of the power of congregations, That in regard the French Discipline, chap. v, and

Confession of Bohemia, chap. xiv, and the letter from Classis of Walcheren, owned and approved by the synod of Zeeland' along with 'other Reformed churches, [to] give some power of church government and censures to the consistory of each particular congregation.'[77]

Gillespie, far from just agreeing with the Walcheren classis's emphasis on the power of the keys being in the particular church's eldership, also indicated this was in keeping with the Reformed churches on the continent. The confession of Bohemia (1535) stated that the 'keys of the Lord, or rather the administration and power of those keys, is given and handed over first to the leaders and ministers of the Church, then to any Christian congregation, no matter how few members are in it'.[78] With such sentiments on the continent, it becomes clearer why Baillie could not convince theologians such as Rivet and Voetius to condemn the Apologists. Gillespie then went on to note that the Scots had asserted this prerogative of the particular church 'in our second paper concerning church government given to the Grand Committee'.[79] This is the paper that the Scots handed into the Grand Committee after the publication of the *Apologeticall Narration*, and we can see from Baillie's letters that it caused significant problems back in Scotland.

Baillie wrote to Spang describing how much trouble Gillespie's position was for the Scots. Baillie stated, 'We gave in, long agoe, a paper to the great Committee, wherein we asserted a congregationall eldership, for governing the private affaires of the congregation, from the eighteenth of Matthew.' This got the Scottish commissioners, as Baillie said, into 'a pecke of troubles'.[80] David Calderwood, the don of Scottish presbyterianism, 'censured [the Scots] grievouslie' for submitting such a paper to Parliament. Calderwood angrily reminded the Scots 'that our Books of Discipline admitts of no Presbyterie or Eldership but one', and the commissioners put themselves 'in hazard to be forced to give excommunication, and so entire government, to congregations, which is a great stepp to Independencie'.[81] This is all part of a story we will look more closely at in chapter 8. For at the same time that the *Narration* exposed tensions between Parliament and the assembly, it also accelerated efforts at accommodation between the Scots (under Gillespie's leadership) and the Apologists.

CONCLUSION

From a perspective taken from the assembly of divines and Parliament, we can present a very different picture of the *Apologeticall Narration* than that offered by the historiography. As an assembly-related document we should see it as only nominally important, with very little impact on the assembly debates. Rosemary Bradley stated that the 'presbyterians were unanimous that the five brethren had injured the assembly by their sudden publication of the Apology'.[82]

Yet, she based this assertion on a comment by Adam Steuart. Steuart was not an assembly member, and he was writing against John Goodwin, also not an assembly member. However, we see here that the assembly of divines was by no means united against the *Narration,* if indeed they were against it at all. This new perspective highlights the dangers of letting the pamphlet debates outside the assembly tell the story of what was going on inside. Historians' insistence on a reductive binary conflict model of 'presbyterian verses independent' has made it far too easy to use these external pamphlets as lenses through which we read all ecclesiological debates of the 1640s.

The *Apologeticall Narration* was not a breaking of the godly alliance; indeed, it was quite the opposite.[183] Nearly three years earlier, as we saw in Chapter 1, there was agreement surrounding the platform of church government presented in the *Petition Examined.* The alliance had begun to fray between 1642 and 1643 with the publications of a variety of ecclesiological pamphlets, including Charles Herle's treatise against independency. The pressure on the godly alliance was only going to increase with the forthcoming debates on the presbytery.

In 1645 the New England divines John Allin and Thomas Shepard, lamenting the gulf that had grown between the presbyterian majority and congregational minority in England, asked, how is 'this wound ... now so wide and deep, that at the first was presented to the world so small, or scarce any at all?'.[184] They then stated, 'When the Prelates petitioned for their government, because the Reformers were not, nor could ever agree upon one Forme: it was professed that in six Points ... all did agree, and doubted not but if the Prelates were downe, all would agree in one.'[185] And thus, we come full circle, back to 1641, the *Petition Examined,* the platform of church government, and the unity of the godly discussed earlier in this book. Allin and Shephard saw the Westminster assembly as having disrupted the alliance that was publicly professed in the *Petition Examined* in 1641. They cited Charles Herle who had, in their opinion, tried to keep the godly together, when he stated that the distance between the brethren was so 'narrow, as if one plaster more might seeme to have healed it'.[186]

Shepard and Allin also understood that the *Apologeticall Narration* was an effort to keep the Calamy house group united around the platform established at Aldermanbury: 'Wee thought that ... meeke *Apologetick Narration* gave a faire opportunity of closing with brethren in such things as they professed to concur in.' But now, they continued, some of those 'six points' of agreement in the *Petition Examined* are the 'greatest bones of contention'. To the minds of Allin and Shepard, the public consensus in the *Petition Examined* ended when the assembly of divines failed to defend articles five and six, which gave the particular church 'her owne power and authority' and stated that assemblies were 'expedient' for the 'good and edification' of the churches under that assembly.[187] From the perspective of these New England divines, the presbyterians had moved away from an agreement made in 1641 that had promised to unite the godly once the prelacy fell. As we shall see in the coming chapters, it was English presbyterians who neutered the rights of particular churches. All this might seem like partisan whitewashing if it were not for the evidence presented in the preceeding chapters of this book.

The *Apologeticall Narration* was not a full statement of the Apologists' polity. Such a document would have elicited a reprimand from both the assembly and Parliament, and the assembly had already agreed – against the Apologists' repeated requests – that no platform was allowed until the specifics of church polity had been sorted. Indeed, whenever the London presbyterians chose to cite the polity of the Apologists they chose Cotton's *Keyes of the Kingdom*, rather than the *Narration*. Similarly, the *Narration* was not, as William Haller has said, a call for wider religious liberty, which would have horrified the assembly, Parliament, and the Apologists themselves. Furthermore, as we will see in the following chapters, the polity in the *Narration* was shared by many English and Scottish presbyterians. The real controversy over the *Narration* was in its capacity to risk an international crisis and to prefigure the 'grand debate' yet to be had between Parliament and its own assembly of divines.

NOTES

1 'The real "Grand Debate"' is a phrase utilised by Chad Van Dixhoorn referring to the Erastian controversy. C. Van Dixhoorn, 'Politics and Religion in the Westminster Assembly and the "Grand Debate"', in R. Armstrong and T. O'hAnnrachain (eds), *Alternative Establishments in Early Modern Britain and Ireland: Catholic and Protestant* (Manchester: Manchester University Press, 2013), pp. 129–148.

2 Powell, 'Dissenting Brethren', pp. 97ff.

3 See below, p. 108.

4 For more on this point, see chapters 5 and 6 of this book.

5 See chapters 3 and 7.

6 *20. Junii, 1643. A particular of the names of the licensers, vvho are appointed by the House of Commons for printing; according to an order of the Lords and Commons, Dated the 14. of June, 1643* (London, 1643).

7 T. Goodwin, P. Nye, S. Simpson, J. Burroughs et al., *An Apologeticall Narration* (London, 1644), frontispiece. Three years later a royalist claimed that Herle 'confessed to me that he had modified many expressions' in the *Apologeticall Narration*. J. Hall, *A true account and character of the times* (1647), p. 4. Bradley, 'Jacob and Esau', p . 125.

8 Bradley, 'Jacob and Esau', pp. 69–70.

9 Thomason has the date at 2 May, 1643. *Catalogue of the pamphlets, books, newspapers, and manuscripts relating to the Civil War, the Commonwealth, and Restoration, collected by George Thomason, 1640–61* (London, 1908), vol. 1, p. 256.

10 C. Herle, *The Independency on Scriptures of the Independency of Churches* (London, 1643), preface, not paginated.

11 Vivienne Larminie, 'Herle, Charles (1597/8–1659)', *Oxford Dictionary of National Biography*, Oxford University Press, Sept 2004; online edn, May 2006, accessed 21 July 2010; Baillie, *Letters and Journals*, vol. 2, pp. 415–416.

12 *Mercurius Britanicus: Communicating the affaires of great Britaine: For the better Information of the People, 20* (2 January–11 January 1644), p. 160; P. Heylyn, *Mercurius Aulicus, Communicating the intelligence and affaires of the Court to the rest of the Kingdome* (week ending 6 January, 1644), pp. 762–763; see also Bradley, 'Jacob and Esau', p. 126. For Thomason dating see *Thomason Catalogue*, vol. 1, p. 304.

13 *Mercurius Britanicus, 20*. p. 160.

14 Goodwin, Nye, Simpson, Burroughs *et al.*, *Apologeticall Narration*, p. 24.

15 Lightfoot, *Journal*, pp. 50–51. See chapter 8 of this book for more on this.

16 *Two letters of great concernment* (London, 1645), p. 7. See also, Lightfoot, *Journal*, p. 119.

17 *Two letters*, p. 7.

18 Goodwin, Nye, Simpson, Burroughs *et al.*, *Apologeticall Narration*, p. 12.

19 Ibid., pp. 12–13.

20 Ibid., p. 13.

21 See chapter 6 of this book.

22 *Reformation of church-government in Scotland, cleared from some mistakes and prejudices* (1644). The diarist Thomas Juxon refers to the *Narration* and *Reformation Cleared* together, but offers no commentary as to how he connects them. T. Juxon, *The Journal of Thomas Juxon, 1644–1647* (Cambridge: University of Cambridge, 1999), pp. 43–44.

23 Kim, 'The Debate on the Relations between the Churches of Scotland and England during the British Revolution (1633–1647)', p. 212.

24 Paul, *The Assembly of the Lord*, p. 581.

25 See below, chapter 7.

26 L. Kaplan, 'Presbyterians and Independents in 1643', *English Historical Review*, 84 (1969), 244–56, p. 255; B. Gustafsson, *The Five Dissenting Brethren: A Study on the Dutch Background of their Independentism* (Lund, 1995), pp. 9–10; Bradley, 'Jacob and Esau', pp. 127–128; W. M. Hetherington, *History of the Westminster Assembly of Divines* (Edinburgh: J. Johnstone, 1843), pp. 188–189.

27 Goodwin, Nye, Simpson, Burroughs *et al.*, *Apologeticall Narration*, p. 30, italics mine.

28 Paul, *Narration*, p. 42.

29 Paul, *The Assembly of the Lord*, p. 91.

30 See below, chapter 7.

31 S. Simpson, *The Anatomist anatomis'd* (London, 1644), p. 4.

32 See above, pp. 7, 29.

33 R. Baillie, *A dissuasive from the errours of the time* (London, 1645).

34 R. Baillie, *The Disswasive from the Errors of the Time* (London, 1655), p. 44.

35 See below, p. 97.

36 This is a primary reason for Paul dismissing the date for the *Narration*.

37 Bradley, 'Jacob and Esau', pp. 124–125.

38 Juxon, *Journal*, pp. 40–41.

39 See B. M. Gardiner, *A Secret Negociation with Charles the First, 1643–1644*, Camden Miscellany (1883), vol. 8; *Letters original from King Charles I* (Cambridge University Library: Baker MSS, Mm.I.46).

40 The other plot is popularly known as Brooke plot. For an overview of both see S. R. Gardiner, *History of the Great Civil War*, 4 vols (London: Windrush, 1987), vol. 1, pp. 262ff.

41 Baillie, *Letters and Journals*, vol. 2, pp. 133–134.

42 Lightfoot, *Journal*, p. 126.

43 S. Marshall, *A sacred panegyrick* (London, 1644).

44 T. Nutt, *To the right honourable, the knights, citizens and burgesses, of the House of Commons assembled in Parliament* (London, 1643); W. A. Shaw, *A History of the English Church during the Civil Wars and under the Commonwealth 1640–1660*, 2 vols (London: Longmans, Green, 1900), vol. 1, p. 94; Van Dixhoorn, *MPWA* (vol. 2), p. 294; Lightfoot, *Journal*, p. 50; *An Exhortation vnto the learned divines assembled at Westminster to set an order touching fayth and religion in the Church of England* (Amsterdam, 1643).

45 Van Dixhoorn, *MPWA* (vol. 2), pp. 328, 352. See also, Edwards, *Antapologia*, pp. 5–6.

46 Goodwin, Nye, Simpson, Burroughs et al., *Apologeticall Narration*, p. 15.

47 Van Dixhoorn, *MPWA* (vol. 2), p. 584.

48 Henderson reminded to the assembly not to carry themselves 'as adversaryes out of the assembly, a suggesting to write pamphlets to the prejudice of the assembly', Van Dixhoorn, *MPWA* (vol. 3), p. 98.

49 I am grateful to Dr Chad Van Dixhoorn for pointing this out to me.

50 Van Dixhoorn, *MPWA* (vol. 3), p. 259.

51 Gillespie, *Notes*, p. 98.

52 Goodwin, Nye, Simpson, Burroughs et al., *Apologeticall Narration*, p. 21.

53 Ibid., p. 21.

54 See chapters 7 and 8 of this book for more on Erastianism.

55 By presbytery here, I am not referring to the local presbytery of elders, but a gathered body of presbyters from multiple churches.

56 Goodwin, Nye, Simpson, Burroughs et al., *Apologeticall Narration*, p. 19.

57 Ibid., p. 19.

58 Ibid., p. 23.

59 I am grateful to Dr Chad Van Dixhoorn for sharing this information with me.

60 Van Dixhoorn, *MPWA* (vol. 2), p. 576.

61 Ibid., p. 576.

62 Bradley, 'Jacob and Esau', p . 127; Paul, *The Assembly of the Lord*, p. 292. Sears McGee is one notable exception to this group, but McGee fails to see where the Walcheren

letter did disagree with the *Narration*. J. S. McGee, 'Francis Rous and "Scabby or Itchy Children": The Problem of Toleration in 1645', *Huntington Library Quarterly*, 67 (2004), pp. 401–422, p. 412.

63 Lightfoot, *Journal*, p. 192.

64 Ibid., p. 192.

65 Ibid., p. 199; Van Dixhoorn, *MPWA* (vol. 2), pp. 581ff.

66 Lightfoot, *Journal*, p. 199.

67 Baillie, *Letters and Journals*, vol. 2, pp. 143, 144, 146, 147.

68 Ibid., vol. 2, p. 165.

69 Coffey, *Rutherford*, p. 202.

70 Bonar (ed.) *Letters of Samuel Rutherford*, pp. 618, 619; Van Dixhoorn, *MPWA* (vol. 3), p. 498.

71 Webster, *Godly Clergy*, pp. 319–320.

72 I am grateful to Alexander Campbell for discussions on Robert Baillie's ecclesiology and very much look forward to his Cambridge PhD on Baillie, 'The Political and Religious Thought of Robert Baillie (1602–1662)'.

73 D. Stevenson, 'The Radical Party in the Kirk, 1637–45', *Journal of Ecclesiastical History*, 25 (1974), pp. 136–139.

74 Baillie, *Letters and Journals*, vol. 1, p. 90.

75 Ibid., vol. 2, p. 85.

76 Stevenson, 'The Radical Party in the Kirk, 1637–45', pp. 162, 164.

77 Ibid., p. 178.

78 I am grateful to Alexander Campbell for pointing this out to me.

79 V. Pearl, 'London Puritans and Scotch Fifth Columnists: A Mid-seventeenth Century Phenomenon', in A. E. J. Hollaender & W. Kellaway (eds), *Studies in London History* (London: Hodder and Stoughton, 1969), p. 320.

80 Ibid., p. 326.

81 Ibid., p. 328; E. Williams Kirby, 'The English Presbyterians in the Westminster Assembly', *Church History*, 33.4 (1964), pp. 418–428.

82 Van Dixhoorn, *MPWA* (vol. 1), p. 24.

83 I am grateful to Dr Chad Van Dixhoorn for sharing this information with me.

84 Baillie, *Letters and Journals*, vol. 2, p. 201.

85 Ibid., vol. 2, p. 353; vol. 3, p. 285; see also, Bradley, 'Jacob and Esau', p. 25.

86 G. Yule, *Puritans in Politics: The Religious Legislation of the Long Parliament 1640–1647* (Oxford: Sutton Courtnay, 1981), p. 143.

87 Pearl, 'London Puritans', pp. 324–325.

88 Baillie, *Letters and Journals*, vol. 2, p. 160. I am grateful to Dr Laura Stewart for discussions on Baillie.

89 Cotton, *The Way of Congregational Churches Cleared*, vol. 2, p. 20.

90 Pearl, 'London Puritans', p. 325.

91 For a very different, and more adulatory assessment of Baillie, see Hetherington, *History of the Westminster Assembly of Divines*, p. 149.

92 Lightfoot, *Journal*, p. 199.

93 The *Coole Conference* reappears in the minutes of the assembly on 6 May in its completed form, along with John Goodwin's *M. S. to A. S*. John Goodwin's pamphlet was ordered to be committed to the same committee already established to 'consider of the letters [of which there were now two] from the classis of Walacria and province of Zealand and the booke entitled *The Coole Conference*', and this committee was to 'make a report to this assembly what they find in [*M. S. to A. S.]* that may reflect upon this assembly or the Commissioners of Scotland or the churches in Walacria'. J. Goodwin, *M. S. to A. S. [i.e. Adam Steuart]* (London, 1644); N. Holmes, *A Coole Conference between the Scotish Commissioners' Cleared Reformation and the Holland Ministers' Apologeticall Narration* (London, 1644), p. 53.

94 Lightfoot, *Journal*, p. 199.

95 J. Coffey, *John Goodwin and the Puritan Revolution: Religion and Intellectual Change in Seventeenth-century England* (Woodbridge: Boydell, 2006), p. 109.

96 For more on their view of the magistrate see below, pp. 106ff.

97 Coffey, *John Goodwin and the Puritan Revolution*, p. 111; G. Gillespie, *Wholsome severity reconciled with Christian liberty* (London, 1644), pp. 2–3.

98 A. Zakai, 'Religious Toleration and Its Enemies: The Independent Divines and the Issue of Toleration during the English Civil War', *Albion: A Quarterly Journal Concerned with British Studies*, 21 (1989), 1–3, p. 18; W. Walwyn, *The compassionate Samaritane* ([London], 1644), pp. 1–2.

99 Baillie, *Letters and Journals*, vol. 2, p. 184.

100 Ibid., vol. 2, p. 184.

101 Norton, *Answer*, pp. 19–20.

102 In letter to Spang in mid-May 1644, Baillie stated, 'The two books which I have sent yow last, will informe [Apollonius] more of their mind; little Dr Homes, the author of "The Coole Conference," "M. S. against A. S." is John Goodwin of Coleman Street'. Baillie, *Letters and Journals*, vol. 2, pp. 180–181.

103 The only recorded comment by the congregationalists that may be connected to the *Narration* on 6 March was by Thomas Goodwin. His comment was tantalisingly unfinished in the transcription, 'Move ther ware mistakes ...'. It is not known what mistake Goodwin is talking about. Van Dixhoorn, *MPWA* (vol. 2), p. 584.

104 Ibid., p. 584.

105 Ibid., p. 584.

106 Baillie, *Letters and Journals*, vol. 2, p. 186.

107 Ibid., vol. 2, p. 144.

108 Ibid., vol. 2, p. 144.

109 Ibid., vol. 2, p. 144.

110 Paul, *The Assembly of the Lord*, p. 376.

111 Ibid., p. 377.

112 Ibid., p. 381.

118

113 See Dr Temple's complaint, Gillespie, *Notes*, p. 100.

114 Baillie, *Letters and Journals*, vol. 2, pp. 155, 165, 170, and 239. These comments from Baillie reflect frustration with both the letter from the Walcheren and the letter from Zealand.

115 Goodwin, Nye, Simpson, Burroughs *et al.*, *Apologeticall Narration*, pp. 12–13.

116 Baillie, *Letters and Journals*, vol. 2, p. 165.

117 Ibid., vol. 2, p. 159.

118 Ibid., vol. 2, p. 193.

119 Ibid., vol. 2, pp. 170, 180.

120 Paul, *The Assembly of the Lord*, pp. 269–271.

121 Baillie, *Letters and Journals*, vol. 2, p. 146. Baillie was referring to Nye's citation of Gillespie's *Assertion*.

122 Lightfoot, *Journal*, p. 169.

123 Gillespie, *An Assertion*, preface, not paginated; Lightfoot, *Journal*, p. 169.

124 Ibid., p. 169.

125 I am grateful to Dr Chad Van Dixhoorn for pointing this out to me.

126 For a discussion about the Erastian debates in 1646 see Bradley, 'Jacob and Esau', p. 430.

127 Lightfoot, *Journal*, p. 169.

128 See Gillespie, *Notes*, pp. 26–27.

129 For a summary of newsbook debates see Bradley, 'Jacob and Esau', pp. 156–157; *Mercurius Aulicus, Sunday February 25, 1644* (Oxford, 1643), last page. J. Peacey, 'The Struggle for "Mercurius Britanicus": Factional Politics and the Parliamentarian Press, 1643–1646', *Huntington Library Quarterly*, 68 (2005), 517–543.

130 Van Dixhoorn, *MPWA* (vol. 1), p. 30.

131 Baillie, *Letters and Journals*, vol. 2, p. 146.

132 Bradley, 'Jacob and Esau', p. 157.

133 Baillie, *Letters and Journals*, vol. 2, p. 146.

134 See chapter 7, below.

135 For more on the Apologists' understanding of the magistrate and the church, see Powell, 'The Last Confession: A Background Study of the Savoy Declaration of Faith and Order', chapter 1.

136 Kim, 'The debate on the relations between the Churches of Scotland and England during the British Revolution (1633–1647)', p. 239.

137 W. Bridge, *The Truth of the Times vindicated* (London, 1643), pp. 28–29.

138 J. Burroughs, *Irenicum, to the Lovers of Truth and Peace* (1646), p. 26.

139 Ibid., p. 26.

140 *Jus divinum regiminis ecclesiastici*, p. 75.

141 Van Dixhoorn, *MPWA* (vol. 3), p. 355.

142 Cotton, Goodwin & Nye, *Keyes*, p. 50.

143 G. Gillespie, *Aarons rod blossoming* (London, 1646), pp. 257–258.

144 Van Dixhoorn, *MPWA* (vol. 2), p. 598; Lightfoot, *Journal*, p. 206.

145 Lightfoot, *Journal*, p. 206.

146 'Mr. Goodwin and his partners were very upset to stop the business, and desired a long debate upon it: at last it was put to the question, whether the clause in it, which was this, "The assembly having religiously kept the order of the Houses of this kind," should be left out, as seeming to charge the Apologists with violating that order, and it was voted should be left out', ibid., p. 206.

147 Ibid., p. 206; Van Dixhoorn, *MPWA* (vol. 2), p. 598.

148 House of Lords Journal, *Journal of the House of Lords: volume 6: 1643* (1767–1830), pp. 465–466. Online version.

149 Ibid.

150 House of Lords Journal, *Journal of the House of Lords: volume 6: 1643* (1767–1830), pp. 465–466. Online version.

151 Van Dixhoorn, 'Politics and Religion in the Westminster Assembly and the "Grand Debate"', in R. Armstrong and T. O'hAnnrachain (eds), *Alternative Establishments in Early Modern Britain and Ireland: Catholic and Protestant* (Manchester: Manchester University Press, 2013), pp. 129–148.

152 House of Lords Journal, *Journal of the House of Lords: volume 6: 1643* (1767–1830), pp. 465–466. Online version.

153 Van Dixhoorn, *MPWA* (vol. 2), p. 604.

154 Lightfoot, *Journal*, p. 206; Gillespie, *Notes*, p. 39. 'House of Commons Journal, *Journal of the House of Commons: volume 3: 1643–1644* (1802), pp. 425–426. Online version. Note: Gillespie gets his date wrong, believing de la March to have come to the assembly on 13 March.

155 Van Dixhoorn, *MPWA* (vol. 2), p. 605.

156 House of Commons Journal, *Journal of the House of Commons: volume 3: 1643–1644* (1802), pp. 425–426. Online version.

157 Baillie, *Letters and Journals*, vol. 2, p. 184.

158 Ibid., vol 2, pp. 129ff.

159 Ibid., vol. 2, p. 179.

160 I am grateful to Joel Halcomb for pointing this out to me.

161 Baillie, *Letters and Journals*, vol. 2, p. 165.

162 L. Whitaker, *Diary of Proceedings in the House of Commons, from 8 Oct.. 1642 to 8 July, 1647: a full and detailed account by L[awrence]. Whitacre, M.P. for Okehampton* (British Library: Add. MSS, 31116), p. 246.

163 William Shaw knew of the D'Ewes entry recording Selden's speech and how it related to the Erastian controversy. Shaw, however, does not corroborate this with the Whitaker diary and fails to see the connection to the *Apologeticall Narration*. Robert Paul followed Shaw on this point. Shaw, *English Church*, vol. 1, 301; Paul, *The Assembly of the Lord*, p. 494.

164 House of Commons Journal, *Journal of the House of Commons: volume 3: 1643–1644* (1802), pp. 426–427. Online version.

165 S. D'ewes, *Diary of Sir Simond D'Ewes* (British Library: Harleian 166), f. 32a. I am grateful to Vivienne Larminie who confirmed that Selden did indeed give a speech on this day.

166 Whitaker, *Diary*, p. 246; see also, W. Yonge, *Journals of proceedings in the House of Commons, and of public events in England, from 19 Sept. 1642 to 10 Dec. 1645; kept by Walter Yonge, of Colyton, co. Devon, Barrister at Law, and member for Honiton in the Long Parliament* (British Library: Add. MSS, 18779), fol. 71.

167 Baillie, *Letters and Journals*, vol. 2, p. 129; Paul, *The Assembly of the Lord*, pp. 493–494.

168 McGee was expanding on a claim made by W.K Jordan. McGee, 'Francis Rous and "Scabby or Itchy Children": The Problem of Toleration in 1645', p. 420.

169 Ibid. p. 412; F. Rous, *The ancient bounds* (London, 1645), p. 57.

170 [Goodwin], *M. S. to A. S*, p. 19.

171 Goodwin, *M. S. to A. S.*, p. 8; According to *Mercurius Aquaticus*, Saye and Sele had tried and failed to get Goodwin into the assembly. This could be where Goodwin got his information. *Mercurius Aquaticus or The Water Poets Answer to All That Hath Or Shall Be Writ by Mercurius Britanicus. Issue 16* (Oxford, 1644), C2.

172 See Van Dixhoorn, *MPWA*, vol. 5, for transcriptions.

173 Baillie, *Letters and Journals*, vol. 2, p. 174.

174 Ibid., vol 2, pp. 174–175, 180.

175 Ibid., vol. 2, p. 175.

176 Ibid., vol. 2, p. 175.

177 Gillespie, *Notes*, p. 56.

178 James T. Dennison, Jr, *Reformed Confessions of the sixteenth and seventeenth Centuries in English Translation: 1523–1552* (Grand Rapids, MI: Reformed Heritage Books, 2008), vol. 1, pp. 325–326.

179 Gillespie, *Notes*, p. 56.

180 Baillie, *Letters and Journals*, vol. 2, p. 182.

181 Ibid., vol. 2, p. 182.

182 Bradley, 'Jacob and Esau', p. 204.

183 *Contra*, ibid., p. 127.

184 Allin & Shepard, *A Defence of the Answer*, p. 16.

185 Ibid., p. 16.

188 Ibid., p. 16.

187 Ibid., pp. 16, 23.

Chapter 5

━━━━◆━━━━

Transatlantic confusion

Philip Nye and Thomas Goodwin's publishing of Cotton's *Keyes of the Kingdom of Heaven*, along with their explanatory preface, was a brilliant political and polemical manoeuvre.[1] Reformed divines across the ecclesiological spectrum in England, Scotland and the continent regarded Cotton as one of the greatest puritan divines of their age. His influence at Westminster, as we shall see, was considerable; indeed he was arguably more influential in Old England than he was in colonial ecclesiological development. While the concepts espoused by Cotton were not new to the Apologists, the New England divine did provide Old England with a new scholastic framework for discussing church power.

This chapter will provide a broad summary of the unique congregational polity of the Apologists, using Cotton's *Keyes* as our starting point. We will then look at how Cotton's pamphlet fitted into wider pamphlet debates and how other independent divines rejected Cotton's understanding of the keys. This contextualisation will set the stage for the following chapter, where we will take a more in-depth look at the ecclesiastical keys through Rutherford's engagement with Cotton's polity and how the New England divine responded. We will also see why the revered continental divine Gisbertus Voetius embraced the *Keyes*. Looking at Rutherford and Voetius will enable us to see how the polity of the 'middle-way men' was understood by two reformed churches *outside* England, and thus situate the Apologists and John Cotton in a wider, continental stream of reformed orthodoxy. In chapter 8 we will discuss how the *Keyes* impacted the accommodation attempts of 1644. To date, no scholar has provided a thorough transatlantic analysis of Cotton's polity, and while this chapter is unable to fill that gap, it will nonetheless attempt to provide a basis for how Cotton viewed the church.[2]

In context, the *Keyes* represented the Apologists' final effort to circumnavigate hostile clerical English presbyterians and reach an accommodation with Rutherford and Gillespie. In terms of the debates in the Westminster assembly and its divines, Cotton's *Keyes* should take pride of place over the *Apologeticall Narration*. It was cited repeatedly and positively on the assembly floor by presbyterians – especially Gillespie – as a source of accommodation. Although the Apologists claimed they did not necessarily assent to every assertion, scriptural proof and terminology of the *Keyes*, they nonetheless claimed the 'substance' of the book represented their position.[3] The preface to the *Keyes* will show that Nye and Goodwin were highlighting and amplifying Cotton's understanding of the keys, not dissenting from it.

Many notable Independents on both sides of the Atlantic were frustrated by Cotton's presbyterian-sounding polity. Contemporary writers considered the polity in the *Keyes* to be representative of the Apologists' position, and readily acknowledged it to be distinct from other forms of independency.[4] The Apologists had studiously avoided breaking assembly protocol to publish their own ecclesiological writings, but there was no injunction against publishing someone else's work. The timing of the pamphlet served to soften the blow of Thomas Edwards's *Antapologia* and to diffuse Baillie's ongoing attempts to discredit the Apologists through the writings of continental divines. Cotton's pamphlet exposed fundamental differences between English presbyterians and Scottish presbyterians while simultaneously highlighting similarities between the Scots and the Apologists. In this chapter we will first look at the polemical context of Cotton's *Keyes* and then analyse its ecclesiology.

COTTON AND THE APOLOGISTS

The publication of Cotton's *Keyes of the Kingdom of Heaven* by Goodwin and Nye dismantles two popular historiographical myths. First, through statements in the preface, it demonstrates that Cotton was not the influential catalyst for the Apologists' views on church government, and second, it further supports our argument that the *Apologeticall Narration* was not the most important document produced by the assembly's congregationalists. Baillie, citing Thomas Edwards's collection of scurrilous anecdotes, claimed that Cotton was 'the mis-leader of Master Goodwin and others'.[5] This Cottonian conversion, so Baillie alleged, began while Cotton was hiding in London in anticipation of his New England exile. 'Before his departure from England, by conferences in London, he had brought off Master Davenport and Master Goodwin, from some of the English ceremonies.' And although none of them had the 'least degree of Separation' at the time, 'yet so soon as he [Cotton] did taste the New-English air, he fell into so passionate an affection' of the separation he once 'opposed'.[6] Baillie reported that Cotton set about drawing his 'convert, Master Goodwin, a most fine and dainty Spirit ... by his Letters from New-England, to follow him unto this step also of his progresse'.[7] Michael

Lawrence has already demonstrated conclusively that Goodwin's 'conversion' towards anti-ceremonial congregationalism did not begin with his 1634 meeting with Cotton, nor indeed, did Goodwin demonstrate any particular ecclesiological allegiance to Cotton in the 1630s. Goodwin's 'conversion' to congregational polity was actually a gradual shift in his thinking over time as he reflected on the book of Revelation.[8]

Baillie, writing a year after the *Keyes* was published, was obliquely refuting an important point made by Goodwin and Nye in their preface to Cotton's pamphlet. Goodwin and Nye stated, 'when we first read this of this [*sic*] learned Author ... we confesse we were filled with wonderment at that Divine hand, that had thus led the judgments ... of our Brethren there, and our selves ... here'.[9] These similar 'judgments' were developed 'without the least mutuall interchange or intimation of thought or notions in these particulars'.[10] Therefore, according to Goodwin and Nye, Cotton's ideas were not 'new unto our thoughts', and this should not be a surprise to 'many of our friends', some of whom 'are of a differing opinion, having knowne our private judgments long, as likewise our owne Notes and transcripts written long agoe, can testifie; besides many publike professions since as occasion hath beene offered'.[11]

As this book has demonstrated, the polity of the Apologists had not been hidden, particularly since the Calamy meetings began in 1640/41. Cotton refuted Baillie's claim that he had misled the Apologists in his *Way of the congregational churches cleared*. Cotton stated, 'Is it a misleading to lead men away from the English Ceremonies? Were they Misleaders, who led the Honorable Houses of Parliament to fall off from the Ceremonies?' The thrust of the 1634 conference between Cotton, Davenport and Goodwin was to discuss the already hot topic of 'matters indifferent' and whether or not 'Bishops bee appointed to rule a Diocese, or a particular Congregation'. Cotton argued that if one would agree to the latter, then it infers 'an unavoydable Separation from under the shadow of Diocesan-Episcopall-Government'.[12] Other than that, Cotton flatly denied he had any part in leading Goodwin towards the congregational way, and in this respect Cotton echoed Goodwin and Nye's sentiment in the preface to the *Keyes*. Cotton stated, 'I doe not remember that ever I wrote [to Goodwin] from New-England about our way.'[13]

There were some differences in the way the Apologists and Cotton understood the synod that took place in Jerusalem recorded in Acts 15, but the practical results of their readings were the same.[14] The polity in Cotton's *Keyes* was taken as representative of the Apologists' position by divines inside and outside the assembly. Even the London presbyterian ministers, some of the Apologists' harshest ecclesiological critics, were careful to distinguish between the 'middle-way men' as represented by Cotton's *Keyes* and 'independents' like Nathaniel Holmes.[15]

For Nye and Goodwin in 1644, 'The greatest commotions in Kingdomes have for the most part been raised and maintained for and about Power, and Liberties, of the Rulers and the Ruled, together with the due bounds and limits of either.'[16] The 'controversie' that the Apologists considered the 'lot of these present times' was, 'who should be the first adequate, and compleat subject of that Church-power, which Christ hath left on earth'.[17] The Apologists acknowledged that in response to the power placed in bishops, the clergy of each church became jealous to guard their own rights. It was only a matter of time before the people 'begun to plead and sue for a portion' of that power. Yet 'it was [an] unhappiness' that those who had pleaded for a people's share in the power of the church 'err[ed] on the other extreame ... by laying the plea and claime on their behalfe unto the whole power', holding that elders 'did but exercise that power for them, which was properly theirs'.[18] The divines who held this position, including Robert Parker, John Paget and John Robinson – although each coming to different practical conclusions – believed Christ had placed the power of the keys 'radically and organically ... in the people onely'. On this point, the congregationalists set the stage for the unique polity Cotton was espousing and that they believed.

'THE RIGHT DISPOSAL OF THE POWER THEREIN': THE THEOLOGY OF THE *KEYES*

For Nye and Goodwin 'the substance' of Cotton's *Keyes* was, 'That very Middle-way (which in our Apologie we did in the generall intimate and intend) between that which is called Brownisme, and the Presbyteriall-government, as it is practised'.[19] That 'middle-way' was between the former, who 'put the chiefe (if not whole) of the rule and government unto the hands of the people, and drowns the Elders votes (who are but a few) in the major part of theirs', and the latter, who take 'the chiefe and principall parts of that rule (which we conceive is the due of each Congregation, the Elders and Brethren) into this Jurisdiction of a common Presbyterie of severall Congregations'.[20] This 'Presbyteriall-government' does 'thereby ... swallow up, not onely the interests of the people, but even the votes of the Elders of that Congregation concerned'.[21] The two Apologists, therefore, were concerned about the rights of the believers in the church, but were equally concerned about the prerogatives of the elders in that congregation, whom they argued have unique rights within the context of the particular church. In their minds, Cotton was dealing with a topic the assembly, limited by their protocols and procedures, never adequately addressed. Cotton articulated that 'the right disposall of the power' of church polity may 'lie in a due and proportioned allotment and dispersion (though not in the same measure and degree) into divers hands'.[22] This dispersion of power was 'according unto the severall concernments and interests that each rank in his Church may have', rather 'than in an intire and sole trust committed to any one man'.[23]

It seems that Goodwin and Nye were speaking directly to Rutherford in their preface. In April, Rutherford had complained that the independent churches had failed to distinguish between governors and the governed in the church, and did not understand that there were distinct, non-shared powers between the 'judge' (elders) and the 'jury'.[24] The Apologists, writing about a month after Rutherford published his *Due Right*, used both of these terms in the preface to the *Keyes* to make the exact same point Rutherford had made.

The first chapter of Cotton's *Keyes* discussed Matthew 16:19 and defined the keys of the kingdom. Cotton began with a summary statement,

> the keys of the kingdom are the Ordinances which Christ hath instituted to be administered in his Church; as the preaching of the Word (which is the opening and applying of it) also the administring of the Seals and Censures: For by the opening and applying of these, both the gates of the Church here and of heaven hereafter, are opened or shut to sons of men.[25]

The sovereign power of the keys belonged to Christ alone, who was 'said to have the Key of David, to open, and no man to shut: to shut, and no man to open'.[26] The keys were metaphorical objects for 'the power of opening and shutting, as they do thereby binde and loose, retain and remit; in opening, they loose, and remit; in shutting they bind, and retain'. The subjects to be 'bound and loosed' were both the sin and the person committing those sins. This binding and loosing the sin of the sinner was achieved 'partly in the conscience of the sinner, and partly in his outward estate in the Church' which was expressed as *in foro interiori*, or *in foro exteriori*. When a sinner's conscience was bound by a particular sin, then the church moved to either censure or excommunicate, based on the 'quality and desert of his offence'.[27] But when that sinner repented, his conscience was loosed and the 'gates of holy communion' were reopened.

These keys were given to Peter. As with the Apologists' arguments about Matthew 16:19, Cotton noted that Peter was 'considered not onely as an Apostle, but an Elder also, yea, and a Believer too, professing his faith, all may well stand together'.[28] Cotton wanted to show that 'there is a different power given to all these, to an Apostle, to an Elder, to a Believer, and Peter was all these'. He 'received all the power which was given by Christ to any of these, or to all these together'.[29] As Goodwin had noted both in his writings and in the assembly, this first mention of church power was 'indefinite' and inclusive of all sorts of power and subjects of that power.[30] Cotton later used the same language Goodwin used, stating, 'When Christ Promised the keyes to Peter, though he spake Indefinitely, keyes, yet he meaneth universally all the keyes of the kingdom of Heaven.'[31] Cotton also cited Augustine, who interpreted Matthew

16:19 to mean that Peter received the keys 'in the name of the church', for the church encompassed all those things. According to John 20:21, 23, Christ gave the power to bind and loose specifically to the Apostles.[32] Cotton maintained that the Apostles also receive an Apostolic power in Matthew 16:19, and that the Apostles were forerunners of the elders. In that sense his arguments would have agreed with Seaman's proposition in October 1643.[33] Yet, as the Apologists had argued, Matthew 16:19 could not be *limited* to that proposition. Therefore, elders had a unique share in the keys, and the body of the church also had a power of the keys. Yet there is an important distinction here. Cotton considered the body to be a 'Fraternitie with the Presbytery'.[34]

Therefore, the whole power of the keys is given to the whole church, rightly constituted with elders and believers taken together. At this stage, Cotton connected Matthew 16:19 to Matthew 18:17, 18. As Goodwin noted, Christ 'having spoken this indefinitely in Matthew 16. 18, 19, here in Matthew 18. 15, 16 he particularly determines the Seat, and Subject of this Ecclesiastical power'.[35] In the procedure of rebuking a sinner through confrontation, he was to be confronted first privately and secondly with witnesses, and finally the church was to be told about the offence.

> And if he shall neglect to hear them, tell it unto the church: but if he neglect to hear the church, let him be unto thee as an heathen man and a publican. Verily I say unto you, Whatsoever ye shall bind on earth shall be bound in heaven: and whatsoever ye shall loose on earth shall be loosed in heaven.

Cotton believed the connections to Matthew 16:19, particularly as they related to the binding and loosing, were obvious. Since the power to bind and loose was given to Peter as he represented the whole church, in all its constituent parts, so the church in Matthew 18:17, 18 encompassed both elders and the congregation. The import was that this seat of all church power was not the body or elders, but believers and elders as together they made up a particular church.[36] A church rightly ordered, with elders and a company of Christians, was the 'Subject and Seat of this Grand Charter of the keys'.[37] Goodwin argued that the church could not be the first seat of all church government, or recipient of all the keys, until it consisted of elders and saints together.[38]

Goodwin and Nye were careful to highlight their agreement with Cotton in the ways that it differentiated them from the 'independents'. Cotton noted that the keys had typically been 'distributed' into two categories, the 'Key of Knowledge' and the 'Key of Power'. The 'Key of Power' was then subdivided into the 'Key of Order' and the 'Key of Jurisdiction'. This distribution within the 'Key of Power' was the heart of church government and, as Cotton noted, 'current both amongst Protestants and Papists'.[39] Cotton seems to have been silently quoting John Hart from his well known debate with John Rainolds, where Hart stated, 'To be short, *the keyes* of the church may be divided, into *the keye of knowledge*, and *the key of power* ... *The key of power*, is either of order, or jurisiction.'[40] Cotton himself had also used this distinction in his earlier sermons. In his sermons on Canticles, preached in the late 1620s and published in 1642, he said that the keys of the kingdom of heaven were two, 'one of knowledge ... the other Jurisdiction', and even back then he believed that both were given to Peter in Matthew 16:19.[41]

Some presbyterians disagreed with the subdivision of the key of power. The English presbyterian John Ball had argued that power and jurisdiction could not be separated and both of these, therefore, were subsumed under the key of power.[42] In other words, for Ball, there could be no power of the keys where there was no ability to exercise the power of the keys. The presbyterian ministers of London made the same refutation when they stated that neither 'the Power of Order' nor the 'Power of Jurisdiction' could be given to the 'multitude of the faithful by the Scriptures ... for, the whole multitude and every one therein, neither can, nor ought to intermeddle with any branches of that power'.[43] For many English presbyterians, power (whether order or jurisdiction) in the 'whole body' would mean that the people would have a role in preaching, administration of the sacraments, ordination and excommunication. As the presbyterian divine Daniel Cawdrey complained, 'A key in all mens judgment, that ever writ of the power of the Church, carries in the notion of it, a power and authority, properly called, power in government.'[44] There could be no power without jurisdiction. And therefore, the 'Key of Power', understood as connoting order and jurisdiction, must reside in the elders alone. The people could not have any share of the power, because that would mean they would need to have the authority to exercise that power.

Both Cotton and the Apologists agreed the people did not share in the elders' powers, but they disagreed that this meant the people had no power at all. The defect in the standard distribution of the 'Key of Knowledge' and the 'Key of Power' was effectively twofold: the key of knowledge is left without any power, and conversely all *church* power (i.e. order and jurisdiction) resided exclusively in the elders of the church.[45] Therefore, Cotton re-organised the way the keys were defined and distributed.

In his letter to the Colossians, Paul extolled the church: 'For although I be absent in the flesh, yet am I with you in the spirit, joying and beholding your order, and the steadfastness of your faith in Christ.'[46] Paul praised the church for their 'order' and 'faith'. Therefore, Cotton saw two keys, the key of knowledge (which Cotton also called the key of faith) and the key of order.[47]

As we approach these distinctions, we should note that although Cotton based his distinctions on scriptural proofs, he nonetheless conceded that there would be those who 'out of love to Antiquitie' would prefer to use the standard 'distribution of the keyes'.[48] Cotton admitted, 'we would not stick upon the words rightly explained', but he nonetheless hoped his readers would apply these conceptual distinctions if not the verbal distinctions.[49]

Key 1: The key of knowledge

The first key opened the door to a saving knowledge of Jesus Christ. Cotton equated knowledge with faith by citing Christ's words in Luke's Gospel, 'Woe unto you, lawyers! for ye have taken away the key of knowledge.'[50] Christ claimed that the religious leaders were denying their followers access to the kingdom of heaven by taking away the 'key of knowledge'. Such knowledge, Cotton stated, 'whereby a man hath power to enter into heaven, is only Faith, which is often therefore called Knowledge'.[51] The key of faith belonged to every believer, 'by grace through faith', and with it the believer 'entereth into the kingdom of heaven, both here and hereafter'.[52] Therefore the proper subject of the key of knowledge was all the faithful, whether or not they belonged in the church. In this sense, the key of knowledge gave access to the mystical church. But the mystical church was only one subject of one part of the keys; the key of knowledge was not properly an ecclesiastical key until believers and elders were united in a church. The mystical church was not the recipient of all the keys, as some English presbyterians would have it.[53] As Goodwin noted, 'not any company of Christians, but such as embodied together into, and setled Order of a Church, are the Subject and Seat of this Grand Charter of the keys, or the Ecclesiastical power'.[54] Once in the church context, the key of knowledge/faith functioned properly as a means of encouragement, charity, and discipline, where, according to Matthew 18, the believer may not admonish without help from the elders.[55]

Key 2: The key of order

The key of order addressed the way people act within the church. This second key 'is the power whereby every member of the church, walketh orderly himself, according to his place in the Church'.[56] A rightly ordered church existed when each person knew his or her role and stayed within the confines of that role. This key of order was given to all members of the church, whether elders or brethren. Members of the church had a power to walk orderly according to their calling in that church. Because every member had a unique role within the church Cotton could introduce his next, perhaps most significant, distinction. Within the key of order there were two keys, 'a key of power, or interest: and the key of authority and rule'. Cotton called the former key the key of liberty, and this key belonged to the people in the church context. The key of authority (also called rule) belonged to the elders alone. They were separate and distinct keys, yet related insofar as they were both subsumed under the 'Key of Order'.

As Goodwin and Nye stated, 'we conceive the Elders and Brethren in each Congregation, as they are usually in the New Testament thus mentioned distinctly apart', who meet in one assembly and yet 'have two distinct intersts'.[57] Through the key of order the elders had authority and the people their distinct share of power. A properly ordered church meant the people were the first subject of church liberty and the elders were the first subject of church authority, 'and both of them together are the first subject of all church-power needfull to be exercised within themselves, whether in the election and ordination of officers, or in the censure of offenders in their own body'.[58] Goodwin and Nye compared this power structure to a town corporation, in which the common council and the company of aldermen possessed distinct roles, where the consent of both was needed. Therefore, although the power of the elders was distinct, a church act was incomplete without the consent and concurrence of both parties.[59]

First key of order: the key of authority
Thus, Cotton proceeded to define the various roles encompassed within the 'Key of Order'. The first key, the key of authority, addressed the power of the elders. Not only was there a distinction between the two parties (elders and people) and the power given to them, but the 'multitude' was, 'by the command of Christ, to be subject and obedient' to the elders, and the elders' authority should 'guide them in their consent'.[60] In this regard, the two Apologists were emphasising, and indeed amplifying, the unique power the elders had over the congregation. In the elders resided the 'ultimate, formall Ministeriall act of binding and loosing', and this authority stood in contrast to the power in the brethren 'which must yet concurre with theirs' because they 'have a greater and neerer interest and concernment in those affaires, over which these [elders] ... are set as Rulers'.[61]

Goodwin and Nye compared this power to the authority of a parent over their 'virgin daughter' in a matter of marriage. The daughter had a power, insofar as she must agree to the marriage in order to the make the marriage valid. Yet the parents had a power, indeed duty, to guide her in that choice, and the daughter had a duty to obey them and should submit to their decision. The daughter's power 'doth arise to the notion of an extrinsicall authority; whereas that power which is in her, is but simply the power of her own act, in which her own concernment doth interest her free by an intrinsicall right'.[62] This organisation would be similar to an aristrocracy tempered by a democracy. The people have a share in the government, having voted and therefore implicitly consented to laws, and yet the Nobles have been set over them, those Nobles having 'a formall sanction ... [of] rule and authority'.[63]

This distinction is vitally important to understanding the polity of the Apologists. They argued that Christ gave both the authority to the elders and an interest and power to the brethren. The power was not shared, nor could either party deprive the other of their power. Against those who believed all church power resided primarily in the brethren of the church, the Apologists argued that if that were the case, 'all that is said in the New Testament about [the elders'] rule, and of the peoples Obedience to them' would be nothing more than 'metaphors, and ... [would] hold no proportion with any substantial reality of Rule and Government'.[64] These commands towards obedience to elders could be found in the oft-cited passages of 1 Timothy 5:17 and Hebrews 13:7, 17.[65] In Paul's letter to Timothy he reminds him that there is unique authority in him as a presbyter, and in the epistle to the Hebrews the reader is told to obey and submit to those who rule over them. In his letter to Titus, Paul says that he is to 'speak, rebuke, and exhort, with all authority'.[66] Cotton enumerated various examples where the elders exhibit their unique authority, which include calling the church together, dismissing the church, examining officers and members before being brought into the church, and rebuking, charging, and directing the spiritual lives of the members. The elders alone had the power to ordain new elders, although the church elected them.

Protecting the elders' authority from mob rule was something common to the polity of the Apologists and the presbyterians. The congregation had the power to choose its officers, yet both the office and the power in that office was committed directly to the elders, 'immediately from Christ'. Against the separatists, no 'authority' existed in the members that could be communicated to the elders. Because the people were weak and unskilful in comparison to the elders whom Christ had gifted, Christ had placed not only a 'directing' power but also a 'binding' power in the elders. In that way, the people could do nothing without the elders, and nothing could be 'esteemed validly done unlesse done by them'.[67] The people should therefore submit to their elders because the elders' power from Christ is an ordinance of Christ.[68] Again, this dynamic was a crucial distinction from the position of 'independents'.[69] This 'key of authority', although distinct from the power in the members and residing in the elders alone, only existed in the context of a particular church and in connection with its members. This was very similar to the arguments put forth by John Ball when he challenged the 'independency' of the New England churches. Ball claimed that 'the power and authoritie whereunto a Minister is elected, is not in the people that elect him, but from Christ the King ... who out of power doth conferre that office upon him'.[70] Cotton could agree with Ball against many 'indendendents' that church authority was only in the elders, but for Cotton that did not necessarily mean that people had no church power at all.

Second key of order: the key of liberty
The key of liberty was the second key subsumed under the 'key of order'. It was here that the Cotton tried to account for the rights of the saints in the church. A particular church was composed of both elders and saints. Thomas Goodwin stated that the elders did not receive 'power from the People as Officers, yet a

virtual power, concurrence and assistance ... as such from the presence of the Saints'.[71] The brethren of the church, as distinct from the elders, were the subject of what Cotton called the 'key of liberty'. In Paul's letter to the Galatians, he tells them, 'Brethren, you have been called to liberty.'[72] This 'liberty', although by no means the same power as that of the elders, was a power invested in the people of the church to prevent 'the tyrannie, and oligarchy, and exorbitancy of the Elders'.[73] Cotton quoted the continental reformer Martin Bucer, who said, '*Potestas penes omnen [sic] Ecclesiam est; Authoritas ministerii penes Presbyteros & Episcopos.*'[74] And thus, Cotton claimed the people had a power of 'libertie and privilege' that was distinct from the key of authority.

The best example of how to understand the interplay between the elders' key of authority and the brethren's key of liberty is through Cotton and the Apologists' understanding of Matthew 18:17–18, and how it related to excommunication.[75] Christ commanded the offended Christian to attempt repentance and reconciliation privately. If that failed, then they were commanded to 'tell the church'. For these congregational divines, that could not mean 'tell the elders' alone, much less 'tell a presbytery of gathered elders from various churches'. Of course, if Matthew 16:19 refers to the Apostles and the elders after them as the recipients of the keys, it is not a large exegetical step to insist that 'church' in Matthew 18 could mean elders alone.

However, Goodwin claimed that even if the presbyterians could prove that 'church' meant elders – a premise Goodwin denied – it still meant elders *within* a particular church.[76] Goodwin argued that the presbyterians who believed 'church' referred to elders in a particular congregation were those who considered the particular church to be '*ecclesia prima*'. They believed Matthew 18 referred to elders in a particular congregation because the initial process of discipline in Matthew 18:15–17 involved one 'brother' in a particular church approaching another 'brother' and furthermore assumed that the members were already involved in the process of discipline.[77] Cotton argued that the believers had 'power ... and privilege to expostulate with their Brethren, in the case of private scandals, according to the rule, Mat. 18.15, 16'. But in the case of a 'public scandall' the whole church had the 'power and priviledge to joyn with the Elders in inquiring, hearing, judging, of publick scandals' and so bound [censured] the offenders and loosed [forgave] them.[78] He cited the punishing of the incestuous adulterer in Corinth, where Paul tells the church, who Cotton presumed had gathered together with the elders, 'to deliver the incestuous person over to Satan'.[79]

Cotton carefully pointed out that the people's role in judging the accused was 'not an act of authority'. He cited the English courts as an example. 'The Jury, by their verdict, as well as the Judge by his sentence, doe both of them judge the same malefactor.' The jury's 'verdict is but an act of their popular liberty: In the Judge it is an act of his judiciall authority'.[80] For practical purposes the elders would have thoroughly examined the case beforehand in order 'to prepare ... [and] ripen it for the Churches cognizance'.[81] Therefore, the church's power to bind and loose was only in their right to consent, concur, and question what the elders had done in private. The judge and the jury cannot act independently of each other, and yet the state charged them to fulfill distinct functions. In this regard, the elders' power was unique, yet only actuated in the context of the particular church. Thomas Goodwin gave this example:

> Tho' the Elders be as the Loadstone; yet as to the Virtue and Efficacy of the Loadstone, depends upon its being set in Steel, so the virtual Blessing of the Elders' Actions in matters Jurisdiction (which are the highest Acts of Church government) depends upon their being in the midst of the Saints, that concur with them.[82]

The elders' power could not be carried away from the 'seat' in the church. This would mean, necessarily, they could not carry their unique power away from the church to a synod of multiple presbyteries.

Therefore, in terms of excommunication, the church should follow the lead of the elders, but the elder did not have the power to ignore legitimate concerns postulated by the congregation that may 'gainsay' the elders' decision. Conversely, the elders' authority should not be 'judged vain and fruitlesse and effectuall [sic], to draw men to obedience'.[83] The people in the church, according to Cotton, did not have the final say in excommunication, or censure, because 'he is not thereby censured till upon the sentence of the Presbytery'.[84] Edmund Calamy would cite Cotton's *Keyes* positively on the assembly floor regarding this very point. The people, Calamy argued from Cotton, do not have the *suffragia decissiva* (deciding vote).[85]

The elders, therefore, could not be called a church, and a church could not be called elders, but taken together they were the church made up the whole first subject of church power. The two had distinct roles that were ordained by Christ and therefore meant to be obeyed. Cotton is very clear that the scriptures prohibited the abuse of the people's liberty. The sotieriological call to freedom in the Gospel was, for Cotton, analogous to the freedom *to obey* that a member has in the context of a particular church.[86]

THE *KEYES* IN CONTEXT: TRANSATLANTIC CONFUSION AND THE PAMPHLET DEBATES

Before assessing the international reception of Cotton's *Keyes*, we first need to pause and assess how the publication of the *Keyes* reflected the climate inside and outside the assembly of divines and how it has been incorrectly understood in relation to Cotton's others publications. At some point after his arrival in New England and before 'the Suppressing of Bishops in England' Cotton began work on what would become known as *The Way of the Churches of Christ in New-England*. According to Cotton, this pamphlet should never have been printed. He had been asked by various brethren in New England to 'Draw up an Historicall Narration of our Church-way together with some familiar grounds of the same'.[87] Evidently Cotton's fellow divines-in-exile did not entirely agree with the book and therefore the project was scuttled.[88] It seems that a copy of the manuscript was picked up, without Cotton's permission, and taken to England where it took on a life of its own.[89] The manuscript became well known in England, for it was cited often.[90] Cawdrey stated that the manuscript 'went up and down in the dark'.[91] This was not the first time this had happened to Cotton. In 1637 he wrote to his friend John Dodd about a catechism going around England in his name, asking Dodd, 'I pray you ... to beare witnesse from me I doe not owne it, as having never seene it: although may be, sundry things in it, were delivered by me, which I doe acknowledge.'[92] This is not surprising since Cotton was somewhat of a celebrity in England, and even for those who may have disagreed with his polity he was nonetheless considered a spiritual grandfather by many English divines.[93]

For our purposes, we should note that Cotton's manuscript version of *The Way of the Churches of Christ* was a primary target in Rutherford's *The Due Right of Presbyteries*, printed in April 1644. Very much in keeping with Rutherford's *A Peaceable Plea*, *Due Right* was a gentle, yet direct, confutation of Independency. Rutherford was careful to say, 'I heartily desire not to appeare as an adversary to the holy, reverend, and learned brethren who are sufferers for the truth', for we are 'Sonnes of one father ... [and therefore] to dispute is not to contend.'[94] Unlike many polemical pamphlets that sweeten the preface, only to rage in the content, Rutherford maintained his respect throughout the work. This kindness does not diminish the fact that he had very real problems with independency, and more importantly, the apparent 'independency' being espoused by Cotton's *Way of the Churches of Christ*.

Rutherford's first, and primary, concern with Cotton's manuscript was that too much power (i.e. the keys) had been given to the believers of the church at the expense of the elders. This was precisely why Cotton set about writing the *Keyes* in order to clarify his beliefs. It also explains why Goodwin and Nye were responsible for bringing Cotton's *Keyes* to print. Our goal here is to map out how Cotton's *Way of the Churches of Christ* influenced the subsequent publication of his *Keyes*. Notably, Rutherford never mentioned the *Apologeticall Narration* in his *Due Right*. This omission would be odd if, as the current historiography argues, the *Narration* initiated a full-scale war between presbyterians and 'independents'. Yet, when the assembly's most able presbyterian polemicist published his massive tome against independency only three months after the *Narration* was published, he made no mention of it. Presumably Rutherford saw a difference between the polity of the Apologists and the polity being espoused in Cotton's *Way of the Churches of Christ*.

The Keyes should be regarded as Cotton's most cogent and well thought-out articulation of his congregationalism. It should not, however, be seen as 'the most complete' statement on New England congregationalism.[95] There were very important differences between what Cotton espoused and what many of his New England brethren believed, including, for example, Thomas Hooker. We are not sure whether Cotton knew the extent to which his *Way of the Churches of Christ* had been circulated. Given the time and distance between New England and England, he may not have known when he published the *Keyes* that Rutherford had been preparing a document in response to a manuscript he had written almost ten years earlier.[96] There was further confusion when Cotton wrote an actual response to Rutherford's *Due Right*, for the general theme of Cotton's rejoinder was that Rutherford had interpreted the manuscript of Cotton's *Way of the Churches of Christ* to have given more power to the believers in a church than Cotton had intended. Cotton claimed that Rutherford's concerns would have been ameliorated had he had Cotton's *Keyes*.[97]

By the time Cotton responded to Rutherford, the Scottish divine, in reaction to Cotton's *Keyes*, had desisted from attacking Cotton's polity. Indeed, by 1646, Rutherford was citing Cotton's *Keyes* as an authority in matters of the unique powers of the elder and the role of the magistrate in relation to the church.[98] However, the presbyterian polemicist Cawdrey delighted in exposing the perceived inconsistencies between Cotton's *Way of the Churches of Christ* and the *Keyes of the Kingdom* and how Cotton's polity was at variance with other independent writings such as Thomas Hooker's *Survey*.[99] Rutherford never accused Cotton of being inconsistent, and he readily recognised that Cotton and Hooker had different views of church power.[100]

In his first response to Cawdrey, Cotton made it clear that he did not perceive himself to be inconsistent, although he perhaps could have been clearer. Nonetheless, Cotton continued, 'it were no just matter of calumny if in some latter Tractate I should retract, or express more commodiously, what I wrote in a former less safely'.[101] Furthermore, 'Augustine (as much above me, as the Moon to a little star) lost no whit of his Reputation in the Church, by writing two whole Books of Retractions of his own Opinions and Expressions.'[102] However, even with such an admission, Cotton did not waste much time attempting to dismantle Cawdrey's accusations. John Owen would take on this role after Cotton had died.[103] In any event, given Rutherford's positive reaction to Cotton's *Keyes*, these perceived inconstancies were more of a concern to a man like Cawdrey than they were to Rutherford.

The background to this dispute has led to confusion in the historiography. The independent divine Nathaniel Holmes used Cotton to fan flames of discord, much to his own benefit. Scholars have assumed that Cotton and Nathaniel Holmes were working collusively in 1644 and 1645.[104] This would seem to be an accurate conclusion given that Holmes is the one who brought Cotton's *Way of the Churches of Christ* to publication. However, we learn from Cotton – and indeed from Holmes – that *The Way of the Churches of Christ* was published against Cotton's will.

As we noted in chapter 4, the *Apologeticall Narration* did not result in an ecclesiastical war amongst assembly divines. The *Narration*, however, was used by some peripheral figures to flame a pamphlet war. As previously stated, Holmes also used the Scottish commissioners' *Reformation of Church-Government in Scotland Cleared* for the same ends. Holmes, writing anonymously, wove the two pamphlets together in order to create the spectre of conflict within the assembly between the Scots and the congregational divines.[105] This document, entitled the *Coole Conference*, was arranged in such a way as to portray the Apologists as being the victims of the intractable and inflexible Scottish commissioners. Insofar as historians have placed undue emphasis on the pamphlet warfare as representative of the debates inside the assembly, the *Coole Conference* has only served to reinforce this storyline. The assembly, however, was not impressed. Someone delivered Holmes's *Coole Conference* to the assembly in an uncompleted form, and the divines quickly moved to distance themselves from the images of disorder and conflict portrayed by Holmes. They were wise to do so, for the *Coole Conference* had started a fire that would burn all through the pamphlets of Alexander Forbes, Adam Steuart, and John Goodwin, and most conspicuously, through Thomas Edwards's *Antapologia*. This was only the beginning of Holmes's mischief.

For men like Rutherford, clarity had been established with the publication of the *Keyes*. For Holmes, Cotton's *Keyes* served to discredit his own position. Therefore, quite against the desire of Cotton, and probably against the wish of the Apologists, Holmes published *The Way of the Churches of Christ* after Cotton's *Keyes* was published. Cotton's errant manuscript, written in the previous decade, was now in the public domain; it was published a year after Cotton's *Keyes*, and it opened Cotton to the accusations of logical inconsistency. Whereas Cotton's *Keyes* had served to highlight the similarities with the Scottish presbyterians, Holmes's intervention empowered men like Cawdrey and other English presbyterians desperate to lump all 'independents' into one ecclesiological category and to show as much clear water between the Apologists and the presbyterians as possible.

INTERNECINE DISPUTES: HOOKER, HOLMES AND 'ZEAL FOR THE FRATERNITY'

Cotton recalled the situation in this way: 'sundry yeares after the Treatise of the *way* had been finished, and carried to England, and (as I hoped) suppressed ... It seemeth some Brother there ... got a Copy of it', and 'He caused his

Copy of the *Way* ... to be Published in Print'.[106] That brother was Holmes and, according to Cotton, he was 'zealous of the Authority of the Fraternity, and perceiving that their Authority was not so fully Acknowledged in the *Keyes* as in the *Way*'. In other words, Holmes was worried that Cotton had not given the full power of the keys to the believers of the church. Cawdrey took advantage of this very real discrepancy between *The Way of the Churches of Christ* and Cotton's *Keyes*.[107] The difference highlights Holmes's reason for printing Cotton's manuscript *after* the *Keyes* was published. Holmes's version of Cotton's *Way* stated that the 'church hath the lawfull Authoritie to proceed to ... censure' all their 'Officers' should they commit an unlawful crime or teach heretical doctrine. Whereas, in the introduction to the *Keyes*, Goodwin and Nye stated that the people cannot 'proceed to any publique censures, without they have Elders over them'.[108] Cotton, in the *Keyes*, wrote, 'Excommunication is one of the highest acts of Rule in the Church, and therefore cannot be performed but by some Rulers.'[109]

In other words, Holmes wanted to represent Cotton to have said that the people hold all church power, even in a situation *without* elders. Cotton admitted that his *Way* was 'imperfect' and that 'It troubled me not a little, as knowing, That the Discrepant Expressions in the one, and in the other, might trouble friends, and give Advantage to Adversaries.'[110] Heightening Cotton's anxiety was the fact that there were multiple, and seemingly different versions of his manuscript travelling around England. Holmes admitted as much and asked for Cotton's pardon when he wrote his preface to *The Way* in 1645, saying, 'wee had not the fairest Copie, nor knew wee, till the Book was neer done, that there was a better to be had, nor to this day yet ever saw it'.[111] According to Cotton's grandson, Cotton Mather, whereas the published version of Cotton's *Way of the Churches of Christ* 'may have in it a little more of the Morellian tang,' those words were 'none of Mr. Cotton's'. Indeed, Mather claimed to have an unpublished version copy of Cotton's *Keyes* where Cotton was even more assertive against the 'Brownistical arguments', and here Cotton maintained that 'in the government of the church, authority is peculiar to the elders only'.[112] Apparently, even the presbyterian emphasis in Cotton's *Keyes* was toned down before it was published!

It was not only Holmes who worried that Cotton sounded too presbyterian in his *Keyes*. The great New England divine, Thomas Hooker, was equally frustrated. When Cotton had finished his *Keyes* Hooker came 'downe from Connectiquol, to consult with the Elders here about his Book'. Hooker's 'book' was his famous *The Survey and Summe of Church Discipline*.[113] When Cawdrey wrote his second attack on Cotton, he made a three-column chart where he attempted to expose the discrepancies between *the Way*, the *Keyes*, and Hooker's *Church Discipline*.[114] Cotton acknowledged the discrepancy between his *Keyes* and Hooker's *Discipline*, but the reasons for the discrepancy are striking and important. When Hooker came to visit Cotton in Connecticut, he told Cotton that he disagreed with his *Keyes*. Hooker, as Cotton says, 'pleaded seriously for the Placing of all Church power, primitively, in the Body of the Church'.[115]

Hooker was complaining about a point of difference that made Cotton's, and the Apologists', understanding of the keys unique from that of other 'independents', who believed that the 'primum subjectum' of the keys was solely in the believers in the church. Hooker felt, as did Holmes, that Cotton's *Way of the Churches of Christ* had left the door open to that understanding, whereas the *Keyes* had closed the door. Cotton said that Hooker did not prevail with him 'to lter [sic] the Placing of the First Subject of the Power of the Keyes, from what I had delivered in the Treatise of the *Keyes*'.[116] Cotton also noted that his 'Brother Hooker' dissented from him in print, after the *Keyes* had been published. 'It is true that [Hooker] taketh the Church of Covenanted Believers to be the first Subject of the power of the keyes.' If by that Hooker 'meane[s] that they are the first Subject of all Church-Power properly' then Cotton could not consent with him.[117]

Cotton acknowledged that some sided with *The Way of the Churches of Christ*, and that others sided with the *Keyes*, and therefore he 'suffered both to stand as they did, especially seeing I could not help it, the Book of the *Way* being published without my Consent' and 'both the *Way* and the *Keyes* being disperst into many hands (past my Revoking) and Refuted by some'.[118] Whereas Cawdrey argued that Cotton had put church government in the hands of the multitudes, others countered that Cotton had placed too much power in the hands of the elders in a particular church.[119] Indeed, Cotton later told Cawdrey that he allowed for all this despite the fact that 'the Doctrine of the *Way* (in such few Points wherein it differeth from the *Keyes*) was not then mine when the *Keyes* were published'.[120] Indeed it was 'much less mine' when Holmes published a corrupted version of the *Way* almost a year after the *Keyes* was published and many years after the *Way* was actually written. Holmes achieved his penance by publishing Cotton's corrective response to Rutherford entitled *The Way of congregational churches cleared*. Holmes did not endorse Cotton's *Churches Cleared*, but ambivalently noted it was a 'fair Additional to the models (afore printed) of the Church way'.[121]

It may be easy to dismiss Cotton as a man attempting to save face. Yet we need only read Rutherford to see that some presbyterians did not perceive an inconsistency in Cotton's writings. Rutherford wrote a massive refutation of Thomas Hooker's *Survey and Summe of Church Discipline* entitled *A survey of the Survey of that summe of church-discipline penned by Mr. Thomas Hooker*. This was to be expected, since Hooker's pamphlet was by and large an attack on Rutherford's *Due Right of Presbyteries*.[122] Nevertheless, Rutherford was careful to point out the weaknesses in Hooker's arguments when compared to Cotton's *Keyes*. Rutherford lamented Hooker's pamphlet was 'inferior, not a little, to the arguments of learned M. Cotton'.[123] Indeed, Rutherford used Cotton against Hooker many times and repeatedly stated that when Hooker argued against Rutherford, he was also arguing against Cotton.[124] One can see why Hooker pleaded with Cotton to retract his *Keyes*.

BAILLIE'S COTTON PROBLEM

We do not know when Goodwin and Nye received Cotton's *Keyes of the Kingdom*, but we know they had it by early May 1644. Goodwin and Nye registered Cotton's *Keyes* with the Stationers Company on 14 May 1644.[125] This was only six days after Thomas Edwards's diatribe against the *Narration*, the *Antapologia*, was registered.[126] Here is yet another example of why Baillie's views do not reflect the opinions of the other Scots. On 17 May 1644, only eight days after Edwards's *Antapologia* was registered at the Stationers Company and three days after the *Keyes* was registered, Alexander Henderson told the assembly, 'Not to carry yourselves as adversaryes out of the assembly, a suggesting to write pamphlets to the prejudice of the assembly.'[127]

Still, Baillie was at precisely the same time encouraging the publication of the greatest polemical attack on the assembly's congregationalists to date, Edwards's *Antapologia*.[128] However, the Preface to Cotton's *Keyes* carefully refrained from any attack on the presbyterians, and studiously avoided mentioning assembly debates. The work only received positive responses when mentioned on the assembly floor. Indeed, the *Keyes* should be considered as reaching out to the Scots, not arguing against them. Perhaps Goodwin and Nye refrained from publishing Cotton's *Keyes* in May because they were waiting for Thomas Edwards to make his next move. On 7 June, Baillie wrote to Spang saying that 'there is a piece of twentie-six sheets, of Mr. Edwards, against the Apologetick Narration, near printed, which will paint that faction in clearer colours than yet they have appeared'.[129] Baillie knew that the Apologists had a document in hand from Cotton, but he was not quite sure how they would use it.[130]

The central purpose of Edwards's pamphlet was to expose the schismatic tendencies of the Apologists. Although he could never prove that the Apologists were schismatic, he was a master at 'guilt by association'. In that sense, Holmes's *Coole Conference* and John Goodwin's answer to Adam Stuart had set the stage for, and even provoked, Edwards. As long as more 'independents' like John Goodwin and Nathaniel Holmes acted as if they were carrying the public banner for the Apologists, Edwards's task was an easy one. Furthermore, as the Apologists were bound to remain silent in terms of bringing debates into the public sphere, Edwards could write without fearing a bold rejoinder. Edwards used this to his advantage. He demanded time and time again that the Apologists respond to him, saying that if they did not he would take their silence as a validation of his accusations. In actual fact, the Apologists were not allowed to respond to Edwards, and when they asked the assembly for permission to respond to the aspersions cast upon them in 1644, the assembly refused to allow them to do so.

The *Keyes* was registered at a time of great anxiety for Baillie. He had seen the efforts by Gillespie to reach out to the Apologists, and the Scottish commissioners were reprimanded by Scottish covenanter David Calderwood for sounding too much like 'independents'. Baillie immediately began to ramp up his cross-channel effort to discredit the congregational divines. He had heard that Apollonius was about to write to the Apologists, asking them to explain their views on church government.[31] Sometime around 3 May, Baillie sent his cousin Spang two pamphlets, 'to inform [Apollonius] more of the ['independents'] mind'.[32] The two books were the 'little Dr. Homes['s] ... "The Coole Conference" [and] "M. S. against A. S."' by 'John Goodwin of Colemen Street'.[33] Baillie had no problem tying the pamphlet warfare around the necks of the Apologists. He also sent two other books to Apollonius that were unnamed, although we are not left totally in the dark as to which books they were.

When Apollonius wrote to the Apologists, he listed the books he had used as his basis for understanding their polity.[34] The Apologists had written only one of the books listed, and that was the *Apologeticall Narration*. The list also included writers the Apologists would never have accepted as fully representing their polity, such as Katherine Chidley and John Canne.[35] This book transmission was all part of Baillie's uphill battle to get more continental reformed divines to write against the Apologists. In his letter to Apollonius, Baillie lamented, 'It's marvelled, that the rest of your provinces and professors will not follow the gracious and charitable example of Zeland.'[36] In his following letter to Spang he cried, 'Will neither Rivet nor Voetius follow the example of brave Apollonius?'[37] In this context we can see why Baillie eagerly awaited Thomas Edwards's *Antapologia*.

Around this same time, Spang sent Baillie a manuscript from Alexander Forbes written against the 'independents', and Baillie requested that Spang find a way to get it published for England. This document was eventually licensed by Baillie's friend, James Cranford, and was printed around 14 June, the same day as Cotton's *Keyes*.[38] Thomason picked up a copy of Cotton's *Keyes* the same day he received Forbes's *An Anatomy of Independency*.[39] It was probably not coincidental that the *Keyes* was published on the same day the Apologists received their first direct attack from Baillie's Cranford circle. The *Anatomy* resulted in the only response given by any of the Apologists during 1644. Simpson responded with his *Anatomy Anatomized*, which functioned to clarify factual errors about the Apologists' experiences in Holland before they returned to England.[40] It seems the assembly allowed Simpson to proceed with this publication, for Simpson defended himself from Forbes's claim that the Apologists did not think elders lawful because the 'keys' belonged first to the 'faithful' in a church.'[41] Simpson knew that this pamphlet from Forbes was just the first volley of attacks licensed by Cranford. Simpson said, 'there is an Antapology in Presse, or a Collection of such faults as either mens mistakes and malice', and this '*Anatomist* is a foreunner to that, as some few great drops before a shower.'[42]

Baillie's anxious anticipation was assuaged on or around 13 July when Edwards's *Antapologia* made its debut. The book, however, was preempted by the publication of Cotton's *Keyes of the Kingdom* just a few weeks before. The very publication Baillie hoped would expose the inconsistencies and fallacies of the Apologists had been neutered by a document that was to be embraced by two of his prestigious fellow commissioners, Rutherford and Gillespie. On 5 July Baillie blandly said to Spang, 'receave a late piece by Cotton'. In that same letter he continued, 'I wish Voetius [were] ingaged'. And indeed, it seems he was losing his help from Apollonius as well, for he stated, 'Hold on Apollonius'.[43] The following week he wrote Spang again, stating, 'I wish againe and againe, that Apollonius and Voetius were moved to write.'[44]

The *Keyes* had actually scored two victories against Baillie: on the one hand, it brought the Apologists closer to Rutherford and Gillespie; and on the other, it diffused Baillie's ability to procure critiques from the continent. We already noted how the letters from Zeeland sided with the Apologists in terms of the power of the elders in a particular church, but now Cotton's *Keyes* took the support a step further. Even when Baillie finally succeeded in getting Apollonius to write a more comprehensive attack on the 'independents', Apollonius still cited Cotton's *Keyes* approvingly and continued to insist that the power of excommunication resided in the particular church's presbytery.[45] One can see why Baillie later said that Cotton was the mightiest of all his 'opposites'.[46]

Baillie's frustration that the continental divines refused to follow orders and contribute to his anti-independent campaign reached its height when Baillie realised that the University of Utrecht refused to fall in line and that Gisbertus Voetius was about to give his 'approbation of the Cotton's Keyes [as] ... consonant to truth, and the discipline of Holland'.[47] It is impossible to know whether Baillie truly did not understand ecclesiological variations on the continent, or if out of political desperation he simply did not care. What is true is that while the polity espoused by the Apologists may have offended some English divines, it had a claim to the Reformed tradition outside of England. And it is to the Scottish and Dutch tradition that we now turn.

NOTES

1 George Yule called the publication a 'masterstroke', given the stature of Cotton. Yule, *Puritans in Politics*, p. 134.

2 For useful overviews of Cotton's career and context see, L. Ziff, *The Career of John Cotton: Puritanism and the American Experience* (Princeton, NJ: Princeton University Press, 1962), Bush (ed.), *Correspondence*, pp. 1–67.

3 Contra C. G. Pestana, *The English Atlantic in an Age of Revolution, 1640–1661* (Cambridge, MA: Harvard University Press, 2004), pp. 72–73.

4 E.g. Baillie, *A Dissuasive*, p. 110; *Jus divinum regiminis ecclesiastici*, p. 116.

5 Baillie, *A Dissuasive*, Table of Contents.

6 Ibid., p. 56.

7 Ibid., p. 56.

8 Lawrence, 'Goodwin', chapter 3.

9 Cotton, Goodwin & Nye, *Keyes*, preface, not paginated.

10 Ibid., preface, not paginated.

11 Ibid., preface, not paginated; Cawdrey mocks this as a 'miracle', D. Cawdrey, *Vindiciæ Clavium: or, A Vindication of the Keyes of the Kingdome of Heaven, into the hands of the right Owners* (1645), Epistle to the reader, not paginated.

12 Cotton, *The Way of Congregational Churches Cleared*, vol. 2, p. 24.

13 Ibid., p. 26. Burroughs had also sought Cotton's advice in 1630 as to whether he should leave Norwich and accept a living by Lady Jane Bacon in Tivetshall, Bush (ed.), *Correspondence*, pp. 151–156.

14 The Apologists claimed that they would not 'have used the same terms to expresse ... prophecying'. But Cotton claimed that he did not believe himself to disagree with them. Cotton stated, 'I must againe Professe as I did before, that I do not know wherein I Dissent from them: unlesse it be that I Allow somewhat more liberty to the Prophecying of private Brethren, then they do.' Cotton, Goodwin & Nye, *Keyes*, preface, not paginated; J. Cotton & J. Owen, *A Defence of Mr. John Cotton from the imputation of Selfe Contradiction* (1658), pp. 74–75.

15 *Jus divinum regiminis ecclesiastici*, pp. 96ff, 114, 118ff.

16 Cotton, Goodwin & Nye, *Keyes*, preface, not paginated.

17 Ibid., preface, not paginated.

18 Ibid., preface, not paginated.

19 Ibid., preface, not paginated.

20 Ibid., preface, not paginated.

21 Ibid., preface, not paginated.

22 Ibid., preface, not paginated.

23 Ibid., preface, not paginated.

24 Rutherford, *Due Right*, pp. 4, 320–321.

25 Cotton, Goodwin & Nye, *Keyes*, p. 2.

26 Ibid., p. 3, Revelation 3:7; 'And to the angel of the church in Philadelphia write: These things saith he that is Holy, He that is true, He that hath the key of David, he that openeth, and no man shutteth; and shutteth, and no man openeth.'

27 Ibid., p. 3.

28 Ibid., p. 4.

29 Ibid., p. 4.

30 Goodwin, *Government*, p. 55.

31 Cotton & Owen, *A Defence of Mr. John Cotton*, p. 15.

32 'So Jesus said to them again, "Peace to you! As the Father has sent Me, I also send you." And when He had said this, He breathed on *them*, and said to them, "Receive the Holy Spirit. If you forgive the sins of any, they are forgiven them; if you retain the *sins* of any, they are retained' (John 20:21–23).

33 Cotton, Goodwin & Nye, *Keyes*, pp. 10, 32.

34 Ibid., p. 4.

35 Goodwin, *Government*, p. 55.

36 Ibid., p. 55.

37 Ibid., p. 53.

38 Ibid., p. 50.

39 Cotton, Goodwin & Nye, *Keyes*, p. 6.

40 J. Rainolds, *The summe of the conference betwene Iohn Rainoldes and Iohn Hart* (London, 1584), p. 105. See also, A. Willet, *Hexapla: that is, A six-fold commentarie vpon the most diuine epistle of the holy apostle S. Paul to the Romanes. The First Booke* (Cambridge, 1611), p. 528.

41 Cotton, *A brief exposition of the whole book of Canticles, or Song of Solomon*, p. 187. Bush (ed.), *Correspondence*, pp. 133–134. Timothy Van Vleteren requested a copy of Cotton's Canticles in 1629.

42 Ball, *A Friendly Triall*, p. 243; *Jus divinum regiminis ecclesiastici*, p. 105.

43 *Jus divinum regiminis ecclesiastici*, p. 103.

44 Cawdrey, *Vindiciæ Clavium*, p. 11.

45 Cotton, Goodwin & Nye, *Keyes*, p. 6.

46 Colossians 2:6.

47 Cotton, Goodwin & Nye, *Keyes*, p. 7.

48 Ibid., p. 10.

49 Ibid., p. 10.

50 Luke 11:52, 'Woe unto you, lawyers! for ye have taken away the key of knowledge: ye entered not in yourselves, and them that were entering in ye hindered.'

51 Cotton, Goodwin & Nye, *Keyes*, p. 7, citing for example Isaiah 53:11, 'He shall see of the travail of his soul, and shall be satisfied: by his knowledge shall my righteous servant justify many; for he shall bear their iniquities.' Also see John 17:3, 'And this is life eternal, that they might know thee the only true God, and Jesus Christ, whom thou hast sent.'

52 Ibid., p. 7.

53 See above, chapter 3.

54 Goodwin, *Government*, p. 53.

55 Cotton, Goodwin & Nye, *Keyes*, p. 11.

56 Ibid., p. 11.

57 Ibid., preface, not paginated.

58 Ibid., p. 33.

59 Ibid., preface, not paginated.

60 Ibid., preface, not paginated.

61 Ibid., preface, not paginated.

62 Ibid., preface, not paginated.

63 Ibid., preface, not paginated.

64 Ibid., preface, not paginated. Margaret Sommerville saw these distinctions, but simply concluded that most, if not all, independents believed the same thing that Cotton did. M. R. Sommerville, 'Independent Thought, 1603–1649', University of Cambridge, PhD thesis (1981), pp. 94–102.

65 1 Timothy 5:17, 'Let the elders that rule well be counted worthy of double honour, especially they who labour in the word and doctrine.' Hebrews 13:7, 17, 'Remember them which have the rule over you, who have spoken unto you the word of God: whose faith follow, considering the end of their conversation', 'Obey them that have the rule over you, and submit yourselves: for they watch for your souls, as they that must give account, that they may do it with joy, and not with grief: for that is unprofitable for you.'

66 Cotton, Goodwin & Nye, *Keyes*, p. 20.

67 Ibid., preface, not paginated.

68 Ibid., preface, not paginated.

69 It is something that Rutherford took notice of when he wrote against Thomas Hooker. He pointed Hooker to Goodwin's and Nye's preface as having 'judiciously' defended the unique ministerial authority within the elders of the church. S. Rutherford, *A Survey of the Survey of that Summe of Church Discipline* (London, 1658), p. 309.

70 Ashe & Rathband, *A Letter*, p. 73.

71 Goodwin, *Government*, p. 64.

72 Galatians 5:13, 'For, brethren, ye have been called unto liberty; only use not liberty for an occasion to the flesh, but by love serve one another.'

73 Cotton, Goodwin & Nye, *Keyes*, p. 12.

74 Ibid., p. 12.

75 For more on this see chapter 7 of this book.

76 This is an argument the presbyterians will make for analogical representation in a synod of presbyteries.

77 Goodwin, *Government*, p. 62.

78 Cotton, Goodwin & Nye, *Keyes*, p. 13.

79 Ibid., p. 14. 1 Corinthians 5:4–5, 'In the name of our Lord Jesus Christ, when ye are gathered together, and my spirit, with the power of our Lord Jesus Christ, To deliver such an one unto Satan for the destruction of the flesh, that the spirit may be saved in the day of the Lord Jesus.'

80 Ibid., p. 14.

81 Ibid., p. 14.

82 Goodwin, *Government*, p. 64.

83 Cotton, Goodwin & Nye, *Keyes*, preface, not paginated.

84 Ibid., p. 14.

85 Van Dixhoorn, *MPWA* (vol. 3), p. 320.

86 Cotton, Goodwin & Nye, *Keyes*, p. 9.

87 Cotton & Owen, *A Defence of Mr. John Cotton*, p. 36.

88 Ibid., p. 36.

89 Ibid., p. 36; Bush (ed.), *Correspondence*, p. 381, fn. 3.

90 See for example, Rutherford, *Due Right*, chapter 1.

91 Cited in Cotton, *The Way of Congregational Churches Cleared*, vol. 2, p. 5.

92 J. Cotton, 'John Cotton to John Dodd', in Bush (ed.), *Correspondence*, p. 272.

93 I am grateful to Michael Lawrence for pointing this out to me.

94 Rutherford, *Due Right*, preface, not paginated.

95 *Contra* Ha, *English Presbyterianism*, p. 126.

96 Thomas Shepard claimed 'that oftimes it is not possible for us [New England divines] to take notice of ... objections, and return an answer under a yeare or almost two years', Shepard & Allin, *A Treatise of Liturgies*, p. 4.

97 Cotton, *The Way of Congregational Churches Cleared*, vol. 2, pp. 20–21.

98 S. Rutherford, *The Divine Right of Church-Government and Excommunication* (London, 1646), pp. 236, 560.

99 See D. Cawdrey, *The Inconsistencie of the Independent way with Scripture and it self* (London, 1651); Cawdrey, *Vindiciæ Clavium*, front page.

100 Rutherford, *A Survey of the Survey of that Summe of Church Discipline*, p. 26, 112, 141, 165, 190.

101 Cotton, *The Way of Congregational Churches Cleared*, vol. 2, p. 4.

102 Ibid., p. 4.

103 E.g. D. Cawdrey, *Independencie a great Schism* (London, 1657); D. Cawdrey, *Independency further proved to be a Schism* (London, 1658); J. Owen, *A review of the true nature of schisme* (Oxford, 1657).

104 Bradley, 'Jacob and Esau', p. 290. Bremer, *Congregational Communion*, p. 164; Ziff, *Career of John Cotton*, p. 34.

105 Baillie claimed that the author was Holmes, Baillie, *Letters and Journals*, vol. 2, p. 180. For more on Holmes's involvement see Bradley, 'Jacob and Esau', pp. 183ff.

106 Cotton & Owen, *A Defence of Mr. John Cotton*, p. 38. Cotton's use of the *Way* here

referred to *The Way of the Churches of Christ in New England*, not to be confused with the *Way of the Congregational Churches Cleared*.

107 Cawdrey, *The Inconsistencie of the Independent way*, p. 40.

108 J. Cotton, *The Way of the Churches of Christ in New England* (London, 1645), p. 45; Cotton, Goodwin & Nye, *Keyes*, preface, not paginated.

109 Cotton, Goodwin & Nye, *Keyes*, p. 16.

110 Cotton & Owen, *A Defence of Mr. John Cotton*, pp. 38–39.

111 Cotton, *The Way Of The Churches of Christ in New England*, preface, not paginated; Holmes tried to minimise the difference between Cotton's *Keyes* and this book. He cited a letter from Cotton that came 'in the very nick of time' where Cotton claimed that there were 'logical differences' but not related to 'Doctrine of Divinitie, or Church Practice'. Holmes also inserted stars where he could not agree with Cotton. See ibid., epistle to the reader, not paginated.

112 C. Mather, *Magnalia Christi Americana* (London, 1702), p. 28.

113 Cotton & Owen, *A Defence of Mr. John Cotton*, p. 38.

114 Cawdrey, *The Inconsistencie of the Independent way*, pp. 40f.

115 Cotton & Owen, *A Defence of Mr. John Cotton*, p. 39.

116 Ibid., p. 39. This is not to suggest Cotton disowned every aspect of these congregational writings. Cotton stated, 'If I knew where the Pinch of difficulty lay, I would Addresse my selfe, to give them fuller satisfaction either by condescending to them, or giving them just reason why I could not. Meane while I have learned (through Grace) not to fall out with my Brethren for greater differences in judgment then those be' ibid., pp. 78–79. Cotton was happy to write a preface to Norton's *Answer* to Apollonius, with the caveat that he disagreed with Norton on the first subject of church power. Norton, *Answer*, pp. 10–18, 14.

117 Cotton & Owen, *A Defence of Mr. John Cotton*, p. 51.

118 Ibid., p. 39. See also J. H. Tuttle, 'The Writings of the Rev. John Cotton', in *Bibliographical Essays: A Tribute to Wilberforce Eames* (New York: B. Franklin, 1924), pp. 363–380, pp. 149–150.

119 Cotton, *The Way of Congregational Churches Cleared*, vol. 2, p. 15

120 Cotton & Owen, *A Defence of Mr. John Cotton*, p. 39.

121 Cotton, *The Way of the Churches of Christ in New England*, preface, not paginated.

122 For a summary of Hooker's response to Rutherford, see S. Bush Jr, *The Writings of Thomas Hooker: Spiritual Adventure in Two Worlds* (Madison, WI: University of Wisconsin Press, 1980), pp. 110–119.

123 Rutherford, *A Survey of the Survey of that Summe of Church Discipline*, p. 26.

124 See above, p. 138.

125 *A Transcript of the Registers of the Worshipful Company of Stationers; from 1640–1708 A.D.* (1913), vol. 2, p. 115.

126 Ibid., p. 113.

127 Van Dixhoorn, *MPWA* (vol. 3), p. 98.

128 Baillie, *Letters and Journals*, vol. 2, p. 181.

129 Ibid., vol. 2, p. 190.

130 Ibid., vol. 2, p. 190.

131 Ibid., vol. 2, p. 180.

132 Ibid., vol. 2, p. 180.

133 Ibid., vol. 2, pp. 180–181.

134 Norton, *Answer*, p. 20.

135 Ibid., p. 20.

136 Baillie, *Letters and Journals*, vol. 2, p. 181.

137 Ibid., p. 189.

138 A. Forbes, *Anatomy of independency* (London, 1644). It was registered on 13 June, and Thomason had it by 14 June. *Transcript ... Company of Stationers*, vol. 1, p. 118; *Thomason Catalogue*, vol. 1, p. 328.

139 *Thomason Catalogue*, vol. 1, pp. 328–329.

140 Simpson, *The Anatomist anatomis'd*, pp. 8ff.

141 Forbes, *Anatomy of independency*, p. 26; Simpson, *The Anatomist anatomis'd*, p. 12. Bradley, 'Jacob and Esau', p. 263.

142 Simpson, *The Anatomist anatomis'd*, p. 4.

143 Baillie, *Letters and Journals*, vol. 2, p. 202.

144 Ibid., vol. 2, p. 202.

145 W. Apollonius, *A consideration of certaine controversies at this time agitated in the kingdome of England, concerning the government of the Church of God* (London, 1645), p. 100.

146 Baillie, *The Dissuasive ... Vindicated*, preface.

147 Baillie, *Letters and Journals*, vol. 2, p. 240.

Chapter 6

John Cotton and the
'Best Reformed Churches'

While the Assembly pursued a church government that was in keeping with the best reformed churches, the publication of Cotton's *Keyes* changed the terms of the debate. Whereas the previous chapter analysed Cotton's ecclesiological impact on debates in and surrounding the Westminster assembly, we will now look at the influence of his polity in its international reformed context. By looking at the reception of Cotton's *Keyes* in the wider reformed tradition, we are forced to reassess the debates over polity within England.

John Cotton's *Keyes of the Kingdom of Heaven* elicited two opposite responses and exposed the variety of presbyterian polities on offer in 1644. It had the effect of isolating clerical English presbyterianism from the reformed churches in Scotland and in Holland. Daniel Cawdrey, the London presbyterian and assembly member, would later build a polemical career against Cotton's *Keyes*. He decried Cotton's view of church government as full of weakness and inconsistencies.[1] Although Cawdrey's fellow English presbyterians in London gave more respect to the 'middle-Way men' represented in Cotton's *Keyes* than to those of the 'Brownistical way', they nonetheless called the former's position 'a rotten foundation, and a tottering superstruction'.[2] The London ministers knew that Cotton and the Apologists gave a unique key of authority to the elders, they nonetheless chafed at the 'key of liberty', which to them was 'a new Key, lately forged by some new lock-smiths in Separation-shop, to be a pick-lock of the power of Church officers, and to open the door for popular government'.[3] The *Keyes* also exposed a split between divines in the assembly and English divines outside. Indeed, Cotton's *Keyes* was cited only positively on the floor of the Westminster assembly.[4]

Rutherford, Gillespie and Henderson marvelled at Cotton's *Keyes*. Rutherford praised how close Cotton came to the Scottish way, and he was happy enough with the document to tell the entire Westminster assembly, 'When

I read through that treatise of *The Keys of the Kingdome of Heaven*, I thought it an easy labour for an universall pacification, he comes soe neare unto us.'[5] Gillespie cited Cotton's *Keyes* positively in print and referenced it repeatedly, and only positively, in the Jersualem Chamber. Even Baillie, the only commissioner to write books specifically aimed at Cotton, conceded several years later, 'I do not deny that Mr. Cotton hath, and ever hath had, since first I heard of his way, so high an estimation in my mind, that I do preferre him to all my Opposites.' Baillie cited Cotton in a list of the ablest minds of the 'British Churches', which also included Rutherford, Gillespie, and Goodwin.[6] Indeed, Cotton said that he had received a letter from England claiming that 'Mr Rutherford ... offered to the Dissenting brethren, That if they would come up to the Treatise of the *Keyes*, themselves [the Scots] would meet them there.'[7]

Whereas October 1643 helped us to see a uniquely English debate, the Scots' engagement with Cotton's *Keyes* helps us see how these two minority groups in the assembly understood each other without the English presbyterians adding a layer of rhetorical complexity. W. D. J. Mckay, noting similarities between Gillespie and Nye, wondered 'how close the two sides may have been in reality outside the polemical context of the assembly'.[8] This chapter will attempt to answer that question. By analysing the similarities of Cotton and Rutherford, along with the context in which those similarities were brought to light, we will be able to better understand why Nye could tell the Westminster assembly, 'Ther is more than 2 or 3 or 4 partyes in the assembly', and if the 'government of Scotland layed downe, those you call independents will come nearer to it than many in this Assembly'.[9]

Gisbertus Voetius, arguably Europe's greatest living theologian at the time, not only endorsed Cotton's *Keyes*, but also adjusted his own polity to agree with Cotton's scholastic framework. We will analyse how Voetius understood the reformed orthodoxy of the Apologists' polity and how he appropriated much of the congregational divines' terminology in his own writings, and how he was able to distinguish between the polity espoused by the 'middle-way men' and the more 'extreme independents', like John Canne, that lived in the Low Countries. We will argue that an understanding of Voetius's ecclesiology will force historians to adjust their understanding of English presbyterians, and further clarify why Gillespie was willing to accommodate the Apologists.

RUTHERFORD RESPONDS

In April 1644 Rutherford responded to Cotton's manuscript version of *The Way of the Churches of Christ*, which the New England divine had penned almost ten years earlier. Rutherford had begun writing his response at some point before December 1643, and Baillie anxiously awaited its publication, calling it Rutherford's 'large book against Independents'.[10] Baillie, of course, failed to note that Rutherford's *The Due Right of Presbyteries* addressed a very particular strain of independency. Rutherford's response was awkwardly situated between a document that Cotton never intended for publication, and the pamphlet Cotton considered to be the most accurate representation of his polity. When Cotton responded to Rutherford he noted that the Scottish divine had read more into his initial manuscript than Cotton had intended, and that his meaning was 'more fully and distinctly opened in the small treatise of the Keyes'.[11] Rutherford had made undiscriminating comparisons between Cotton's *Way of the Churches of Christ* and other independent tracts. Therefore, in his response Cotton further demonstrated the differences between his congregationalism and the independency refuted by Rutherford and reviled by many English presbyterians.

The first two-thirds of Cotton's response to Rutherford, *The Way of the congregational Churches Cleared*, attempted to refute the charges of inconsistency and anarchy that Baillie and Cawdrey had levelled at him after the publication of the *Keyes*.[12] Baillie had published his *Dissuasive*, a book heavily reliant upon Thomas Edwards for sources, attacking Cotton's inconsistencies.[13] Both Baillie and Cawdrey were in Thomas Edwards's circle of London ministers, and we are therefore not surprised to find their tracts loaded with innuendo, rumours and general disdain for any ecclesiological position espoused by Cotton. More than once Cawdrey misquoted Cotton, thus prejudicing the argument.[14] Unlike Rutherford, Cawdrey and Baillie continued to critique Cotton after the *Way of the Congregational Churches Cleared* appeared.

Cotton attempted to lead the reader away from the rhetorical strategies deployed by Baillie and Cawdrey. He stated that it would be a 'loss of time and labour' to respond to Cawdrey, whose writings 'are but collections out of the writings of others, who have more distinctly and elabourately disputed the cause'.[15] Cotton focused his disputations on the keys. Cotton's attitude towards Cawdrey and Baillie was one of intellectual dismissiveness, whereas he engaged Rutherford as one who 'excelleth in acuteness and Scholastical Argumentativenes'.[16] There was certainly a stylistic difference in the way Rutherford and Cotton engaged each other, and the ways Cawdrey and Baillie engaged Cotton. Cotton and Rutherford were scrupulous in their attention to syllogistic forms, whereas Baillie and his team of polemicists, including Edwards and Cawdrey, abandoned scholastic argumentation in favour of a more accusatory style.[17]

In another similarity to Edwards, Cawdrey's frustration with Cotton, by his own admission, was partially born out by Cotton's choice to engage Rutherford and not Cawdrey.[18] Rutherford, for his part, never offered a rejoinder to Cotton's response.[19] This is in stark contrast to Cawdrey, who built a career mocking Cotton and the polity he espoused. Whereas Cawdrey, and the London presbyterian ministers, were horrified to think of any power residing within the congregation, Rutherford was more interested in the nature of the power given to the congregation, and whether or not a congregation without elders could be the first subject of the power of the keys.

Rutherford's starting point in *Due Right* was Cotton's first proposition in *The Way of the Churches of Christ*. It should be noted that Rutherford's citation of this proposition is proof that the copy published by Nathaniel Holmes was from a different manuscript source: Rutherford's citation of the manuscript version is different from Holmes's published version.[20] Cotton was always careful to demonstrate where someone was utilising a corrupted version of his original manuscript, and therefore his silence in responding to Rutherford indicates Rutherford had a version closer to what Cotton had originally written.[21] Cotton re-quoted the proposition cited by Rutherford, indicating that Rutherford's manuscript source was more accurate than Holmes's copy.

> That the Church which Christ in the Gospell hath instituted, and to which he hath committed the Keyes of his Kingdom, The power of binding and loosing, the Tables and Seals of the Covenant, the Officers and Censures of his Church, the administration of all his publike Worship and Ordinances, is Coetus Fidelium, a company of Believers, meeting in one place every Lords day, for the administration of the holy Ordinances of God to publike edification.[22]

In response, Cotton focused on two of Rutherford's questions regarding the proposition. We will take each question in turn, along with Cotton's response, in order to clarify Cotton's understanding of the particular church and how that understanding reflected upon Rutherford's view of the church.

> Question 1: 'If a company of believers and saints builded by faith, upon the rock Christ, and united in a Church-Covenant, be the only instituted visible Church in the New Testament, to which Christ hath given the keys.'[23]

We will not spend much time on this first point, because the premise itself goes beyond anything Cotton actually said or believed. The thrust of Rutherford's first question was whether or not the faithful in the church were the first subjects of all church power, and were therefore the 'only instituted visible church which Christ hath given the keys'. Did the visible saints make up the church, or were they part of the church? Rutherford argued that they were stones for the house, but they were not the whole house. The reason for this was that the people in the church could not administer that which properly belongs to the ministers of the church, namely, the 'Ordination of Pastors, and election of Officers, administration of the seales of grace, and acts of Church censures'.[24] Rutherford cited John Robinson's *A justification of separation* and Henry Ainsworth's *A true confession of faith* as examples of counter-arguments, along with Cotton's *Way of the Churches of Christ*, which had argued that a church was a 'perfect church' even when it lacked pastors to administer God's sacraments.[25] This would mean that ministers 'are but only accidents and not parts, not integrall members of a constituted Church'.[26]

According to Rutherford, the proper 'instituted Church of the New Testament is an organicall body of diverse members ... of Elders governing and a people governed'.[27] Elders were an integral and essential part of the visible church.[28] Interestingly, Rutherford acknowledged that 'a single congregation ... [is] the onely visible Church instituted in the New Testament. Nothing can be said against this'.[29] However, because this church must consist of elders and people governed, and elders were required to administer the acts of church government and discipline, it would therefore be improper to call a church 'an instituted visible church' before there are 'governours'.[30] The people were not the officers, nor were the officers the people, and if they were both essential parts of the church then it is impossible that all the keys could be given to a church without officers. This was precisely the same language used by the Apologists, and perhaps gives us further indication as to why Rutherford did not include them in his attack on Cotton, whom at this stage he regarded as being in the genetic line of 'separatists' like Ainsworth and Robinson.

Cotton's response was simple. He rightly stated that the word 'onely' was not in his proposition: he never indicated that the visible church is only a company of believers, without the elders.[31] He never intended to 'exclude the Organical Church (a Church furnished with all her officers) from being an instituted Visible Church' nor did he mean the 'Coetus Fidelium, a company of believers without officers' to be the instituted visible church.[32] Similarly, the officers were not given to the church 'as meer adjuncts given to a Subject' but as integral parts of the church, given for 'completing the integrity and perfection of it'.[33] He stated he never 'intended to invest a Church of Believers (without officers) with all the powers of the Keyes'. There is nothing that Cotton disagreed with in Rutherford's various 'distinctions, or conclusions raised up against' his proposition. Cotton therefore passed quickly on to Rutherford's next question.[34]

> Question 2: 'Whether or not Christ hath committed the Keys of the Kingdom of Heaven to the Church of Believers, which as yet wanteth all Officers, Pastors Doctors, &c.'[35]

This question was really the thrust of Rutherford's critique of Cotton's *Way of the Churches of Christ* and of independency in general. Do members of a church have all powers necessary for church governement without the need of elders? As Cotton pointed out, 'M. Rutterford doth chiefly aime at this conclusion; To prove that the Keyes are not given to a Church of professed Believers, destitute of Pastors and Teachers', but Cotton rejoined that this is '[a] conclusion [Rutherford] is pleased to frame unto himself, but had not occasion to collect it from any words in my Proposition'.[36] Cotton noted that his original proposition, which he expanded upon in his treatise on the *Keyes*, 'speaketh not of a Church that wanteth all officers'.[37] Rather Cotton, as we have noted earlier, insisted that the power of the keys was given to a whole church that included elders. The real question, from Cotton's perspective, was not whether the elders had authoritative power, but whether the acts of the believers in the congregation can be called a 'church-power' at all.

The question of stewardship was an important point in the debate. For in Matthew 16:19 Christ, by giving Peter the keys, makes him a steward of the house of God. Rutherford stated that the keys are given to the ministers 'who are stewards of the mysteries of God, 1 Cor.4.1. And servants of the house by office, 2 Cor.4.5 … and to behave themselves aright in Gods house, I Tim.3.16'.[38] Christ, who has the Key of David, is the supreme ruler of his church, and the stewards are given the keys to rule the church on his behalf.[39] However, a church of believers without officers could not be stewards of the house of God.[40] To emphasise this point, Rutherford marshalled a variety of sources, including Schindler, Musculus, Calvin, Beza, Pareus, Chrysostom, Augustine, Whitaker, Bullinger, and Zwingli. Rutherford summarised: 'I think, while of late, never interpreter dreamed, that in the Text Mat. 16. the keys of the Kingdom of Heaven are given to all believers'; rather, the keys were given 'only to the stewards of the house'.[41]

Cotton, however, never denied that keys were given to elders in the church. Cotton conceded that the verses cited by Rutherford indeed proved 'that the Keyes were promised and given to Stewards and officers'.[42] Cotton further acknowledged, and agreed with Rutherford, that 'a company of professing Believers' without officers are not stewards in the house of God. 'But this we deny', Cotton continued, 'that all Keyes, all kind of Power in the Church, is promised and given to the officers of the Church, solely and solidly'.[43] He argued that Christ gave all 'Office-power' only to the officers and that the Brethren in a church ought never to usurp that power, but he denied that all power should be considered 'officer-power'.[44] His point was that there was more power in the Scriptures than the power belonging to officers alone. Cotton acknowledged Rutherford's citations. 'The Testimonies which he alledgeth … [prove] that the Keyes signifie power, and Authority, and that Stewardly, or Officer-Power, is given to the Officers of the Church', but none of these theologians proved that all power was office power, or that the keys only refer to one type of power, or that believers had no power at all.[45] The one point that all commentaries and annotations seemed to agree upon was that the power of the keys at least partly included ministerial stewardship. However, although it was an argument from silence, Cotton could claim that those who only reference ministerial authority in Matthew 16:19 do not necessarily claim that believers in the church have no power at all. They simply argued that the believers in the church were not given ministerial power.

Cotton therefore made two assertions regarding the power of the keys. Firstly, a church without officers has indeed received 'some part of the Power of the Keyes', such as the 'Power to receive Members, to elect Officers, and to do other such Church Acts, as do not require Office-Rule, or Office-Power'.[46] Secondly, a church 'hath in it a Radical or Virtual Power, whereby it may call forth such Officers, as may Administer all those Acts of office-Rule, or Power, which of it self without them, it could not exercise'.[47]

From Rutherford's perspective the questions, as they arose from Matthew 16 and 18, came back to the problem of representation. He went back to the distinctions Bridge had made in the assembly. Were the keys given to all believers through Peter, or did Peter receive the keys for the good of believers, or did Peter represent 'the person of Apostles, Pastors, and Church-guides'.[48] Bridge had similarly claimed that Peter received the keys either representing the whole church, for the benefit of the church, or on behalf of the church.[49] Here Rutherford cited Paul Baynes, Robert Parker, and the Catholic Sorbonnists against what he believed to be Cotton's assertion that the keys are given to a church of believers apart from the officers. He argued that the church was not capable 'as a subject' to exercise the gifts of 'Pastors and Doctors'. Rather, Pastors and Teachers were gifts *to* the church. However, the church was capable of receiving these gifts 'as the object, and end, because the fruit and effect of these gifts redoundeth to the good of the Church'.[50] Cotton later argued that there was a difference between the first subject of church power, and the 'first Subject Recipient' of that power.[51] An elder could be the first subject of church authority, but the church could be the 'first Subject Recipient' of that power. Cotton used the analogy of a dowry: 'A wife may be the first subject of her own Dowry, but yet the Husband is the first Subject Recipient of his wife with her Dowry.'[52]

Cotton stated that Rutherford had presumed more than he intended: 'Though I said the Keyes were given to a Church of Believers, whereof Peter was one ... [I only intended] that [the believer] had his share in the power of the Keyes', not that Peter in his capacity as believer 'had his share in the whole power of the Keyes'.[53] Peter had other powers of the keys as well, 'as an Elder, and as an Apostle immediately given Him by the Lord Jesus.' Secondly, Cotton did 'not understand the safety of that speech; That Pastors and Teachers are Gifts of which the Church is not capable, as a Subject'.[54] According to Paul's letter to the church in Ephesus, Christ gives pastors and teachers to his church, and therefore the church is the recipient subject of them.[55] Cotton used the popular metaphor of the eye and the body. The eye was given to the body and the body was the recipient subject. The body itself could not see, but it could see through the eye. Therefore, the church could not exercise the role of ruler and teacher by itself, but the church could exercise power through their elders. Thomas Goodwin used the same language when he stated, 'Although the Eye is that member that doth see for the Body; yet it hath the Virtual Efficacy that inableth it to see, from its being placed in the Body.'[56] Therefore the church was not merely the object and end (or recipient) of the pastors' gifts. For Cotton 'Pastors and Teachers' were given to the church as 'Integrall' parts of the church. The body of believers was also an integral part. Therefore officers and the body were 'intrinsecall and essentiall to a Totum Integale, not extrinsicall, as the object'.[57]

If the believers in the body were merely the object of the elders' gifts, then they were non-essential parts of the church, something Rutherford himself would certainly reject. Before we get into more detail, we should state that Cotton considered himself to be in line with Rutherford, despite Rutherford's misreading of Cotton's earlier pamphlet. Cotton believed, with Rutherford, that the 'Church is not capable of exercise of the Pastors and Doctors place, and therefore is not the first subject of their Office-power'.[58]

This dialogue tapped into a longer line of debate, and Rutherford was keenly aware of this when he cited Robert Parker, Paul Baynes and the Parisians as authorities. Cotton conceded that these divines stated that 'the fruit and effect of the gifts of the Pastor and Teacher doth redound to the good of the Church'.[59] But Parker and the Parisians gave more power to the body of the church than Cotton was willing to give, namely, 'that the Church is not onely the object and end, but the first subject of all Church-Power'.[60] Frank B. Carr claimed that Cotton learned from Parker that a particular church was the first subject of the power of the keys. But Carr – the only person who has written extensively on Parker – fails to fully understand the differences between Parker and Cotton and to notice that Cotton did not go as far as Parker.[61] Robert Parker, as we have noted, believed that Christ gave the keys to the whole church, and that the elders received their power derivatively from the church. As Parker stated, 'The authoritie of rectors was given to the church by Christ, resteth not in the whole church, but conditionally to be communicated to rectors to the edification of the whole.'[62] So Parker also deployed the eye-body metaphor, but came to a slightly different conclusion. For Parker the church of believers was 'superior' to the pastors and teachers, and the eye was therefore subordinate to the body.[63]

In the section of Paul Baynes cited by Rutherford, Baynes sounded more like Cotton and the Apologists than did Parker. He stated that the 'Ordinarie power with the execution thereof, was not given the communitie of the Church, or to the whole multitude of the faithful' insofar as the multitude was not 'the immediate and first receptacle, receiving it ... and virtually deriving it to others'.[64] By denying that the body was the first subject of church power, Baynes positioned himself against the Sorbonnists. He also claimed that Martin Luther and Philip Melancthon wrongly held to this conclusion based on their interpretations of Matthew 16:19.[65]

In response to Rutherford's later claim that no 'interpreters' believed that the keys were given to the body of believers, 'but onely to the stewards of the house', Cotton cited Luther and Melancthon, along with William Whitaker,

Martin Bucer and Augustine, against him.[66] Whereas Parker believed power was originally in the body of the church, Baynes believed that a unique power was given to the elders, not derivatively through the body. Adding to the complexity, Cotton agreed with Baynes's belief that 'the visible Church instituted by Christ and his Apostles, to which the Keyes are given, is not a Diocesan, or Provinciall, or National Assembly, but a particular Congregation'.[67] Goodwin also cited Baynes as an authority in the matter of the bounds of the particular church.[68] So it follows from Baynes's argument that the particular church was the first subject of church power, but he believed that the subject included only the elders. When Cotton said that he differed somewhat from Baynes' description of the first subject of the power of the keys Cotton did not mean he therefore agreed with Parker. Parker and Baynes both had elements in common with Cotton and the Apologists, but neither of them fully represented their polity.

Stephen Brachlow claimed that Parker contradicted himself by saying, on the one hand 'ministerial power' rested more principally in the church, whereas on the other hand 'full power to govern' rested more principally in the elders. Brachlow believed that Parker (and William Ames with him) resolved this contradiction with a distinction between the 'possession and use of power' that could only be found in a church that was 'partly democratic and partly aristocratic'.[69] More recently, Michael Winship has argued that Parker's position was that of a congregationalist in the tradition of Henry Jacob, though Parker 'gave more power to synods than other congregationalists'.[70] Yet, what Brachlow called a contradiction and what Winship calls congregationalism, was precisely the points where Parker influenced so many English presbyterians.[71]

As we will remember from chapter 3, the question of 'power' and 'jurisdiction/use of power' caused no end of confusion at the Westminster assembly. Cotton and the Apologists never believed the people possessed or used the unique authorial power of the keys. It was common currency in the 1640s to describe a church as partly monarchical (under Christ the king), partly aristocratic (under the elders), and partly democratic (under the people). For Parker, the power of the elders was derived from the people, and at that point the ministerial power rested more principally upon the elders than upon the church. Cotton and Rutherford also believed in this construct, but understood it in a very different way than Robert Parker. In Cotton and the Apologists' unique construct of the keys there could be a power in the elders and a power in the people, but those powers were distinct.[72] The elders were the first subject of the elders' power and the church was the first subject of the church's power.[73] Rutherford believed the people could have the right to vote for their pastors, but he would not call this anything more than a 'popular power of the keys'. Thus we are introduced to complex logical concepts of 'virtual' and 'formal' power.

'Virtual and Formall' power

Rutherford argued that 'there is a power virtuall, not formall in the Church of believers'.[74] This power was distinct from the 'formall' ordinary power that came directly from Christ to the elders. This formal power could not come from believers because they did not possess the elders' power. The virtual power in the people included the ability to 'supply the want of ordination of pastors, or some other acts of the keyes simply necessary'.[75] The people in essence or effect had the power to do that which they should not do when they have elders. For Rutherford this was an extraordinary power, not an ordinary or official power. He used the example of a church on an island where all the elders had died. In such extraordinary cases the people could ordain pastors (something that should normally be done by the elders alone). Rutherford cited a number of Spanish Thomists on this point, along with the Apologists' friend Gisbertus Voetius.[76] We should remember that though Rutherford's *Due Right* was published in 1644, he was addressing what he perceived to be an inconsistency in the independent position as espoused by Cotton several year earlier. He was not refuting the Apologists and he could not have known that Cotton's *Keyes*, which Voetius would endorse, was forthcoming.

Cotton felt that Rutherford had caught himself in a peculiar dilemma. If, as Rutherford argued, the church had received no power of the keys (and we understand the keys as the basis of all church power), then it would follow that a church that lost all its elders on an island would cease to be a church, something Rutherford would deny. Cotton therefore called into question the legitimacy of such a distinction between 'formal' and 'virtual' power. The 'formal' and 'virtual' powers were very familiar to Cotton. They were rooted in the teachings of the Jesuit Francisco Suarez and were part of the curriculum taught at Cambridge when Cotton was a student.[77] 'I confesse, I do not well understand, how a man in case of necessity hath any virtual power to do this or that Act, but he hath also a formall power to do such an Act in that case of necessitie.'[78] For Cotton 'virtuall' and 'formall' power must be either of the same kind, or the same in 'Analogy'.[79] Cotton was concerned that Rutherford, in his effort to protect the unique authority of the elders, had made every act of the 'Brethren of the church (who are no officers) as no Acts of power at all, and consequently, no part left to the People in the power of the Keyes'.[80] Cotton used the relationship between a people and their king to prove his point. People who chose a king did not have formal sovereign power. The people did have a virtual sovereign power to give kingly authority, yet this authority never existed in the people. However, they had the formal power to yield up themselves unto subjection to the king.[81] The people never had the king's power, but that did not therefore mean they had no state power. In other words, the peoples' power was not merely 'extra-ordinary'. They did have a formal power, but the formal power was a different power from that of the king.

As Cotton noted, should the presbytery of a particular church be removed by death, then according to Rutherford's allocation of the keys to the elders alone, the church would cease to be a church.[82] Of course, Rutherford said quite the opposite, but his way of argumentation, according to Cotton, left him vulnerable to the accusation. By indicating all power and exercise of that power resided in the elders alone, Rutherford was, according to Cotton, making elders the only integral and essential parts of a church. 'Take away all power of Action, and operation from a Church and you take away the church it self.'[83] Cotton once again drew an analogy from the state. If some catastrophe destroyed Parliament and the king, then England would not cease to be a commonwealth. 'The Body of the People may solemnly assemble together, and chuse out of themselves new Magistrates.'[84]

Once again, we are brought to the issue of different types of keys distributed in Matthew 16:19. Cotton believed that the people in a church had the power to elect ministers, and this was 'indeed, a privilege, or liberty, [but it is not] therefore Authority'. The power of authority only belonged to elders as the 'first subject', and the authority came immediately from Christ. On this point Cotton agreed with Rutherford that the ordination of a pastor by the believers on an island destitute of elders does not mean the people have, or ever had, authoritative power. In this case they would have the power of authority 'virtually', but not 'formally'. Election of a pastor was no act of 'authority' just as election of a king was no act of 'kingly authority'. Only the officers of the church were given, as the first subject, the formal power to exercise the keys of authority.

However, Cotton believed that the body of believers had another type of power. Both Rutherford and Cotton cited the passage in I Samuel when David, starving and running from Saul, ate the bread that had been set-aside for ceremonial purposes, although this was forbidden under Israelite law. Yet from a case of necessity David was right to eat. Whereas Rutherford called this a 'virtual' power, Cotton rejoined that it was a 'formal' power because the moral law necessarily trumped the ceremonial law. Therefore while Rutherford articulated that the power exercised in the case of necessity could only be 'virtual and extra-ordinary', Cotton believed that it could be both virtual and formal. It was virtual in regards to establishing the authority and establishing the context (church) and subject (believer) for that 'authority', and it was formal insofar as they were acting out the real power they had in subjecting themselves to the king.[85]

So Cotton could conclude that the body of the church 'that hath formall power to make one Relative ... hath an analogicall Power, to set up ... [its] correlative'.[86] Just as the king and subject were relatives, so were elders and people. A 'correlative' must necessarily have a reciprocal relationship with something else (a church implies elders, and vice versa). The Power was analogical because the people only had the elders' power virtually, but they did have the formal power to establish their authority. This is where Cotton's scholastic terminology provided a way forward in understanding a real power in the people, but he was still able to say it was not a formal ministerial power. Cotton later stated, 'For though the Brethren have not a *formall Power* to exercise the *Pastorall ministry* of the word and Sacrament, yet they have a *virtuall power* to exercise them by choosing ... Officers as have a *formall power*, to exercise the same.'[87]

The exchange between Cotton and Rutherford illustrates why we should see the publication of Cotton's *Keyes* as a way for the Apologists to reach out to the Scots for accommodation. The Apologists did not offer an olive branch to the Scottish divines out of fear of being outmanoeuvred by a more cogent system of polity, but they reached out to the Scots because the polity of the Scots was closer to the Apologists than perhaps any other group of divines in the Westminster assembly. The Apologists had worked closely with Gillespie and Alexander Henderson three years before, and knew exactly the common ground they shared. Thus we can see why, upon reading the *Keyes*, Rutherford told the 'Dissenting Brethren, That if they would come up to the Treatise of the Keyes, themselves [the Scots] would meet them there'.[88]

GISBERTUS VOETIUS

Gisbertus Voetius was the greatest authority on the church in the Netherlands, and one of the brightest theological minds on the continent during the mid-seventeenth century. Douglas Nobbs states, 'The University at Utrecht became an international centre for Calvinists under his academic guidance ... he was at heart a "scholastic sage" who was the greatest controversialist of the century.'[89] Jonathan Israel has called him Utrecht's 'doyen of *theological practica*', and Keith Sprunger called him 'the mightiest Dutch Puritan of them all'.[90] Voetius's *Desperata Causa Papatus* (1635) was considered a triumph of anti-papal polemic; in a generation used to citing authorities from the past, English and Scottish divines regularly quoted it.

It was not without reason, therefore, that Baillie desperately tried to get Voetius to write against the Apologists, as we saw in the previous chapter. Baillie's failure to procure a response from Voetius is telling: for one thing, it further indicates that Baillie was a state-agent working to secure a victory on behalf of the Covenantors rather than a man interested in the particulars of ecclesiastical debate. Only a year earlier, Baillie had dismissed Voetius because he sounded too much like Robert Parker. Baillie stated: 'I confesse I am verie evill satisfied with Voetius's Theses of Synods ... he sticks so to Parker's grounds of mutuall association and ecclesia prima, that I wish he had written nothing in this purpose', although he was careful to also tell Spang to keep this complaint private.[91]

It is difficult to explain his fool's errand in 1644, given that Baillie knew at least something of Voetius's polity, although he might have believed that Voetius would come around once he encountered Rutherford's arguments. In the same letter to his cousin in 1643 Baillie mentioned that 'Mr Samuel Rutherfoord hath much more readie for the presse of that subject [of Parker's polity].'[92] However, this hypothesis is hard to believe given that Rutherford's *Peaceable Plea* had been in print for over a year and was, as we have seen, aimed primarily at the polity of Robert Parker. We also know that part of Baillie's methodology was to send Spang a variety of independent manifestos, including works by John Canne, in an attempt to link all of them directly to the Apologists. It was certainly true that Voetius had nothing but scorn for the 'extreme independency' of men like John Canne.[93] However, Voetius knew and was in communication with the Apologists while they were at the Westminster assembly, and by his own admission he knew that John Canne believed in a different brand of polity than the 'middle-way men'.[94]

Baillie's was a high stakes game: he repeatedly, and with great risk, demanded responses from Dutch divines who disagreed with Parliament's involvement with the Church and also disagreed with many presbyterians' view of 'ecclesiae primae'.[95] Yet he believed that if he could close the doors on the Apologists' claim to be in the tradition of the 'best reformed churches' then one more obstacle – no matter the collateral damage – would be removed from the Covenanters' path. Baillie grossly misunderstood the nature and basis from which Voetius's ecclesiological viewpoints arose. Voetius believed that the first subject of all church power was a church of visible saints, made up of elders and people covenanted together, and that any power above that church must exist by the voluntary consensus of the people. Baillie had heard through his sources that Voetius was about to endorse Cotton's *Keyes*, but, unbeknownst to the Scottish divine, Voetius was about to do more than endorse it. Cotton's *Keyes of the Kingdom* was not only approved of by Voetius, but the language, and much of the structure of the pamphlet was fully and uncritically co-opted into Voetius's famous *Politicae Ecclesiasticae*, a point overlooked by historians of the English church. The very themes Voetius adopted were precisely the aspects of the Apologists' polity that partially assuaged Rutherford's fears of anarchical power in the church.

Before taking a closer look at Voetius's polity, we should reiterate that Voetius was quite capable of distinguishing between separatists and the congregationalism espoused by the Apologists. Robert Parker had in a small way influenced Voetius, as Bouwman and Nobbs have noted.[96] However, neither of these historians noted the significance of where Voetius departed from Parker. Voetius appreciated Parker's emphasis on the role of the elders in ruling the church, and Parker's emphasis on representative power was attractive to Voetius, as it was to John Paget (an English clergyman who pastored in Amsterdam) and many other English presbyterians. However, Voetius disagreed with Parker for the same reasons that Cotton and the Apologists did: none of them believed that all types of ecclesiastical power rested in the people alone as the first subject. Therefore, Voetius opposed the independency of John Canne, William Best, Henry Ainsworth and even the famous congregationalist divine, John Davenport.[97] English 'separatists' existed in abundance in Holland, so Voetius was keenly aware of the dangers they presented.[98] This is an important point to stress, given that much of the historiography of the Apologists has been told via the pamphlets and petitions of a few London presbyterian ministers.[99] Indeed, we are reminded that 'radicalism' is a matter of perspective; what seemed 'radical' to many English presbyterians in London may have seemed like a logical strand of reformed polity to others.

Voetius's multi-volume *Politicae Ecclesiasticae* was a treatise primarily about the power and rights of the particular church and secondarily about its relationship to other visible churches and the universal church. It is a rich source that deserves much more study than this book can offer.[100] Voetius rejected the presbyterian arguments that the particular church was a derivative of the Universal church. This was what Goodwin called the 'descendendo' position. 'Voetius attacked the hierarchic principle of virtual representation by which authority descended from the whole' universal or catholic church 'to the particular' church.[101] He went to great lengths to emphasise 'a covenant of visible saints as the essential characteristic of the visible church, and consequently, the share of the people in its government and the primary and indestructible nature of the particular church'.[102] Moreover he, like the Apologists, believed that the first subject of church power was the whole particular church made up of both elders and the people. At this point his polity began to mirror Cotton's.[103] Voetius saw this polity as also belonging to Thomas Goodwin and Nye.[104] For him both the key of liberty and the key of authority, taken together, were the 'first operator of all church-power needful for [a church] to exercise within themselves'.[105]

Like the Apologists, Voetius 'denied that all ecclesiastical power was in the ministry or consistory; but he equally denied that it was in the people distinct from, and by them delegated to, church organs'.[106] He distinguished himself from Parker and other 'independents' in that he believed the two powers were distinct, and one was not derived from the other. Taken together, the people and the elders were the whole church.[107] The power in the people was not derived from the elders or 'vice versa', no more than, as Voetius argued, 'the right eye derives its sight from the left'.[108] In order to describe this distinction Voetius borrowed the language of Cotton. Voetius stated that there are distinct church powers distributed to different 'subjects' in the church. In the people was the key of 'libertatis' (liberty) and in the elders was the key of 'autoritatis' (authority).[109] This distinction in church powers was entirely reliant upon

Cotton's *Keyes*.[110] Voetius possibly had already developed the concept of the division of the power of the keys prior to reading the *Keyes*. Indeed, as we have shown, the Apologists believed in this distinction well before they received the *Keyes*. Nonetheless, Cotton provided a linguistic framework for articulating these concepts. Indeed, Voetius used a variety of words to describe the various types of power, but he retained the conceptual distinctions.

This statement regarding the keys of liberty and authority was only the first of many examples of Voetius's reliance on Cotton's *Keyes*. In his *Politicae Ecclesiasticae*, the Dutch divine began to outline the variety of ways the people could exercise the key of liberty and the elders could exercise the key of authority. These sections mirrored the corresponding sections of Cotton's *Keyes*. Voetius outlined the various powers of the keys and utilised the same sub-points, phraseology and scriptural proofs that Cotton used to describe the key of liberty in the people and the key of authority in the elders. Voetius, although operating with Cotton's distinctions in mind, allocated Cotton's points under slightly different categories.[111] There were three meta-categories of church power: (1) teaching authority, (2) administrative power and (3) judgment and discipline.[112]

We are primarily concerned with the third category, since it discusses the people's role in church government. Here, under this third heading, Voetius subdivided church power into four separate categories utilising Cotton's distinctions between the peoples' power and the elders' power. He then allocated Cotton's descriptions under those four headings. The first two headings, 'Potestatem ordinis & regiminis' and 'potestatem jurisdictionis', concerned the power of the people.[113] These categories were aided by Cotton's fourth chapter, 'Of the subject to whom the Key of Church privilege, power, or Libertie is given'.[114] For Cotton this power of liberty was given to the people of the church and included the rights to choose elders, receive new members, excommunicate and restore the penitent to membership.[115] However, Voetius divided Cotton's categories into the powers the people had alone (e.g. choosing elders) and those powers they shared with the elders (e.g. excommunication). Voetius then placed Cotton's 'special acts' of those 'to whome the Key of Authority is committed (i.e. the elders)' under the third and fourth headings, 'potestate regiminis' and 'potestate jurisdictionis'.[116] This latter division of the elders' power mirrored the way Cotton divided the people's power. There are acts unique to the leaders of the church, such as calling the church together and ordination, and acts that the elders share with the people, like excommunication.[117] Voetius later claimed that removing the people from a role in church government was outside the tradition of the reformed churches on the continent.[118] So in Voetius's mind the jurisdictional power of the church represented the centre of a Venn diagram, where the powers of the people and the power of the elders overlapped. If anything, Voetius's linguistic adjustments were an improvement on Cotton's *Keyes*.[119]

VOETIUS, THE APOLOGISTS AND THE UTILITY OF SYNODS

Since church power impacts the function of synods and classes, we will attempt to offer a sketch of how these debates over the particular church's power illustrated the complexity of understanding the role of synods. This book cannot provide a full analysis of the debates over the role of synods, which would require another book altogether.[120] Yet the emphasis on the allocation of power at the particular church level has ramifications on the understanding of structures over and above particular congregations. Voetius's emphasis on the particular church being the first and proper subject of all church power has significant ramifications on how we are to understand the Dutch churches and their views of classes and synods. Given the preceding discussions on the power of the keys, it is not possible to distinguish congregationalists simply on the basis of the existence of synods. Nor can 'independents' simply be defined as those who wanted synods to have advisory power, while presbyterians wanted synods to have church power analogical to, or even superior to, the particular church.

Voetius provided a very helpful platform for clarifying the Apologists' position vis-à-vis other reformed churches, for through Voetius we also encounter two of his contemporaries, Robert Parker and John Paget. Robert Parker influenced Voetius's thought and John Paget was himself influenced by Voetius. By using Voetius as our starting point, we will see how Parker's influence on the Dutch actually distanced the Dutch churches from many presbyterians in England and Scotland, and we will see that Paget's arguments against Davenport, Robinson, Canne and Ainsworth actually came quite close to the position of the Apologists. We will first briefly examine how the Apologists understood the power of synods, and then we will see how Voetius viewed their position and how it fit into the larger Dutch tradition.

The presbyterians, both Scottish and English, repeatedly pointed out that Cotton used the Jerusalem council in Acts 15 as the basis for a formal synod of messengers sent from other associated churches for counsel. The London presbyterians extensively cited Cotton's description of synods and were particularly keen to point out that, in Cotton's words, synods were 'authoritative [and] juridical'.[121] In the preface to the *Keyes*, the Apologists claimed they did not entirely follow Cotton in seeing the gathering in Acts 15 as a formal synod. Nor did they think the Apostles were making authoritative decrees in their capacity as 'ordinary elders'.[122] Rather than a formal synod, the Apologists believed the gathering 'was an Assembly of the Church of Jerusalem, and of the Messengers from the Church of Antioch alone; that were farre remote each from other, and now electively met'.[123] This meeting was meant to arbitrate the 'deciding of that great Controversie risen amongst them at Antioch, which they found to bee too difficult for themselves'.[124] Cotton later claimed that the

Apologists did not 'herein Dissent from me'. Cotton agreed that the churches of Antioch and Jerusalem 'were too far remote to stand in a set, or combined Association, and therefore [the Apologists] may well deny it to be a Formall Synod according to the Forme of Synods ... in the Prebsyteriall Churches'.[125]

The Apologists, according to Cotton, essentially believed the assembly in Jerusalem was a synod. It had 'true matter and forme of a just Synod', for the 'efficient cause of the Synod, the Church of Antioch sent messengers; and the Church of Jerusalem (whose officers were sent unto) they freely gave them a meeting, and the Church with them.' The distinction between Cotton and the Apologists seemed to be a matter of terminology, because Cotton claimed that two churches meeting had the 'necessary being' of a synod, just as much as many churches meeting together. 'The forme of a Synod they had, in Arguing, and disputing, the case in hand, and freely giving in their Judgements from Scripture grounds' and concluding the matter with the 'Joynt consent of the Apostles, Elders, and Brethren'.[126] Both Cotton and the Apologists believed the 'brethren' were present at the decision made in Jerusalem.

There was an important distinction to be made between the Apostles functioning in their 'Apostolicall Power' with their unique ability and authority to explain obscure passages and ratify their conclusions 'with some greater Plerophory of the mind of the Holy Ghost' and their functioning as elders. Cotton believed that in allowing the members of the church and the elders to dispute, vote, and publish their opinions in a letter, 'herein they Acted as Ordinary Elders and messengers of churches'.[127] This reflects Cotton's position on Matthew 16:19, where Peter represented the Apostles, the elders, and the people. The result of Cotton and the Apologists' exegesis was the same: the power of the synod did not extend further than 'Ministeriall Doctrinall power' and it did not brandish 'the sword and power of Excommunication'.[128]

Many presbyterians argued that the synod had the power to excommunicate on the basis that all power to bind and loose was committed to the elders alone in Matthew 18:17, 18.[129] Cotton and the Apologists believed that this passage was in reference to the particular church, whereas presbyterians argued by way of analogy that if the elders represented the church, and the elders were the ones told of the offence, then there could be recourse to a higher court of gathered elders from multiple churches. As we discussed in the previous chapter, although the Apologists also believed an elder's authority was unique, and not derived from the believers, it was nonetheless an authorial power that could only be actuated in the context of a particular church, where believers were present. Thus Acts 15, where Luke tells us that the brethren were, in some measure, procedurally involved with the decision handed down, is hermeneutically connected to Matthew 16:19 and Matthew 18:17–18. The locus of binding church power was still in the particular church, and was never, nor ever could be transferred to a classical presbytery, or synod, where believers were not present. Therefore the binding authority in Acts 15 was existent only because of unique and extraordinary apostolic authority.

When Burroughs wrote his *Irenicum* on behalf of the Apologists he outlined six points where the presbyterians and the congregationalists agreed on synods, and one point where they disagreed.[130] It is has been incorrectly suggested that Burroughs was more presbyterian than his congregational brethren.[131] Burroughs in fact was clear that his position represented the Apologists. Their view on synods was not a new development, as they could trace their beliefs back to their days in exile. 'I doe not in these [points on synods] deliver onely mine owne judgement ... I stand charged to make it good to be their [my brethren's] judgments also.'[132]

Burroughs stated that these six points had been the opinion of the Apologists as far back as their exile in Holland. He stated that these views 'hath been both theirs and mine for divers yeares, even then when we never thought to have enjoyed our owne Land againe'.[133] First, congregations have a duty, and are bound in conscience, to give account of their ways to other churches around them. Second, 'Synods of other Ministers and Elders about them are an ordinance of Jesus Christ for the helping of the Church against errors, schismes, and scandals.' Third, these synods are to admonish churches with the authority of Christ. Fourth, 'they may declare men or Churches to be subverters of the faith ... to shame them before all the Churches about them'. Fifth, 'they may by a solemne act in the name of Jesus Christ refuse any further communion with them, till they repent'. Finally, they may proclaim 'in the name of Jesus Christ' that errant people or churches 'are not to be received into fellowship ... or communion ... with any ... [other] Churches of Christ.' For Burroughs 'the very knot of the controversie, between those who are for the Presbyteriall, and those who are for the congregationall way', was in the seventh point, the ability of the synod to excommunicate a person or a church. Even Rutherford was forced to admit to this point. Rutherford stated that the Dissenting Brethren gave much power to a synod, but because they did not give excommunication, they gave nothing.[134] We can see a similar list written by the presbyterians of the Westminster assembly, describing the nine points of 'use' of synods they saw in the Apologists' polity. This list was published in the assembly's *The Grand Debate*, which we can take as a summary of the debates on the assembly floor.[135]

One main critique Burroughs had of the presbyterian position concerned their insistence that the seventh point on excommunication was more effective than the six points he outlined above. Burroughs could not see how the presbyterian system was different in consequence from the powers of a congregational church. A synod, with the authority of Christ, put the church out of communion with the other churches, and 'are not such persons or Congregations put out of the Kingdome of CHRIST, and put under the power of Sathan consequently?"[36] The goal of excommunication was to work on the conscience of the sinner and to bring him to repentance, and Burroughs failed to see how the presbyterian synod's ability to 'excommunicate' was any stronger than to tell churches to refuse to associate, receive, or commune with a sinner or sinning church. In other words, for Burroughs, the consequences were the same. In both systems, the sinner or sinning church was outside the communion of godly churches. Burroughs anticipated the question 'But what if Congregations refuse ... to regard admonitions?'[37] He would not accept that one who had refused to obey a congregational synod's declaration would be more probably to obey a synod that had excommunicated him. A person or a church that was intent on erring would do so in either model. Furthermore, he thought that the magistrate should be made aware of what the synod has decreed, and was meant to assist and reinforce the judgment of the synod's decree. The assembly presbyterians noted this positively when they said the Apologists' declaration of non-communion could be 'ratified and backed with the authority of the Magistrate, to the end it may be more effectual'.[38]

Contrary to the claims of the Erastians, the magistrate did not take this action as an officer of a church, nor was his duty primarily spiritual. A subverter of the faith, or a heretical and schismatic church, was a danger to the state, and the magistrate should move to stop those who refuse the synod's decrees. But, on this point, Burroughs conceded, the congregationalists were not different from many of the English presbyterians. And the assembly presbyterians themselves recognised how close the Apologists came to them in terms of the power of the synods, saying, 'Our brethren acknowledge ... so much concerning Synods and their usefulnesse, as is sufficient to warrant not onely the lawfulnesse of their use, but also the standing use of them.'[39] But the presbyterians also acknowledged that their fundamental differences came down to the fact that the Apologists believed Matthew 18 meant that all church power was in the particular church.[40]

The congregationalists eventually made an adjustment in their understanding of synods. They came to believe that synods were, as Thomas Goodwin stated in May 1644, 'ordinances of Christ'.[41] The catalyst for this change seems to have been either the accommodation attempts in early April or Cotton's *Keyes*, which claimed that synods were 'an Ordinance of Christ'.[42] Indeed, Goodwin's description of the power of synods describes just how much power the Apologists had conceded: 'we acknowledge elective occasional Synods' for cases such as 'Male-Administration, or an unjust proceeding, in the Sentence of Excommunication, and the like we acknowledge Appeals or Complaints may be made to other Churches; and the Elders of those Churches met in a Synod', and these synods 'may as an Ordinance of Christ, Judge and Declare that Sentence to be Null, Void, and Unjust'. This 'ordinance of Christ' to declare and judge was amplified by the Apologists' claim that churches' obeying a synod was an ordinance Christ.[43] While this concession only provided the briefest outline of the Apologists' understanding of synods, it nonetheless gives us a better framework for understanding why Voetius could follow the congregationalists on this point as well.

Voetius not only followed Cotton's description of the keys' allocation in the particular church: he also acknowledged the validity of Goodwin and Nye's description of the utility and necessity of synods in the preface to Cotton's *Keyes*. Goodwin and Nye provided a limited summary of the Apologists' position on synods, because providing a specific defence in print in 1644 would have broken assembly protocol.[44] Voetius made particular reference to Goodwin and Nye's statement that synods were useful in cases of 'Mal-administrations and healing dissentions *in particular* congregations, and the like cases'.[45] And although they granted all the powers to those mentioned above, the Apologists also made it clear that a synod was 'not armed with authority and power of Excommunicating or delivering unto Satan, either the Congregations or the Members of them' because they were 'to leave the formall act of this censure to that authority which can onely execute it, placed by Christ in those Churches themselves'.[46] Such associations and assemblies 'should not intrench or impaire the privilege of intire Jurisdiction committed unto each Congregation (as a libertie purchased by Christ's bloud)' but leave that Church to exercise its powers 'untill they abuse that power, or are unable to manage it; and in that case onely to assist guide, and direct them, and not take on them to administer it for them, but with them, and by them'.[47]

Voetius agreed with Goodwin and Nye that churches should resort to synods in the case of maladministration only. And although the synod could assist, guide and direct, it did not have jurisdiction. Jurisdiction, for Voetius, only belonged to the particular church.[48] He also believed that while the synod was to assist, guide and direct its churches, it could never co-opt or assume the power that uniquely belonged to the particular church.[49]

Douglas Nobbs has noted that for Voetius, 'a covenant was the essential characteristic of the visible church, and consequently, the share of the people in its government and the primary and indestructible nature of the particular church'.[50] Voetius firmly believed that all churches were equipped with all ecclesiastical authority to exercise within themselves, and that no church could be set over another church.[51] Therefore, 'Divine Right claims was not to Voetius a sufficient basis' for the presbyterians' claims: 'he insisted that divine right had to be accepted by voluntary consent before it could be the basis of the visible church.'[52] Voetius held that the particular church was the *ecclesia prima* of all church power, and therefore the synod or classis could not be subjects of any power of the keys, nor could the power of the particular church be derived from the universal church. Voetius rejected calling a synod a church, and he rejected the constituting of a national church with its own church power, because that would mean setting one church above another church. Nobbs has noted that on this point Voetius's position was influenced by Robert Parker, whose notion of a 'basic or prime (prima) church' was 'the gathering of the faithful into a single congregation'.[53] John Paget shared a similar conception of the basic church.

VOETIUS, PAGET AND PARKER

When Paget wrote against 'extreme independents', he was desperate to protect men like Robert Parker, Paul Baynes and Voetius from being co-opted by Canne or Davenport. Paget's primary critique of the 'independents' in the Low Countries was that they did not give enough power to synods. Because modern scholars have been unable to distinguish between different types of congregationalists, they have failed to notice that the basis for Paget's polity was the main critique Rutherford levelled at the 'independencie' of Robert Parker.

Paget emphasised that the power of synods came from an ordinance of Christ. Nevertheless, he proclaimed that 'though we hold that Classes and Synods are most necessary and profitable for the well-being of the Church ... yet doe we not hold that the essence & being of the Church doth consist in this'.[54] As early as 1635 Voetius had already argued that 'Each Church ... hath its proper form of an Ecclesiastical Body or Society, so its endued with its proper Government and Jurisdiction' which this church exercises 'Independently in respect of al other churches'.[55] However, Paget claimed that a consociation of churches could willingly come together and give power to a synod of their own making.[56] Similarly, Voetius believed that 'ecclesiastical power was primarily and originally in the particular churches', but there could be synods or classes that 'arose from the desire of those churches to strengthen their own power in cases where each church had not sufficient power'.[57]

Cotton and the Apologists likewise argued for an 'association' or 'consociation' of churches, but the synod thus formed may not 'be perverted, either to the oppression or dimunition of the just libertie and authoritie of each particular Church within it self'.[58] Therefore the classis and synod was nothing more than an aggregate of their constituent members; there was no inherent power in these consociations, and any power those synods had was derived from the individual churches.[59] Thus 'the whole power was and continued to remain in the churches as the source, and was exercised by them as causa principalis, but was in the classes and synods by delegation'.[60] Years later when Nye reflected on the polity of Parker he stated that 'though that Jurisdiction which hath its rise in a particular church be pumped up into a Classis or a Synod', this power is 'but the same it was before. Synods, saith Parker out of Chamier, *Nullam habeant authoritatem* &c. They have no Authority but what is derived from particular Churches, So Voetius.'[61]

This last point was very important to John Paget, and he attempted to use it against John Davenport. Davenport cited Voetius's *Desperata causa papatus*, which said the church was the proper first subject of all power, 'Which aught to be and to remaine so proper to the Church, that it, neither may be snatched away by the authority of others, nor lost by their voluntary concession, nor committed to the trust of any other'.[162] Paget was quick to say that he agreed with this statement, but he denied its consequences, namely that Voetius supported Davenport's argument that synods were merely advisory. Paget argued that Voetius believed that synods had more power than simply of 'counsel and admonition', but he was not clear as to what power Voetius believed they actually had.[163] He argued that Voetius believed there was ecclesiastical jurisdiction in the synod, yet he did not describe the nature of that jurisdiction.[164] Paget, writing in 1638, could not have known how Voetius would interact with the Apologists and Cotton. Still, Paget's reading of Voetius placed the Dutch divine in the hermeneutical tradition that would make Cotton's *Keyes* ripe for appropriation. By 1644 Voetius had adjusted his position away from Robert Parker and John Paget, who believed the saints were the first subject of church power, and towards a model that distinguished between both the types of keys and the recipients of those keys.

Although much more work needs to be done on Paget, it seems that he did not believe that synods had the power to excommunicate. Thomas Goodwin claimed that the 'Learned Presbyterial Writer [Paget] acknowledgeth that none of the Reformed Churches ever practised it.'[165] Indeed, Goodwin also pointed out that when Low Countries held a synod to deal with the Arminian (remonstrant) congregation and Anabaptists, both of whom were worthy of censures and committed 'gross Errors', yet 'none of them were Excommunicated' by that synod.[166] Voetius also denied that synods could have the highest power, namely the power to bind and loose, although he was careful to give a great deal of power to synods. For example, he came to believe that a church could not excommunicate or call a minister without the advisory involvement of a synod. Bouwman believed that this may indicate a shift towards presbyterianism, but Douglas Nobbs rightly notes that Voetius always believed that the particular church was the only source of jurisdiction. Voetius denied that the synod had any right to excommunicate a church or individuals from a church.[167] Any synod could only act insofar as the church, as a covenanted body of visible saints, was willing to consociate with other churches and allow for a synod to advise. This was not a *jure divino* presbyterian polity.

All of this helps us better understand the variety of presbyterians in England during this period, as illustrated by the various understandings of the nature of synods and their respective powers. When the first Smectymnuan tract came out in 1641, the authors claimed, 'Wee reade in Scripture, of the Churches of *Iudea*, and the Churches of *Galatia*; and why not the Churches of *England*? Not that we denie the *Consociation*, or *Combination* of Churches into a Provinciall or Nationall Synod for the right ordering of them.' Charles Herle similarly argued for consociation of churches in early 1643.[168] At this date, the emerging English presbyterians were of one mind: churches may consociate. Eventually, the language of consociation was dropped in favour of subordination.[169] It should be carefully noted that the assembly presbyterians coalesced around the word subordination as means of accommodating disparate presbyterian views. An examination of the London Provincial assembly's *Vindication of the Presbyteriall-Government* helps us understand this accommodation. Edmund Calamy was involved in both of the Smectymnuan publications in 1641 and he also took the lead in the Provincial assembly's *Vindication* in 1649. The London presbyterians argued that Matthew 18, 'by a parity of reason, proves a subordination of Congregations unto Synods'.[170] It may seem that there was little difference between the assembly's document and the Provincial assembly's *Vindication*. However, there was a variety of definitions of subordination.

Paget and Voetius spoke of subordination, but they meant something entirely different than the presbyterians in the London Provincial assembly. For Paget, in the Reformed churches, there 'is no one head-Church, that hath more authority then another, all Congregations are equall, independent of each other', and all these congregations 'are equally and mutually subject to the Synod consisting of many', but their dependency 'is onely in regard of many combined'.[171] So the subordination was predicated upon the consociation and delegated from the constituent churches. The London presbyterians could not stomach any of these distinctions because they allowed the people power – even if it was power delegated by representation. Although they readily recognised that the 'middle-way men' were distinct from other 'independents' on the basis of their understanding of the keys, they nonetheless called this schema borrowed from Cotton a 'rotten foundation'.[172] Cawdrey, who represented those more clerical English presbyterians close to James Cranford, disapproved of all Cotton's distinctions that Voetius embraced.[173]

By 1649, Edmund Calamy was a moderating influence in the London Provincial assembly.[174] The emphasis on subordination gave cover to those clerical English presbyterians in London, many of whom still did not believe the particular church had a share in governing the church. On the other hand, Parker, Paget and Voetius believed that those churches who consociated should submit to the synod, but not because the synod was a church itself. This ecclesiology was entirely different from the polity espoused by the London Provincial assembly. These presbyterians argued from *Jure divino* that the synod was a church properly speaking, with the keys invested in the synod. The churches should submit not because they had consociated, but because they were subordinate bodies under the church governing it. Hence, the Westminster assembly tried to avoid this question of where church power lay every time it came up for discussion.

Indeed, much of the assembly's frustration was predicated upon the fact that the Apologists and Cotton believed in a consociation of churches, but denied the jurisdiction of those consociations. Thomas Goodwin knew about this friction, and although the *Grand Debate* did not contain congregational re-rejoinders to the presbyterians' responses, we can find Goodwin's response in his *Government of the Churches of Christ*. He stated that the 'very Principle which the Assembly doth go upon to Establish this power in Synods and Presbyteries' given in the *Grand Debate* is 'That as Families are bound to joyn into some Congregational church, so those Churches into Association together: and these joyned in a New Congregation, gives them power over each other.'[75]

Goodwin sympathised most with Paget's type of presbyterianism. '[T]his association of Churches, gives the whole a power over each of these Churches', and 'Tho' we wholly assent not to this latter, yet supposing it (and it is one of the best and fairest grounds of the Presbyterial way)', it cannot 'extend to a power of Excommunicating any of these Churches so associated'.[76] This attraction to consociation presbyterianism further explains the Apologists' commonality with the Smectymnuans in 1641. The London presbyterians placed a greater emphasis on subordination, as evidenced in the *Vindication*. The London Provincial assembly, while attempting to respect the rights of the particular church, viewed association and subordination in more clerical terms. They believed that the church in Matthew 18 could only mean the elders.[77] Therefore, an assembly made of associated churches meant an association of elders who constitute a church because the elders carried all church power with them from the particular to the synod.

A great deal of confusion arose from these debates over who was the first subject of church power and how it related to Matthew 16:19 because so many views existed on the subject. Without coming to a concrete conclusion in October 1643 as to who Peter represented when he received the keys, Matthew 18 was allowed a broad range of interpretations. We have established that early on Robert Parker, John Paget and many English presbyterians followed the line that the people were the first subject of all church power, but the elders exercised that power on their behalf. This understanding was certainly held in some Dutch traditions. With this model, one argued from the particular church via delegation and representation up to the power of a synod. However, this view was unreasonable to Rutherford, whose *Peaceable Plea* struck at the heart of Parker's basis of ecclesiology. Rutherford had two fundamental problems with Parker. First, he rejected outright the claim that all the keys of the kingdom are given to the believers in any church.[78] Second, he rejected Parker's claim that since a church 'may be without synods; therefore Synods are no ordinances of Christ'.[79] We know the Apologists also rejected both of these premises, and we can see why in the eyes of Rutherford, Cotton and the Apologists' understanding of the diversity of keys and recipients was actually closer to the Scottish model than to the English tradition borne out of Robert Parker.

From John Paget's perspective in 1638, Voetius was very much in the same tradition as Robert Parker. By 1644, Voetius had adjusted his polity to reflect the uniqueness of the elders' authority, while retaining the rights and privileges of the people. Yet Voetius remained committed to a role of synods with power derived from its constituent members. How did this ecclesiology differ from Parker's position?

CONCLUSION

We typically understand a congregational polity as pertaining to the rights of the people. Yet for the 'middle-way men', it was also about protecting the rights of the elders. The rights of the elders could be violated in two different directions: from the side of the Brownists whose 'rule and government ... [in] the hands of the people ... drowns the Elders votes (who are but a few) in the major part of theirs', and from the opposite 'Presbyteriall-government' where the right of the elders were 'swallow[ed] up ... into this Jurisdiction of a common Presbyterie of severall congregations'.[180] In the mind of the Apologists, the clerical impulse of their polity was crucial. The Parker model troubled them because the elders' power was merely derivative, while the presbyterian model bothered them because the rights of the elders were diluted into a body of other elders from other churches. But in the Apologists' mind and in the mind of Voetius, the unique 'Authority' of the elders in the church actually credited a synod with more respect since it was not the people's authority being refracted back to the churches, but the authority of men who had been acknowledged with a unique, non-derivative power from Christ meeting together to discuss weighty matters. Thus they deserved respect and their council should be acknowledged by nature of their being men who received the keys of authority. From the perspective of the presbyterians who followed Robert Parker, the Apologists seemed unwilling to give enough power to the synod. From Rutherford's perspective, these same presbyterians seemed to rely on popular authority as the basis of synodical authority, which was unstable and, worse, had no biblical basis. In many ways, the 'middle way' found a path through this seeming contradiction. Voetius could believe that the Reformed churches always held place for the people to exercise power, but he also recognised that the people could not exercise authorial jurisdiction in normal circumstances. The model described by the Apologists and Cotton's interpretation of Matthew 16:19 allowed for a unique role of the elders that was distinct from, but connected to the people.

Here it seems the *clerical* English presbyterian position was the most unique in the Reformed tradition. Historians' failure to grasp the nature of power and the presence of a strong Reformed tradition that allowed people a role in church government, has led them to incorrectly place all types of English presbyterians into the continental stream of polity. In reality at least two, seemingly contradictory, streams existed. One was very much born out of the clerical position, typified by Seaman, Burgess, Cawdrey and the London ministers in 1645. These divines believed that power resided exclusively, and as the first subject, in the clerics. The other was born out of Robert Parker and typified by John Paget and Stephen Marshall. They believed that the people were the first subject of church power, but the exercise of that power rested exclusively in the elders.[181] The Scots pointedly rejected both of these English traditions, as would Voetius and the Apologists. In terms of the particular church, the Scots, the Dutch and the Apologists espoused a middle way between these two English traditions. But, we should be careful to note that this 'middle way' was not simply in *reaction* to the English traditions. Of course, all the presbyterians could coalesce around the concept of a synod, but because the assembly divines did not settle the issue of the first subject of church power the question of synods was left open to a wide range of interpretations. We will highlight this problem in the next chapter, as we turn back to the debates on the assembly floor.

NOTES

1 Cawdrey, *The Inconsistencie of the Independent way*, pp. 38–39.

2 *Jus divinum regiminis ecclesiastici*, p. 116.

3 Ibid., p. 116.

4 For examples see Van Dixhoorn, *MPWA* (vol. 3), pp. 269, 320, 355, 360–362, 408; Gillespie, *Notes*, pp. 83, 98, 99. London presbyterians outside the assembly designed much of their *Jus divinum regiminis ecclesiastici* against Cotton's arguments.

5 Van Dixhoorn, *MPWA* (vol. 3), p. 543. See, for example, S. Rutherford, *A Survey of the Spirituall Antichrist* (London, 1648), p. 177.

6 Baillie, *The Dissuasive … Vindicated*, preface, p. 86.

7 Cotton & Owen, *A Defence of Mr. John Cotton*, p. 38.

8 W. D. J. McKay, *An Ecclesiastical Republic: Church Government in the Writings of George Gillespie* (Edinburgh: Rutherford House, 1997), p. 245.

9 Van Dixhoorn, *MPWA* (vol. 3), 285.

10 Baillie, *Letters and Journals*, vol. 2, p. 161.

11 Cotton, *The Way of Congregational Churches Cleared*, vol. 2, p. 21.

12 Cawdrey wrote anonymously in his first pamphlet against Cotton and the Apologists, probably because he was a member of the assembly. Cawdrey, *Vindiciæ Clavium*, frontispiece.

13 Bush (ed.), *Correspondence*, p. 176.

14 Cotton, *The Way of Congregational Churches Cleared*, vol. 2, p. 2; Cotton & Owen, *A Defence of Mr. John Cotton*, p. 65.

15 Cotton, *The Way of Congregational Churches Cleared*, vol. 2, p. 19; A. Hughes, *Gangraena and the Struggle for the English Revolution* (Oxford: Oxford University Press, 2004), p. 262.

16 Cotton, *The Way of Congregational Churches Cleared*, vol. 2, p. 20.

17 For more on Cotton's use of syllogism in his exegesis, see E. H. Davidson, 'John Cotton's Biblical Exegesis: Method and Purpose', *Early American Literature*, 17 (1982), 119–138, p. 127. Ann Hughes has shown that Edwards's style lacked 'logic and coherence'. Hughes, *Gangraena*, p. 55.

18 Cawdrey, *The Inconsistencie of the Independent way*, p. 39.

19 See, for example, Rutherford, *A Survey of the Spirituall Antichrist*, p. 177.

20 Compare Rutherford, *Due Right*, p. 1; Cotton, *The Way of the Churches of Christ in New England*, p. 1. See chapter 5 for discussion of Holmes.

21 Compare the following two copies of the same quotes. Cotton, *The Way of the Churches of Christ in New England*, pp. 19, 20; Rutherford, *Due Right*, p. 1.

22 Cotton, *The Way of Congregational Churches Cleared*, vol. 2, p. 19.

23 Rutherford, *Due Right*, p. 2.

24 Ibid., p. 3.

25 Rutherford cites the wrong section of Ainsworth's confession. It seems he was following Robinson's citation of the same section of Ainsworth. Robinson's marginal note cites article 37 of Ainsworth's *Confession*, when it was actually article 34. Ainsworth, *A True Confession of the Faith*, not paginated; Robinson, *A justification of separation*, p. 106; Rutherford, *Due Right*, p. 3.

26 Rutherford, *Due Right*, p. 3.

27 Ibid., p. 3.

28 Ibid., p. 6.

29 Ibid., p. 4.

30 Ibid.

31 Cotton, *The Way of Congregational Churches Cleared*, vol. 2, p. 20; see also Cotton, *The Way of the Churches of Christ in New England*, p. 1.

32 Cotton, *The Way of Congregational Churches Cleared*, vol. 2, p. 20.

33 Ibid., p. 20.

34 Ibid., p. 21.

35 Ibid., p. 21; Rutherford, *Due Right*, p. 6.

36 Cotton, *The Way of Congregational Churches Cleared*, vol. 2, p. 25.

37 Ibid., p. 21.

38 Rutherford, *Due Right*, p. 10. 1 Corinthians 1:4, 'I thank my God always on your behalf, for the grace of God which is given you by Jesus Christ'. 2 Corinthians 4:5, 'For we preach not ourselves, but Christ Jesus the Lord; and ourselves your servants for Jesus'

sake.' 1 Timothy 3:16, 'And without controversy great is the mystery of godliness: God was manifest in the flesh, justified in the Spirit, seen of angels, preached unto the Gentiles, believed on in the world, received up into glory.'

39 Revelation 3:7, 'And to the angel of the church in Philadelphia write; These things saith he that is holy, he that is true, he that hath the key of David, he that openeth, and no man shutteth; and shutteth, and no man openeth.'

40 Rutherford, *Due Right*, p. 10.

41 Ibid., p. 11.

42 Cotton, *The Way of Congregational Churches Cleared*, vol. 2, p. 30.

43 Ibid., p. 30.

44 Ibid., p. 30.

45 Ibid., p. 30.

46 Ibid., p. 22.

47 Ibid., p. 22.

48 Rutherford, *Due Right*, p. 7.

49 Van Dixhoorn, *MPWA* (vol. 2), p. 237.

50 Rutherford, *Due Right*, p. 7.

51 Cotton & Owen, *A Defence of Mr. John Cotton*, p. 50.

52 Ibid., p. 50.

53 Cotton, *The Way of Congregational Churches Cleared*, vol. 2, p. 22.

54 Ibid., p. 22. The printer wrongly attributes the first line of the quotation to Rutherford.

55 Ibid., p. 22. Ephesians 4:8–11, 'Therefore He says: *"When He ascended on high, He led captivity captive, And gave gifts to men."* (Now this, *"He ascended"* – what does it mean but that He also first descended into the lower parts of the earth? He who descended is also the One who ascended far above all the heavens, that He might fill all things.) And He Himself gave some *to be* apostles, some prophets, some evangelists, and some pastors and teachers.'

56 Goodwin, *Government*, p. 64.

57 Cotton, *The Way of Congregational Churches Cleared*, vol. 2, p. 23.

58 Ibid., p. 23.

59 Ibid., p. 23.

60 Ibid., p. 23.

61 F. B. Carr, 'The thought of Robert Parker (1564?–1614) and his influence on puritanism before 1650', University of London, PhD thesis (1964), pp. 293–294; cf. Cotton, *The Way of Congregational Churches Cleared*, vol. 2, pp. 13, 20.

62 Parker, *De Politeia Ecclesiastica* [trans.], 97r; see also Carr, 'The thought of Robert Parker (1564?–1614) and his influence on puritanism before 1650', pp. 165, 169.

63 Stephen Brachlow briefly addresses this topic. S. Brachlow, *The Communion of Saints: Radical Puritan and Separatist Ecclesiology, 1570–1625* (Oxford: Oxford University Press, 1988), p. 173.

64 Baynes, *The diocesans tryall*, p. 83.

65 Ibid., p. 83.

66 Cotton, *The Way of Congregational Churches Cleared*, vol. 2, p. 31.

67 Ibid., p. 23.

68 Goodwin, *Government*, p. 57.

69 Brachlow, *The Communion of Saints*, pp. 172–173.

70 Winship, *Godly Republicanism*, p. 97.

71 For more on this point see above, chapter 3.

72 Cotton & Owen, *A Defence of Mr. John Cotton*, pp. 33, 34.

73 Ibid., pp. 48ff.

74 Rutherford, *Due Right*, p. 7.

75 Ibid., p. 7.

76 Ibid., p. 8.

77 I am grateful to Richard Serjeantson for pointing this out to me.

78 Cotton, *The Way of Congregational Churches Cleared*, vol. 2, p. 23

79 Ibid., p. 23.

80 Ibid., p. 25.

81 Ibid., p. 24. Bridge addresses this topic in his pamphlets against Henry Ferne.

82 Cotton, *The Way of Congregational Churches Cleared*, vol. 2, p. 35.

83 Ibid., p. 35.

84 Ibid., p. 36.

85 Ibid., pp. 22–26.

86 Ibid., p. 24; see also, Cotton & Owen, *A Defence of Mr. John Cotton*, pp. 53–54.

87 Cotton & Owen, *A Defence of Mr. John Cotton*, p. 7.

88 Ibid., p. 38.

89 D. Nobbs, *Theocracy and Toleration: A Study of the Disputes in Dutch Calvinism from 1600 to 1650* (Cambridge: Cambridge University Press, 1938), p. 130.

90 J. I. Israel, *The Dutch Republic: Its Rise, Greatness and Fall, 1477–1806* (Oxford: Clarendon Press, 1995), p. 477; Sprunger, *Dutch Puritanism*, p. 361.

91 Baillie concludes with, 'bot this to yow onlie', Baillie, *Letters and Journals*, vol. 2, p. 65.

92 Ibid., p. 65.

93 M. Bouwman, *Voetius over het gezag der synoden* (Bakker, 1937), p. 53.

94 W. Bridge, *A Sermon preached before the Honourable House of Commons, at their Publique Fast, Novemb. 29. 1643* (London, 1643), p. 22; Bouwman, *Voetius*, pp. 54–55; Edwards, *Antapologia*, p. 232.

95 See above, chapters 3 and 4.

96 Bouwman, *Voetius*, pp. 49–53; Nobbs, *Theocracy and Toleration*, pp. 174–176.

97 Bouwman, *Voetius*, pp. 54ff, 58, 132, 135, 335.

98 Nobbs, *Theocracy and Toleration*, p. 173; Sprunger, *Dutch Puritanism*, chapter 3.

99 The quintessential example is Tolmie's *Triumph*.

100 Only two authors have studied the ecclesiological components of Voetius's work. See Bouwman, *Voetius*, and Nobbs, *Theocracy and Toleration*.

101 Nobbs, *Theocracy and Toleration*, p. 147.

102 Ibid., p. 172.

103 This is something that M. Bouwman noticed in 1937. Bouwman proves that Voetius is reliant upon Cotton for his understanding of the power of the keys. He does not, however, make any effort to understand the English context. Much of what I will say is an attempt to summarise, amplify and make accessible his assessment. I am very grateful to Anthony Milton for pointing me to Bouwman's work. Bouwman, *Voetius*, p. 56.

104 Ibid., pp. 56, 337.

105 Ibid., pp. 335–336.

106 Nobbs, *Theocracy and Toleration*, p. 165.

107 G. Voetii, *Politicae Ecclesiastiae* (Amstelodami, 1663), vol. 1, p. 220.

108 Ibid., p. 220.

109 Ibid., p. 118. Here Voetius states, 'there are those who attribute the key of authority and power to the consistory of elders and members' and he then proceeds to allocate those powers according to Cotton's model. Therefore 'those' is undoubtedly referring to Cotton, Goodwin and Nye. Bouwman, *Voetius*, 335; Voetii, *Politicae Ecclesiastiae*, p. 118.

110 Bouwman, *Voetius*, p. 56.

111 Ibid., p. 366.

112 I am greatly indebted to Gerald Bray for his help in translating the following sections of Voetius. Voetii, *Politicae Ecclesiastiae*, p. 118.

113 'the power of order and government' and 'the power of jurisdiction', ibid., p. 120.

114 Cotton, Goodwin & Nye, *Keyes*, p. 12.

115 M. Bouwman has provided a comprehensive list of Voetius's literal reliance upon Cotton in the Appendix of his *Voetius over het gezag der synoden*, although I have included examples here. Bouwman, *Voetius*, pp. 435ff; Cotton, Goodwin & Nye, *Keyes*, pp. 12–23; Voetii, *Politicae Ecclesiastiae*, pp. 119–122. Cotton stated, 'as the brethren have a power of order, and the priviledge to expostulate with their Brethren, in case of private scandals, according to the rule Mat. 18. 15, 16. So in case of publike scandal, the whole Church of the Brethren have power an priviledge to joyne with the Elders … and the same Brethren of the same Church, as well as the Elders, he intreateth to forgive the same incestuous Corinthians upon his repentence, 2 Cor. 2. 7, 8.' So Voetius follows, 'Quod expostulare possint non tantum seorsim in casu privatae offensae et scandali, Matt 18:15, 16, sed et collectim una presbyterio in scandu publico, immo et judicare Matt 18. 17 coll. Cum 1 Cor. 5 v. 2, 5, 22 … Quod potestatem habeat lapsos et poenitentes ad reconciliationem admittende 2 Cor. 2 v. 7, 8.'

116 Voetii, *Politicae Ecclesiastiae*, pp. 120–121.

117 An example of the former: 'A fourth act of their rule is, the ordination of officers (whom the people have chosen) whether elders or deacons, I Tim. 4. 14, Acts 6. 6.' Voetius

177

follows, 'Quod instituant et solemniter introducant presbyteros, 1 Tim. 4. 14 cum Actor. 6. 6.' Cotton, Goodwin & Nye, *Keyes*, p. 21; Voetii, *Politicae Ecclesiastiae*, p. 121; see also Bouwman, *Voetius*, p. 439.

118 See Powell, 'Dissenting Brethren', pp. 248–253.

119 Bouwman claimed that Voetius took the 'rough edges' off of Cotton's framework. Bouwman, *Voetius*, p. 336.

120 For summary of the debates see *The grand debate concerning Presbitery and independency by the Assembly of Divines convened at Westminster by authority of Parliament* (London, 1652).

121 *Jus divinum regiminis ecclesiastici*, pp. 249, 250.

122 Certain men were telling the Christians in Antioch and Judea that they must be add circumcision to their faith. The council in Jerusalem was asked for advice and told the representatives in from Antioch that they need not add Jewish legal customs to their Christian faith. Act 15:1–29. Cotton, Goodwin & Nye, *Keyes*, preface, not paginated.

123 Ibid.preface, not paginated.

124 Ibid., preface.

125 Cotton & Owen, *A Defence of Mr. John Cotton*, p. 76. This may have been, in part, due to a comment made by Rutherford, who noted that Cotton and the Apologists 'contradict' each other over the exegesis of Acts 15. Rutherford, *A Survey of the Spirituall Antichrist*, p. 10.

126 Cotton & Owen, *A Defence of Mr. John Cotton*, pp. 76–77.

127 Ibid., p. 78.

128 Cotton, Goodwin & Nye, *Keyes*, preface, not paginated.

129 Polly Ha provides a good background on earlier presbyterians' synecdochal use of Matthew 18:17–18; Ha, *English Presbyterianism*, pp. 57–58.

130 These six points are quotes from Burroughs, *Irenicum*, p. 43.

131 Tom Webster, 'Burroughes, Jeremiah (*bap.* 1601?, *d.* 1646)', *Oxford Dictionary of National Biography* (Oxford: Oxford University Press, 2004), www.oxforddnb.com/view/article/4106, accessed 2 April 2011.

132 Burroughs, *Irenicum*, p. 47. See also, Burroughs, *Vindication*, p. 11. It was not unusual for the Apologists to allow one of their own to write on behalf of the rest. This can be shown in the newly rediscovered *Principles of Christian Religion* manuscript. Although the *Principles* have sixteen articles, the majority of authors signed the document after article eleven. The remaining five chapters are signed by Nye and Sydrach Simpson 'on behalf of ourselves and others'. *Principles*, 116v.

133 Burroughs, *Irenicum*, p. 47. These two paragraphs are taken from ibid., pp. 43–44.

134 Rutherford, *A Survey of the Survey of that Summe of Church Discipline*, pp. 459–460.

135 I am grateful to Chad Van Dixhoorn for pointing this out to me.

136 Burroughs, *Irenicum*, p. 44.

137 Ibid., p. 46.

138 *The Grand Debate*, 138ff. For a full discussion on the presbyterians' counter arguments to the Apologists, see pp. 137ff.

139 Ibid., p. 138.

140 See below, chapters 7 and 8.

141 Van Dixhoorn, *MPWA* (vol. 3), p. 98.

142 Gillespie, *Notes*, p. 41; Cotton, Goodwin & Nye, *Keyes*, p. 23.

143 Goodwin, *Government*, p. 139.

144 Cotton, Goodwin & Nye, *Keyes*, preface, not paginated.

145 Ibid., preface, not paginated.

146 Ibid., preface, not paginated.

147 Ibid., preface, not paginated.

148 Bouwman, *Voetius*, pp. 336–338. I am extremely grateful to Dr Dirk Jongkind for assistance in the translation of Bouwman's Dutch to English.

149 Ibid., pp. 336–338.

150 Nobbs, *Theocracy and Toleration*, p. 172.

151 Cited in P. Nye, *The Lawfulnes of the Oath of Supremacy, and power of the King in Ecclesiastical affairs* (London, 1683), p. 116.

152 Nobbs, *Theocracy and Toleration*, p. 170.

153 Carr, 'The thought of Robert Parker (1564?–1614) and his influence on puritanism before 1650', p. 163.

154 J. Paget, *A Defence of Church-Government, exercised in Presbyteriall, Classicall, & Synodall Assemblies* (London, 1641), p. 33

155 Nye, *The Lawfulnes of the Oath of Supremacy*, p. 118.

156 Paget, *A Defence*, p. 96.

157 Nobbs, *Theocracy and Toleration*, p. 166.

158 Cotton, Goodwin & Nye, *Keyes*, p. 57.

159 Nobbs, *Theocracy and Toleration*, p. 166.

160 Ibid., p. 167.

161 Nye, *The Lawfulnes of the Oath of Supremacy*, p. 112

162 J. Davenport, *An apologeticall reply to a booke called an ansvver to the unjust complaint of VV.B.* (Rotterdam, 1636), pp. 242–243.

163 Paget, *A Defence*, p. 120.

164 Ibid., p. 120.

165 Goodwin, *Government*, p. 205.

166 Ibid., p. 205.

167 Bouwman, *Voetius*, pp. 336–337, 388.

168 Smectymnuus, *An answer*, pp. 80–81; Herle, *The Independency on Scriptures of the Independency of Churches*, p. 1; Bradley, 'Jacob and Esau', p. 233.

169 *The Grand Debate*, pp. 139ff. For an overview of how many English presbyterians argued for subordination of synods see, *A Vindication of the Presbyteriall Government*, pp. 22–26.

170 *A Vindication of the Presbyteriall Government*, p. 25.

171 Paget, *A Defence*, p. 112.

172 *Jus divinum regiminis ecclesiastici*, p. 116.

173 Cawdrey, *Vindiciæ Clavium*, pp. 10ff.

174 I am grateful to Elliot Vernon for clarifying the important distinctions between those London presbyterians who wrote *Jus Divinum Regiminis* and those who wrote the *Vindication*.

175 Goodwin, *Government*, p. 206.

176 Ibid., p. 206.

177 *A vindication of the Presbyteriall-Government, and Ministry* (London, 1650), p. 49.

178 Rutherford, *Peaceable Plea*, chapter 1.

179 Ibid., p. 214.

180 Cotton, Goodwin & Nye, *Keyes*, preface, not paginated.

181 There was undoubtedly a wide range of presbyterian positions that fell somewhere in between.

Chapter 7

Presbyterian coalitions

In the first two months of 1644, Parliament's most contentious piece of wartime legislation and the assembly's most momentous propositions collided in the Jerusalem Chamber. On 19 January, while the assembly was preoccupied with the pressing question of ordination, Cornelius Burgess presented two relatively uncontroversial propositions on church government from the First Committee – one of three standing Committees in the assembly. First, 'The scripture holdeth out a presbytery in a church.' Second, 'A presbytery consisteth of ministers of the word, and such other public officers, as have been already voted to have a share in the government of the church.'[1] The first two propositions did not receive any recorded debate. It was the 'Third Proposition', introduced on February 1 that forced the assembly into its first discussion on presbyteries and synods through February and March 1644. These entropic debates culminated in the voting through of this one vital proposition (*viz.* the 'Third Proposition) – the first and only *affirmative* proposition on presbyterianism. The 'Third Proposition' was as momentous as it was short. Indeed, the assembly spent nearly six weeks debating this one proposition: 'That divers churches may be under one presbyteriall government.'[2]

In the previous chapter we saw how foreign churches regarded certain strains as outside the reformed tradition. This chapter primarily focuses on the first three weeks of those debates and how they served to highlight the variety of presbyterian polities emerging on the floor of the assembly. The importance of the topic is highlighted by three facts. Firstly, all the themes covered in the first six chapters of this book surface the assembly's discussions. Secondly, parliamentary interest in the assembly's proceedings was at its highest point during February. Thirdly, it quickly became apparent that the presbyterians had to reach an agreement within their own majority before they could accommodate the Congregationalists and that would unalterably change the complexion of the assembly.

February shared two similarities with the controversy of October 1643: firstly, the Apologists again tried – and failed – to begin with a platform of church government; secondly, the congregationalists lost exegetical ground on the second of their two most fundamental verses of their polity. Both debates reflected the anxiety held by all parties that there was no settled opinion on the dicey topic of church power. In both October and February the Apologists were outmanoeuvred on procedural grounds. The main difference, as we shall see in this chapter, is that the Scots were present. The Scots initially supported the congregationalists methodology, but with pressures from back home and facing a potential schism within the English presbyterian ranks, quickly changed tactics.

For reasons that will be explained in chapter 8, though the assembly voted to affirm the Third Proposition in early 1644, the divines did not send the proposition for parliamentary approval until the end of the year. The time in between represented the slow death of congregationalism at Westminster and the dashing of any hopes for a national church predicated upon congregational principles or even an accommodation of the Apologists polity. The Apologists – as we shall see – were victims less of their own obstinacy than of intra-presbyterian factionalism and political exigencies.[3]

PARLIAMENTARY DIMENSION

Before approaching these debates in early February, we need to see how they mapped onto seismic shifts occurring within the concurrent Parliamentary power structures. Parliamentarians who had been most frustrated with Lord General Essex's dilatoriness – including Saye and Sele, Wharton, St John, and Vane, Jr – had been pushing for a new way to monitor the war effort for months.[4] The tensions between the war party and Essex had only increased throughout the autumn of 1643.

Essex's brief victory at Gloucester and outmaneuvering of Charles' attempt to prevent him from returning to London in early September only served to make Essex more 'erratic and self-aggrandizing'.[5] Matters were made worse when Charles decided to utilise Irish Catholic forces to invade England. Essex 'refused to resume the field' and, instead, for the second time argued 'that Parliament should take the opportunity for a negotiated peace'.[6] The war party was not keen to have its own military leader telling it when to seek peace with Charles.

By October 1643 – the same month that the Westminster assembly took up its initial debates on church government – the House of Commons was pondering the need for a new permanent council of war.[7] The problem was that the existing supervisors of the war effort, the Committee for Safety, had no real authority to demand that Essex take up arms. The committee was never given 'any empowering ordinance from Parliament', and for those parliamentarians who had risked the most in the rebellion, this impotency was an increasing source of frustration.[8]

As Essex's army faltered and Parliament was faced with the prospect of outright defeat, the Committee for Safety came to be regarded as one of the principal obstructions to Parliament's success.[9] But by late January 1644 the Committee for Safety's leader, John Pym, was dead, the Scottish army was crossing the northern border back into England and London was abuzz with Charles's various foiled plots against the city. All this provided the impetus for a new committee to govern the war effort. The creation of this new committee, the Committee for Both Kingdoms, would represent the first of two significant political and religious realignments that would occur over the ensuing twelve months.[10] By January this parliamentary spat began to spill over into the Westminster assembly.

The month of January seemed to be a time when, in the build-up to the establishment of the Committee for Both Kingdoms, the peace party members and war party members each struggled to point the assembly in a direction that favoured their own respective interests. On 3 January (around the same time the *Apologeticall Narration* was published) the Lords asked the Commons to appoint Essex to the Westminster assembly. The Commons agreed, but perhaps anticipating Essex's influence in the assembly also made Arthur Hesilrige, a member of the war party, and Edward Reynolds, an Essex ally, members of the assembly.[11] During the next few weeks, the attendance of Parliamentarians in the assembly increased considerably.

The primary question throughout the month of January surrounded the ordination of ministers. The Lords seemed particularly concerned that London citizens were not receiving the sacraments due to the lack of ordained ministers in the capital.[12] It was proposed that a committee of ministers be assembled in London to ordain new ministers. Though this ad hoc committee was widely seen to be a temporary solution to an extraordinary situation, it caused a great deal of anxiety in the assembly.[13] The Apologists thought it established presbyteries before the topic had even been debated.[14]

Some in the Assembly attempted to avoid the charge of creating a presbytery by saying that such a committee called to ordain would be able to do so on the basis of their being ministers, rather than on the basis of their association in a presbytery. As Wayne Spear has noted, this was a 'dangerous and inconsistent' position. As we saw in chapter 1, the Aldermanbury divines argued the power of order and jurisdiction lay in elders associated in a presbytery, not by virtue of the office they held.[15] The Scots and the congregationalists were both concerned with a possible resurgence of episcopacy, and this proposal seemed to leave that option open.[16] Indeed, Selden shocked the Scots by noting England's current laws stated none could ordain but a 'bishop, with some presbyters'. Since this law still stood, Selden continued, and the assembly had 'sworn to preserve the laws of the kingdom', the Solemn League and Covenant was no 'excuse for ignoring the law of the Land'.[17]

There clearly was as sense of urgency on the floor of the assembly. No doubt the proposal was appealing to Parliamentarians (perhaps a majority of them) who favoured some sort of reduced episcopacy, but to the Scots, it fell altogether short of the requirements laid out in the Covenant. It was also at this time that Wharton revealed that he, Nye and John Goodwin had served Parliament as a decoy in the Ogle plot.[18] This was a stark reminder to those in attendance that the king was more than willing to divide and conquer London, especially if presbyterianism was a casualty. Pembroke repeatedly urged haste, claiming that the church and kingdom would burn down before the assembly came to any solution.[19] Saye, on the other hand, tried to delay any immediate resolution on the question of ordination.

By this point in the debate, days before the ordinance for the Committee for both Kingdoms would be introduced, we find Pembroke, Salisbury, Wharton, Howard, Saye, Northumberland, Waller, Essex and other unnamed Lords in regular attendance. One wonders if Pembroke and his allies were hoping to establish this ad hoc committee with parliamentary oversight before Scottish troops crossed the border and before Saye could push through his bill for the Committee for Both Kingdoms. In the end, it did not matter. On 29 January news was brought to the assembly that Scottish troops had crossed the border into England, and Burgess presented a 'declaration from the Scots, wherein they justify themselves in their coming'.[20]

This was undoubtedly welcome news to the Scottish commissioners in the assembly. They knew they were not enormously popular in Parliament, and one can see that throughout the month of January and into early February they were constantly adjusting their strategy as they navigated the impatient Covenanters back in Scotland and suspicious English presbyterians in the assembly. Meanwhile, the Scots continually felt that their agenda for church reform was being sidelined in favour of uniquely English problems. But the Scots also knew that the English needed the Scottish troops, and, in any event, the Solemn League and Covenant required that the Scots be present for any decisions regarding the joint war effort.[21] Saye seized this opportunity to change the course of the entire Westminster assembly. Three days later, on 1 February, Saye shepherded a proposal through the Lords that ultimately gave birth to the Committee for Both Kingdoms, 'to order and direct whatsoever doth or may concern the managing of the war ... and whatsoever may concern the peace of his Majesties kingdoms'.[22] It is probably not coincidental that on 2 February Saye also urged the assembly of divines to lay aside the ongoing question of ordaining London ministers and move directly into the debate we will discuss in this chapter.[23]

If anything, interest in the assembly debates only increased with the first real debate over presbyterian government. By the time the Apologists began their counter-arguments to the proposition, the assembly was so full of nobles and MPs that they ran out of space in the Jerusalem Chamber.

The setting aside of the pressing question of ordination was certainly connected to the concurrent efforts of leading Scottish commissioners and English parliamentarians to streamline both religious reform and the war. Given that Parliament was not united in its support of Scottish presbyterianism, one sympathises with William Shaw's description of these early debates as 'theoretical, premature, [and] merely declaratory'. [24] Yet, as we shall see, the Third Proposition was designed to give cover to all types of presbyterianisms, without yet committing England to any particular one, and while nonetheless sending a message to the Scottish covenanters that England took the Covenant stipulations seriously.

We will look at two issues surrounding this debate. First, we will look at the procedural manoeuvring that brought about the debate over the Third Proposition, how Thomas Goodwin recollected these events, and why he believed the Apologists had been placed in an impossible situation. The difficulty was that the Apologists not only had to defend their belief that the particular church had all the power of church government, they had to do so while objecting to a proposition that was left purposefully vague. Second, we will examine how the Apologists sought to defend the rights of the particular church using the language of the keys. The main line of attack used by the Apologists against the proposition was through the power of excommunication. For the Apologists this highest act of church power was limited to the particular congregation, and their arguments were based primarily in 1 Corinthians 5 and Matthew 18.

FEBRUARY 1644: OFFENCE OR DEFENCE?

In February 1644, like the previous October, the Apologists found themselves on the short end of a procedural stick. This time, however, it was the Scots who had outmanoeuvred them. The commissioners, under political pressure from the Covenanters, made a tactical decision that would later make aspects of their polity far more difficult to defend.

When the Grand Committee introduced the Third Proposition on 1 February, Nye tried to stop this proposition from being debated. He cited a platform of church government written by the Scottish commissioners as a model for a preferable method for debating church government. As Gillespie recorded in his notes for that day, 'Mr Ney said, That the Scots commissioners had given in to the grand committee, a system of the whole church government.' According to to Gillespie, Nye 'desired that the assembly might go on it that method, beginning at the beginning with the government of particular congregations'. [25]

185

We know there were two papers handed into the Grand Committee, on 10 November 1643 and 24 January 1644, and Nye was probably referring to the former.[26] These papers have been presumed to be no longer extant, but they can be recreated through various sources. We noted in chapter 4 that these papers were, in some measure, the beginning of an accommodation dialogue between the Apologists and the Scots. Lightfoot recorded some contents of the first paper. It was clear that the Scots agreed with the Apologists on officers, understood the particular church to be *ecclesia prima*, and began their description of church government with particular elderships and moved upward from there.[27]

Nye, therefore, in citing the Scots' papers as his preferred methodological model, wanted the assembly to follow the Scottish model and start with the particular church and work upward to synods. It seems during the assembly's initial attempt at accommodation in November 1643, an agreement had been made that the assembly should use this method. Given that the Scots submitted their first paper on 10 November, and that paper began with the particular church, it seems the Scots were involved with the committee.[28]

In response to Nye's request, Gillespie stated that 'we [the Scots] were well content the Assembly should take their own order, and not be tie themselves to ours'.[29] The Scots were content to reverse the order of their own official statement on church government and allow the assembly to debate the proposition regarding many particular churches under one presbytery. They anticipated that the Apologists would agree with them concerning the particular church, and most probably saw an opportunity to first codify the power of synods of elders from multiple churches, where they would receive virtually no opposition from English presbyterians – a manoeuvre the Scots would be forced to repeat in September 1644.[30] It was becoming clear that their primary problem was not the congregational divines, but keeping the various presbyterian polities, and the men who espoused them, on the same page.

Something had spooked the Scots. There was intense political pressure from some Covenanters back in Scotland who believed the commissioners were sounding too independent.[31] We know that the assembly itself 'laid by ... severall Papers received from the Reverend Commissioners of the Church of Scotland'.[32] It may have been that sheer political pressure from some powerful Covenanters in Scotland forced the Scots to fall in line with the presbyterian majority in the assembly at this early, yet crucial, point in the debate. At some point before these February debates the Scots had suffered the same defeat as the Apologists had in October 1643.

Like the Apologists, the Scots had wanted to begin with a church platform and define church government from there.[33] It may be that the assembly's rejection of this was, in part, the reason why Gillespie and the Scots were willing to take a step back and let the majority lead the way through the initial debates on presbyterianism in the assembly. And we must keep in mind that it was the Covenanters back in Scotland who were pressuring Parliament for a more aggressive adherence to the Solemn League and Covenant. No doubt the formation of the Committee for Both Kingdoms was behind Gillespie's comments.

As non-voting members the Scots were limited in their capacity to manage a variety of influential – and comparably dogmatic – English presbyterians. They needed the majority in order to secure a presbyterian platform, and they knew that following the Apologists' – and their own – methodology of ecclesiological argumentation would end any alliance with the English presbyterians. The problem was that by the time the assembly tried to define the boundaries of particular churches in May 1644, it was less amenable to protecting the privileges of the particular churches than the Scots had anticipated.

The assembly decided that the Apologists should present their objections to the proposition before the assembly began to debate support of the topic.[34] In bringing forth those objections, the Apologists sought cover under the Scots numerous times, citing over and over again the Kirk's understanding of the particular church. Later in the same month Gillespie once again recorded Nye as saying, 'The divines of Scotland and in the Netherlands acknowledge that a single congregation is a true integral church, with intrinsical government.'[35] Thomas Goodwin would later state that the Scots' paper called the particular church 'the *ecclesia prima*'.[36]

GOODWIN REMEMBERS

Historians have missed the fact that Goodwin used his personal assembly notes to provide a retrospective on these specific assembly debates in his *Government of the Churches of Christ*. From Goodwin's perspective, this month was so pivotal and ultimately detrimental to the congregationalists' position that he took a break from his polemical defence of congregational polity to narrate what happened at the beginning of the debates over presbyterianism. He saw February 1644 as the beginning of the end of the alliance that had begun three years before. But that unravelling was not predicated upon any open declaration of warfare; it was instead a matter of the Apologists finding themselves once again in a procedural predicament: they felt forced to present their prescriptive rationale for congregational power via dissent from what they considered to be an inherently vague proposition. Goodwin claimed that it was the 'wisdom of the assembly' to limit the proposition debated in February 1644 to congregations that '*may be*' governed by 'a fixed and constant Assembly of Presbyters and Elders'.[37] This purposeful avoidance of explicit *jure divino* presbyterianism worked against the Apologists. From Goodwin's perspective, the Apologists were placed in an impossible position based on the two inherently vague phrases 'may be' and 'presbyteriall government'.[38]

First, as we have already noted, the assembly decided that the Apologists should bring their objections forward prior to the assembly's presentation of their positive arguments for a presbytery over multiple congregations. Therefore, because of the phrasing of the proposition and because it had not yet been clarified by the assembly, the Apologists were limited to dissenting from what a church 'may be' rather than what a church 'should be'.[39] Goodwin linked the discussions of February 1644 with the debates of October 1643 when the assembly decided to argue from the particulars of church polity upward to a platform rather than vice versa. Goodwin noted that when the assembly began its debates over church government in October, it decided that it would waive two propositions: 'That there is a certain standing ordinary Term of Church government, held forth in the Directions given to the Apostles, or the Examples of those Churches we read of in the Scripture, erected by their guidance', and 'That there ought to be no other, than what is by Institution'.[40] Goodwin, after reminding the reader of the anti-prelatical parties' efforts in 1640/41, noted that this was exactly how they had argued against diocesan episcopacy in order 'to prove that the Government of the Church of Bishops, may not be'.[41] We are thus reminded that the congregationalists had indeed provided a platform for church government in the *Petition Examined*, and tried to get the assembly to settle on a platform in October 1643.

As we saw in earlier, the assembly's methodology in October 1643 hindered the Apologists' ability to defend their position on Matthew 16:19, and now it was to haunt them as they attempted to address Matthew 18:17, 18. Goodwin anticipated that many in the assembly would have disagreed with a platform of congregational government if the Apologists had been allowed to present it. '[T]he consequence would have been denied by many of our Brethren, that hold *all power of Government, to be in a Congregation*, but not solely or only', for those who held this position could also say 'classical government over many congregations, may yet be.'[42]

To overthrow this position in February, the Apologists would have had to argue, 'first, that an Ecclesiastical Government may not be set up (unless warranted by Institution) over many congregations, that have it by Institution themselves'. And secondly, the Apologists would have had to demonstrate 'that Scriptures do not hold forth by Institution, an Ecclesiastical Government in classes, &c. over many Congregations'.[43] The problem, according to Goodwin, was that in order to prove either of these points the Apologists would have had to violate assembly protocol and enter into a new 'General Head about Institutions, Namely, *That what in Church-Government is not by Institution, may not be*'.[44] However, the assembly had already decided what type of church government the Scriptures instituted and cloaked it under what '*may be*'. They allowed the congregationalists to present their negative arguments before the assembly defined presbyterian government positively. 'Our Brethren',

Goodwin stated, 'not undertaking to prove an Institution of the Presbyterial Government, all our answers to their Arguments, had answerably still fallen short of disproving the Institution of that Government.'[45]

The second difficulty for Goodwin was that there were at least four different types of presbyterian polities in the assembly. The proposition, stated as it was, 'upon a meer, *It may be* ... allows the greatest Latitude and compass to the affirmers of it, for their defending of it' and therefore 'paves the way for passableness with all Men, of all sides whatever'. In this way, the proposition allowed for those who believed in *jure divino* presbyterianism, and those who did not (like the Erastians) to take cover under the ambiguous phrase, 'may be'.[46] As Goodwin noted, our 'difficulty was increased further also, and yet no less from the vast indefiniteness, and indeterminate Ambiguity and uncertainty of that other Term [*Presbyteriall Government over many congregations*]'. This 'admit[s] many Variations, and includes in it severall patterns of Government, and also differing Constitutions of those Congregations'.[47] Although the Apologists failed to persuade the assembly of their position, they succeeded in ferreting out variant counter-arguments that exposed numerous presbyterian polities within the assembly. Goodwin recorded the presbyterian polities that he had observed in February.[48]

The Apologists asked the assembly to clarify what form of presbyterianism was meant in the proposition. The first view held that churches would fall under the jurisdiction of a presbyteriall synod. There might be a two-fold presbytery, or associated elders, over many congregations. One might have argued for the 'Ordinary and Standing Government thereof', and therefore the greatest matters pertaining to each congregation should be regularly brought to that presbytery 'as belonging to their Jurisdiction'. The congregation should not proceed in weighty matters until 'Warranted by the Sentence of a Higher Presbytery'.[49] A second view held that a presbytery or meeting of elders from several churches would be convened in the case of schisms and contentions, whether in difficult cases or doctrinal matters, where the elders of a particular church might need to seek direction and council. It was also a means for neighbouring elderships to assist when an eldership of a particular congregation had 'scandalously managed their Government, or wrongfully Excommunicated'.[50] This second view was the Apologists' position, and Goodwin included the congregational position as one of the 'presbyterian' options.

Knowing that the majority of the assembly would line up behind the first position, Goodwin further noted a subdivision of it. In the first variety, pastors in a presbytery over multiple churches were properly pastors in every sense of the word. They were elders over multiple churches in a region and cared for each church 'in their courses and rounds' by preaching, teaching, etc., in each church. This custom was practised in some cities in Holland. Ministers in three or four parishes preached 'in a circular way to each ... [church] in their course'.[51] The people were related to one another as one church, but met in fixed congregations as a matter of convenience. A second variety of the first category said that a synod was a 'Presbytery unto' all churches under them 'for Acts of Discipline; yet they are Pastors or Elders fixed in their Relations properly, but to one Congregation, to perform Duties thereunto, and not unto the rest'.[52]

This second variety could also be further divided into two sub-categories. The first form held that 'the Elders of these many Congregations have no share of Government in publick Admonitions or Censures, nor bear no Rule in those congregations, they are respectively affixt to', but, as in the time of the prelacy, all matters of discipline, admonishing and censures, are immediately 'brought to the common presbytery of Elders, set over them for all Government'. The other form was that practised in Scotland, where many congregations had proper and peculiar pastors, and were thereby distinct churches. These churches were the *ecclesiae prima*, 'as those to whom the Notion and true Nature and State of a Church doth first belong'. They have the power of church suspension and admonition in themselves. 'There is only this difference, that when it comes to the great matters of Ordination or Excommunication, these are taken up to the great Presbytery.'[53] Goodwin concluded:

> In these unlimited and incomprehensible Senses [types of Presbyteriall government], was this proposition (the first Born of all that follow about this Government) propounded to the debate, although we urged upon the Assembly, that they would specifie and determine, which of these Governments they intended, and would maintain, but it would not be granted, nor any thing added for the limitation thereof: as [must be] no [rather be] in stead of [it may be] not [over many Churches] in stead [of many Congregations.] The advantage of which, on their part, was a liberty to defend it in any of these Senses, and each upon the lowest Terms [it may be] for the proposition might vary, and alter with any of these shapes.[54]

Thus for Goodwin, by 22 February 1644 the 'Grand Debate' was over. The presbyterian majority had outmanoeuvred the Apologists. The assembly had refused to define a presbytery too specifically in order to keep as many presbyterians in favour of the proposition as possible. While we must stress that these were Goodwin's reflections, and therefore biased towards the congregational view of the assembly, it nonetheless supports what we have seen in the minutes and pamphlets associated with the assembly. The assembly had a number of presbyterian polities on offer, and there was greater danger of a breakdown *within* the presbyterian majority than there was of a failure to come to agreement with the Apologists. In the early months of the assembly, the Apologists were the victims of intra-presbyterian squabbles. They were not simply the delay tacticians as has been portrayed in the historiography.[55] The confusion is particularly evident when we take a look at the actual debates on the assembly floor.

THE DEBATE

While the Apologists spoke against the Third Proposition, they also attempted to give prescriptive proofs about congregational polity. And it seems the way they discussed their views was calculated to expose the variety of opinions emerging in the assembly. To set the stage for their first arguments against the Third Proposition, the Apologists argued that elders must be connected with the congregations they ruled and taught, responsibilities that would be impossible to perform if they also had to rule over other churches through a presbytery of elders. As Burroughs noted, 'the power of ruling' in such a presbytery 'is larger than [the elders'] power of preaching'. This argument harkened back to a verse used by both the Apologists and the Smectymnuans, Acts 28:20, where Paul tells the Ephesian elders, 'Take heed therefore unto yourselves, and to all the flock, over the which the Holy Ghost hath made you overseers, to feed the church of God.'[56] Ruling (overseeing) and preaching (feeding) were bound together in the Apologists' minds. The flock that was to be fed by the word must also be the same flock that is governed. Or, as it was argued against diocesan episcopacy, an elder governing and preaching must be coextensive.[57]

Seaman, however, indicated that just as a minister by ordination was made a minister in the 'general visible church', so he was also made a minister to all churches, particularly those within provincial presbytery boundaries.[58] Elders from many churches ruled over other congregations where they were not ministers, and that jurisdiction was mediated through the presbytery over those churches. As De Witt has written: 'elders in a presbytery have an immediate relationship to the presbytery and mediate in and by the whole they have relation to the particular churches under it'.[59] Seaman believed that the elders in a presbytery over multiple churches, by virtue of their relationship to the visible universal church, were a true church even if those elders were not assigned to particular churches. The Scots, however, believed the elders joined a presbytery over multiple churches by virtue of their ordination into a particular church. Again, the positions divided along the lines of whether the church power was placed in the universal church and passed derivatively downward to the particular, or whether, like the Scots and the Apologists believed, the particular church was the *ecclesia prima*.

The Apologists tried to protect the prerogatives of the particular church through two well known biblical descriptions of excommunication, Matthew 18 and 1 Corinthians 5. In Matthew 18 Christ commanded the offended party to 'tell the church' as a requisite step in a process of discipline that may lead to excommunication, and Paul's letter to the church in Corinth commanded the Corinthians to put the incestuous man out of their midst. The Apologists divided their argumentative duties throughout early February. Thomas Goodwin and Burroughs led the arguments regarding 1 Corinthians, while

Bridge took the lead with an exegetical defence of Matthew 18. The sections of Scripture, in the mind of the Apologists, were hermeneutically bound together. Matthew 18:15–20, as we have seen, was intimately connected to Matthew 16:19, since both passages discuss 'binding and loosing' and therefore both impact how the keys of power were allocated. The passage 1 Corinthians 5 was, as Burroughs noted, 'the only example' of discipline and therefore must be followed.[60] On 13 February, Goodwin stated, 'In this, I Cor. V. is the only instance of excommunication, and answers Mathew 18.' Both verses mention 'the meeting together: and εν μεσω αυτων [gathered together] in the one [Matthew 18], and εκ μεσου υμων [from among you] in the other [1 Cor. 5]: and "delivering to Satan" in the one, is "accounting a publican and heathen"'.[61] The two sections were mutually interpretative. One provided the Christological basis for excommunication, and the other provided a specific example.

The Apologists attacked the idea that a synodical presbytery had the power of excommunication by arguing that the power of excommunication belonged exclusively to the particular church. The difficulty for their position was that they had to defend not only their belief that a particular church had all the power of church government in itself, but also their belief that a presbytery had no binding jurisdiction over particular churches. The debates in February were only meant to address the latter point, something the Apologists could not do without asserting the former. They had to make all these arguments knowing full well they had to engage with multiple forms of presbyterianism. Their long discourses that asserted the power of the particular church were met with two concluding responses from Rutherford and Gillespie.

GILLESPIE'S GHOSTS

An underlying issue in all of these debates was the people's role in church government. Paul tells the Corinthians, 'In the name of our Lord Jesus Christ, when ye are gathered together, and my spirit, with the power of our Lord Jesus Christ, To deliver such an one unto Satan for the destruction of the flesh, that the spirit may be saved in the day of the Lord Jesus.'[62] The question was how to understand the Greek word συναχθεντων, which meant, 'gathered together'. Did it mean, as the Apologists argued, that the people gathered with the elders, or did it mean the elders gathered alone, or could it also mean elders gathered together in a synod over multiple churches? Lurking in the background was the question of whether the people needed to be involved in the discipline process and what kind of power, if any, they had in it. Goodwin cited the practice of the Church of Scotland, that 'doth not excommunicate, but with the consent of the people'.[63]

Charles Herle summarised what was more than probably on the minds of many in the assembly. He cited Pareus and Cartwright, who 'understand this gathering together, [in] I Cor v., of the presbytery, unless we fall into the Brownist's opinion, that all the people have the power; for they that are gathered together' to deliver the incestuous man over to Satan, did so 'by the authoritative jurisdiction received from Christ'.[64] Rutherford countered that this excommunication, and indeed other excommunications, was performed 'coram populo', but popular consent was only one part of excommunication.[65] Seaman, however, argued that while he would allow the people to be present at the declaration of the punishment, nonetheless, 'The decree and the act of excommunication are acts of power, and the people have nothing to do in it.'[66] In all of these arguments resided the often-confusing discussion of the keys of power and jurisdiction.

On 13 February Goodwin began addressing this issue head on, using the precise language he and Nye would use a few months later in their introduction to Cotton's *Keyes*. Goodwin stated, 'the power of excommunication belongs to the elders of Corinth met together with the churches'. The assembly accounts around this point become somewhat cryptic. Lightfoot did not record much detail, and Gillespie seemed to be recording his responses to Goodwin as he recorded Goodwin's speech. Nonetheless, Gillespie noted that Goodwin 'acknowledgeth that the people had an interest of presence only, the elders the exercise of jurisdiction'.[67] Goodwin added, '[I] deny not that the people have an interest, not of presence, but of power (not authority)'.[68]

Thus, Goodwin introduced that important distinction between power and authority we have already discussed. He then used the same analogies he would use in the preface to the Cotton's *Keyes*, saying that decisions made by the elders and people were 'as when the alderman and common council' meet together. '[T]he alderman have authority, but yet the common council have an interest.'[69] He also cited the relationship between a father and child on the subject of marriage, in which 'the father hath the authority to command, yet the child hath an interest and power'. So, the people in a church 'having consciences of their own, must have their own power referred, though the elders only have the authority'.[70] Nye added, '[we] would strive a middle way betwixt no interest and jurisdiction', and would further prove 'that those two notions of power and jurisdiction are separable ... So our debates here are of authority, but not of jurisdiction'.[71] The people did not have jurisdiction in the way Protestants have traditionally defined the term, but they had a share in the church's power, a share in a church order that did not rise to the level of jurisdiction. On this point, the difference was whether the people needed to be present at the pronouncement of excommunication, and, more divisively, whether they had a vote in the matter.

Bridge picked up the same theme when he stated that 'the power of the whole to purge out, to judge, &c. (I Cor v.), is somewhat more than consent, and less than jurisdiction'.[72] There was an 'actual personal joining of the people with the elders in excommunication, which yet amounts not to juris-diction'. Bridge cited the example of public prayer, where the people joined the preacher but it was the preacher alone who would lead and guide the praying. In the same way, the power of jurisdiction resided only in the elders, but the people could join in excommunication.[73] Goodwin added that the Apolo-gists 'differ so far from the Brownists, that they hold the people, without the officers, cannot excommunicate'.[74] In this regard, Goodwin stated, 'the people had a power, yet without authority'.[75] This emphasis on the elders' unique authority was what we would expect from the Apologists. Robert Paul, missing the importance of this distinction for the Apologists' polity, concluded that by making this argument they demonstrated 'ambivalence' as they strained 'as far as they could in the direction of the [presbyterians]'.[76] But this was not a strain, nor was it a reach; it was a point of polity, as we have seen, that was fundamental to their ecclesiological system.

Before this discussion ended, Lightfoot recorded a fascinating episode that related directly to the Scottish position vis-à-vis the Apologists in the assembly. As the debate drew to a close, John Philip, the only assembly divine with experience in New England, 'interposed, and would prove, out of Mr. Gillespie, that the power of the keys belongeth to every congregation collectively taken', and furthermore, 'excommunication is to be in the presence of the people'.[77] Philip was citing Gillespie's *Popish Ceremonies*, which had served as a basis for the Scottish/congregational alliance in 1640/41. Gillespie did not record this comment in his notes. Lightfoot, however, said that Gillespie answered: 'That [Mr Philip] wronged the author of that book: so that that book doth plainly say, that excommunication doth apply, and only belong, to the officers.'

Although Gillespie's 1637 tract did not make this point as clearly as he remem-bered, we know that by this time Gillespie believed that the power of excommu-nication belonged to the officers alone. The Apologists would have agreed with Gillespie because they firmly believed that jurisdiction (which they preferred to call authority) belonged to the elders, and the people's power was in their 'interest' and nearness to the case. The English presbyterian Herbert Palmer hit on this point of confusion when he added, '[I have] yet to learn that an act of power and jurisdiction should be power, and yet not jurisdiction.'[78] Palmer could not see how people could have power without also having jurisdiction.

The Apologists were not keen to let Gillespie forget what he had said several years ago. While they remained careful not to name Gillespie, they were not as shy to cite his own work against him. Thus, when the Apologists summarised these assembly discussions in the *Grand Debate* they once again went to Gillespie's *Assertion of Discipline* to prove that a classis could not overrule the decision of a congregation. The Apologists reminded the reader that Gillespie cited Zepperus, Zanchius and Voetius to prove the local presbytery could not excommunicate without the people's consent. How much more would this be true, therefore, of a classical presbytery overruling the decisions of a particular church?[79] It would fall to Bridge to try and clear the air in his exegesis of Matthew 18.

WILLIAM BRIDGE AND A VARIETY OF PRESBYTERIANS

On 16 February 1644, Bridge gave the most robust defence of the congregational way thus far in the assembly. We are fortunate that the extant assembly minutes for 1644 begin on 15 February, for this defence also constitutes our only example of Bridge's articulation of church government. The Yarmouth divine, as Joel Halcomb has shown, was, in terms of church practice (orthopraxy), the most influential congregational divine of the revolutionary period.[80] While Bridge was widely revered for his works on practical theology he published few sole-authorship pamphlets on polity. Bridge's proposition was that church government should be 'according to the mind of Christ & his word revealed'.[81] His syllogistic minor was 'that every perticular congregation should have power within itselfe'.[82] The proof for the minor, and indeed the focus of Bridge's speech, was Matthew 18:15–20.[83] This passage was the second half of the theological basis for congregational polity and its understanding of the keys. The binding and loosing introduced by Christ in Matthew 16 is mentioned again in Matthew 18, but this time it is, from the congregational perspective, delimited within a particular church. Bridge's speech further exposed the variety of presbyterian polities in the assembly: some presbyterians agreed with Bridge and drew away from the presbyterian majority.

Bridge began his argument by addressing the greatest power given to the church by Christ. Bridge stated that the highest power in the church was excommunication (binding and loosing) and where the power to excommunicate rested; therefore, 'That which hath the power of the highest censure is the highest power.' Bridge added that 'this [particular] church hath [the power] & noe apeale from it'.[84] The particular church 'should entirely exercise jurisdiction within itself', and therefore the proposition for a presbytery over multiple churches could not be granted.[85] Bridge claimed that the word *ecclesia* was used forty-eight times in the New Testament, but never in reference to a presbytery alone.[86] Christ gave the keys to every minister, but just as most divines agreed that an elder could not ordain without other elders, so Bridge argued ministers exercised the keys in conjunction with the particular church. The elders' 'seat of jurisdiction' was in a particular church.[87]

Thomas Goodwin picked up the same theme in the next session, when he answered objections on behalf of Bridge and the rest of the Apologists. The question, he stated, 'is not wthether [*sic*] officers be meant but the officers of what church?'[88] This distinction further accentuated the clerical nature of the congregationalists' position. Even if the Apologists were willing to concede that 'tell the church' meant 'tell the officers/elders', it was 'still the Officers of a particular Church, for there is a Presbytery in every Church'.[89] We need not restate the Apologists' distinguishing position on the power of the keys, which we examined earlier. Yet, on the assembly floor these points were distinct enough from the separatist position on the keys that Calamy described the Apologists' position on Matthew 18 as, tell the 'officers "before the church" or "in the presence of the church"'.[90]

Bridge rejected the prevailing opinions within the various presbyterian groups in the assembly. Against the Erastians, Bridge said that Christ could not be referring to a civil court, since excommunication was a spiritual matter and not meant for a civil court, 'because obstinacy is not the object of a civill censure'.[91] Connectedly, Matthew 18 could not mean the Jewish church, with its ecclesiastical courts, like the Sanhedrin. According to Goodwin, a general principle of the 'presbyterian Government' was that classical synods and national assemblies were analogous to the New Testament Jewish church.[92] In the New Testament the supreme council and juridical court in Jerusalem consisted of the High Priest sitting over priests, scribes and leading citizens.[93] Some presbyterians argued from Matthew 18 that Christ had in mind 'a bench or a court' that the people could resort to, as was the case in Jerusalem. As Goodwin noted, they believed there could be a council of elders that ruled, but did not teach in church.[94]

Since some of the divines believed the New Testament church had not yet come into existence when Christ spoke in Matthew 18, there was a debate as to whether Christ was referring to an existing model (Jewish synagogues overseen by Sanhedrin councils) or to the new church Christ would yet build. Against the former position, Goodwin cited from John Cameron that the Sanhedrin were never once called *ecclesia*, even in the Septuagint, where one would expect to find the Greek rendering of the Old Testament word for Sanhedrin.[95] A third argument was that Christ was referring to Old Testament institutions in Matthew 18. In response, Goodwin stated that even if Matthew 18 used Old Testament language, it was nonetheless in the context of Matthew 16:18 before it, where Christ promised 'to build his church'. 'And as [Christ] speaks of New Keys that are to be given ... so he would have a New Church Distinct from the former.' Although the Apostles may not have known all the details of what the church would look like, Goodwin asserted that the Holy Spirit would eventually reveal the fullness of the meaning of the church Christ would build. A New Testament corollary was that although Christ spoke many times of his resurrection, the Apostles did not comprehend its meaning until Christ revealed it to them.[96]

Marshall, Calamy and Herle tended to believe that Matthew 18 could, by way of analogy, refer to an assembly of elders ruling over a group of churches. John Selden, Thomas Coleman and John Lightfoot – leading Erastians –

believed that this exegesis was proof the civil authorities should have a role in the excommunication process. Some of them would ultimately question whether a church could have any role in excommunication – an argument that would offend members more than most arguments of the Apologists. Selden believed that the ruling elders was the state which acted in place of the civil Sanhedrin and had the right to excommunicate. Marshall tried to disprove Selden, but Lightfoot recorded, 'I confess, [it] gave me no satsifac- tion.'[97] Coleman bluntly stated, 'The Jewish sandhedrin was not a spirituall court.'[98] Gillespie had a unique understanding of the Sanhedrin. Distin- guishing between church and state, Gillespie separated a 'civil Sanhedrin' from an 'ecclesiastical Sanhedrin'.[99] The excommunication pertained to the latter since it was purely a spiritual matter, thus foreshadowing elders in a church. Goodwin denied that Gillespie's distinctions could ever be proved.[100]

Considering the number of nobles and MPs in attendance, Bridge's state- ment, distancing himself from the Erastians, was bold. However, Bridge left the door open for an important role for the magistrate. Anticipating a complaint that a person who had been wrongly excommunicated had no recourse for appeal, Bridge said that he '[may] [c]omplaine to the magistrate, though the censure be spirituall, the wrong may be civill'.[101] Marshall, however, understood Bridge to have said that the excommunicated may appeal to the state, and therefore Bridge was giving the state the rights Marshall believed only belonged to the spiritual courts. Marshall believed the magistrate was meant to be a 'helper' but not part of the appellate process. Bridge clarified himself: 'I did not say ther should be an apeale to the magistrate, but the person wronged may complaine to the magistrate.'[102]

According to Bridge, the magistrate was the keeper of the peace, and an errant church was a threat to the body politic. A wronged person could complain to the magistrate, but the magistrate acted as the protector of the church, not as a part of the church.[103] Rutherford echoed Bridge's distinc- tion in his *The Divine Right of Church Government and Excommunication*. 'If the Church erre and fail against the Law of Christ' in a matter of discipline, 'the oppressed man in a constituted Church may have his refuge to the godly Magistrate and complain, but he cannot appeal, for an appellation is from an erring judge to an higher judge.'[104] The magistrate was never given the power of the keys.[105] We can see here how the power of the keys informs our under- standing of the Erastian debates as well.

Bridge concluded of the church in Matthew 18, 'If not the civill court nor [the] Jewish sanhedrin nor the bishop, then either church universall, nationall [or] Presbyteriall.' Citing the Catholic Cajetan, Bridge stated that the verse speaks of two or three being gathered together in the process of discipline, and therefore it cannot refer to a universal or national church.[106] Nor can Christ mean 'any forraigne presbitery that lyes without the congregation because the word ecclesia' is not used to mean a presbytery over other churches.[107] This charge from Christ was meant for the church that the 'offended brother' was part of, but that brother was neither a member of a larger presbytery nor a part of that presbytery. The Apologists believed excommunication was the highest form of church power, and belonged only to a particular church. Giving that power to a synod would violate the prerogatives of the only instituted church in scripture.

Bridge knew the influence of Parker's theology on many English presbyterians, and attempted to turn Parker's arguments against them by channelling John Ball. Bridge argued backwards from a classical presbytery to a particular church. 'If the presbitery be meant, then it is the representative church & then the power will be in the people, & not only the power, but the exercise of that power, because what is in the representing must be first in the represented'.[108] This line of argumentation granted even more power to the people than the Apologists did in their polity. Gillespie, who did not speak during this debate, later recorded his own private responses to Bridge's speech and conceded, 'Though the power be originally in the people, yet divines that say so, restrict the *exercitium* to the elders.'[109] Marshall's response indicated that the English presbyterians had not yet completely abandoned the principles set forth by Parker. 'I would not greatly stand at the word "representative"; if [it] meane that some have power given from Christ not delegated by others to exercise in the name & for the good of the whole, I know noe danger of this.'[110] Marshall also defended the point that the first churches were particular churches.[111] Many of Marshall's arguments were similar to that of the Apologists, and different from that of the clerical English presbyterians. Elders could be delegated from the body, yet retain power that came from God alone. Marshall then went one step further, saying that those elders could carry this unique power to a larger presbytery.[112]

Bridge then cited Voetius twice to indicate that even with a larger presbytery the church did not lose its unique prerogatives as a church. The people in a church, according to Voetius, could resist a larger presbytery if they deemed the presbytery to be in error.[113] Voetius also argued that however a church may associate with another church, 'yet in the midst of all this correspondency, it remains a church'. The concern here was that the line 'tell the church' was interpreted by many presbyterians to be 'tell the classis [or synod]', because a particular church 'is but a part of the classical church, and so is told when the classis is told'.[114] The Apologists often cited foreign divines, including the Scots, in defence of their understanding of the rights of a particular church.

Only a few days after Bridge's speech Nye would state, 'The divines of Scotland and in the Netherlands acknowledge that a single congregation is a true integral church with intrinsical government.'[115] Once again, Gillespie in his personal notes cleverly used the Apologists' arguments against them.

Gillespie stated, the church 'is bound' to obey their own presbytery 'as a congregation is bound, to obey their own eldership. I turn over the objection against himself'.[116] Nye and Goodwin would make precisely this point in the preface to Cotton's *Keyes*: that the people were bound to obey their elders because of the unique authority vested in the elders.

In none of these debates did the Apologists deny the utility, indeed the necessity, of synods of elders from multiple churches. Indeed, as we have seen, a shift occurred in the Apologists' thinking on synods over the course of 1644. Bridge, towards the end of his speech, said, 'I am not against the lawfull use of sinods; they dogmatically [*sic*] ... They may pronounce them [people or churches] subverters of the faith that doe the contrary.'[117] The minutes omit a few lines at this point, although it seems Lightfoot recorded the gist of Bridge's comments.[118] '[Bridge] plainly held that synods might declare who is an enemy to the truth; but to excommunicate or censure him for that, belongs to particular congregations.'[119] Nye had already made this point several days earlier: 'Mr Nye did confess how nearly they came to us; as they held classical and synodical meetings very useful and profitable; yet possibly agreeable to the institution of Christ.'[120] But Nye questioned 'Whether these meetings have the same power that "*ecclesia prima*", or one single congregation has?'[121] By the autumn of 1644 it was widely acknowledged that the Apologists believed in the existence of synods, yet, as we shall see, it was the power that those assemblies possessed that was the sticking point. Again, we need to remember that this debate was discussed in terms of Matthew 18, from which the Apologists argued that the power of excommunication rested only in the particular church. In the end, this disagreement over excommunication was the fundamental difference between the presbyterians and the congregational divines.

The Apologists' long discourses that asserted the power of the particular church were met with a wide variety of responses. We have already noted the Erastian, Scottish, and English presbyterian understandings of the Sanhedrin court. But in terms of how to understand the 'church' in Matthew 18, the assembly exhibited a range of ripostes. John Selden did not believe that Matthew 18 was related to a particular church, since the church had not yet come into existence. Therefore, the verse did not discuss jurisdiction.[122] The English presbyterian Richard Vines, who throughout demonstrated sympathy with aspects of the Apologists' position, agreed that a church was not yet in existence. Nevertheless, he believed that the passage instructed on jurisdiction. Thus, Vines could support the Apologists' distinction between the elders' jurisdiction and the people's power. Quite surprisingly, Vines conceded that Matthew 16:18–19 instructed on the 'society of the faithfull', whereas Matthew 18 instructed on the officers exercising that power.[123] Vines stated, 'I take for granted upon the principles of our brethren that it cannot be meant to extend to the community in poynt of jurisdiction, equally.'[124] While it is true that scholastic argumentation often meant finding common ground with an opposing viewpoint with the goal of luring the opponent into a contradiction, Vines, it seems, sympathised with the allocation of the keys given in the Apologists' ecclesiology. However, Vines questioned why the Apologists could not go one step further and continue the power chain upward to a larger presbytery.[125]

Marshall argued, 'If [Bridge] by a perticular congregation he meane such a congregation as hath elders & brethren compleatly, as many ably transact all businesse concerning themselves, I doe not dissent from him.'[126] Marshall further denied, along with Bridge, that 'church' in Matthew 18 could mean a 'universal church'.[127] However, for a variety of reasons he did not believe this denial prevented a larger presbytery from having jurisdiction. Gataker thought Matthew 18 did not instruct on church censures but instead provided an example of how to handle personal conflict. 'The intent of the discourse is to resolve a case of conscience, how farre a Christian may proceed against a brother that hath done him some wrong before he proceed.'[128]

CONCLUSION

One can see why Lord Saye and Sele, towards the end of the February discussions, complained that the 'Presbyterial men' do not seem to agree amongst themselves.[129] 'On one [congregational] side it is clearly expressed; I think it is not soe in the other [side].'[130] Indeed, Saye and Sele perceived 'a double opinion' on the presbyterian side: '1. That many congregations are such churches as are compleate & have their officers', whereas '2. Others say that those many congregations doe but make up one church consisting of more pastors & elders not assigned to one congregation as their proper chardge, but in generall.'[131] J. R. De Witt saw Saye and Sele's speech as specifically calculated to infuriate the presbyterians. Indeed, according to De Witt and Robert Paul, who follows him on this point, Saye and Sele's suggestion that the presbyterians were divided and the 'independents' were on the same page is 'scarcely believable'.[132] De Witt, in particular, chaffs at the suggestion that the presbyterians were not united in polity.[133] The historiographical consensus has been that the 'leaders of the conservative majority were willing to embrace the Scottish system'.[134] Yet, De Witt and Paul have failed to account for the strength and tenacity of the various English presbyterian positions.

We should not miss the pressure politics placed on the assembly. John Adamson has argued that 'few pieces of legislation before the Self-Denying provoked fiercer divisions within, and between, the two Houses' than the bill to create the Committee for Both Kingdoms.[135] And therefore it should be all the more surprising to see that during the same roughly three-week period the Committee was being formed and debated, the same Peers and

Parliamentarians at the centre of those debates took some of their most active roles in the Westminster assembly. If Saye and Northumberland were 'adroitly managing the bill's introduction', as Adamson suggested, the level to which these Peers are doing double duty as assembly members is impressive.[136] Indeed, at the very moment Essex was attempting to curtail the powers being given to the Committee for Both Kingdoms, he was repeatedly appearing in the Westminster assembly.[137]

Robert Paul has argued that Saye 'entered the fray in support of his Independent' friends'.[138] Yet in early 1644 Robert Baillie called the Saye–Northumberland group the 'good partie'. At this stage, Baillie, and apparently the Scots, clearly sided with the war party and saw them as their closest allies. On the one hand, we see Adamson arguing that Saye is the leader of the Scottish delegation's closest allies in London, and on the other we have Robert Paul arguing that Saye was a power-broker for Independency. This is a perfect example of historiographical divergence in political and religious narratives. We can certainly track the breakdown of the relationship between Saye and the war party by the end of 1644, but, as we shall see, Saye was delicately managing the assembly both to placate the Scots, to provide breathing space for the Apologists, and all the while ensure Parliament retained ultimate oversight of religion in England.

As we look ahead in the minutes, these often-conflicting agendas would continue to slow the progress of assembly debates. Furthermore, we need to remember that, at this stage, Baillie considered Saye an ally. Their relationship would not deteriorate for several months. It seems, rather, that Saye was ensuring some sort of presbyterian polity was put in place, but attempting to prevent any *specific* (especially Scottish) type of presbyterianism from being established. In the short run, he may have gotten more than he bargained for. What we will see is that Saye's endeavour to allow for a variety of opinions on presbytery, ended up unleashing a large coalition of presbyterians strong enough to sideline the congregationalists.

More calculating than Saye and Sele's statement was Philip Nye's controversial comments – on the same day Saye and Sele spoke – citing Gillespie's *Assertion* as describing Scottish presbyterianism as being a power alongside Parliament, rather than answerable to it. As we discussed in earlier, these portentious comments broached the unwelcome topic of Erastianism. Yet, in context, it is not surprising that by 22 February Nye took the opportunity to expose further distinctions within presbyterianism. Indeed, a few months later, Gillespie recorded Nye stating, 'The Assembly differeth as much amongst themselves as against his party', and he then enumerated at least several different kinds of polities being offered in the assembly.[139]

If, for example, the decision had been made in October 1643 that the Scriptures held for a church government by Institution, it would have opened the door to the question of *jure divino*, which would have split the Scots and the Erastians. Had the congregationalists been allowed to start with a platform of church government, as they had requested, it would have divided the presbyterians, for each group had fundamental beliefs they shared with the Apologists but did not share with each other. We can see this potential for disarray when we look at the debates of both October 1643 and February 1644, for when the Apologists argued in *defence* of Matthew 16:19 and Matthew 18 – their two fundamental passages for congregational polity – it always brought out differences amongst the presbyterians. Thus a positive platform early in the assembly would have only caused confusion and frustration within the presbyterian majority.

The assembly needed to keep the presbyterian majority together in order to procure any sort of settlement. In these early months of the assembly, the divines in the majority achieved this unity linguistically and procedurally. The decision to construct the very first proposition on presbyterian government with a measure of ambiguity (viz. *may be*) provided cover for all the presbyterian parties. Had the assembly opted to start with a platform of church government first they would have risked alienating one or more presbyterian party. As a minority in the assembly, the Scots, at this early stage, needed the majority more than they needed another minority to agree with them.

The Scots wanted the assembly to codify the prerogatives of the synod, but they also needed it to be done without violating the rights of a particular church. As the congregationalists' February defence drew to a conclusion, Rutherford and Gillespie added their views. Rutherford stated, 'Nothing that hinders a dispute more than when thing[s] are proved that are not denied.' Gillespie said, 'It doth not belong to this debate whether a particular congregation have the power intire in itselfe; that will be in debate afterwards.'[40] The Scots had no problem with the arguments brought forth to protect the rights of the particular church, especially from Matthew 18. But they denied that these rights prevented a presbytery from having jurisdiction over multiple churches. The Third Proposition dealt only with a presbytery over many churches: to discuss the rights of the particular church was out of order.

The Scots had to be very careful here. There were many English presbyterians who would deny that the particular church had any share in the power of the keys, and perhaps many were still unsure how the particular church fitted into the equation. Since the congregationalists were not at this juncture offering a proposition for a congregational polity, when the assembly voted down the Apologists' objections it merely meant that the Apologists' view on the congregational church did not disprove the proposition on presbyteries over particular churches.

Bridge tried to establish the principle that the power of excommunication belonged to a particular church, but this topic, more than anything, risked dividing the presbyterian majority. Comments made by other divines indicated the delicacy of the topic at hand. Selden called the debate over excommunication the 'greatest questions that can be debated'.[141] Gataker waved off the topic as something the assembly had not yet agreed to debate.[142] If the divines had found the question of recipient of the keys a source of so much confusion and tension in October 1643, there is little surprise they were reticent to broach the topic at a moment when they merely wanted to say there 'may be' a presbytery over multiple churches. The Scots probably anticipated giving the rights of excommunication to the local church once presbyterianism was approved by the assembly and by Parliament. They got more than they bargained for. By May, when the assembly debated the rights of the particular church, the clerical English presbyterians already had the upper hand, and many of them were already denying that the particular church had the power of excommunication unto itself. The Scots soon realised, however, that the rights of the particular church were a necessary causality of the increasingly delicate political climate.

In the midst of all of these debates, the first letter came in from the church of Walcheren. Thus we are brought back to the *Apologeticall Narration* and the issue of accommodation between the Scots and Apologists. The first order of business on the assembly floor after the Walcheren letter to Parliament had been approved on 7 March 1644 was to create another committee on accommodation.[143] The immediate impact of the continental reaction to the *Apologeticall Narration*, far from dividing the Scots and the Apologists, actually initiated a period that accentuated their similarities. But the long-term consequences of accommodation became one of the most frustrating and elusive endeavours in the Westminster assembly.

NOTES

1 Shaw, *English Church*, p. 255.

2 Lightfoot, *Journal*, p. 131; Spear, 'Covenanted Uniformity', pp. 253, 254.

3 *Contra* De Witt, *Jus divinum*, p. 106. Baillie also noted the obstinacy of the Apologists between December 1644 and February 1644. Baillie, *Letters and Journals*, vol. 2, p. 129.

4 J. S. A. Adamson, 'The Triumph of Oligarchy: the Management of War and the Committee of Both Kingdoms, 1644–1645', *Parliament at Work: Parliamentary Committees, Political Power, and Public Access is Early Modern England* (2002), 101–127, p. 105.

5 Adamson, 'The Triumph of Oligarchy', p. 103.

6 Adamson, 'The Triumph of Oligarchy', p. 104; Scott, *Politics and War*, p. 63.

7 Adamson, 'The Triumph of Oligarchy', p. 104.

8 Ibid., pp, 102–103

9 Ibid., p. 103.

10 Ibid., p. 107.

11 Van Dixhoorn, *MPWA* (vol. 1), p. 489.

12 Lightfoot, *Journal*, pp. 116ff; House of Lords Journal, *Journal of the House of Lords: volume 6: 1643* (1767–1830), pp. 382–384, www.british-history.ac.uk/report.aspx?compid=37433, accessed 6 August 2013.

13 Ibid., pp. 120–121, 125.

14 Spear, 'Covenanted Uniformity', p. 297.

15 Ibid., p. 299.

16 Paul, *The Assembly of the Lord*, p. 213.

17 Lightfoot, *Journal*, p. 121; Paul, *The Assembly of the Lord*, p. 223

18 See above, chapter 4.

19 Lightfoot, *Journal*, pp. 129–130; Spear, 'Covenanted Uniformity', p. 299.

20 Lightfoot, *Journal*, p. 130.

21 Woolrych, *Britain in Revolution*.

22 Gardiner, *History of the Great Civil War*, p. 305.

23 Shaw, *English Church*, p. 168.

24 Ibid., p. 168.

25 Gillespie, *Notes*, p. 9.

26 Van Dixhoorn, *MPWA* (vol. 2), p. 312. See also, ibid., p. 489.

27 Lightfoot, *Journal*, pp. 50–51.

28 In September 1644, Goodwin pointed out, 'In the first committee it was first determined to begin with congregations'; Van Dixhoorn, *MPWA* (vol. 3), p. 268.

29 Gillespie, *Notes*, p. 9.

30 See below, chapter 8.

31 Baillie, *Letters and Journals*, vol. 2, p. 21.

32 *The Answer of the Assembly of Divines ... unto the Reasons given in to this Assembly by the Dissenting Brethren [T. Goodwin and six others, 22 Oct. 1645] of their not bringing in a model of their way; and since published ... under the title of A Copy of a Remonstrance, etc* (London, 1645), p. 6.

33 Ibid., p. 10.

34 Gillespie, *Notes*, pp. 9–10; Lightfoot, *Journal*, p. 131. Lightfoot was absent these days and records what he was told; Paul, *The Assembly of the Lord*, p. 250.

35 Gillespie, *Notes*, p. 25.

36 Van Dixhoorn, *MPWA* (vol. 2), p. 511. Years later Nye still cited Rutherford's *Due Right of Presbyteries* as having emphasised the same point. 'The power of jurisdiction,' argued Rutherford, 'is as perfect & compleat in one single congregation, as in a provincial, as in a national, yeah as in a Catholick visible body'. Nye, *The Lawfulnes of the Oath of Supremacy*, p. 107; cf. Rutherford, *Due Right*, p. 307.

37 Goodwin, *Government*, p. 176.

38 Ibid., pp. 176ff.

39 Ibid., p. 176.

40 Ibid., pp. 176, 177.

41 Ibid., p. 177.

42 Goodwin, *Government*, p. 177.

43 Ibid., p. 177.

44 Ibid., p. 177.

45 Ibid., p. 177.

46 Ibid., p. 176.

47 Ibid., p. 176.

48 Ibid., p. 177.

49 Ibid., p. 177.

50 Ibid., pp. 178–179.

51 Ibid., p. 178.

52 Ibid., p. 178.

53 Ibid., p. 179.

54 Ibid., p. 179.

55 De Witt described the congregationalists' debates in February 1644 in this way, 'The debate on presbytery ... reveal[ed] that intractableness and rigid adherence to formal principle with iron resolve and utter carelessness for the consequences marked, not the presbyterians, but their opposites the Independents', De Witt, *Jus divinum*, p. 106.

56 Gillespie, *Notes*, p. 13.

57 Goodwin, *Government*, p. 76. This is also a point drawn in the *Grand Debate*, *The Grand Debate*, p. 3, 4.

58 Gillespie, *Notes*, p. 12.

59 De Witt, *Jus divinum*, p. 108.

60 Gillespie records that Burroughs stated that the example is binding, whereas Lightfoot only recorded that he said 'it must be followed'. Gillespie, *Notes*, p. 14; Lightfoot, *Journal*, p. 139.

61 Lightfoot, *Journal*, p. 148.

62 I Corinthians 5:4, 'In the name of our Lord Jesus Christ, when ye are gathered together, and my spirit, with the power of our Lord Jesus Christ'.

63 Lightfoot, *Journal*, p. 143.

64 Gillespie, *Notes*, p. 15.

65 Gillespie, *Notes*, p. 15; Lightfoot, *Journal*, p. 144.

66 Lightfoot, *Journal*, p. 145; Gillespie, *Notes*, p. 16.

67 Gillespie, *Notes*, p. 17.

68 Ibid., p. 17.

69 Ibid., p. 17.

70 Ibid., p. 17.

71 Lightfoot, *Journal*, p. 150.

72 Gillespie, *Notes*, p. 19; Lightfoot, *Journal*, p. 154.

73 Gillespie, *Notes*, pp. 19–20.

74 Ibid., p. 20.

75 Lightfoot, *Journal*, p. 155.

76 Paul, *The Assembly of the Lord*, p. 259, 260.

77 S. Hardman Moore, *Pilgrims: New World Settlers & the Call of Home* (New Haven, CT; London: Yale University Press, 2007), pp. 123–124; Lightfoot, *Journal*, p. 156.

78 Lightfoot, *Journal*, p. 156.

79 *The Grand Debate*, p. 39; Gillespie, *An Assertion*, p. 121.

80 See J. Halcomb, 'A Social History of Congregational Religious Practice during the Puritan Revolution', University of Cambridge, PhD thesis (2010).

81 Van Dixhoorn, *MPWA* (vol. 2), p. 498; Lightfoot records the statement in the negative: 'That government which is not according to the mind of God and his word revealed, is not to be admitted.' Lightfoot, *Journal*, p. 159.

82 Van Dixhoorn, *MPWA* (vol. 2), p. 498.

83 Matthew 18:15–20, 'Moreover if thy brother shall trespass against thee, go and tell him his fault between thee and him alone: if he shall hear thee, thou hast gained thy brother. But if he will not hear thee, then take with thee one or two more, that in the mouth of two or three witnesses every word may be established. And if he shall neglect to hear them, tell it unto the church: but if he neglect to hear the church, let him be unto thee as an heathen man and a publican. Verily I say unto you, Whatsoever ye shall bind on earth shall be bound in heaven: and whatsoever ye shall loose on earth shall be loosed in heaven. Again I say unto you, That if two of you shall agree on earth as touching any thing that they shall ask, it shall be done for them of my Father which is in heaven. For where two or three are gathered together in my name, there I am in the midst of them.'

84 Van Dixhoorn, *MPWA* (vol. 2), p. 498.

85 Gillespie, *Notes*, p. 21.

86 Van Dixhoorn, *MPWA* (vol. 2), pp. 498–99.

87 Ibid., p. 500.

88 Ibid., p. 508.

89 Goodwin, *Government*, p. 62.

90 Van Dixhoorn, *MPWA* (vol. 2), p. 517.

91 Ibid., p. 498.

92 Goodwin, *Government*, p. 169. Goodwin provides a lengthy discussion on the relationship between the Old Testament Sanhedrin and the New Testament church. Ibid., pp. 166–176.

93 'Sanhedrin', in D. N. Freedman, *The Anchor Bible Dictionary* (New Haven, CT: Yale University Press, 1992).

94 Goodwin, *Government*, p. 169.

95 Ibid., pp. 57–58.

96 Ibid., pp. 59–60.

97 Lightfoot, *Journal*, p. 166.

98 Van Dixhoorn, *MPWA* (vol. 2), p. 529.

99 McKay, *An ecclesiastical republic*, p. 17.

100 E. Nelson, *The Hebrew Republic: Jewish Sources and the Transformation of European Political Thought* (Cambridge, MA: Harvard University Press, 2010), p. 113; Goodwin, *Government*, p. 170.

101 Van Dixhoorn, *MPWA* (vol. 2), p. 500.

102 Ibid., p. 506.

103 For more on the Apologists' view of the magistrate see Powell, 'The Last Confession: A Background Study of the Savoy Declaration of Faith and Order', chapter 2.

104 Rutherford, *The Divine Right of Church-Government and Excommunication*, p. 580.

105 See for example, ibid., p. 252.

106 Bridge cited Cajetan on this point. Gillespie, *Notes*, p. 21; Lightfoot, *Journal*, p. 160; Van Dixhoorn, *MPWA* (vol. 2), p. 499.

107 Van Dixhoorn, *MPWA* (vol. 2), p. 499.

108 Ibid., p. 496; Thomas Goodwin describes it this way, 'The first and primary institution, must fall upon particular congregations, as seats or bounds of the first power, whether the Institution be supposed to fall upon them as Churches, or as a Presbytery. If it falls on them as Churches, the greater churches consisting of many congregations are but *Ortae*, or *Sprung* of this. If it falls them as a Presbytery, they are but compounds, and Decompounds', Goodwin, *Government*, p. 63.

109 Gillespie, *Notes*, p. 21.

110 Van Dixhoorn, *MPWA* (vol. 2), p. 502.

111 Ibid., p. 517.

112 Ibid., p. 500.

113 Gillespie, *Notes*, p. 21; Van Dixhoorn, *MPWA* (vol. 2), p. 499; Gillespie, *Notes*, p. 21.

114 Gillespie, *Notes*, p. 21; Van Dixhoorn, *MPWA* (vol. 2), p. 499.

115 Gillespie, *Notes*, p. 25.

116 Ibid., p. 21.

117 Van Dixhoorn, *MPWA* (vol. 2), p. 500.

118 Ibid., p. 500, fn. g.

119 Lightfoot, *Journal*, p. 161.

120 Ibid., p. 144.

121 Ibid., p. 144.

122 Van Dixhoorn, *MPWA* (vol. 2), p. 528.

123 Ibid., pp. 503–504, 514.

124 Ibid., p. 504.

125 Ibid., p. 504.

126 Ibid., p. 502.

127 Ibid., p. 501.

128 Ibid., p. 512.

129 Lightfoot, *Journal*, p. 170.

130 Van Dixhoorn, *MPWA* (vol. 2), p. 532.

131 Ibid., p. 532.

132 De Witt, *Jus divinum*, p. 114; Paul, *The Assembly of the Lord*, p. 273.

133 De Witt is particularly annoyed by E. W. Kirby for making this suggestion, De Witt, *Jus divinum*, p. 92; see also E. W. Kirby, 'The English Presbyterians in the Westminster Assembly', *Church History*, 33 (1964), pp. 418–428, p. 420.

134 Paul, *The Assembly of the Lord*, p. 273.

135 Adamson, 'The Triumph of Oligarchy', p. 107.

136 Ibid., p. 106.

137 Lightfoot, *Journal*, pp. 132–135.

138 Paul, *The Assembly of the Lord*, p. 233.

139 Gillespie, *Notes*, p. 68.

140 Van Dixhoorn, *MPWA* (vol. 2), pp. 520, 526.

141 Ibid., p. 520.

142 Ibid., p. 529.

143 Ibid., pp. 605, 606.

Chapter 8

The rise of the Dissenting Brethren

The chaotic political and ecclesiological debates of 1644 find their beginning and their end within the elegantly vague Third Proposition. The time in between saw shifts in religious and political allegiances that ultimately, and irrevocably, changed the complexion of the debate for the future of England's church. As we saw in the previous chapter, with the voting through of the Third Proposition in early 1644 a presbyterian settlement seemed inevitable. At that point the question of accommodating the Apologists' polity within that presbyterian system came to the fore. Early in the accommodation process the Scots and the Apologists came close to a resolution for accommodation in their own private meetings, but it was not long before English presbyterians put a stop to these efforts. Like the historiography of the *Apologeticall Narration*, the story of how those accommodation attempts began, and failed, has suffered from the Whiggish tendency to blur the lines between accommodation and toleration.

William Haller argued that the *Narration* called for religious toleration and 'represented a large if not confused body of opinion outside the assembly', and the most recent study on the accommodation attempts of late 1644 has argued that Parliament and the Apologists wanted to secure a wide toleration for those godly separatists.' As we argued in chapter 4, the *Narration* was not a call for religious toleration, and therefore we should not be surprised to find that the Apologists' accommodation attempts that same year were not an effort to protect separatist voices outside the assembly. The story of accommodation is a complex one, compounded by the changing tides of war, politics, and theological differences within the assembly. However, when we take into account what we have studied thus far, the questions of church power and differences within the presbyterian majority help provide a cipher through which we can understand the variety of accommodation attempts that were made in 1644.

In this chapter we will study efforts to find an accommodation with the Apologists and how those attempts ultimately resulted in an open dissent by the congregational divines. The immediate context of the first attempt at an accommodation was, as we studied in the previous chapter, the passing in the assembly of the Third Proposition on presbyterial church government and the international controversy surrounding the *Apologeticall Narration* in March. In early 1644 the Scots, though facing occasional opposition from certain types of English presbyterianism in the assembly, felt they had significant parliamentary support. They were still allied with influential men like Sir Henry Vane Junior, Oliver St John and Lord Saye and Sele. Their troops had only recently crossed the border to support a relatively weak parliamentary army. While the Covenanters in Scotland had tasked them with the very specific assignment of ensuring the establishment of a system of presbyteries in England, they nonetheless felt they still had enough political capital in London to negotiate with the Apologists. In this accommodation effort, the Scots were initially acting as the accommodators in the face of an increasingly belligerent group of English presbyterians while simultaneously navigating pressure from an increasingly impatient government back in Scotland.

The second accommodation attempt was a parliamentary-initiated committee to force the assembly to find an accommodation in the autumn of 1644. As summer changed to autumn in 1644, the Scots began to fall out of favour with Saye and the war party and their troops were eclipsed by Cromwell's success in the battlefield. Those parliamentary victories set in motion a series of events that led to the Scots finding themselves less and less influential in Parliament, thus increasing the pressure from the Scottish Covenanters for England's Parliament to force the codification of a presbyterian church settlement.

With shifting political allegiances we see a shift in tactics by the Scots in the assembly. Here we will see that when the Scots took Newcastle in the Autumn of 1644, the commissioners – adroitly led by Gillespie – seized the moment and convinced the assembly to finally send the Third Proposition up to Parliament. By the end of 1644, Gillespie had almost single-handedly led the assembly away from the Apologists and many of the Aldermanbury divines. He repeatedly instructed the divines – against the repeated protests of the Apologists – to temporarily set aside the thorny question of particular church power. Weighing the risks, the Scots saw that supporting the rights of the presbytery was better politically than discussing the rights of the local church. The latter was the basis for their agreements with the Apologists and men like Marshall, Herle and Calamy, but that alliance was no longer worth protecting, given the influence of the clerical presbyterians at Parliament.

The presbyterians had the advantage of sidelining the complex questions of church power and coalescing around the practicalities of presbyterian government. After years of internecine squabbles, and months of erudite debate, the assembly could only muster this one vague *affirmative* proposition on presbyterian church government, one that reflected a multitude of ecclesiological positions: 'The scripture doth hold forth, that many particular congregations may be under one presbyterial government.'[2] This was a proposition no presbyterian would disagree with, but one the presbyterians wrongly thought the Apologists could support. By the end of 1644, the assembly began to codify a presbyterian compromise that would keep the presbyterian majority from fracturing.

MARCH 1644

Leading the initial assembly attempt for accommodation in March 1644 was Richard Vines. Historians have presumed Vines's sympathies to have lain with a reduced episcopacy, although he eschewed a *jure divino* claim to that position.[3] Yet his comments in the assembly offer a different picture. His contributions throughout 1644 reveal a very accommodating Vines who was very concerned to define the rights of the particular church. Lightfoot recorded Vines giving a speech discussing 'how near they [the 'Independents'] came towards us, and [he] hoped some accommodation might be betwixt us.'[4] The minutes record Vines's speech about the Apologists:

> 1. They consent to presbyteryes & sinods. 2. They can looke upon a presbitery as an ordinance of Christ. 3. They may summon & convent. 4. If he doe apeare as he ought to doe, a presbitery hath a speciall authority in the name of Christ. 5. If he be refractory, they may declare his fault either in that congregation ... In matter of doctrine they will ascribe very much. Put case: the congregation shall patronize the sin of this man; what can the presbytery doe? 1. Can we excommunicate the whole land? I cannot come up to that. Then it must ly upon a non communion, if only the poynt stickes about this formall part of jurisdiction.[5]

Marshall agreed that the differences between the independents and the assembly presbyterians were 'aliquid'.[6] Even Seaman, recognising the amount of power the Apologists were willing to give to synods, was forced to say, 'If they give more to presbiteryes than in their booke [*Apologeticall Narration*], I desire they would set it down *in scriptis*.'[7] This is a fascinating statement, for far from rebuffing the Apologists for their *Narration* – on the very day the assembly was dealing with the assembly's letter to Parliament regarding the Walcheren letter – Seaman actually wanted them to publish another document in which they were more assertive in their views of synods!

> That afternoon (7 March) the assembly set up a committee for accommodation in order to reach an agreement with the Apologists. Regarding the committee, Vines stated, 'That we may take up soe farre as the brethren [the Apologists] can goe. That they can looke [upon] the presbitery as an ordinance of God, & that ther may be a

conviction of brother offending'. Bridge responded, 'We have allwayes been very ready to acomodation; other businesses have setled into acomodation, therefore move that ther may be a committy.'[8]

Lightfoot reported that a committee consisting of Mr Henderson 'among others' made some overtures of accommodation. The assembly chose six members for the committee, 'Mr Seaman, Mr. Vines, Mr. Palmer, Mr. Goodwin, Mr. Bridges, [and] Mr. Burroughs'.[9] With the exception of Vines, the assembly had put together a committee that represented either end of its ecclesiological spectrum: The congregational divines on the one end, and the more clerical English presbyterians on the other. On the latter end, Seaman rejected the views shared by both the Scots and the Apologists that any power of the keys, in measure, was to be found in the particular church. To him this ecclesiology was tantamount to the argument put forth by libertines and socinians.[10] Herbert Palmer likewise defended clerical hierarchy on the assembly floor.[11]

The 'other businesses' of accommodation Bridge referred to were probably the unofficial accommodation meetings that had already been taking place between the Scottish commissioners and the Apologists. We must remember the Scots were non-voting members of the assembly, so any effort to accommodate the Apologists was going to be limited to the Scots' ability to influence the presbyterian majority. By creating the official committee, the assembly ended up removing a basis for accommodation between the Scots and the congregationalists.

Certain members of the assembly, and particularly the Scots, saw the danger of allowing this committee to move forward without a moderating force. So, after another motion, 'Mr. Marshall and Mr. Nye' were added to the committee.[12] From a political perspective, these two divines were considered the *sine qua non* of any sort of accommodation between their respective groups. Marshall's appearance would immediately help Vines temper the clerical English presbyterians. From both Gillespie and Baillie we learn that the Scots requested – and were granted – permission to join the committee.[13] The Scots did not want the more clerically minded English presbyterians like Palmer and Seaman to scuttle the Scots' previous efforts at accommodation with the congregationalists. Baillie hinted that these previous meetings had been going on: 'We were glad that what we were doing in private should be thus authorized,' and we have 'mett some three or four times alreadie, and have agreed on five or six propositions'.[14]

In a matter of three days, the members of the committee produced four separate accommodation documents. The first document represented the Scots' and the congregationalists' previous attempt at accommodation; the second represented Vines's propositions; the third was the Apologists' response to Vines's propositions; and the final document represented a compromise of the previous two. I have analysed the contents of these lists elsewhere.[15] What is important to see, for our purposes, is that once again it was the Scots and the Congregationalists struggling against the clerical Presbyterians to protect the rights of the particular church, especially within the context of a settled Presbyterian system.

We can see Seaman and Palmer's fingerprints on the final accommodation document through what it leaves out. The Scots and Apologists had agreed on a proposition that stated, 'Where a congregation may be furnished with a sufficient eldership, they may have the same power in cases concerning themselves.'[16] That proposition was dropped. The final document makes no mention of the powers of the particular church; it simply leaves the whole question to the side.

This would explain Gillespie's last comments regarding the accommodation committee in his notes. When the final list of proposals was submitted to the assembly, Gillespie said the Scots added this proviso: 'These propositions we assent unto, supposing that particular congregations have that power which we conceive respectively to be due unto them.'[17] Furthermore, we learn from Gillespie that during these meetings the Scots had written a 'paper containing eight propositions concerning particular congregations'.[18]

Something, or, rather, someone in the committee for accommodation was alarming the Scots by threatening the rights of the particular church. The committee was able to vote through the accommodation proposals, but Seaman and Palmer undoubtedly had a majority behind them on the assembly floor that would have never allowed for a set of propositions that did not give the keys of jurisdiction to a synod over multiple churches. Seven months later, Goodwin confirmed that Gillespie's fears were real when he reminded assembly, 'Ther was a committee of accommodation ... [and] the sticke was in the power of perticular congregations.'[19]

For that reason the first committee for accommodation and its propositions disappeared.[20] The last we hear of it on the assembly floor was on 22 March, when it was ordered 'to continew the former committee. They are to make report unto this assembly upon this day forthnight'.[21] Neither the minutes nor the journals record anything else regarding the committee. There are clues, however, as to why the accommodation attempts failed. Baillie's letters seem to indicate that the accommodation attempts fell apart once English divines got involved. On 3 May Baillie stated, 'When we have any truce with the Independents anent our Presbyterie, we fall in new warrs with others.' There was a 'great party' in the assembly who 'in opposition to Independencie, will have no ecclesiastick court at all, bot one presbyterie for all the congregations within its bounds'.[22] Baillie sent this letter two days after Gillespie had tried – and failed – to get the assembly to protect the power of the particular church against Seaman's opposition.

We are reminded in this episode that both the Scots and the Apologists were minority groups in the assembly, and only one of the two had voting privileges. They needed the English majority to achieve an accommodation, but within that majority was a very influential group that would never have allowed such an accommodation. Robert Paul concluded that during these debates in April and May, there was a majority forming in the assembly that was willing to invest presbyteries with the same powers Bishops once had, and that the 'deepest' divisions seemed to be within the presbyterian parties.[23]

Baillie, not surprisingly, represented a very different picture to his cousin in mid-April 1644. 'The Independents are resolute to give their reasons against us', which Baillie suspected would result in an 'open schisme: [and] lykelie after that, we will be forced to deal with them as open enemies'.[24] The events of the next two weeks showed that while Baillie might have considered the congregationalists 'his enemies', Gillespie and Rutherford were by no means of the same mind. There were aspects of Seaman's views on church government that were every bit as alarming to Gillespie as they were to the Apologists. Contrary to Baillie's claim, accommodation was still very much in play, especially as it concerned the Scots and the Apologists. In May 1644, the problem facing the Scots came from other presbyterians, not from the Apologists. Their decision to follow the assembly's methodology in February had come back to haunt them.

MAY 1644: 'A LITTLE DISTASTE FOR THE SCOTS'

Having established the Third Proposition on presbytery earlier in the year, and seeing that their initial accommodation attempt had been thwarted by certain English presbyterians, the Scots realised it was time to bring the assembly back to the important question of church power in the particular church. On 1 May 1644, Gillespie noted that his 'desire' in this debate about particular congregations was 'That in regard [to] the French Discipline, chap. v., and the Confession of Bohemia, chap. xiv., and the letter from the Classis of Walcheren owned and approved by synod of Zeland in their letter, all these and other Reformed churches give some power of church government and censures' to the elders 'of each particular congregation'.[25] Gillespie also stated that the Scots had asserted this 'in our second paper concerning church government given in to the Grand Committee'.[26] This was probably the paper the Scots had submitted on 24 January 1644, which they then backed away from to allow the assembly's majority to begin with the proposition about presbyteries over multiple churches. Gillespie's concern related to a proposition that was being debated in the assembly which concerned whether the particular eldership in a church had the right to exercise church discipline. Seaman, according to Gillespie, believed there should be one presbytery over multiple churches in one city (e.g. one presbytery over London), 'and no eldership, with the least power of church censure in a congregation'.[27] The day before, Seaman had argued that 'discipline by the common presbitery ... was better' and that multiple elders would be too much of a burden for one church to handle.[28]

This is another important clue into the failure of the preceding accommodation attempts. Seaman's position was not only impossible for the Apologists to embrace, but, for Gillespie, it was counter to the entire Reformed tradition. Baillie, however, in trying to get the Dutch to give less power to the particular church, had warned Spang privately that Seaman dismissed Voetius and the classis of Walcheren for not giving the ordinary power of excommunication and ordination to the 'Classes' instead of 'parochiall Consistories'.[29] At the same time Gillespie was trying to ward off Seaman and his followers, Baillie was writing Spang telling him to send letters that would strengthen Seaman's hand.

The letter Gillespie referred to was the *first* letter, from Walcheren, which we discussed in earlier. The 'Synod of Zeeland' had written another letter which the assembly received on 29 April, and according to Gillespie, although it promised a greater response to the *Apologeticall Narration*, it nonetheless owned the policy of the Walcheren letter, namely that the particular elders in a church had the power of excommunication. The assembly minutes recorded that there 'came to us [the assembly] out [of] Zealand to the same tenor of those of Walachria: and the same dislike of the Apologetic narration'.[30] Baillie was pleased to receive this letter, but lamented Parliament's 'woefull way' and that they would probably not publish the letter from Zeeland, because, like the Walcheren letter, it touched upon the issue of the magistrate. Indeed, it was just as Baillie feared, for once again the issue of the magistrate played into the hands of the Apologists and resulted in Parliament refusing to publish the letter.[31] But more problematically for Baillie, the letter actually drew attention to Gillespie's similarities to the Apologists.

According to Lightfoot, on 1 May 'Mr Henderson first moved, "That we might give due to particular churches"' and requested that the Scottish commissioners' paper – the paper referred to by Gillespie above – be given to the Grand Committee to be read.[32] The text of this paper is absent from the historical record. The ongoing debate between Gillespie and Calderwood that would take place over the next three years concerning the matter of excommunication seemed to start in May 1644. That same month, right before the assembly began debating whether the particular church had any right of excommunication, Baillie recorded that the Scots had 'long agoe' handed in 'a paper to the great Committee wherein we asserted a congregationall eldership, for the governing the private affaires of the congregation, from the eighteenth of Matthew'.[33] Calderwood 'censured us [the Scottish commissioners] greivouslie for so doing'. Calderwood claimed that the Scots only allowed for one Presbytery and that putting 'excommunication, and so entire government, to congregations ... is a great stepp to Independencie'.[34] According to Baillie, the commissioners were in a 'pecke of troubles' over the situation. And this probably explains, at least in part, the Scots' initial hesitation to follow their own platform of church government two months earlier.

From the context of Scottish church history one can see why Baillie had trouble keeping the Scottish commissioners on task. In 1645 Gillespie sent 'a Directory of excommunication' to Scotland, and Calderwood soundly rebuked it. Again, Calderwood denied that the particular church's presbytery had any power in church government. Gillespie thus recounted the history of the Scottish church, pointing out from the records of the General assembly and Scotland's *First Booke of Church Discipline* that the particular presbyteries were in Scotland twenty years before they had Synods.[35] There was great irony in Gillespie citing Scottish history back to Scotland's greatest church historian. (Interestingly, it was David Calderwood's massive *Altare Damascenum* which the Apologists cited as one of the greatest influences of their polity.) The *First Booke of Discipline* gave unqualified freedom to the people to choose their elders, and it placed considerable power in the congregation in all-important matters relating to the church, particularly excommunication.[36] Although it had been ultimately rejected when it was first written, the *First Booke of Discipline* was published anonymously by Calderwood in 1621. Calderwood, it seems, used the same printer for both his *Altare* and the *First Booke of Discipline* that printed many of Henry Ainsworth's writings during those same years.[37] Much later, when Calderwood wrote his famous *The True History of the Church of Scotland*, published in 1678, he included a truncated version of *The First Booke of Discipline*. Not surprisingly given his disputes with Gillespie in 1645, the section on excommunication is virtually written out of Calderwood's *History*.[38]

In the Scottish General assembly of 1647, Calderwood tried to block the publication of both papers submitted by the Scots to Parliament's Grand Committee in 1643 and 1644. According to Baillie, Calderwood rejected these papers because 'they held forth a session of a particular congregation to have a ground in Scripture, which he, contrare to his Altar of Damascus, believes to have no divine right, but to be only a commission, which a delegate power from the Presbyterie tollerat in our Church for a time'.[39] This frustration on Baillie's part highlights another one of his polemical quirks. On the one hand he complained to Spang about the Walcherens giving power of excommunication to the particular church, but on the other he marvelled at Calderwood for not believing the exact same thing.

In 1621, Calderwood had argued strenuously for the power of the particular church's elders, and '[that] to call the particular congregations in the countries extended in length and breadth of about … cities, the church of these cities, is absurd, a no where to be found'.[40] At this early date, Calderwood believed that Scripture did not teach that a church is coterminous with a 'countrie'. Rather, a church is limited to the size of a city or town where the elders could exercise 'ordinarie jurisdiction in the Church wher they governed'.[41] In fact, John Spottiswoode, Archbishop of St Andrews, had evidently 'spread a rumour, that M David Calderwood is turned Brownist'.[42] This is an important point, for it gives us greater clarity into why the Apologists – and indeed, many Scots – were indebted to Calderwood. Calderwood later shifted to a position where the particular churches' power was purely derivative of the presbytery, which was more like Seaman than like Gillespie.

Taking all of these examples together, there seems to be a case to make that this 'second paper' handed into the grand committee that Gillespie referred to is the Gillespie manuscript on excommunication published with his notes on the assembly debates. The editor is unable to date the document, but he suspects it was an anti-Erastian piece written against Selden's speech on excommunication during the February 1644 debate discussed earlier in this chapter. The manuscript is entitled *Church Censures to be Dispensed by Church Officers, jure divino.*[43] In the manuscript, Gillespie critiques Calderwood for not holding that officers in a particular church could exercise excommunica-tion. Furthermore, 'Argument 7' of the document states, 'The power of church discipline is intrinsical to the Church, that is, both they who censure, and they who are censured, must be of the church, I Cor. V. 12, 13.'[44] It was Nye – also in February 1644 – who, after being denied the request to follow the method-ology of the Scots' paper handed into the Grand Committee, went on to cite the Scots who believed that a single congregation has 'intrinsical government'.

On 19 May 1644, Rutherford wrote a letter to Lady Boyde, and through a few cryptic comments we can ascertain his thoughts regarding the Apologists and the question of the particular church. Firstly, he refers to Goodwin and Burroughs, although 'mighty opposites of the presbyterial government', as being his 'friends, even gracious men', although he follows this with a quali-fier: 'so I conceive of them'.[45] This seemed to indicate that Rutherford was aware that he dissented from other Scottish commissioners, and Baillie's letters around that time convey a very different opinion of the Apologists than that held by Rutherford. In this letter, Rutherford also revealed something of the debates going on in the assembly in May. He stated, 'We are to prove that one single congregation hath not power to excommunicate, which is opposed not only by Independent men, but by many others.'[46] It is hard to know exactly where Rutherford places himself on this spectrum. Is the assembly meant to prove this? Or are the Scots? Clearly there were many in the assembly who hoped to prove just as much, but we know that Henderson and Gillespie hoped to prove the particular church *did* have the right to excommunicate, and that the Scots had handed in their paper to the Grand Committee stating that they believed excommunication belonged to a particular church's presby-tery *jure divino*. In the matter of particular churches, Rutherford did, 'to some degree', support the congregational divines in defending the rights of people to gather into particular churches by voluntary consent, even from outside rigidly defined parochial boundaries.[47]

Gillespie wanted to await the Grand Committee's response to their submitted papers. Gillespie feared that the assembly would fall headlong into discussions about the power of presbyteries without having concretely established the rights of the local church. He admitted that if, for example, the churches in London had no power of censure within their respective bounds, it would mean that the London common presbytery would have the 'impossible task' of trying to do all the work in the precinct. In this point he was critiquing Seaman's position. 'Now Mr. Seaman's grounds would make but one presbytery in one city, yea, in London itself, in whose hands all censures, less and more, shall be.'[48] And indeed this was an English presbyterian position; a church might function as a church without a particular eldership, for the common presbytery still oversaw the church and could provide ministers when needed.[49]

As it turned out, Seaman succeeded in preventing the Scots from getting any further in their efforts to protect the particular church's power. The majority of the assembly followed Seaman in having the proposition regarding the power of the particular church's elders in discipline set aside completely.[50] Thus, by early May the Scots were horrified to find that their gambit of securing of the synod's role in February had actually endangered the rights of the local church. The Apologists were similarly frustrated, but only because the assembly found itself trying to balance competing positions on synods, whereas they believed there would have been a wider consensus on the power of particular churches. And thus we see the ramped up efforts for accommodation between the Scottish commissioners and the Apologists in late spring of 1644. Many English presbyterians, in reaction to the congregationalists, were going too far in the other direction.[51] The fears of the Scots and Apologists were entirely justified. In the debates of the first two weeks of May, Seaman further exposed the clerical emphasis of his presbyterianism. With the thorough analysis Paul gives to these particular debates, we need only highlight areas relevant to our particular narrative.[52]

Charles Herle, in response to Seaman, stated, 'It seems strange that a single congregation having pastor & elders should not be ordinarily a church.'[53] Stephen Marshall claimed that Seaman 'takes it for granted that a perticular congregation may not be a church'.[54] Seaman responded that although it be a church, it 'is never integrally intire till it be associated with neighbour congregations, if they may associate'.[55] According to Gillespie, Seaman argued that 'There is no warrant from Scripture that there must be a ruling elder in each congregation.'[56] Seaman also rejected the Scottish (and congregational) position that each church needed a plurality of elders.[57]

There was another brief exchange, recorded by Gillespie, that reflects the precise language found in Cotton's *Keyes*, which was registered at the

Stationers' company during these debates. In these debates, Gillespie argued before the assembly that election 'doth ordinarily belong to the congregation', because the people's election was not a matter of 'jurisdiction and authority' like excommunication and ordination were.[58] Seaman responded, 'That in all these particulars the people have no power at all, but are merely passive, that is, they have a measure of liberty, and a privilege of consent, but the power is only in the presbytery.' Cotton, like Seaman, would argue that the people had 'liberty and privilege'. Cotton believed that this was indeed a 'power', although not a power of jurisdiction and authority.[59] Goodwin responded to Seaman with the precise example he used in his preface to the *Keyes*: 'Election in the hands of officers is an act of authority, as parents choosing a husband for their daughter is an act of authority, though the daughter's election is not.'[60] Interestingly, Seaman seemed to agree, adding, 'The Lord Mayor is chosen by the city, but authoritatively only by the council.'[61] Now, for an added measure of complexity, it seemed Seaman saw a role for the people, without the unique prerogatives of their particular elderships!

None of this is to suggest that Seaman was the only person who held to this position, for he evidently had enough support to stymie the accommodation attempt and to lay aside Scottish papers on church government. Nor do I suggest we replace one standard 'enemy' of the congregationalists (the Scots) with another (Seaman). Seaman had been a close friend of Nye's before the assembly and would work for him as a 'trier' in the Interregnum. But it is clear that Seaman reflected a constituency in the assembly that regarded both the Scots and the Apologists as threats to ministerial prerogatives at the larger, regional – indeed, national – level.

Indeed, during these early May debates, Lighfoot recorded that the 'Scots' commissioners did conceive that we [viz. the assembly] did not here come near enough to them' when the assembly began to assert that a congregation only needed one elder. This only annoyed the assembly, and Lightfoot noted that the commissioners were 'answered again and again, and the debate raught to a great length, and to a little distaste of the Scots'.[62] Not only had the Scots realised that their efforts to give rights to the particular church were failing, but the assembly seemed to be curtailing the number of elders in each church. With the emphasis on the presbytery over multiple churches many divines apparently believed a plurality of local elders would be redundant.

As late as May 1644, the Scots knew a basis for accommodation existed with the congregationalists – despite their very real differences. Surprisingly, while we find men like Herle, Vines and Marshall trying to moderate between the English presbyterians and the Apologists, the Scots seemed to be a moderating force as well. It could be that the Scots wanted to settle an accommodation with the Apologists in order to ensure a presbyterian settlement. If the

Apologists were assured that they would be accommodated, then there might be less resistance to many presbyterian arguments.

Again, we are given a very different picture of Gillespie and Rutherford than the one painted by David Mullan, who concluded that any accommodation from the Scots was a 'forbearance [that] had nothing to do with compromise and everything to do with looking the other way'. Indeed, Mullan continues, 'For the Scots, accommodation meant not a meeting in the middle, but ultimately a shift of the independent into the presbyterian camp.'[63] This was true of Baillie, but not necessarily of Gillespie. His type of presbyterianism, however, was very attractive to the Apologists because of its emphasis on the rights of the particular congregation. But as the spring turned to summer it seemed increasingly probably that the clerical English presbyterians would obstruct any accommodation between the Scots and the Apologists. In early May they succeeded in setting aside the question of the power of the particular church, disappointing both the Scots and the Apologists.

However, the Apologists had an ace up their sleeve. For in that first week of May, they registered Cotton's *Keyes of the Kingdom* with the Stationers Company. The *Keyes* addressed the power of the particular church in ways that would certainly appeal to the Scots. It was this document that exposed the deep structural similarities between the Scots and the Apologists – and would only be cited positively on the assembly floor. Rutherford would later state on the assembly floor, 'When I read through that treatise of *The Keyes of the Kingdome of heaven*, I thought it an easy labour for an universall pacification, he comes soe neare unto us.'[64] Similarly, Nye stated, 'Ther is more than 2 or 3 or 4 partyes in the assembly', if the 'government of Scotland layed downe, those you call independents will come nearer to it than many in this Assembly'.[65] The Apologists hoped that publishing the *Keyes* would reinvigorate an accommodation, and they hoped to rely on the Scots to lead the way. Unfortunately for the Apologists, the fortunes of the Scots were about to change.

AUTUMN 1644: THE POLITICS OF ACCOMMODATION AND DISSENT

As summer of 1644 turned to autumn, Parliament and the assembly experienced another shift in political and ecclesiological allegiences.[66] With the success of Manchester and Cromwell in northern England, many in the war party began to view the Scottish army as redundant, and their popularity in Parliament was quickly eroding.[67] Falling out of favour with their former allies in the war party, Saye and Sele, St John and Vane influenced the tactics of the Scots throughout late 1644.[68] Out of sheer political necessity, the war party was initially willing to tolerate a slight movement towards Scottish presbyterianism but they were never interested in re-creating the kirk in England.[69]

By the end of 1644 the Scots discovered that the war party no longer needed – or wanted – their help in the fight with Charles. Thus began a gradual shift of the Scots towards Essex and those who would more readily support a quick settlement with the King.[70]

The Scots not only changed political allies, they needed to form alliances in the assembly with divines had opposed months before. In August 1644 an increasingly frustrated Scottish Parliament dispatched Warriston to London with a 'passionate' letter to Parliament and the assembly of divines to hasten the completion of church uniformity in accordance with the Solemn League and Covenant.[71] The Scots quickly realised that in order to get a system of presbyterianism through Parliament, they would have to keep the Erastians and other presbyterians in the assembly on the same page. In the autumn of 1644 the assembly was debating on several fronts, within committees, in plenary sessions, and in simultaneous accommodation committees.

Partly as a result in these changes, the assembly and Parliament were growing increasingly suspicious of one another. The previous spring the assembly had sent its twelve doctrinal propositions on ordination to Parliament. After dragging its feet on the matter, Parliament returned a revised version of the directory for ordination to the assembly in August.[72] To the horror of many divines, Parliament had omitted the doctrinal part of the document, removed references to presbytery from the practical section, and written its own preface. Adding insult to injury, the assembly could not even debate these revisions unless so ordered by Parliament.[73] The Scots were infuriated by Parliament's meddling.[74] Many English divines were similarly frustrated. On 9 September the assembly was informed of Essex's disastrous defeat in Cornwall and 'began a tumultuous discussion about the causes of God's displeasure with Parliament's forces.' They spent their time debating who was to blame, 'with some pointing the finger at parliament, some the assembly itself, and some the nation'.[75]

Rutherford, for example, complained that previous attempts at accommodation had failed.[76] Calamy saw this defeat as being due, in part, to Parliament ignoring parts of the ordination clauses voted on in the assembly.[77] The assembly boldly drew up a list of twelve 'sins' committed by Parliament. These sins included Parliament's failure to prosecute sectarians or those who had not kept the covenant, their unwise use of money and resources, the lack of care of protection of ministers in England, and the neglect of catechising its citizens.[78] In the end, cooler heads prevailed and the assembly decided not to send their accusations up to Parliament.

The event underscores the fact that at the very point the assembly was once again turning its thoughts to church government, the tensions between the divines and the Parliamentarians had grown considerably. Parliament was frustrated with the assembly's sluggishness in developing a church for

England, and at Parliament's insistence the assembly once again turned their attention to the issue of church government.[79] The question of presbyterian church government, effectively set aside since the previous February, could be avoided no longer. Robert Paul, with good reason, called this phase of debates the 'final clash' over the increasingly divisive issue.[80] It was during these few short months, from September through November, that the assembly debated the majority of the issues that would make their way into the document known as the *Grand Debate*. In retrospective reports, these debates would be remembered as some of the most controversial periods of the assembly.

There were two important debates going on simultaneously during this period. In the assembly the divines once again revisited church government. Outside the Jerusalem chamber parliamentarians and assembly divines were engaged in a Parliament-initiated committee for accommodation. As assembly members were involved in both the assembly debates and accommodation meetings, we are not surprised to find overlap in the issues that began to further alienate particular parties in the assembly. As the assembly discussed how to approach this next period of debate of church government, Thomas Goodwin stated, 'Ther was a committee of accommodation ... the sticke was in the power of the particular congregations.'[81] The very issue that complicated the accommodation attempt in the spring of 1644 – for some surprising reasons – would stretch across both the assembly debates and accommodation debates. We will look first at the Assembly situation, then the accommodation efforts, and then how they overlapped and ultimately resulted in the open dissent of the Apologists.

On 4 September – like in October 1643 and February 1644 – the assembly found itself at an impasse as to exactly how to proceed in their discussions on church government.[82] The Grand Committee tried to expedite the assembly's proceedings and sent a report asking the assembly to address three questions in order: 'Whether there be such an ordinance as excommunication. 2. Whether a single congregation may excommunicate. 3. Whether a classical presbytery may excommunicate.'[83] According to Gillespie, the Scots – though disagreeing with this methodology – refrained from speaking against the questions when the Grand Committee penned them.[84] However, the Scots were less sheepish on the assembly floor. Henderson reminded the assembly that while the Grand Committee was designed for expediting the development of a system of church government, this recommended method of proceeding would not achieve that goal.[85]

Marshal, Vines and others then recommended that the assembly follow an alternate, but similar, procedure offered in by Committee for the Summary.[86] This committee was created the previous spring when Burgess, Gataker, Reynolds and Vines joined the assembly's representatives already on the Grand Committee in order to expedite the drafting of a 'whole businesse of [church] discipline'.[87] When this Summary committee presented its recommendations on 14 May 1644 it 'outlin[ed] a plan which would begin with the government of the local congregation'.[88]

Initially, the assembly was split between the English divines and Apologists who were on the Grand Committee on one side and the Scots, Erastians and clerical English presbyterians on the other. Marshall pointed to both committees' recommendations and highlighted the common theme in both reports, 'Begin wher you will, it is excommunication you must fall upon; from congregations you reason a fit order to assemblyes.'[89] Herle similarly pointed out, 'if you meane a draught in all the parts of it [church government], then you must dispatch the power of a congregation'.[90] It was here that Goodwin referred to the previous committee for accommodation, which fell apart over the issue of 'the power of the perticular congregations'.[91] For the members of both committees tasked with expediting a settlement on church government, it was clear that they could not develop a system of church government without first sorting out the power of the particular church.

As we saw earlier, the Scots had initially offered to the assembly the method of proceeding from the local church upward, but they withdrew it after complaints from the Covenanters back in Scotland, and agreed to let the assembly pursue its debate over the 'Third Proposition'. Calamy reminded the assembly of their February 1644 votes, 'I desire to mind you of the method of the assemby [*sic*] itselfe hath taken; they began first with presbyteryes.'[92] As we noted early in this book, the voting through of the Third Proposition prematurely addressed the question of presbyterianism. Now, seven months later, when they actually began to debate presbyterian church government, the assembly found itself hamstrung by its own votes.

Gillespie, Rutherford and Henderson repeated their tactics from the previous February. The Scots asked the assembly to lay aside the question of church power entirely, or as Dr Joshua Hoyle noted, 'First make the house and then furnish the roomes.'[93] For them the assembly had not yet fully addressed the question of presbyteries and, as Rutherford stated, 'we have already determined what a presbytery is, but many in the Assembly will say it is not fully proved'.[94] Lord Maitland and Gillespie urged the assembly to first prove the existence of '4 sorts of Assemblyes'. Gillespie offered two reasons for this way of proceeding. Firstly, he argued that it would help with the current peace negotiations with Charles, because the king could not possibly understand what type of church government was being offered without its principal parts being codified.[95] Henderson seemed skeptical on this first point, reminding the assembly that 'The king hath often said, 'Thinke you that ever the church of England shall be governed by Assemblyes?''[96] To others, it seemed foolhardy to presume the king would be satisfied with a system of assemblies and presbyteries without telling him what power those governing bodies had.

Herle stated, 'To offer the king a government in 4 assemblyes and not tell him what that is, he will reject it tell him the perticulars.'[97]

The second, and most important, reason Gillespie pressed the assembly to focus on assemblies first was that 'it is better to begin with these things wherein the assembly is unanimous, than with the most knotty things wherein difference is like to be'.[98] Given what we have discussed throughout this book, it should not come as a surprise that the question of church power was something the assembly wanted to avoid. The question of whether or not the elders in a particular church had all the church power necessary to govern was what had gotten the Scots into trouble with men like Seaman the previous May. It was a topic that repeatedly exposed the differences within the presbyterian majority, as displayed by the debate on 4 September. Vines, for example, did not see how the assembly could possibly define church government without first defining what powers the church, and its assemblies, possessed. Vines said, 'Excommunication is government, & all ecclesiasticall government resolves itselfe into that.'[99] Not everyone in the assembly agreed. For the Erastians, for example, excommunication and church government were two separate things.

It was Vines's statement that risked dividing the presbyterians – something the Scots had to avoid in order to secure a presbyterian system. There was indeed wide agreement in the assembly that there should be several sorts of assemblies governing over the particular churches. Gillespie cited Cotton's *Keyes of the Kingdom of Heaven* as a proof that the Apologists agreed with the Scots on assemblies, and that the Scots themselves agreed with Cotton.[100] Goodwin stated that there were such things as national assemblies – though he questioned whether they were standing bodies, and whether there were such things as 'provincial assemblyes'.[101]

Calamy conceded that they could move forward along the path of discussing the assemblies first, but he warned the assembly that they would encounter trouble when they came to discuss the power that was in those assemblies. He stated, 'All our Reformed churches that agree in the *thali* [kind], yet they differ in the power in severall classes.'[102] Calamy's comments further validate what we discussed regarding Voetius and Paget, namely, that there was no settled agreement on the kind of power that existed in governing bodies over particular churches. Nye followed by stating, 'If you will pitch upon that in which all the Reformed churches doe agree, you must begin with congregations.'[103] This is an important point, because Nye's statement risked ferreting out the clerical English presbyterians as not in keeping with the Reformed tradition, something the Scots wanted desperately to avoid. Some English presbyterians, to the horror of many in the assembly, denied that the church – in any form – had the right to excommunicate, and other English presbyterians denied that the particular church was allowed to excommunicate.

It is not coincidental, then, that only days later Baillie dispatched more letters to Spang complaining about the Reformed churches. He was still not pleased with the results of his efforts, claiming that the 'unkindess of all the Reformed churches to us at these times is great'.[104] He once again rebuked Spang for a letter from Utrecht that did not attack 'Independencie' and for Spang's failure to secure support from 'Diodati and the Parisians'. He became particularly nervous immediately after the Scots' victory in Newcastle, fearing that Voetius was going to write a book endorsing John Cotton's *Keyes of the Kingdom of Heaven* 'as consonant to truth, and the discipline of Holland'.[105]

Baillie was well informed of Scottish troop movements, and that may help explain Gillespie's and the other Scottish divines' insistence on discussing the existence of synods before discussing church power. Ballie's concern about the Covenanters' waning influence is underscored by his obsession with Newcastle. His letters from late August to the middle of September 1644 indicate that Scottish troops were edging closer to Newcastle. Baillie knew that if the Scots could occupy Newcastle, their chances of pressing through a church government predicated on a system of presbyteries and synods would improve considerably. Ever the pragmatist, Baillie knew that the fortunes of presbyterianism relied less on theological argument and more on military tactics.[106] If the Scots could delay a question of church power long enough to secure votes on the existence of presbyteries, then they could exert greater pressure on Parliament to accept those votes. Whether by design or not, that is exactly what happened.

In the meantime, the Scots succeeded in persuading the assembly, including the congregationalists, to first debate 'That it is lawful and agreeable to the word that the church be governed by several sorts of assemblies'.[107] This was similar to a paper the Scots had handed in the previous November (1643) which stated that the 'four sorts of assemblies' was a fundamental aspect of Scottish church government.[108] The stage was now set for some of the most difficult and complex periods of the assembly. The first question on the existence of assemblies would be followed by a debate about the subordination of assemblies (23 September), then church censures (4–8 October) and finally excommunication (14–25 October). During the period leading up to the question of subordination the assembly produced three relatively uncontroversial propositions.[109] The question of church power had been temporarily sidelined, but the assembly found it hard to ignore. While we will not cover these debates in detail, we will tease out how the question of church power ultimately brought an end to hopes for accommodation while protecting the presbyterian majority. As long as the assembly kept itself on task, in this case proving the existence of synods and assemblies, it could, by and large, keep the presbyterian majority together and the debates would move along according to their laborious scholastic design. But the latent issue of church power always lurked underneath and proved impossible to avoid when the assembly debated subordination of one governing assembly to a higher one. The question of excommunication proved to be the straw that broke the camel's back.

On 23 September, the assembly turned its attention to the subordination of assemblies. Once again the questions of power sidelined the previous year came to the fore. Nye reminded the assembly that there was a division in the assembly between some who thought 'that the power of church government is chiefly in the church universal, the inferior assemblies being only for the relief of it', and others who thought 'that the power is in congregations, and superior assemblies, for relief and help to them only'. This latter opinion, Nye claimed, was 'the opinion of the most part of the Assembly'.[110] Goodwin had made the same argument about the division in the assembly the previous October – though it is interesting that Nye claimed the majority of the assembly followed the *ascendendo* position. Vines and Herle noted that sidelining the question of power would prove problematic when the assembly would try to figure out how one assembly appeals to another assembly. Seaman, certainly placing himself in the *descendendo* camp, stated, 'begin with the power, & the power of the highest', and Marshall countered, 'Begin first with that power & authority the lowest of them all hath.'[111]

Nye and Gillespie closed ranks and reminded the assembly they were not to address the question of power, but merely the question of whether there is a subordination of various types of ecclesiastical synods (namely, congregational, classical, and synodical).[112] Nye stated, 'It is not yet determined ... what is the power.' And Gillespie agreed, stating, 'This is spoken to good purpose.'[113] Once committed to this debate over subordination the Scots and the Apologists, for different reasons, knew that assigning power to these assemblies would prove problematic. If there is one theme we see from the Scots through all the debates (in both the assembly and Grand Committee), it was the commitment to steer the assembly away from the question of power.[114] As we saw earlier, neither the Scots nor the Apologists believed in ascending or descending power. Henderson knew that those who argued for appeals from a lower body to a higher 'supposeth there is some power in all these from whom the appeal lies'.[115] Unlike the English, the Scots did not believe that power could be trans-ferred upward or downward, but they believed it was given by God to each assembly directly. The Apologists agreed, but they claimed that the power of church government was only given to the particular church. They believed in assemblies, but not as courts with jurisdiction.[116]

Before examining the debates on excommunication, we should briefly turn our attention to the second committee for accommodation that had been meeting concurrently, because it is here, on the matter of excommunication in mid-October, that the two enterprises collide on the assembly floor. Only eight days after the Scots persuaded the assembly to ignore the Grand Committee's procedure in debating church government, the House of Commons ordered

That the Committee of Lords and Commons appointed to treat with the Commissioners of Scotland, and the Committee of the Assembly, Do take into consideration the differences of the opinions of the members of the Assembly in point of Church-government, and to indeavor an union if it be possible: And in case that cannot be done, to indeavor the finding out some way how far tender consciences who cannot in all things submit to the same Rule, which shall be established, may be borne with according to the Word, and as may stand with the publicke peace; That so the proceedings of the Assembly may not be so much retarted.[117]

The Grand Committee, upon the advice of Stephen Marshall, appointed a sub-committee for accommodation. When St John and Vane shepherded this accommodation order through the House of Commons, Robert Baillie was livid. He saw this as a betrayal by two men who owed their influential parliamentary status to the Scots.[118] As we will see, the immediate context suggests this was the Grand Committee's way of forcing the assembly to address the questions they had ignored a few days before.

Baillie claimed that Marshall connived to keep the Scots off this sub-committee, and, given that it was the Scots who were largely responsible for side-stepping the Grand Committee's advice, there could be some truth in that claim. Baillie also claimed that part of Marshall's subterfuge was to put 'Vines, Herle, Reynolds, Seaman, and Palmer' on the committee, but when they 'see us [the Scots] excluded, by Marshall's cunning, would not joyne'.[119] This account is obviously false. According to Gillespie's notes, the published records, and the minutes, the men Baillie listed were clearly on the committee, and as we noted earlier, were some of the most open to accommodation. The official documents note that Vines was the 'Chaire-man of that sub-Committee'.[120] Furthermore, according to Gillespie, Marshall told the Scots that when the sub-committee differed from the Scottish form they would alert the Scots 'or if need be, desire our presence in the Sub-Committee, though they would not trouble us unnecessarily'.[121] Around this time we see an increasing dissonance between Baillie's accounts and the other assembly records. Baillie's journals record a visceral loathing for this committee, and particularly for Marshall, whom he was beginning to regard as a mere agent of the Apologists.[122] Once again, this attitude does not comport with Gillespie's own records of these meetings, or Gillespie's and Rutherford's overall desire to accommodate the Apologists.

What marks these debates, as recorded by Gillespie, is just how much they dealt with the questions left unresolved because the assembly bypassed the Grand Committee's recommendation to start with church power. At the sub-committee for accommodation's initial meeting there was confusion as to whether, as some Grand Committee members believed, the order applied to reconciling existing divisions in the assembly, or as Nye, Goodwin and Marshall believed, it applied to all 'issues on which differences could arise in later debates'.[123] Calamy and Goodwin noted that this meeting 'intends not a sifting of all opinions different, but of practical differences which may hinder men from living as brethren in peace together'.[124]

On the first day of the committee meetings Herle stated, 'The order speaks of all the differences, of which are chiefly three: 1. Some are for the congregational way only; 2. Some give power of censures to congregations, yet acknowledge appeals; 3. Others give the whole power to the classes.'[125] It will be helpful here to restate what the Grand Committee had initially asked the assembly to address: 'Whether there be such an ordinance as excommunication. 2. Whether a single congregation may excommunicate. 3. Whether a classical presbytery may excommunicate.'[126]

They are virtually the same comments, though the Grand Committee postulated questions, while Herle stated them as facts. The assembly was indeed divided between those three groups, though they increasingly disliked pointing out the distinctions. Calamy and Reynolds said, 'It is not fit to make three sorts: for the difference betwixt two of these sorts is only intellectual,' a statement which was designed to unite disparate presbyerian parties. Marshall and Vines countered that it was indeed practical to note the division, because it dealt with excommunication, which, as Vines had told the assembly only days before, *is* church government. Seaman added that 'the distinction of intellectual and practical differences is most necessary'.[127]

Tantalisingly, Seaman and Burgess had urged that the best way forward was for the Dissenting Brethren to write about their difference with the Scottish form of church government. Only a few days earlier Nye had claimed the Dissenting Brethren were closer to the Scots than many others in the assembly. Such a document would have made for fascinating reading, but St John stated that it was too much to ask the Dissenting Brethren to dissent from an existing form of church government, since the assembly was developing its own church government for England. This comment makes one wonder just how much the Apologists wanted parliamentary involvement in their attempts to accommodate. In the end, the Grand Committee decided to appoint a sub-committee for accommodation.

The sub-committee returned two lists to the Grand Committee. On 20 September they returned 'severall Propositions, concerning the Government of particular congregations, and Ordination, &c'. On 11 October they brought in propositions 'concerning Classes and synods[,] [a]nd what might be the way of accommodation for the dissenting brethren to enjoy Congregations amongst us, according to their principles'.[128] The printed documents italicise the portions of the propositions where the Apologists 'differ from the Propositions of the rest of the sub-comittees or do express their desires a part from them'.[129]

The sub-committee found a remarkable level of common ground and gave a considerable deference to the power of the particular church. In their first proposition on the particular church, the sub-committee agreed, without any dissent, 'That a congregation having such officers, as the word of God holds out, both for preaching and governing, is a Church that hath power in all Ecclesiastical affairs, which do only concern itself.'[130] The Grand Committee questioned whether this included ordination and excommunication. Marshall noted that it could not include ordination since the votes on ordination had already passed through the assembly, but 'excommunication is comprehended for the Assembly hath not yet taken excommunication from congregations'.[131] It seems that Marshall, Herle, Vines and Temple were able to push their position on excommunication in the particular church in the sub-committee despite the assembly choosing another route and before the assembly began their debates over the subject. This was bound to cause tension with Grand Committee members such as Seaman.

The third proposition on the particular church confirmed that the officers of the church had all the power voted to them by the assembly – the power of the keys from October 1643 – but that the people in the church also had a voting role in suspension and excommunication.[132] The sub-committee said that even if the officers judge one to be excommunicated, yet if the church 'judge not', the officers may not proceed; similarly, the church may not excommunicate without the help of officers.[133] Again, this was a standard argument from the Apologists throughout the previous years. There was disagreement in the committee as to whether a church may excommunicate without the assistance of a classis, but even here, Marshall stated, 'To say that in no case the congregation may proceed against the advice of the classis, is more than the Sub-committee thinks.'[134] It was also certainly more than a majority in the assembly believed.

Around mid-October, the Grand Committee, its sub-committee, and the Westminster assembly began to collide. Therefore, we need to briefly look at what had been happening in the assembly while the sub-committee for accommodation was meeting. On 23–24 September, four days after the Grand Committee named the sub-committee, the discussion in the assembly transitioned from the existence of the 'several sorts of assemblies' to the subordination of these several sorts. The assembly found it harder and harder to delay the question of church power.

The moment the assembly came to discuss the types of powers held by these assemblies, namely church censures and excommunication, the assembly once again ran up against this problem of church power. On 8 October, the third committee presented the proposition, 'It is lawful and agreeable to the word of God, that all foresaid assemblies have some power to dispense church censures.'[135] Marshall, Calamy and Herle moved that the assembly should 'begin with the greatest censure of all, excommunication'.[136] Once again, Gillespie pushed the assembly to avoid the question of excommunication for the time being, because 'the Assembly will be more divided about excommunication' than about the question of assemblies having the power to administer other censures.[37] That assemblies could administer punishments such as admonition, temporary suspension from the Lord's table, and reproof for sins was surely not going to be as contentious as assigning the power of excommunication to any assembly. The assembly agreed and the proposition passed that same day.

Three days later, on 14 and 15 October, the issues of excommunication, the prerogatives of the Grand Committee and the role of the sub-committee for accommodation all collided on the Assembly floor. The Grand Committee wrote the assembly of divines demanding to know 'why the assembly had not heeded or even debated its requests to proceed in a particular way upon the question of excommunication'.[38] It was certainly a power play by the Grand Committee, since members of the Grand Committee were also members of the assembly and they all knew that the assembly had ignored the Committee's recommendations. Nonetheless, the scribe drew out of his notes a report, 'showing the Scots Commissioners had pressed the Assembly might first fall upon several sorts of assemblies and their subordination' and that the assembly was now turning to the question of excommunication.[39] In other words, it was the fault of the Scottish commissioners. Palmer immediately questioned whether the Grand Committee had any right to make demands of the assembly, insisting that the assembly only answered to Parliament.

Herle accused Palmer of attempting to divide the Grand Committee. Marshall joined Herle in stating that members of the assembly of divines who were also on the Grand Committee were so by appointment of Parliament and were authorised by Parliament to make such requests. Rutherford pointed out that those who were members of both the assembly and the Grand Committee did not need an answer since they were part of the very discussions that ended in the sidelining of the Grand Committee's recommendations.[40] Herle rejoined that to send an answer just to the Lords and Commons members and not to the whole committee would fundamentally deny that the assembly members were appointed members of the Grand Committee. At this point Seaman intervened, claiming that the Grand Committee was acting outside the scope of its original purpose, 'For the first choyse of this committee, it was not to bring papers from themselves, but receive papers from the commissioners of Scotland. What word Answer have you returned to any of those papers from the Scotch commissioners?'[41]

This reference to the Scottish papers alarmed Gillespie and risked sinking the Scottish agenda of avoiding the question of church power. It was the year before that the Grand Committee had laid aside several papers of the Scottish divines that had claimed that any work on church government should start with the particular church and move up from there. Gillespie told the assembly, '[w]e are not craving an account; it doth not come from us; we have noe hand in it'.[42] Marshall could not withhold his frustration, crying that the assembly would not debate anything but what the Scots were pleased to debate, including 'Many things that they doe not disclaime'.[43] Marshall was onto Gillespie's game: he knew well that the very issues that the Scots would agree with – i.e. power of the particular church – were purposefully avoided, so that even the requests of the Grand Committee, which would have been uncontroversial to the Scots a year earlier, were being delayed.

Later that same day, at a meeting of the Grand Committee and the sub-committee for accommodation, a frustrated Marshall reported that the assembly had not so much as taken the Committee's recommendation into debate. Though, per Gillespie's request, Marshall was forced to add 'That the Assembly hath not yet concluded any thing concerning the method of these questions, but is yet to take the method into consideration.'[44] This demonstrated the lack of power the Grand Committee had over the assembly and undoubtedly served to dampen any hopes that their recommendations on accommodation would be taken seriously. It also precipitated an intense debate in the Grand Committee as to whether they should even send the sub-committee's accommodation propositions to the assembly before sending them to Parliament. Gillespie and the Scots (who were also in the Grand Committee meeting that same day) demanded to know whether these propositions would be referred first to the assembly of divines or to the House of Commons.

At this point the Scots were not beyond threatening the Committee, claiming that if the Committee refused to send the accommodation propositions to the assembly first, the Scots had a 'paper ready to be given in on the whole matter'.[45] Rouse, Tate and Prideaux joined the Scottish opposition to bypassing the assembly, and the Grand Committee acquiesced: it was decided that the assembly should debate the propositions first. This further reflected the waning influence of St John and Vane.[46] However, we should be careful not to see this primarily as the Scots' ability to quash sectarianism.[47] The Scots needed to control momentum, if only for a few days longer until their troops could capture Newcastle. They could do so much more easily in the assembly than they could in Parliament, where their influence had diminished considerably.

Even so, the Scots had their hands full in the assembly as they turned their discussions to excommunication. Between 11 October and 25 October, the differences in the assembly were less between the congregationalists and the presbyterians and more between the various presbyterians.[48] Initially, it was the Erastians who caused the most consternation. Even the most heated debates over presbyterian church government did not come close to the furore generated by Erastian denials that the church could retain the power of excommunication – which, as many divines argued, was itself the basic definition of church government. For example, the Erastian Thomas Coleman stated that the only reason the church in Corinth had church government and the right to excommunicate was 'because they [Corinth] had no civill government'. A horrified Seaman exclaimed, 'No opinion have I heard more prejudiciall to the kingedom & government of Jesus Christ than this: that there is no excommunication.'[49] Robert Paul has rightly noted that for all the intensity one expected in debating excommunication, the topic had 'already lost some of its significance for the larger dispute about church government, because it presaged the Erastian issue'.[50]

On 24 October the assembly found itself once again stuck on the topic of the first subject of church power. This time it was in the context of whether the severall sorts of assemblies which the assembly had voted on had the power of excommunication. Marshall pleaded with the assembly 'to begin with particular congregations' before deciding whether or not assemblies could excommunicate. He once again reminded them that the assembly had not yet dealt with the requests of the Grand Committee. The assembly needed to find out where the power of excommunication resided and then move on from there, and in this case, it needed to determine if the power of excommunication belonged to the particular church. With a nod to the clerical presbyterians Marshall warned, 'If we dispute first the power of the classis, then we must go by way of appeal to higher assemblies, wheras congregations can lay no claim if a classis be made the first subject' of this power.[51] Many English divines argued to begin either at the highest assembly or at the local church, and proceed from there.

Assigning the power of excommunication to any sort of assembly risked leaving the particular church without any rights in the matter. Goodwin warned that there were some in the assembly who would be willing to give the power of suspension to a particular church, but not the power of excommunication; the former not being properly a matter of church government. Seaman alarmed the assembly when he suggested that he believed no man had the power to suspend or excommunicate, whereas Rutherford retorted that it must be done by a plurality of elders. Seaman then accused Rutherford of sounding like a Brownist, insinuating that the Scottish divine would give the congregation the right to dissent from its elders![52] But just when it seemed that the presbyterian factions would split, news came that would forever change the dynamic of the assembly: the Scots had taken Newcastle.

The day before, the Committee for Both Kingdoms had received a letter from the Scots in Newcastle demanding that Parliament end their discussions on church government. On 24 October – the very day the assembly was having these debates over church government – the House of Commons heeded those instructions and voted to instruct the assembly to do the same.[53] On the very next day, 25 October, the House of Commons interrupted the assembly with a demand 'that the assembly send the House a directory for public worship and whatever had been voted about church government, even if incomplete'.[54] On

1 November Warwick and Pembroke presented the assembly with the same letter that had been sent to the Committee for Both Kingdoms. The Commons increased its pressure on the assembly on 7 November by sending a delegation to the assembly ordering extra haste. The assembly, of course, had not yet completed its draft of church government, but made the fateful decision to send up all the votes they had already passed to the assembly. The centrepiece of what the assembly sent up to Parliament was the '3rd Proposition', which had been the source of so much tension some eight months before: 'The Scripture doth hold forth, that many particular congregations may be under one presbtyerial government.'

The Apologists' hopes for an accommodation evaporated, and the fate of a presbyterial government for the assembly was sealed. Immediately, the Apologists were forced to enter an official, and their first, dissent. According to Goodwin, the Apologists hoped to wait 'till the platforme fully made up' before having to decide on any dissent. By 15 November the now officially named Dissenting Brethren had presented their reasons for dissenting to the Third Proposition. This was followed up by there dissent to the subordination of synods with Matthew 18 as the proof text, and this was followed up with a dissenting paper on ordination.[55] All three dissents, with the presbyterian responses, made up the majority of the *Grand Debate*, published several years later.

CONCLUSION

With the sending up of the votes to Parliament and the rise of the Dissenting Brethren, the Scots had won a tactical victory that was long in the making. We can see their plan in gestation early in February 1644 when they allowed the assembly to debate the Third Proposition on presbyterial church government rather than follow their recommended procedure of starting with the particular church and moving upward. This was an initial blow to the congregationalists, who, with good reason, anticipated a great deal of common ground with the Scots. But the Scottish commissioners knew they would lose the support of many of the more clerical English presbyterians if they followed their initial recommended procedure. By starting with the vague clause that many churches 'may be' under one presbytery, there was going to be greater unanimity amongst the presbyterians, whom the Scots needed to keep together if they were going to succeed in achieving the demands of the Covenanters back in Scotland. In the spring they were able to secure some rights for the particular congregation and their elderships, without having to address the thorny issue of church power and excommunication. This strategy continued through the autumn when Gillespie convinced the assembly to set aside the question of church power in favour of affirming the existence of several sorts of assemblies, but this time it was to the dismay of many of the English presbyterians they had worked with since 1644.

Falling out of favour with Parliament, and the increasing tension with the Erastian party (and the Parliamentarians who supported them), the problem of excommunication exposing the various types of English presbyterianism, and the knowledge that Newcastle was on the verge of being captured, meant the Scots had to delay and/or sideline even some of their own personal beliefs in order to ensure Parliament approved a presbyterial system of church government. Baillie knew that in order to defeat the congregationalists (and those presbyterians who supported them) they had to get a presbyterial system to Parliament.[156] Of course, it behoved Parliament to prematurely push votes on the presbyterial government, because it prevented the assembly from defining presbyterianism *jure divino*, or giving rights of excommunication exclusively to the presbyteries without parliamentary involvement.

None of this is to contradict what has been said earlier, that the Scots were not the vanguard of presbyterianism. The minutes and personal records do not indicate significant shifts in the ecclesiological beliefs of many assembly presbyterians. But the Scots, particularly Gillespie, were brilliant tacticians, able to, at times singlehandedly, steer the assembly presbyterians away from open dissention. More often than not, the Scots tried to bridge divisions at Westminster. This was reflected in the committee for accommodation in the spring of 1644. With Parliament and the war party largely on their side, the Scots undoubtedly felt more freedom to attempt to accommodate the congregationalists. However, they abandoned this tactic when it became less feasible. With Cromwell's victories in the summer of 1644, and the Scots' waning support in Parliament, they no longer had the flexibility to accommodate the Apologists. Certainly if we are to believe that Baillie was the Covenanters' eyes and ears in London, we can assume they would not have endorsed such an accommodation. To be sure, the Aldermanbury divines tried repeatedly to provide space for the Apologists to debate their positions, but, it seems, they were also losing influence in the assembly. Indeed, in late 1644, accommodating the congregational divines was not going to secure a presbyterian settlement, and it was certainly not going to appease a majority of English presbyterians who had little willingness to do so.

The Apologists, for their part, would have preferred to help the assembly develop a full platform of church government and then to offer a dissent to particular points of the platform. William Bridge, when he entered his dissent to the Third Proposition and its proofs, stated that he did so, in part, because of the 'unseasonablenesse' of the request.[157] There were undoubtedly several in the assembly who would have preferred to develop a platform. But, as Lazarus Seaman noted, when Parliament demanded that all the votes passed thus far be sent in, it would be 'A great mistake that nothing set up till the whole platforme'.[158] The Apologists' written dissent forced the assembly to think in terms of two parties and thus, from this point forward, one can read the debates in the assembly more clearly as church government debates between congregationalists and presbyterians. As Vines noted, when the Dissenting Brethren submitted their dissent it risked bringing 'the whole controversy upon the stage'.[159] The divines recognised the Apologists' rights to write a dissent (though they debated whether or not the Apologists had brought in new arguments), but they were also forced to make a committee to respond to the Dissent.[160]

Parliament, for its part, was well aware of the Apologists' views on the Third Proposition, many of them having sat through the debates of the previous February. Undoubtedly, many Parliamentarians and assembly divines hoped that the vagueness of the Third Proposition would create space for a congregational accommodation. However, the Dissenting Brethren, whose fundamental ecclesiological belief was that the power of excommunication belonged to the particular church, could not go along with a proposition that did not also explicitly protect the rights of the particular church. It was clear that the assembly was going to give the power of excommunication to the presbyteries over multiple churches, something Burroughs would later call the nub of the entire controversy.[161]

In January 1645 the assembly made one more attempt to resolve their differences over excommunication, although there was still recognition that the topic should be avoided, as it was the most significant point of difference within the assembly.[162] Marshall once again noted that there were the same three differing groups in the assembly (the same three groups we noted above). Henderson and Goodwin, once again, attempted to reach an accommodation. Henderson noted that 'I have heard some of our brethren say if they cold get satisfaction in this [excommunication] they did not see any great difference.'[163] In a remarkable concession – that itself summarised all the debates of 1644 – Rutherford stated that it was pointless for the assembly to determine the first subject of the power of jurisdiction, for 'many writters learned have written accurately of it & yet never setled this controversy ... [indeed] not a protestant synod ... that hath determined it on either side'.[164] Not even, apparently, the synod at Westminster.

It was not that the Scots were against accommodating the congregationalists: indeed, after they were able to secure the votes for presbyterial church government, Gillespie and Rutherford become the most vocal proponents of accommodating them. Throughout 1644 we see the Apologists repeatedly attempt to take cover under the writings of Scottish divines, and we see the Scots, more than any other divines, citing Cotton and the *Apologeticall Narration* in order to mediate with Apologists on the assembly floor. But we must remember that covenanted uniformity did not mean that the English church and the Scottish church would merge; it simply meant – for the Scots at least

– that England should bring itself in closer proximity to the Scottish system of presbyteries and synods.

However much the Scots may have agreed with the Apologists on a number of issues, or even have liked their congregational friends, accommodating their polity was not essential to securing presbyterianism in England. Due to the Erastians and clerical English presbyterians in Parliament, accommodation would probably hinder a settlement. Indeed, in early January 1645, after Marshall reiterated his point that there were three parties in the assembly, Palmer responded, 'One thing I desire may be avoided: not to speake of 3 parteyes.'[165] The presbyterians had coalesced into a majority, and the differences they had with each other no longer mattered as much as the differences they had with the Dissenting Brethren.

When it became apparent that no accommodation was achievable, a clearly disappointed Rutherford said, 'I thinke the saddest session that I ever sate, in regard of the Reverend brethren's renouncing of the whole accommodation.'[166] The Apologists would later insist that the assembly never brought a debate about the particular church's right to the assembly floor, and the presbyterians would counter that they discussed, in general terms, the rights of the particular church on numerous occasions. However, here we are venturing beyond the scope of this book and into the equally complex years of 1645–1647, where once again, war, politics and polity would change the entire complexion of the English state.

Notes

1 Haller, *Liberty and Reformation in the Puritan Revolution*, p. 118. More recently, see Chung, 'Parliament and the Committee for Accommodation', p. 289.

2 See previous chapters.

3 William Lamont, 'Vines, Richard (1599/1600–1656)', *Oxford Dictionary of National Biography* (Oxford: Oxford University Press, 2004), online edn, January 2008, www.oxforddnb.com/view/article/28322, accessed 10 August 2010.

4 Lightfoot, *Journal*, p. 205.

5 Van Dixhoorn, *MPWA* (vol. 2), p. 596.

6 Ibid., p. 597.

7 Ibid., p. 597.

8 Ibid., p. 599.

9 Lightfoot, *Journal*, p. 206.

10 Van Dixhoorn, *MPWA* (vol. 2), p. 240.

11 Jacqueline Eales, 'Palmer, Herbert (1601–1647)', *Oxford Dictionary of National Biography* (Oxford: Oxford University Press, 2004), online edn, January 2008, www.oxforddnb.com/view/article/28322, accessed 10 August 2010.

12 Lightfoot, *Journal*, p. 206; Baillie, *Letters and Journals*, vol. 2, p. 145.

13 Baillie, *Letters and Journals*, vol. 2, p. 147; Gillespie, *Notes*, p. 37.

14 Baillie, *Letters and Journals*, vol. 2, p. 147.

15 Powell, 'Dissenting Brethren', pp. 225ff.

16 Gillespie, *Notes*, p. 37.

17 Ibid., p. 41.

18 Ibid., p. 41.

19 Van Dixhoorn, *MPWA* (vol. 3), p. 268.

20 Spear, 'Covenanted Uniformity', p. 86.

21 Van Dixhoorn, *MPWA* (vol. 2), p. 636.

22 Baillie, *Letters and Journals*, vol. 2, p. 174.

23 Paul, *The Assembly of the Lord*, pp. 322, 345.

24 Baillie, *Letters and Journals*, vol. 2, p. 168.

25 Gillespie, *Notes*, p. 56.

26 Ibid., p. 56.

27 Ibid., p. 56.

28 Van Dixhoorn, *MPWA* (vol. 3), pp. 43.

29 Baillie, *Letters and Journals*, vol. 2, p. 165.

30 Lightfoot, *Journal*, p. 254; Van Dixhoorn, *MPWA* (vol. 3), p. 39.

31 Baillie, *Letters and Journals*, vol. 2, pp. 174, 180.

32 Lightfoot, *Journal*, pp. 256–257.

33 Baillie, *Letters and Journals*, vol. 2, p. 182.

34 Ibid., vol. 2, p. 182.

35 Ibid., vol. 2, p. 505.

36 See above, p. 41.

37 D. Laing (ed.), *The Works of John Knox* (Edinburgh: Wodrow Society, 1848), p. 183.

38 D. Calderwood, *The true history of the Church of Scotland, from the beginning of the reformation, unto the end of the reigne of King James VI* (1678), pp. 25–30.

39 Baillie, *Letters and Journals*, vol. 3, p. 21.

40 D. Calderwood, *The altar of Damascus or the patern of the English hierarchie, and Church policie obtruded upon the Church of Scotland* (1621), p. 82.

41 Ibid., p. 82.

42 Ibid., p. 222.

43 Gillespie, *Notes*, p. 116.

44 Ibid., p. 112.

45 Bonar (ed.), *Letters of Samuel Rutherford*, p. 618.

46 Ibid.

47 Spear, 'Covenanted Uniformity', p. 207.

48 Gillespie, *Notes*, p. 56.

49 I am grateful to Elliot Vernon for pointing this out to me.

50 Gillespie, *Notes*, p. 56

51 Paul, *The Assembly of the Lord*, p. 342.

52 For a summary of debates during April and May, see Paul, *Assembly of the Lord*, pp. 331–381.

53 Van Dixhoorn, *MPWA* (vol. 3), p. 59.

54 Ibid., p. 64.

55 Ibid., p. 66.

56 Gillespie, *Notes*, p. 58.

57 Spear, 'Covenanted Uniformity', p. 220.

58 Gillespie, *Notes*, p. 59.

59 Cotton, Goodwin & Nye, *Keyes*, p. 12.

60 Gillespie, *Notes*, p. 59.

61 Ibid., p. 59.

62 Lightfoot, *Journal*, p. 261.

63 Mullan, '"Uniformity in Religion": The Solemn League and Covenant (1643) and the "Presbyterian Vision"', pp. 259–260.

64 Van Dixhoorn, *MPWA* (vol. 3), p. 543.

65 Ibid., p. 285.

66 V. Pearl, 'Oliver St John and the 'Middle Group' in the Long Parliament: August 1643–1644', *English Historical Review*, 81 (1966), 490–519, p. 516.

67 L. Kaplan, 'English Civil War Politics and the Religious Settlement ', *Church History*, 41 (1972), 307–325, pp. 308–309.

68 Woolrych, *Britain in Revolution*, pp. 297–298.

69 Scott, *Politics and War*, p. 83.

70 Ibid., pp. 84–85.

71 Shaw, *English Church*, p. 175.

72 Van Dixhoorn, *MPWA* (vol. 3), p. 232. The debates surrounding ordination, and how it relates to growing fears of sectarianism outside the assembly, are worthy of a study in their own right. For more on ordination in the assembly see, Shaw, *English Church*, pp. 319–337; Paul, *The Assembly of the Lord*, pp. 392–398; Spear, 'Covenanted Uniformity', pp. 290–313.

73 Marshall told the assembly, 'We are tyed by ordinance to debate nothing here but what we receive order. You dare not name any persons to execute that which you have not the power to examine, the perticulars of it which are fit', Van Dixhoorn, *MPWA* (vol. 3), p. 235.

74 Paul, *The Assembly of the Lord*, pp. 395–396.

75 Van Dixhoorn, *MPWA* (vol. 3), p. 279.

76 Bradley, 'Jacob and Esau', p. 296.

77 Gillespie, *Notes*, p. 67.

78 Ibid., p. 70.

79 Van Dixhoorn, *MPWA* (vol. 3), p. 263.

80 Paul, *The Assembly of the Lord*, p. 97.

81 Van Dixhoorn, *MPWA* (vol. 3), p. 268.

82 The importance of this day's debates is highlighted by the fact that Gillespie's notes resume for the first time since the previous May. Gillespie, *Notes*, pp. 64–65.

83 Ibid., p. 65.

84 Van Dixhoorn, *MPWA* (vol. 3), p. 264.

85 Gillespie, *Notes*, p. 65.

86 It seems that the Scots were not placed on this Committee for the Summary. Van Dixhoorn, *MPWA* (vol. 3), pp. 33–34; Spear, 'Covenanted Uniformity', p. 79.

87 Van Dixhoorn, *MPWA* (vol. 3), p. 34.

88 Spear, 'Covenanted Uniformity', p. 79.

89 Van Dixhoorn, *MPWA* (vol. 3), p. 264.

90 Ibid., p. 266.

91 Ibid., p. 268.

92 Ibid., p. 266.

93 Ibid., p. 265.

94 Ibid., p. 265.

95 Ibid., pp. 265–267; Gillespie, *Notes*, p. 65.

96 Van Dixhoorn, *MPWA* (vol. 3), p. 269.

97 Ibid., p. 268.

98 Gillespie, *Notes*, p. 65.

99 Van Dixhoorn, *MPWA* (vol. 3), p. 265.

100 Ibid., p. 269.

101 Ibid., p. 267; Gillespie, *Notes*, p. 65.

102 Van Dixhoorn, *MPWA* (vol. 3), p. 269.

103 Ibid., p. 269.

104 Baillie, *Letters and Journals*, vol. 2, p. 227.

105 Ibid., vol. 2, pp. 239–240.

106 Paul, *Narration*, p. 444.

107 Gillespie, *Notes*, p. 65.

108 Spear, 'Covenanted Uniformity', p. 229.

109 On 17 September they approved the proposition, 'The Scripture holds forth another

sort of Assemblies for the government of the kirk beside classical and congregational, which we call Synodical.' On the 23rd the assembly voted that 'Pastors and teachers and other idonous persons,where it shall be deemed expedient, are members of those which we call Synodical, where they have lawfull fall thereto.' The clause on expediency was a late addition at the request of the congregationalists. Shaw, *English Church*, pp. 177–178.

110 Gillespie, *Notes*, p. 78.

111 Van Dixhoorn, *MPWA* (vol. 3), p. 330.

112 The next few days were taken up with the Apologists arguing against the subordination of assemblies. Many of these arguments can be found in *The Grand Debate*, pp. 115ff.

113 Van Dixhoorn, *MPWA* (vol. 3), p. 330.

114 This is something Gillespie had to remind the assembly repeatedly. See, for example, Gillespie, *Notes*, p. 79.

115 Ibid., p. 78.

116 Here began the debate over subordination of assemblies, much of which made its way into *The Grand Debate*, p. 113.

117 *Papers ... for Accomodation ... 1644* (1648), p. 1.

118 Baillie, *Letters and Journals*, vol. 2, p. 230.

119 Ibid., vol. 2, p. 236.

120 *Papers ... for Accomodation ... 1644*, p. 3.

121 Gillespie, *Notes*, p. 104.

122 Bradley, 'Jacob and Esau', pp. 305–306.

123 Ibid., p. 305.

124 Gillespie, *Notes*, p. 103.

125 Ibid., p. 103.

126 Ibid., p. 65.

127 Ibid., p. 103.

128 *Papers ... for Accomodation ... 1644*, p. 2.

129 Ibid., p. 3.

130 Ibid., p. 4.

131 Gillespie, *Notes*, p. 105.

132 Ibid., p. 104; *Papers ... for Accomodation ... 1644*, p. 4.

133 Gillespie, *Notes*, p. 105.

134 Ibid., p. 105.

135 Ibid., p. 87; Van Dixhoorn, *MPWA* (vol. 3), pp. 373, 374.

136 Van Dixhoorn, *MPWA* (vol. 3), p. 374; Gillespie, *Notes*, p. 87.

137 Gillespie, *Notes*, p. 87; Van Dixhoorn, *MPWA* (vol. 3), p. 375.

138 This quote is taken from Chad Van Dixhoorn's summary of the debates on 15 October, Van Dixhoorn, *MPWA* (vol. 3), p. 399.

139 Gillespie, *Notes*, p. 92; Van Dixhoorn, *MPWA* (vol. 3), p. 391.

140 Van Dixhoorn, *MPWA* (vol. 3), p. 400.

141 Ibid., pp. 399–400.

142 Ibid., p. 401.

143 Ibid., p. 401.

144 Gillespie, *Notes*, pp. 92–93, 106.

145 Ibid., p. 106.

146 Bradley, 'Jacob and Esau', p. 309.

147 Contra, Chung, 'Parliament and the Committee for Accommodation', p. 299.

148 Many of the questions dealt with the proper recipient of the keys and many of the distinctions we discussed in chapter 3 resurfaced in the matter of who had the juridical power to excommunicate. See for example, Van Dixhoorn, *MPWA* (vol. 3), pp. 418–419.

149 Ibid., p. 393.

150 Paul, *The Assembly of the Lord*, p. 425.

151 Gillespie, *Notes*, p. 96; Van Dixhoorn, *MPWA* (vol. 3), p. 421; Lightfoot, *Journal*, p. 321.

152 Van Dixhoorn, *MPWA* (vol. 3), p. 424.

153 Yonge, *Journals of proceedings in the House of Commons, and of public events in England, from 19 Sept. 1642 to 10 Dec. 1645; kept by Walter Yonge, of Colyton, co. Devon, Barrister at Law, and member for Honiton in the Long Parliament*, vol. 3, pp. 674–676.

154 From summary comments, see Van Dixhoorn, *MPWA* (vol. 3), p. 426.

155 Bradley, 'Jacob and Esau', p. 319.

156 Baillie, *Letters and Journals*, vol. 2, p. 230.

157 Van Dixhoorn, *MPWA* (vol. 3), p. 441.

158 Ibid., p. 441.

159 Ibid., p. 450.

160 Ibid., p. 448.

161 Burroughs, *Irenicum*, pp. 43ff.

162 Van Dixhoorn, *MPWA* (vol. 3), p. 500.

163 Ibid., p. 502.

164 Ibid., p. 40.

165 Ibid., p. 503.

166 Ibid., p. 523.

Conclusion

We began this book with an alliance; we ended it with a Dissent. The time between has proven to be far more complicated than the standard 'presbyterian versus independent' narrative. Indeed, upon a closer inspection of the actual writings of assembly divines, we find high amount variegation within each of those categories. Between 1638 and 1640 the polity espoused by George Gillespie in *Popish Ceremonies* was of a type that the future Apologists believed to be a legitimate basis for an ecclesiastical alliance. Indeed, of all the groups pushing for religious reform in England in 1640/1641, the polities with foreign experience (i.e. the Scots and the future Apologists) were the two that looked the most alike to concurrent observers. Their exegetical similarities resulted in a pamphlet campaign for the abolition and against a reduced episcopacy orchestrated with the approbation of the revolution's leading peers and parliamentarians, who had repeatedly protected, and sought counsel from, the future Apologists and their English (Smectymnuan) presbyterian friends. One important pamphlet generated by this alliance, the *Petition Examined*, proffered a platform of church government that many Scottish and English presbyterians supported.

The breakdown in the Aldermanbury alliance really began as an English controversy. The evidence demonstrates that many of the English presbyterians moved away from those who would become the Apologists between 1640 and 1644. This became apparent during the Westminster assembly's first debate over church government in October 1643. In that purely English debate we began to see just how different aspects of the English ecclesiological tradition were from wider post-Reformed orthodoxy. To many, at that point, the Apologists fully developed congregational polity was closer to the continental Reformed churches than the strain of clerical English presbyterianism that was beginning to exert its influence at Westminster.

In the initial debates on church government the Apologists (in keeping with what the godly alliance had done three years earlier) tried, and failed, to get the assembly to begin by outlining a platform of church government. Guided by clerical presbyterians such as Lazarus Seaman, the assembly instead decided to identify the disparate parts of the church (elders, deacons, etc.) before arranging them into a form of government. Beginning the debate with Matthew 16:19 and the power of the keys, the assembly quickly realised that there was no settled reformed position on whom church power passed to after Peter – whether it was visible saints, elders, presbyteries, synods, national assemblies etc. The clerical presbyterians were able to convince many in the assembly who agreed that the keys were given to the local church, to delay the controversial question for another time by voting through a proposition stating that the Apostles – represented by Peter – were the recipients of church power. To create and maintain a presbyterian majority, it was becoming clear that vital topics of church polity had to be avoided.

Months later two leading Apologists, Nye and Goodwin, published John Cotton's *Keyes of the Kingdom of Heaven* because it largely mirrored the way the Apologists had discussed the power of the keys in the Assembly in October 1643 and provided a basis for accommodation with the Scots, who, of all parties, had most actively pursued an accommodation with the congregational divines. Scottish and English presbyterians marvelled at Cotton's *Keyes*. Presbyterians and congregationalists cited it positively during the assembly with surprising regularity. Leading Continental divines regarded it as an influential reformed work on church government and refused to gainsay it. Had it not been for men like Seaman, Baillie and Burgess the *Keyes* could have been a basis for an accommodation between the presbyterians and the apologists. But these clerical presbyterians repeatedly scuttled any accommodation attempts in early 1644.

The Apologists published their famous *Apologeticall Narration* in January 1644. Far from a call for ecclesiastical warfare, the *Narration* was an attempt to keep the alliance that had formed three years earlier from coming apart. We cannot understand the context of the *Narration* without having understood the *Petition Examined*, written three years earlier. When taken in context, we find that the *Narration* was not a source of tension on the assembly floor. Indeed, the only times we find it cited in the minutes, it is referred to as a source of accommodation. The *Narration*, through Baillie's machinations, briefly foreshadowed the real 'grand debate' over Erastianism that would take place between Parliament and the assembly in the coming years. When foreign churches followed Baillie's plea to reject the *Narration*, they ended up critiquing it on the basis of its deference to Parliament, while still supporting the rights of the particular church's elders to excommunicate. The latter position was something Baillie's clerical allies in the assembly rejected. The most siginifiant controversy surrounding the *Narration* was that it nearly caused an international political crisis and, that, in turn, increased suspicions between Parliament and the assembly.

To understand the year leading up to the first official dissent of the Dissenting Brethren, we looked at how the 'Third Proposition' (the first and only affirmative proposition offered on presbyterian government) effectively bookended the debates of 1644. The Scots tried to get the assembly to address the particular church, but under pressure from Calderwood and other Covenantors, they decided to allow the assembly to debate the Third Proposition, which stated that many churches 'may be' under one presbytery. The proposition was vague enough to achieve a presbyterian détente, but ended up empowering the clerical presbyterians who – to the Scots' frustration – repeatedly sidelined any question over the local church.

By the end of 1644, when the Scots found they had lost favour with their former allies in the parliamentary war party, they took advantage of their success at Newcastle to force the assembly to send the Third Proposition (the only affirmative proposition on presbyterian church government the assembly ever passed) to Parliament for approval. While this forced the Apologists to enter their first Dissent, it nonetheless assured the increasingly anxious Covenanters that Westminster would embrace some sort of presbyterian polity. Though many Scots and many English presbyterians agreed with the Apologists on the power of the particular church, losing the clerical presbyterian support would have been far more deleterious to a church settlement than losing the Apologists. At the end of 1644 the variegated presbyterian polities had themselves been corralled into a coalition that, from that point onward, could broadly be defined as 'presbyterianism'. To some presbyterians the Third Proposition was vague enough to include the Apologists, to others the vagueness left the door open to ultimately exclude them. The Apologists could not take the risk of submitting to the proposition given that this latter group had demonstrated its strength over the course of the previous year by repeatedly obstructing any discussions on church power.

PRESBYTERIANS VERSUS RADICALS?

This book seeks to challenge several prevailing ways by which ecclesiological debated have been studied. The first, as already mentioned, is this reductionistic debate between two opposed ecclesiastical parties. As we have seen, the binary motif that has dominated the historiography of the Puritan Revolution, with its casual use of words like 'enemy' and 'warfare', turns scholastic disputation into something that was utterly foreign to puritans trained during the period of 'high orthodoxy'. These divines, particularly the ones coming from the Cambridge tradition, were trained in such a way that the closer they were together on any given point, the more intense the debate.[1] And, in any event, the hottest disputes were reserved for the theological debates, which took up far more of the assembly's time than the question of church government. While the debates over ecclesiology could get intense, only when disputing Christology did assembly members call each other heretics.[2]

The overreliance on vituperative pamphlet debates written by non-Assembly members has certainly contributed to the argument for binary conflicts. In this book we made extensive use of polemical writings, but we saw that choosing pamphlets written by those actually involved in national church reform paints a very different picture from one utilising those written by men who were outside the assembly. For example, the assembly did not permit the Apologists to respond to Thomas Edwards, and thus studying Edwards' view of religious debates gives us just that, Edwards's view. However, a careful reading of Rutherford, Gillespie, Calamy, Herle and any number of other 'presbyterians' involved in the Westminster assembly allows us to study an actual debate between a number of competing polities. And, as we have seen, that dialogue defies easy categorisations, and certainly does not mirror the style and substance of those men, like Edwards and John Goodwin.

This warfare model does not take into account relationships between these leading divines across a larger thirty-year period. When looking forward, the evidence shows that George Gillespie, for example, was seeking counsel directly from Voetius on how to accommodate congregationalists well after his departure from the assembly. We also see that the Smectymnuan divines rejoined the Apologist friends in order to craft – and to lead – Cromwell's national church-vetting system during the Interregnum. From a larger perspective, the Assembly actually forced a limited, if intense, division within a group that spent most of the time between 1630 and 1660 either agreeing, or agreeing to disagree.

If one sets out to make the Apologists radicals, one will invariably succeed. By not analysing the important theological and ecclesiological distinctions within the wide range of 'radicals' he studied, Murray Tolmie has generated an influential narrative of the Apologists that is virtually unintelligible given what we have studied in this book. For Tolmie, the fact that the Apologists actually met with or even knew more radicals figures outside the assembly means that the Apologists must have been clandestine radicals themselves. 'Working together', however, should not be confused with 'agreeing with one another'. No one accuses the Scots of being secret independents for working with the future Apologists in 1640–41. Further, Chad van Dixhoorn has recently demonstrated how much English presbyterians, even in the mid-1640s, were regularly meeting with 'separatist' friends.[3]

This book has shown that the Apologists' approach to ecclesiological debates exhibited all the hallmarks of reformed scholastic humanism, rooted first and foremost in the Scriptures. The Apologists did not understand themselves to be tolerationists, independents, political moderates, radicals or schismatics, despite the narratives historians want to tell. Such conclusions have been drawn with very little consideration of what the Apologists actually thought and believed. The goal in this book is not to challenge the veracity of such claims, but to create a framework – based on close readings of the sources – that enables us to reassess those concepts.

Developing a 'highly unique doctrine' was not an admirable academic attribute in reformed orthodoxy.[4] As reformed scholastics, the English puritans believed in catholicity, insofar as they 'explicitly aimed to stand within the tradition of the entire church [and] made no pretence of originality, or of developing "true doctrine".[5] These divines, mindful of the circumstances they were in, could (and did) marshal the works of the church fathers, ancient philosophy, 'trajectories of argument belonging to the medieval tradition', and the writings of their theological and philosophical opponents in their own theological development, while still maintaining a strong sense of catholicity within the reformed tradition.[6] They could look at the tradition of the past and look towards the future without considering themselves to be 'radical'.[7] Similarly, recent claims that the Apologists were seeking a *via media* between two ecclesiastical extremes need to be tempered by the fact that a *via media* is not only reactionary.[8] The 'middle way' was not 'moderation' insofar as it had an exegetical basis, not merely a positioning against extremes.

These divines could study theology *and* ecclesiology 'through the lens of [the] distinction [of] theology as an expositive, contemplative, polemical, and practical science'.[9] Ecclesiology could be irenic (expositive and contemplative) as well as being polemical (defensive and apologetic).[10] Reformed scholastics did not understand these to be contradictory approaches, nor did many feel the need to sacrifice dogmatic beliefs on the altar of irenicism. Moderation was not necessarily an eschewing of truly held beliefs in favour of consensus. When considering 'consensus' and accommodation from a tactical standpoint, we should remember that some influential Calamy house presbyterians and the Apologists could work together because their differences were in 'lesser things', not because they papered over their differences or believed them to be unimportant.

ANGLOCENTRICISM

Anglocentric historiography is one significant reason we have received so many misleading and decontextualised narratives within puritan ecclesiological studies. This is, again, exemplified by the overly casual use of subjective terms such as 'radical', 'conservative', or 'moderate'.[11] What was 'radical' to English presbyterians like Thomas Edwards or Daniel Cawdrey was not necessarily 'radical' outside of England. English opinions about English debates have become the sole arbiter of what was inside and outside the reformed camp. We tend to forget that England's prelatical church was itself considered 'radical' (or 'conservative') within different continental reformed traditions. Ecclesiastical debates in Caroline nonconformity created a climate in England during the 1640s that undoubtedly made many English divines more sensitive to the spectre of separatism. However, the most vituperative pamphlets generated against independency typically came from peripheral figures that were not central to the Parliament sanctioned efforts at national church reform.

Contrary to the arguments of Murray Tolmie, who privileges these peripheral figures, it is quite clear that the Apologists actually desired a national church. Anthony Milton's forthcoming work will seek to demonstrate how we need to have a more expansive understanding of what the 'Church of England' was, what it might have become, and how the Apologists fit into the new framework. Nonetheless, we must also remember that England was part of a 'larger network of intellectual commerce between British Protestants and Protestant thinkers on the continent'.[12] Furthermore, the vision of a 'true international church ... reflected decades of close interaction and mutual influence with foreign divines and churches which may have indeed seemed less "foreign" to Puritan consciences than the persecuting prelates' of England.[13]

However much pamphlets written by men outside the assembly wanted to convince England that the Apologists had no legitimate claim on a reformed ecclesiological heritage, these opinions need to be balanced by those of respected continental divines like Gisbertus Voetius who thought the type of presbyterian polity in which the people had no power was outside the reformed trajectory. This is why Edwards and Baillie desperately wanted Voetius to disown the Apologists, and why they failed in getting Voetius and other continental divines to do so to their satisfaction. But, the polity espoused by Seaman and Cornelius Burgess was, to Gillespie and to Voetius, outside the reformed tradition because of its failure to see the particular church as having necessary powers of jurisdiction. While it is true that living in the Low Countries could have exposed the Apologists to separatists, the Apologists also engaged with the leading lights of reformed orthodoxy. Thomas Goodwin, therefore, could say to the assembly with some credibility, 'We [the Apologists] doe hold more things with the reformed churches than many in this Assembly doe.'[14]

This will have a bearing on another aspect of this study, namely the transatlantic reception of New England's ideas. While Francis Bremer, Carla Gardina Pestana and Susan Hardman Moore have all recently accentuated how important the New England experience was to those involved in the English Civil Wars, we have still not intertwined the two events. Again, led by a select number of anti-independent pamphlets, historians have attempted to analyse the radicalisation of New England divines and how those views may have influenced Old England independents. The ecclesiological thoughts of notable New England divines like Thomas Hooker and John Cotton are seen as essentially the same, yet leading divines at Westminster and in Holland were able to clearly distinguish between the two. Indeed, when we take a look at the Westminster assembly as well as its international context, we see that seminal figures such as John Cotton and his unique views of polity had a massive influence on a variety of leading divines in the early 1640s. How widespread Cotton's influence was something that deserves more study, but we can say with confidence he was an important divine in the eyes of those involved in national church reform.

It was not without reason that the Westminster assembly sought to develop a model of church government in keeping with the 'best reformed churches'.[15] To date, however, historians have given little attention to what reformed churches outside of England thought of the ecclesiological debates at Westminster. It has been well established that concepts in covenant theology, such as the *pactum salutis*, developed as part of a regular pamphlet dialogue with continental theologians.[16] Yet, little attention has been given to how this communication was reflected in questions over church government. Work has been done on military and commercial relations between England and the Low countries, but this has not been equally applied to religious discourse. Even when studying the seventeenth-century puritanism in the Low Countries, the focus is on debates between transplanted English divines, rather than what celebrated Dutch theologians thought of England's debates.[17]

LOOKING BACKWARDS

The topic of who and what influenced the Westminster divines is perilous. Of course, given their commitment to *Sola Scriptura*, we should be cautious in assigning purely derivative motives for ecclesiological development. This conflict motif has also generated more recent suggestions that congregationalism developed in reaction to presbyterianism. This type of denominational historiography privileges a pre-existent, static presbyterian polity over avantgarde separatists.[18] As we have seen, types of presbyterianism can be said to have developed in reaction to each other, and where the line between presbyterian and congregationalism was drawn was far from settled at Westminster. Rather than reducing ecclesiological development to reactionism, we should simply note that scholastic engagement was one of many methods for clarifying and developing one's own views on any given topic.

Furthermore, as Richard Muller has pointed out regarding theological development, these divines, academically saturated in scholastic humanism, were quite capable of appropriating ideas from people with whom they disagreed, while leaving others' ideas to the side.[19] The congregationalism of the Apologists was no more the product of one straight line of ecclesiological thought than was covenant theology, the complex origins of which continue to perplex and fascinate theologians. Given their understanding of authority and power in the particular church, we find the Apologists had more in common with the early Stuart divine Walter Travers – considered by some historians a paragon of English presbyterian thought – than they did with Henry Jacob, whom they never cited in their writings nor mentioned in their speeches.

We need always to proceed cautiously when attempting to chart an ecclesiological lineage. Early Stuart historians too often draw grand conclusions about the 1640s based upon debates that took place a generation earlier.[20] Recent historiographies have placed a great deal of weight on the foundational influence of the 'English presbyterian' Walter Travers and the 'congregational "independent"' Henry Jacob. However, in the surviving minutes of the Westminster assembly we have only one recorded reference to Travers (and this only in a side-reference for a theological point), and no mention of Henry Jacob. On the other hand, Robert Parker was cited by a variety of different ecclesiological positions, each attempting to utilise his writings to defend their own position.

The evidence does not suggest that congregational polity in the 1640s was simply derivative of an earlier non-conformist debate in England. This conclusion does not allow for the distinction between 'early orthodoxy (1560–1620)', which van Asselt calls the 'skeleton of high dogmatics', and 'high orthodoxy (1620–1700)', which was 'characterized by increasing precision in its theological apparatus'.[21] Even John Cotton's influence was limited. The Apologists could agree with him in some important points regarding elders and the people's power, and yet happily retained the standard verbiage of 'jurisdiction' and 'order'.[22]

Although I have attempted, to borrow Patrick Collinson's words, a 'horizontal and lateral' study of the Apologists, I do not intend to imply radical discontinuity with the past.[23] Nor should we proceed in the opposite direction with reductionistic label like 'Amesian' (i.e. followers of William Ames).[24] From that perspective the Apologists could just as easily have been associated with 'Parkerians' or 'Zanchians', reference points so remote as to have lost any descriptive power.

Michael Winship has recently argued that Massachusetts' congregationalism developed because Bay Colony divines encountered Plymouth separatists. He states that had this encounter not occurred, 'the odds of Massachusetts' puritans hitting upon their particular version of congregationalism are not entirely unlike those of monkeys typing Shakespeare'.[25] Yet whatever influence Plymouth separatism had on John Cotton, it does not explain how men like Voetius, Gillespie and Goodwin developed surprisingly similar views of church power reading a wide variety of reformed and post-reformation divines. Unless, of course, one wants to argue (no doubt to the shock of many historical theologians) that Voetius, in appropriating Cotton, was himself influenced by Plymouth.

What Carl Trueman has noted regarding problematic modern views of Calvin's influence in the seventeenth century is equally attributable to ecclesiology: 'questions of continuity and discontinuity need to be set aside, or at least adopted in a highly qualified form'.[26] If anything, we see ambivalence towards influences in Assembly debates, precisely because it was recognised that any non-scriptural authority utilised in a debate (which was relatively rare) was only one piece of a much larger framework of thinking and, in any event, relative only to the particular topic being discussed.[27]

We can, however, map out a universe of influences in the writings and speeches of the Apologists. From the continent they show indebtedness to David Pareus, Girolamo Zanchius, Johan Gerhard and Catholic Sorbonnists and their friend Gisbertus Voetius. In England they seemed to be most influenced by William Fulke, Robert Parker, Paul Baynes and Andrew Willet, and in Scotland by the presbyterian David Calderwood.[28] As we have seen, all of these divines equally influenced many presbyterians. Bridge claimed that of all the 'episcopalian' polities, the 'best' were those described by Baynes, Parker and Didoclavius (Calderwood). If we are to go by sheer number of citations, then pride of place seems to belong to Baynes and Calderwood. Although the more clerical (*descendendo*) version of English presbyterianism, as espoused by Seaman, is very difficult to find in earlier presbyterian writings, it was a remarkably influential position in the assembly.[29] Perhaps the best way forward is to see how the Assembly members could actually assimilate, combine, and ignore various parts of the authorities and confessional traditions to which they showed indebtedness.

IN SUMMARY

From an ecclesiological perspective the Westminster assembly was a bold experiment that was ultimately hampered by its own rigorous search for biblical 'truth'. The assembly was neither the first nor the last religious body to find that the more precise the terms of debate, the more irreconcilable the differences that emerged. In addition, Parliament's oversight, and the unpredictable dynamics of a civil war, proved to be forces the assembly could not ignore. Throughout its first year, the assembly attempted to steer clear of the question of church power, because on that point, more than anything else, there was a wide spectrum of beliefs. When the topic was allowed to surface, it tended to unite parties that we have heretofore understood as enemies. For many English presbyterian divines, the topic of church power exposed a discontinuity with the contintental-reformed tradition. The Scottish commissioners quickly realised that to ensure a presbyterian settlement they would have to prevent the assembly from addressing arguably the most contentious, and complex, issue in the history of the church. Therefore, after 1644 drew to a close Rutherford urged the assembly to concede 'many writters learned have written accurately of it [the power of jurisdiction] & yet never setled this controversy ... [indeed] not a protestant synod ... that hath determined it on either side'.[30]

England changed before the assembly could change England. As revolutionary England shifted from a monarchy to Commonwealth and then to a protectorate, the country was marked by increasingly diverse and increasingly vocal heterodoxies. By that point, many former members of the assembly recognised that a coalition of churches united under strong Reformed confessionalism, with formalised magisterial oversight, was the least bad way to stem the tide of sectarian heresies.

NOTES

1 I am very grateful to Richard Serjeanston for discussing this paragraph with me and providing extremely helpful insights.

2 C. Van Dixhoorn, 'Reforming the Reformation: Theological debate in the Westminster Assembly, 1643–1652', University of Cambridge, PhD thesis (2004), pp. 346, 348.

3 Van Dixhoorn, 'Politics and Religion in the Westminster Assembly and the "Grand Debate"'.

4 Muller, *Calvin and the Reformed Tradition: On the Work of Christ and the Order of Salvation*, pp. 52–53.

5 Van Asselt & Rouwendal, 'Introduction: What Is Reformed Scholasticism', p. 2.

6 Muller, *Calvin and the Reformed Tradition: On the Work of Christ and the Order of Salvation*, pp. 29–30.

7 Van Asselt & Rouwendal, 'Introduction: What Is Reformed Scholasticism', p. 2.

8 See Shagan, 'Beyond Good and Evil: Thinking with Moderates in Early Modern England'.

9 Van Asselt, 'Scholasticism in the Time of High Orthodoxy (ca. 1620 –1700)', p. 100.

10 I am grateful to Dr Mark Jones for discussions on this point.

11 V. Gregory, 'Congregational Puritanism and the Radical Community in England c. 1585–1625', University of Cambridge, PhD thesis (2003), p. 8.

12 Muller, 'Persistent Whiggism and Its Antidotes', in p. 149. See also, P. Ha & P. Collinson (eds), *The Reception of Continental Reformation in Britain (Proceedings of the British Academy)* (Oxford: Oxford University Press, 2010).

13 A. Milton, 'Puritanism and the Continental Reformed Churches', *The Cambridge Companion to Puritanism* (2008), p. 111; R. A. Muller, *Post-Reformation Reformed Dogmatics: The Rise and Development of Reformed Orthodoxy, ca. 1520 to ca. 1725*, 2 edn (Grand Rapids, MI: Baker Academics, 2003), vol. 2, p. 102.

14 Van Dixhoorn, *MPWA* (vol. 3), p. 252.

15 *A solemn league and covenant for reformation and defence of religion* (London, 1643), Article 1.

16 M. Jones, *Why Heaven Kissed Earth: The Christology of the Puritan Reformed Orthodox theologian, Thomas Goodwin (1600–1680)* (Gottingen: Vandenhoeck & Ruprecht, 2010), chapter 6.

17 See, for example, Sprunger, *Dutch Puritanism*.

18 Ha, *English Presbyterianism*, p. 49. Michael Winship makes the same argument, Winship, *Godly Republicanism*, p. 59.

19 R. A. Muller, *After Calvin: Studies in the Development of a Theological Tradition* (Oxford; New York: Oxford University Press, 2003), chapter 6.

20 See, for example, Webster, *Godly Clergy*, p. 328; Ha, *English Presbyterianism*, pp. 103–105; Winship, *Godly Republicanism*, pp. 234–235.

21 W. J. van Asselt, 'Scholasticism in the Time of High Orthodoxy (ca. 1620 –1700)', in W. J. van Asselt (ed.), *Introduction to Reformed Scholasticism*, trans. A. Gootjes (Grand Rapids, MI: Reformation Heritage Books, 2010), pp. 132–166, p. 133.

22 *The Grand Debate*, p. 4.

23 P. Collinson, *The Elizabethan Puritan Movement* (Oxford: Clarendon Press, 1990), p. 527.

24 Webster, *Godly Clergy*, chapter 16 and p. 328.

25 M. P. Winship, 'Godly Republicanism and the Origins of the Massachusetts Polity', *The William and Mary Quarterly*, 63 (2006), 427–462, p. 158.

26 C. R. Trueman, 'The Reception of Calvin: Historical Considerations', *Church History and Religious Culture*, 91.1–2 (2011), 19–27, p. 21; see also, Muller, *Calvin and the Reformed Tradition: On the Work of Christ and the Order of Salvation*, pp. 40–41.

27 Muller, *Calvin and the Reformed Tradition: On the Work of Christ and the Order of Salvation*, p. 40.

28 John Cotton claimed his influences – in terms of the keys and the particular church – were Parker, Baynes, and Ames; Cotton, *The Way of Congregational Churches Cleared*, p. 13.

29 This version of presbyterianism, and its background, would be a worthy topic for further study.

30 Ibid., p. 40.

Index

CPSIA information can be obtained
at www.ICGtesting.com
Printed in the USA
BVOW08s1128040517

483145BV00002B/22/P